A SOCIO-LEGAL THEORY OF MONEY FOR THE DIGITAL COMMERCIAL SOCIETY

This book poses the question: do we need a new body of regulations and the constitution of new regulatory agents to face the evolution of money in the Fourth Industrial Revolution?

After the Global Financial Crisis and the subsequent introduction of Distributed Ledger Technologies in monetary matters, multiple opinions claim that we are in the middle of a financial revolution that will eliminate the need for central banks and other financial institutions to form bonds of trust on our behalf. In contrast to these arguments, this book argues that we are not witnessing a revolutionary expression, but an evolutionary one that we can trace back to the very origin of money.

Accordingly, the book provides academics, regulators and policy makers with a multidisciplinary analysis that includes elements such as the relevance of intellectual property rights, which are disregarded in the legal analysis of money. Furthermore, the book proposes the idea that traditional analyses on the exercise of the lex monetae ignore the role of inside monies and technological infrastructures developed and supported by the private sector, as exemplified in the evolution of the cryptoassets market and in cases such as *Banco de Portugal v Waterlow & Sons*.

The book puts forward a proposal for the design and regulation of new payment systems and invites the reader to look beyond the dissemination of individual Distributed Ledger Technologies such as Bitcoin.

Hart Studies in Commercial and Financial Law: Volume 13

Hart Studies in Commercial and Financial Law

Series Editors: John Linarelli and Teresa Rodríguez de las Heras Ballell

This series offers a venue for publishing works on commercial law as well as on the regulation of banking and finance and the law on insolvency and bankruptcy. It publishes works on the law on secured credit, the regulatory and transactional aspects of banking and finance, the transactional and regulatory institutions for financial markets, legal and policy aspects associated with access to commercial and consumer credit, new generation subjects having to do with the institutional architecture associated with innovation and the digital economy including works on blockchain technology, work on the relationship of law to economic growth, the harmonisation or unification of commercial law, transnational commercial law, and the global financial order. The series promotes interdisciplinary work. It publishes research on the law using the methods of empirical legal studies, behavioural economics, political economy, normative welfare economics, law and society inquiry, socio-legal studies, political theory, and historical methods. Its coverage includes international and comparative investigations of areas of law within its remit.

Volume 1: The Financialisation of the Citizen: Social and Financial Inclusion through European Private Law
Guido Comparato

Volume 2: MiFID II and Private Law: Enforcing EU Conduct of Business Rules
Federico Della Negra

Volume 3: Reforming Corporate Retail Investor Protection: Regulating to Avert Mis-Selling
Diane Bugeja

Volume 4: The Future of Commercial Law: Ways Forward for Change and Reform
Edited by Orkun Akseli and John Linarelli

Volume 5: The Cape Town Convention: A Documentary History
Anton Didenko

Volume 6: Regulating the Crypto Economy: Business Transformations and Financialisation
Iris H-Y Chiu

Volume 7: The Future of High-Cost Credit: Rethinking Payday Lending
Jodi Gardner

Volume 8: The Enforcement of EU Financial Law
Edited by Jan Crijns, Matthias Haentjens and Rijnhard Haentjens

Volume 9: International Bank Crisis Management: A Transatlantic Perspective
Marco Bodellini

Volume 10: Creditor Priority in European Bank Insolvency Law: Financial Stability and the Hierarchy of Claims
Sjur Swensen Ellingsæter

Volume 11: Chinese and Global Financial Integration through Stock Connect: A Legal Analysis
Flora Huang

Volume 12: The Governance of Macroprudential Policy: How to Build Regulatory Legitimacy Through a Social Justice Approach
Tracy C Maguze

Volume 13: A Socio-Legal Theory of Money for the Digital Commercial Society: A New Analytical Framework to Understand Cryptoassets
Israel Cedillo Lazcano

A Socio-Legal Theory of Money for the Digital Commercial Society

A New Analytical Framework to Understand Cryptoassets

Israel Cedillo Lazcano

•HART•

OXFORD • LONDON • NEW YORK • NEW DELHI • SYDNEY

HART PUBLISHING

Bloomsbury Publishing Plc

Kemp House, Chawley Park, Cumnor Hill, Oxford, OX2 9PH, UK

1385 Broadway, New York, NY 10018, USA

Bloomsbury Publishing Ireland Limited, 29 Earlsfort Terrace, Dublin 2, D02 AY28, Ireland

HART PUBLISHING, the Hart/Stag logo, BLOOMSBURY and the Diana logo are trademarks of Bloomsbury Publishing Plc

First published in Great Britain 2024

First published in hardback, 2024

Paperback edition, 2025

A catalogue record for this book is available from the British Library.

A catalogue record for this book is available from the Library of Congress.

Library of Congress Control Number: 2023950160

ISBN: PB: 978-1-50996-967-8
ePDF: 978-1-50996-970-8
ePub: 978-1-50996-969-2

Typeset by Compuscript Ltd, Shannon

For product safety related questions contact productsafety@bloomsbury.com

To find out more about our authors and books visit www.hartpublishing.co.uk. Here you will find extracts, author information, details of forthcoming events and the option to sign up for our newsletters.

ACKNOWLEDGEMENTS

Understanding the legal nature of 'money' throughout the legal-financial history of the world has been a challenging task. Great minds like Aristotle, Sir Thomas Gresham, Lord Holt, Lord Mansfield and Sir Francis Mann have offered us different and interesting analyses on this fascinating subject. However, the dynamic nature of this socio-legal institution, and its evolution in the context of the Digital Commercial Society, exhort us to develop new approaches, one of which the reader will find in this work.

Consequently, one can imagine that an academic effort of this nature cannot be produced without the support from many people. I am very much indebted to Dr Luis Ernesto Derbez who has acted as a mentor and friend, and has encouraged me to pursue this goal, and for providing me the time and the space to grow personally and professionally. I owe him a debt of gratitude that can hardly be repaid.

I will be always grateful to the University of Edinburgh, the Edinburgh Law School, and to their awesome academic and administrative staff, for allowing me to be part of the tradition that has influenced the world since 1583. I had the honour to work under the supervision of Professor Emilios Avgouleas, who was – and is – an influential figure who pushed me to be my best and gave me invaluable advice, influencing my legal thinking. I am also grateful to my second supervisor, Dr Parker Hood, for his thoughtful advice, patience, guidance and for expending considerable time and effort reviewing the multiple drafts that I prepared for the development of this work. Without both of them, this book would not have been possible. I also had the honour and pleasure of having Professor Deirdre Ahern and Dr Longjie Lu as the examiners of the research project that acted as the cornerstone of this work. They were very generous with their time and knowledge, providing me with valuable feedback that has enabled me to develop the book that readers now have in their hands.

I have to add a special thank you to my family of Old College, who created and shared great memories with me, and aided my work in one way or another during the development of this book, especially Alvaro García, Fernando Pantoja, Alberto Brown, Jiahong Chen, Arianna Florou, Francesca Soliman, Ke Song, Yawen Zheng and Qiang Cai. And, of course, to my friends in Edinburgh and Mexico, Alejandro Guzmán, Manuel Giménez, Gabriel Utrilla, Gerardo Rodríguez, Guillermo Alberto Hidalgo and Arturo García, who are the family I chose, and who were a source of constant support.

Above all, I am grateful to my family for their support, patience, indulgence and sympathy throughout this project, in more ways than I could possibly say. This book is for Jesús, Emma, Emma, Yolanda, Claudia and Luca. My parents, Jesús and Emma, who take care of me despite physical distance and whose conversations keep me close to home. My aunt Yolanda, who has supported me in different ways as a second mother. I am lucky to have such a wonderful sister, Emma, who always has believed in me and keeps supporting me independently of the decisions I make. Most of all, I am forever thankful for Claudia, the best and the most beautiful and awesome companion of my heart and mind, and my muse that inspires and guides me to make possible all the things I do. Her love has proved to be the most beautiful treasure in my world. And for Luca, my son, a new source of joy and the light of my world.

I thank you all with all my heart.

CONTENTS

ABBREVIATIONS/ACRONYMS

ABS	Asset Back Securities
AES	Advanced Encryption Standards
AI	Artificial Intelligence
API	Application Programming Interface
ATM	Automated Teller Machine
BIS	Bank for International Settlements
BSA	Bank Secrecy Act
BSD	Berkeley Software Distribution License
CBDC	Central Bank Digital Currency
CDOs	Collateralized Debt Obligations
CGS	Classical Gold Standard
DCS	Digital Commercial Society
DES	Data Encryption Standards
DLT	Distributed Ledger Technologies
ECB	European Central Bank
EFT	Electronic Fund Transfer
EMIR	European Markets Infrastructure Regulation
EPO	European Patent Office
EVM	Ethereum Virtual Machine
FATF	Financial Action Task Force
FINCEN	Financial Crimes Enforcement Network
FIR	Fourth Industrial Revolution
FMC	Financing through Money Creation
FSB	Financial Stability Board

FWS	Financial World System
GFC	Global Financial Crisis
ICOs	Initial Coin Offerings
IEOs	Initial Exchange Offerings
IoT	Internet of Things
IPO	Initial Public Offering
IPRs	Intellectual Property Rights
IT	Information Technology
OS	Open Source
P2P	Peer-to-Peer
PoA	Proof-of-Authority
PoI	Proof-of-Identity
PoL	Proof-of-Location
PoS	Proof-of Stake
PoW	Proof-of-Work
RTGS	Real-Time Gross Settlement Systems
SELT	Singapore Electronic Legal Tender
TBTF	Too-Big-To-Fail
TCTF	Too-Complex-To-Fail
WIPO	World Intellectual Property Organization

LIST OF FIGURES

TABLE OF CASES

Australia

Canada

European Union

The Netherlands

United Kingdom

United Mexican States

United States of America

TABLE OF LEGISLATION

France

Germany

Japan

The Republic of Malta

United Kingdom

United Mexican States

United States of America

International Agreements

Introduction

The disruption and liquidity contraction that followed the Global Financial Crisis (GFC) highlighted the historical hostility against traditional intermediaries.[1] Unsurprisingly, this fundamental crisis of trust has fostered the development of new socio-technological answers, commonly labelled 'financial technology' (FinTech),[2] to deliver alternative financial solutions with the aim of facing the excessive infrastructural and political influence held by those institutions considered too-big-to-fail (TBTF) and/or too-complex-to-fail (TCTF), and promote competition and financial inclusion. Within the FinTech universe, cryptoassets tend to be seen as the purest materialisation of these objectives, eliminating the need for the government and existing financial infrastructures to form bonds of trust on our behalf.[3]

As an illustration of this lack of trust, 10 years after the GFC, the 2018 Edelman Trust Barometer[4] showed how, among the industry sectors analysed,[5] the financial sector was the least trusted independently of its improvement between 2014 and 2018. These findings are more interesting in light of the global distrust in governments shown in the same study,[6] and the public perception, in the 2023 edition of the same Barometer,[7] that governments are less trusted than companies, and seen as sources of misleading information. The interaction of both stakeholders and the projection of the distrust related to them was clearly perceived in the context of the Silicon Valley Bank (SVB) collapse in March 2023.

[1] Niall Ferguson argues that this is not a new phenomenon, given that throughout the financial history of the world, hostility to finance and financiers has been a recurrent issue. See N Ferguson, *The Ascent of Money. A Financial History of the World* (New York, The Penguin Press, 2008) 2.

[2] DW Arner, J Barberis and RP Buckley, '150 Years of Fintech. An Evolutionary Analysis' (2016) 3 *The Finsia Journal of Applied Finance* 22.

[3] I Cedillo, 'A new Approach for "Cryptoassets" Regulation' (2019) 35 *Banking and Finance Law Review* 37, 38.

[4] Edelman, 'Edelman Trust Barometer' (2018), available at www.edelman.com/sites/g/files/aatuss191/files/2018-10/2018_Edelman_Trust_Barometer_Global_Report_FEB.pdf.

[5] Technology, health care, energy, food and beverages, telecommunications, automotive, entertainment, consumer packaged goods and financial services. See ibid.

[6] The 2020 Edelman Trust Barometer shows a change in this trend, but I am cautious in using its results given that they are heavily focused on the perception of the policies put in place to face the COVID-19 crisis. See Edelman, 'Edelman Trust Barometer' (2020), available at www.edelman.com/research/trust-2020-spring-update.

[7] Edelman, 'Edelman Trust Barometer' (2023), available at www.edelman.com/trust/2023/trust-barometer.

I. The FinTech Dragon

During the Edinburgh Art Festival 2017, a discussion relating to a piece by Zoë Walker and Neil Bromwich named *The Dragon of Profit and Private Ownership* took place. In this forum, several people argued that the dragon could represent our international financial system, one that is collapsing in favour of a new generation of 'democratic' and 'decentralised' projects structured around peer-to-peer (P2P) lending platforms, distributed ledger technologies (DLT),[8] cloud computing and machine learning, among other inventions and innovations that underpin today's DCS. Certainly, it is an interesting argument that does not lack appeal, particularly after the GFC. Yet, this naïve approach ignores the cyclical nature that defines our financial systems and the infrastructures that support them, assuming that innovators act as idealised expressions of the *Homo oeconomicus*. As will be shown throughout this book, the spirit of this post-Lehman argument does not reflect the entire picture.

Figure 1 'The Dragon of Profit and Private Ownership' by Walker and Bromwich, with the author

[8] DLT refers to the set of protocols and supporting infrastructure that allow computers in different locations to propose and validate transactions and update records in a synchronised way across permissioned or permissionless networks.

Despite this fact, developers and promoters of cryptoassets tend to support these assumptions, invoking works like FA Hayek's celebrated *Choice in Currency. A Way to Stop Inflation*,[9] in which its author argues that 'the pressure for more and cheaper money, is an ever-present political force which monetary authorities have never been able to resist'.[10] In other words, it is believed that these projects can offer 'democratic' and 'descentralised' alternatives to current socio-political structures – ironic, if we consider that these alternatives tend to be developed around non-democratic algorithmic 'black boxes' that can identify their inputs and outputs, but cannot tell how, when and why one becomes the other.[11]

The spirit of these works, the increasing interoperability among different technology providers, and FinTech projects developed under long global value chains (GVCs)[12] and their network effects, invite innovators to challenge current sovereign prerogatives on money and data sovereignty.[13] Consequently, attracted by the deceptive neutral virtues of software, unsophisticated investors around the world, who have never invested in traditional investment instruments, are rushing to acquire products, such as cryptoassets, which they barely understand. This worrying behaviour was the main source of inspiration for the present work, especially because the first and most popular generation of cryptoassets was constituted around subprime innovations that emerged from a subprime crisis, to offer alternative financial instruments to subprime investors.

Of course, although innovators such as those who follow the ideas of the 'cypherpunk'[14] movement argue, through notions of decentralisation and disintermediation, that they are creating a financial revolution, this is not a new scenario. Just as in the past, pseudo-banking establishments are emerging and seizing on the weaknesses of traditional intermediaries, and – through a new generation of instruments – are introducing new sources of liquidity for businesses and households, not only to borrow, but also to speculate. Consequently, this financial

[9] FA Hayek, *Choice in Currency. A Way to Stop Inflation* (London, Ibi The Institute of Economic Affairs, 1976).

[10] ibid, 15.

[11] F Pasquale, *The Black Box Society. The Secret Algorithms that Control Money and information* (2015, Massachusetts, Harvard University Press, 2015) 3.

[12] A global value chain is constituted by hierarchical networks of actors that are linked in the production and distribution of products and services. These hierarchies are structured around the power that results from the ownership of patent rights, the control of branding and marketing, and the ability to create links for the distribution of products and services. See RW Cox and M Wartembe, 'The Politics of Global Value Chains' in R Kiggins (ed), *The Political Economy of Robots. Prospects for Prosperity and Peace in the Automated 21st Century* (Cham, Palgrave Macmillan, 2018) 17–40, 17.

[13] Generally, one tends to think that the Internet is a lawless zone that fosters the emergence of projects, such as Bitcoin. Nothing is further from the truth. States, in exercise of their data sovereignty, can command considerable control over the network architecture – including certain intermediaries – required to process data. See AK Woods, 'Litigating Data Sovereignty' (2018) 128 *The Yale Law Journal* 328, 360–361.

[14] The cypherpunk movement emerged in the 1990s from a series of meetings of cryptographers with liberal views that were against the actions of the US Government against the research and publication of ideas relating to cryptography. See P Franco, *Understanding Bitcoin. Cryptography, Engineering and Economics* (West Sussex, John Wiley & Sons, 2015) 161.

alchemy is creating in the shadows a new 'dragon' that is taking form through the implementation of the 'virtues' of these new technologies to offer unregulated financial services to sophisticated and unsophisticated consumers alike. One can call this the FinTech Dragon.

II. Financial Innovation

As was stated above, the constitutive elements of our FinTech dragon do not represent something radically new. Financial markets are not constituted by static practices and institutions that exist since time immemorial. They are the outcome of a *Bildungstrieb*[15] that has fostered the development of inventions, innovations and processes of diffusion, which have been used in four major ways: 1) to handle a greatly expanded customer base or foster processes of financial inclusion; 2) to represent different underlying *res* according to the best technology available to substantially reduce costs of processing payments; 3) to liberate the banks from the traditional constraints on time and place;[16] and 4) to introduce new products and services.[17] In other words, to improve the allocation of capital and risk management.[18]

Throughout the financial history of the world, this Schumpeterian[19] chain has taken us from the very conception of money to the emergence of algorithmic trading. One could even argue that financial innovation has played a major role in the healthy evolution of our financial systems, which, in turn, has had positive ramifications throughout our economies.[20] However, it is also possible to highlight

[15] The term *Bildungstrieb* was developed by Johann Friedrich Blumenbach to describe a formative force of 'architectonic' character that fostered the formation of new anatomical structures and functions on an original creature. In this work, this term is used as an analogy to the processes of invention, innovation and diffusion within our financial systems that are materialised through new products and services. A good reference to the original bases of the term can be found in JF Blumenbach, *De generis human varietate nativa* (Göttingen, Vandenhoek, 1795) 84–85; RJ Richards, 'Kant and Blumenbach on the Bildungstrieb: A Historical Misunderstanding' (2000) 31 *Studies in History and Philosophy of Biological and Biomedical Sciences* 11, 17–18.

[16] On this point, Freixas and Rochet develop an interesting formulation of the banking version of Salop's model. See X Freixas and JC Rochet, *Microeconomics of Banking.* (Cambridge, MIT Press, 2008) 68–69; SC Salop, 'Monopolistic Competition with Outside Goods' (1979) 10 *The Bell Journal of Economics* 141.

[17] A Arora, *Electronic Banking and the Law* (London, Banking Technology, 1993) 2–3; A Heertje, 'Technical and Financial Innovation' in A Heertje (ed), *Innovation, Technology, and Finance* (Oxford, European Investment Bank, 1988) 1, 4.

[18] E Avgouleas, 'Regulating Financial Innovation' in N Moloney, E Ferran and J Payne (eds), *Oxford Handbook of Financial Regulation* (Oxford, Oxford University Press, 2017) 660, 660.

[19] Schumpeter was the first to describe the evolutionary trend based on the distinctions among invention, innovation and diffusion, thus highlighting the role of diffusion of successful innovations across firms, sectors and nations. See JA Schumpeter, *Business Cycles: A Theoretical, Historical and Statistical Analysis of Capital Process* (New York, McGraw-Hill, 1939).

[20] WS Frame and LJ White, 'Empirical Studies of Financial Innovation: Lots of Talk, Little Action?' (2004) 42 *Journal of Economic Literature* 116, 116; R Levine, 'In Defense of Wall Street. The Social Productivity of the Financial System' (2011), available at faculty.haas.berkeley.edu/ross_levine/Papers/defense%20of%20wall%20street_post.pdf.

some experiences where the continuous interaction among financial innovation, a very low level of talent, and suboptimal regulatory frameworks[21] resulted in some of the most disastrous financial crises in the history of the world. Examples of this include the *Gebroeders de Neufville* crisis of 1763,[22] the *Overend, Gurney & Company* panic of 1866[23] and, of course, the GFC in 2007–08, which required the intervention of the Bank of Amsterdam, the Bank of England and the Federal Reserve of the United States, respectively, thus configuring some of the financial–constitutional mandates and regulatory tools that currently are in force around the world.

Since the GFC, we tend to relate the negative effects of financial innovation to instruments like asset-backed securities (ABS) and collateralised debt obligations (CDOs), and to institutions, such as Lehman Brothers, Royal Bank of Scotland and even the Federal Reserve. This perception has been highlighted by enthusiasts of new technologies like Jack Dorsey,[24] who argue that the answer for a more stable and inclusive financial system can be found in algorithmic P2P models like that presented in Satoshi Nakamoto's *Bitcoin: A Peer-to-Peer Electronic Cash System*,[25] which one can argue is a 'modern' version of John Law's Money and Trade Considered.[26] However, given that these projects are labelled as 'P2P', these enthusiasts tend to ignore that innovations like blockchain emerge from the same Schumpeterian chain that started with individual works and inventions protected by copyright, and industrial property figures and principles like patents and transformative use, and currently identified through the diffusion processes illustrated

[21] JP Coggan, *Paper Promises. Money, Debt, and the New World Order* (London, Penguin, 2011) 23; JK Galbraith, *Money. Whence It Came, Where It Went* (London, Andre Deutsch, 1975) 302.

[22] In the context of the failure of Gebroeders de Neufville, banks were underdeveloped, unregulated and relied heavily on an innovation structured around the bill of exchange known as the 'acceptance loan'. When the option to repay obligations from drawing these instruments was no longer viable after the conclusion of the Seven Years War, the following liquidity contraction fostered the failure of this bank. See S Quinn and W Roberds, 'Responding to a Shadow Banking Crisis. The Lessons of 1763' (2015) 47 *Journal of Money, Credit and Banking* 1149; I Schnabel and HS Shin, 'Foreshadowing LTCM. The Crisis of 1763' (2003), available at www.bis.org/authors/1763_schnabel_shin.pdf.

[23] Just as in the case of the crisis of 1763, practices related to the bill of exchange and the emergence of 'pseudo banking institutions' known as 'bill brokers', which gradually became discount houses, were in the middle of this crisis. After the restriction imposed by the Bank of England on these 'shadow banks' to access its Discount Window, Overend Gurney adjusted its business model and expanded it into riskier activities, which were the first to suffer the effects of a general collapse in the stock market and a fall in commodities prices, among other externalities in 1866. See H Chubb, 'The Bank Act and the Crisis of 1866.' (1872) 35 *Journal of the Statistical Society of London* 171; R Sowerbutts, M Schneebalg and F Hubert, 'The Demise of Overend Gurney' (2016), available at www.bankofengland.co.uk/-/media/boe/files/quarterly-bulletin/2016/the-demise-of-overend-gurney.

[24] A Frean, 'Bitcoin Will Become the World's Single Currency, Twitter Chief Says.' (2018), available at www.thetimes.co.uk/article/bitcoin-will-become-the-worlds-single-currency-tech-chief-says-66slm0p6b.

[25] S Nakamoto, 'Bitcoin: A Peer-to-Peer Electronic Cash System.' (2008), available at bitcoin.org/bitcoin.pdf.

[26] J Law, *Money and Trade Considered with a Proposal for Supplying the Nation with Money* (Glasgow, R & A Foulis, 1750).

by projects such as, JPM Coin[27] and smart off-line banknotes based on central bank digital currencies (CBDCs).[28] Consequently, as it will be highlighted in this book, most of these diffused innovations rely on intermediaries and infrastructural stakeholders to work and create trust. Furthermore, despite the apparent virtues of these governance schemes, during this process of diffusion, we have witnessed several failures related to cryptoassets projects[29] that in contexts of TBTF and/or TCTF institutions would have required the interpretation of regulations, such as Article 13(3) of the Federal Reserve Act to rescue them under 'unusual and exigent circumstances',[30] just as we witnessed during the GFC.

Acknowledging that the current process of systemic diffusion of the cryptoassets market will not stop in its current state, this work aims to offer the reader a more nuanced analysis of financial innovation focused not only on individual assets such Bitcoin, but also on the role of these innovations in the constitution of new payment systems with their respective payment instruments, infrastructures and intermediaries.

A. A New Challenge: Cryptoassets

Cryptoassets, also commonly referred to as cryptocurrencies, initial coin offerings (ICOs[31]), initial exchange offerings (IEOs[32]), stablecoins, etc, offer us examples

[27] O Wyman and Onyx, 'Deposit Tokens. A Foundation for Stable Digital Money.' (2022), available at www.jpmorgan.com/onyx/documents/deposit-tokens.pdf.

[28] Orell Füssli Ltd Security Printing, 'OFS and AUGENTIC GmbH Reveal the Design of the Offline "Smart Banknote CBDC" Prototype.' (2021), available at www.ofs.ch/de/events-news/news/detail/ofs-and-augentic-gmbh-reveal-the-design-of-the-offline-smart-banknote-cbdc-prototype-1.

[29] For instance, a study developed by Tyler Moore and Nicolas Christin argued that – in the early stages of the evolution of the market – approximately 45% of Bitcoin exchanges like Mt Gox had failed. See T Moore and N Christin, 'Beware the Middleman: Empirical Analysis of Bitcoin-Exchange Risk' in AR Sadeghi (ed), *Financial Cryptography and Data Security* (Berlin, Springer, 2013) 25–33.

[30] Before the changes introduced by the Dodd-Frank Act, Art 13(3) of the Federal Reserve Act authorised emergency actions in 'unusual and exigent circumstances … to discount for any participant, in any program or facility … provided that the Federal Reserve Bank shall obtain evidence that such participant in any program or facility with broad-based eligibility is unable to secure adequate credit accommodations from other banking institutions.' Just as described by Bernanke, Geithner and Paulson, the interpretation of this Article allowed them to help non-bank firms in programmes like the Term Securities Lending Facility (TSLF). See An Act To provide for the establishment of Federal reserve banks, to furnish an elastic currency, to afford means of rediscounting commercial paper, to establish a more effective supervision of banking in the United States, and for other purposes, Pub. 63–43, 23 December 1913; BS Bernanke, TF Geithner and HM Paulson, *Firefighting the Financial Crisis and Its Lessons* (London, Profile Books, 2019) 44–45.

[31] They are known as initial coin offerings given that they present similarities to traditional initial public offerings (IPOs), which involve 'a fundraising event in which an entity offers participants a unique digital asset – often described as a 'coin' or 'token' – in exchange for consideration (most commonly Bitcoin, Ether, U.S. dollars, or other fiat currency).' See *US Securities and Exchange Commission v Kik Interactive Inc* [2019], 19cv-5244 (US), 8.

[32] IEOs are by-products of ICOs, by which companies rely on non-regulated exchanges to offer digital assets in contrast to the P2P model used by other cryptoassets. See Securities and Exchange

of the complexities that courts, legislators and regulators face when they analyse the legal nature and consequences of new technologies and the innovations that result from them. Therefore, it is not surprising to find different legal interpretations regarding a single term, such as 'money', even within the borders of a single nation. For instance, on 22 July 2016, in Miami, Florida, Teresa Pooler J issued an order[33] by which she took a classical functional approach to argue that because cryptoassets are not accepted 'by all merchants and service providers'[34] and their value is uncertain and volatile, they cannot be labelled as money. In clear contrast, on 19 September 2016, Alison Nathan DJ[35] argued that Section 1960 of the Code of Laws of the United States of America (US Code) does not specify what counts as 'money', other than a note that it 'includes … funds';[36] she therefore reasoned that, given that these innovations are liquid assets 'which are generally accepted as a medium of exchange or a means of payment',[37] they could be classified as funds and, consequently, as money.

In the same spirit, one can find different interpretations, warnings and memoranda among other legal documents relating to these cryptographic instruments not only in the USA, but also around the world, that have been issued on this matter since the publication of Nakamoto's white paper.[38] Naturally, the challenging conclusion that one can draw from such documents is that, given these innovations are emerging and evolving quickly, these normative exercises reflect a rush to identify market imperfections and create different regulatory standards to face them. Unfortunately, these exercises have been structured around suboptimal efforts that lack a proper understanding of the legally relevant effects of the technologies involved and their respective value chains, and the legal nature of money. To some degree, these issues are the result of quasi-metaphysical debates among non-monetarists, pragmatists and fundamentalists within regulatory bodies about whether their definitions of 'money' should be focused on narrow measures – those closer to notes and coins – or on broader ones[39] that include different expressions of 'inside money'.[40]

Commission, 'Initial Exchange Offereings (IEOs). Investor Alert' (2020), available at www.sec.gov/oiea/investor-alerts-and-bulletins/ia_initialexchangeofferings.

[33] *The State of Florida v Michelle Abner Espinoza* [2014], F14-2923 FL (US), 5–6.

[34] ibid, 5.

[35] *US v Murgio et al* [2015], 15-cr-00769 AJN (US), 5–6.

[36] Code of Laws of the United States of America (US Code) 44 Stat 778, 30 June,1926 §1960(b) (2).

[37] *US v Murgio et al* [2015], 15-cr-00769 AJN (US), 6.

[38] Nakamoto (n 25).

[39] N Kiyotaki and J Moore, 'Liquidity, Business Cycles, and Monetary Policy' (2001), available at www.princeton.edu/~kiyotaki/papers/ClarendonLec2.pdf.

[40] Inside money can be defined as privately issued assets and liabilities that are used to satisfy contractual obligations, responding to the behaviours of regulated and non-regulated institutions based on the internal factors of each economic context. See N Kiyotaki and J. Moore, 'Inside Money and Liquidity' (2018), available at www.princeton.edu/~kiyotaki/papers/km4-5.6.2018(1).pdf; C Sissoko, 'Why Inside Money Matters?' (2007) 39 Journal of Money, Credit and Banking, 2097, 2097.

B. Introduction to DLT

Before the emergence of Bitcoin, encryption was largely seen as the sole province of the military and cybersecurity experts, but in the Digital Commercial Society (DCS), it is not surprising that this mathematically arcane science has joined the other forces of the Fourth Industrial Revolution (FIR) to help deliver our money intact.[41] Accordingly, with the aim of combatting these informational assymetries, we first have to understand the basics of the technological infrastructure that acts as the *Bildungstrieb* for this market.

While DLT may immediately bring to mind 'blockchain' and 'Bitcoin', can we say that DLT is a synonym for those words? The answer is a partial yes. In general terms, DLTs can be defined as 'data structures to record transactions and sets of functions to manipulate them'.[42] The core components of DLT are its nodes and their connections, which together make up the architecture of each network.[43] Through these structures, developers aim to create complete networks characterised by: 1) the absence of imposed centralised control; 2) the autonomous nature of their subunits; 3) the high connectivity among the descentralised subunits; and 4) the non-linear causality of the network effects.[44] The idea behind Bitcoin was not entirely new and revolutionary; one need only think of the references of Nakamoto's paper[45] and through the offer of DLTs, such as Blockchain, Tangle, Hashgraph and Sidechain. One can even argue that it is an example of sedimentary innovation.[46] After all, to foster its own diffusion, each DLT is developed using different data models and technologies; among which the most relevant are: 1) public key cryptography; 2) distributed peer-to-peer networks; and 3) consensus mechanisms.[47]

The first element has been a requirement for the evolution of electronic commerce following the principles of technology and service neutrality found in normative instruments such as Article 9 of the Directive 2000/31/EC[48] on Electronic Commerce and Article 89 of the Commercial Code[49] of Mexico, which

[41] EH Solomon, *Virtual Money. Understanding the Power and Risks of Money's High-Speed Journey unto Electronic Space* (New York, Oxford University Press, 1997) 227.

[42] NE Ioini and C Pahl, 'A Review of Distributed Ledger Technologies' in H Panetto et al (eds), *On the Move to Meaningful Internet Systems* (Cham, Springer Nature, 2018) 277, 278.

[43] L Enriques, A Romano and T Wetzer, 'Network-Sensitive Financial Regulation' (2019) 451 *ECGI Working Paper Series in Law* 1, 15.

[44] K Kelly, *Out of Control. The New Biology of Machines, Social Systems, and the Economic World* (New York, Basic Books, 1994) 22.

[45] Nakamoto (n 25).

[46] Sedimentary innovations are developed around multiple small modifications to a basic invention. See C Ford, *Innovation and the State. Finance, Regulation and Justice* (New York, Cambridge University Press, 2017) 195.

[47] Ioini and Pahl (n 42).

[48] Directive 2000/31/EC of the European Parliament and of the Council on certain legal aspects of information society services, in particular electronic commerce, in the Internal Market (Directive on electronic commerce) OJ L 178/1, 8 June 2000.

[49] Commercial Code DOF, 13 December 1889.

were based on the content of the UNCITRAL Model Law on Electronic Commerce (1996).[50] To put in practice these principles, in 1976, Diffie and Hellman[51] identified the problems relating to the creation of electronic contracts, and argued that:

> In order to develop a system capable of replacing the current written contract with some purely electronic form of communication, we must discover a digital phenomenon with the same properties as a written signature. It must be easy for anyone to recognize the signature as authentic, but impossible for anyone other than the legitimate signer to produce it. We will call any such technique one-way authentication. Since any digital signal can be copied precisely, a true digital signature must be recognizable without being known.

Consequently, through encryption, we can transform a message or data files (plaintext) into a form (ciphertext) that is unintelligible without a decryption key.[52] The most popular one-way authentication technique is known as a hash function, which is an algorithmic processing of data that, in contrast to an ordinary cipher system, is not invertible.[53] After all, we have to be able to replicate the effects of a traditional signature, which cannot be physically reverted given that when the referred signature is fixed, it alters the carrier with the addition of a substance while it adds information to the *reifier*.[54] Within the universe of hash algorithmic standards, we can mention the NIST Secure Hash Standard and SHA-2, which is constituted around three algorithms: SHA-256;[55] SHA-384; and SHA-512.[56] These are labelled as secure because each is computationally infeasible to find a message related to a specific given message digest, or to find two different messages that produce the same digest. Consequently, any change to a message will result in a verification failure.[57]

In the particular case of DLTs like blockchain, the algorithms are organised using a mathematical structure of branching nodes following a Merkle hash-tree pattern (Figure 2), which was supported by the patent US4309569A.[58] The patent was granted to Ralph Merkle, who filed it in 1979; however, the expiration of the patent in 1999 has allowed developers to incorporate the concept freely into new inventions and diffuse it through the incorporation of OS software.

[50] UNCITRAL, 'UNCITRAL Model Law on Electronic Commerce (1996) with additional article 5 bis as adopted in 1998.' (1996), available at uncitral.un.org/en/texts/ecommerce/modellaw/electronic_commerce#:~:text=The%20MLEC%20was%20the%20first,of%20modern%20electronic%20commerce%20law.

[51] W Diffie and ME Hellman, 'New Directions in Cryptography' (1976) 22 *IEEE Transactions on Information Theory* 644, 649.

[52] Solomon (n 41) 228.

[53] J Dooley, *History of Cryptography and Cryptanalysis* (Cham, Springer International Publishing, 2018) 179–80.

[54] S Mason, *Electronic Signatures in Law* (London, University of London, 2016) 182.

[55] Bitcoin runs using the algorithm SHA-256.

[56] Dooley (n 53) 180.

[57] National Institute of Standards and Technology, 'Secure Hash Standard (SHS)' (2015), available at nvlpubs.nist.gov/nistpubs/FIPS/NIST.FIPS.180-4.pdf.

[58] [1979] US4309569A: 'Method of Providing Digital Signatures'.

Figure 2 The Merkle tree structure of a blockchain[59]

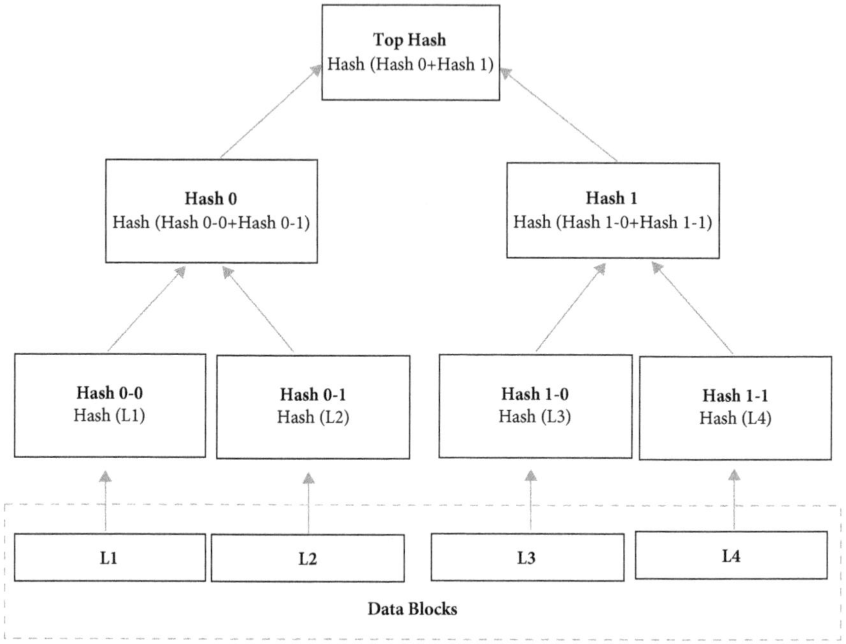

C. The Solution to the Byzantine Generals Problem

The other two technologies involved (distributed peer-to-peer networks and consensus mechanisms) are closely related to a well-known computer science problem known as the Byzantine Generals Problem. As one can see with current electronic money models, the most straightforward way to represent and communicate value is to constitute it around a binary system, ie, a machine-readable string of zeroes and ones.[60] However, such systems exhibit an externality known as the 'public goods' problem[61] because, in absence of cryptographic systems and/or 'black boxes', their data sets can be replicated easily at practically no cost.

There is a belief among computer scientists that a distributed group of people cannot reach consensus in absence of a common clearinghouse, because the

[59] K Werbach, *The Blockchain and the New Architecture of Trust* (Massachusetts, MIT Press, 2018) 13.

[60] LP Nian and DL Kuo Chuen, 'Introduction to Bitcoin' in DL Kuo Chuen (ed), *Handbook of Digital Currency. Bitcoin, Innovation, Financial Instruments, and Big Data* (San Diego, Academic Press, 2015) 6, 15; C Reed, *Electronic Finance Law* (Cambridge, Woodhead-Faulkner, 1991), 111; Franco (n 14) 10.

[61] Public goods are characterised by two main features: 1) non-excludability and 2) non-rivalrous. In this case, this problem allows users to copy computer programs and databases easily and inexpensively even if they are not duly empowered to do it. See MA Lemley et al, *Software and Internet Law* (New York, Aspen Law & Business, 2000) 31.

network would otherwise be at risk of attack from ill-intentioned actors.[62] In theory, the best solution to this problem is the creation of a central registry in a third-party trusted system, as put forward by Leslie Lamport, Robert Shostak and Marshall Pease.[63] The problem is posed through a hypothetical scenario where three divisions of the Byzantine army are camped outside an enemy city in hopes of conquering it. Independent generals command each division of the army and, in order to plan an attack, they need to decide on a common course of action. Yet, the generals can only communicate with one another through oral messages. However, as one can find in innumerable historical and military records, there is a risk that one or more generals are potential traitors who might prevent the loyal generals from reaching an agreement. Given that a solution will not work unless more than two-thirds of the generals are loyal, where there are three generals, no solution can work in the presence of a single traitor.[64]

In most modern payment systems, the database is managed by a central 'settlement institution' (generally a central bank), which acts as the paymaster to commercial banks and payment service providers, holding deposits from each of them, so it can settle obligations among these regulated participants.[65] However, as was seen in incidents related to the activities of the Lazarus group, the Ploutus and the Medusa malware phishing attacks, among others,[66] this paradigm presents a single point of failure, given that, in our digitalised context, our payment systems become huge targets for cyber theft.[67]

Now, to face this problem, distributed systems, such as blockchain, rely on consensus mechanisms that aim to seek agreement and ensure robust network security. They refer to the algorithms that – in the absence of a central node – verify the agreements developed among the various network nodes as to the state of the stored data, thus reflecting the current status of the network.[68] Among these

[62] RE Kahn and PA Lyons, 'Representing Value as Digital Objects: A Discussion of Transferability and Anonymity' (2006) 5 *Journal on Telecommunications and High Technology Law* 189, 190; A Wright and P De Filippi, 'Decentralized Blockchain Technology and the Rise of Lex Cryptographia' (2015) available at https://papers.ssrn.com/sol3/papers.cfm?abstract_id=2580664.

[63] L Lamport, R Shostak and M Pease, 'The Byzantine Generals Problem' (1982) 4 *ACM Transactions on Programming Languages and Systems* 382.

[64] D Schwartz, N Youngs and A Britto, 'The Ripple Protocol Consensus Algorithm' (2014), available at ripple.com/files/ripple_consensus_whitepaper.pdf; Lamport, Shostak and Pease (n 63) 382–84; Wright and De Filippi (n 62).

[65] MT Rosner and A Kang, 'Understanding and Regulating Twenty-First Century Payment Systems: The Ripple Case Study' (2016) 114 *Michigan Law Review* 650, 653.

[66] Carnegie Endowment for International Peace, 'Timeline of Cyber Incidents Involving Financial Institutions' (2022), available at carnegieendowment.org/specialprojects/protectingfinancialstability/timeline.

[67] BP Eha, *How Money Got Free. Bitcoin and the Fight for the Future of Finance* (London, Oneworld Publications, 2017) 19; Franco (n 14) 11.

[68] P Bains, 'Blockchain Consensus Mechanisms: A Primer for Supervisors.' (2022), available at www.elibrary.imf.org/view/journals/063/2022/003/article-A001-en.xml#:~:text=Consensus%20mechanisms%20underpin%20the%20effective,agreed%20on%20by%20most%20nodes; D Hellwig, G Karlic and A Huchzermeier, *Build Your Own Blockchain. A Practical Guide to Distributed Ledger Technology*

mechanisms, are proof-of-work (PoW) and proof-of-stake (PoS), and their respective incentive systems like Bitcoin that take advantage of the governance models that emerge from the structure of the DCS.

D. The Digital Commercial Society and the Digital *Bildungstrieb*

Just as in the case of financial innovations based on DLT, the concept of the DCS is not a novelty. Its origin can be traced back to Scottish Enlightenment in the seventeenth and the eighteenth centuries, which was developed to improve social and economic institutions.[69] Consequently, this paradigm emerged from the understanding that one of the most powerful influences in the greatness and prosperity of a state and, consequently, in the happiness of its citizens, is the driving force of trade,[70] which acts as the *Bildungstrieb* of the evolving markets that define each commercial society. Consequently, one can infer that this model of society, in turn, was an outcome of the break-up of feudalism when every private individual received greater security, in the possession of their trade and their riches, and became a member of a merchant society. Within this society, its members could trade freely with each other under the law,[71] following the paradigm in works such as *De Jure Regni apud Scotos Dialogus*,[72] and the development of growing value chains, which, in turn, fostered the emergence of disciplines like intellectual property law (IP law). This legal discipline became necessary to face the problem of public goods and the operational decentralisation of production, and to break the territorial paradigm that defined the genesis of the schemes of protection, thus fostering the development of GVCs.[73]

These interactions within commercial societies foster the evolution of technology, and change the factors of production and their relationship to technology; after all, markets are not static institutions, but mechanisms for the discovery and development of new endogenous demands[74] that emerge as inputs for our

(Cham, Springer Nature, 2020) 53; AS Yadav, N Singh and DS Kushwaha, 'Evolution of Blockchain and Consensus Mechanisms & its Real-World Applications' (2023) 82 *Multimedia Tools and Applications* 1, 11.

[69] CJ Berry, *The Idea of Commercial Society in the Scottish Enlightenment* (Edinburgh: Edinburgh University Press, 2015) 1.

[70] R Goode, *Goode on Commercial Law* (London, Penguin Books, 2016) 3.

[71] A Smith, 'The Origin and Development of our Property Rights' in A Broadie (ed), *The Scottish Enlightenment. An Anthology* (Edinburgh, Canongate Books, 1997) 475–87; D Hume, 'Of Commerce' in A Broadie (ed), *The Scottish Enlightenment. An Anthology* (Edinburgh, Canongate Books, 1997) 385–397, 388; J Norman, *Adam Smith. What He Thought, and Why it Matters* (Milton Keynes, Allen Lane, 2018) 296.

[72] G Buchanan, *De Jure Regni apud Scotos Dialogus* (Glasgow, Ronerti Urie, 1750) 72–73.

[73] BK Woodward, 'The Roles of Non-State Actors in Lawmaking within the Global Intellectual Property Regimes of WIPO and TRIPs' (2012)14 *International Community Law Review* 33, 33–36.

[74] A Heertje, 'Technical and Financial Innovation' in A Heertje (ed), *Innovation, Technology, and Finance* (Oxford, Basil Blackwell, 1988) 1–13, 4.

dynamic social systems. Building on the theory of dynamic systems,[75] that is the basis for the development of the technologies that have configured our DCS, we define a dynamic social system as a complex set of interconnections of individuals and institutions, endowed with three main elements: 1) a state; 2) an input; and 3) an output. The dynamism of our societies under this paradigm is based on the dynamic nature of the rules of transition by which each society will flow from one state to another. Among these rules is the *lex monetae.*

Just as in the case of the Scottish Enlightenment, we are today witnessing the emergence of a new generation of merchants that are expanding the principles and institutions that configured our real economy to the digital world, and by which they foster the development of new forms of creative collaboration, and even new forms of money that address the new endogenous needs of the DCS. Evidently, the latter could not be possible in absence of the dissemination of knowledge and the diffusion of innovations among peers under participative paradigms, such as user-generated content and open-source software. These models empower users to be increasingly active contributors to developing, rating, collaborating on and distributing digital content, and developing and customising Internet applications.[76] Consequently, we can define our DCS as the fifth stage[77] of the 'natural progress' of our dynamic social systems in which many endogenous needs are addressed – almost immediately – through the development and interoperability of systems created on a collective basis. In different terms, it is possible to argue that each individual that has access to a node of a network within the global network is a potential digital merchant; an individual architect for the development and evolution of our FinTech dragon.

Of course, the control that this new generation of merchants exercises over the Internet goes beyond the notice and takedown model that is actively employed in social media, and it is even possible to argue that it has shaped the development of the Internet by creating new collective systems of enforcement that operate parallel to the law.[78] Despite this, the way in which the Internet is managed is vastly under-studied given that its structure tends to be analysed under the role of international organisations and the role of Internet intermediaries in the standard-setting process that supports the evolution of the network of networks.[79] However, if we want to understand the evolution of our FinTech dragon, we have to pay attention to the GVCs, which are constituted as networks of stakeholders

[75] See J Angeles. *Fundamentals of Robotic Mechanical Systems. Theory, Methods, and Algorithms* (Cham, Springer, 2014) 1.

[76] Organization for Economic Co-operation and Development, 'Participative Web: User-Created Content' (2007), available at www.oecd.org/sti/38393115.pdf.

[77] In the context of the Scottish Enlightenment, several authors developed a model of societal development based on four stages: 1) hunters; 2) herders; 3) farmers; and 4) commerce. Berry (n 69) 38.

[78] NP Suzor. *Lawless. The Secret Rules that Govern Our Digital Lives* (Cambridge, Cambridge University Press, 2019, 60.

[79] A Harcourt, G Christou and S Simpson. *Global Standard-Setting in Internet Governance* (Oxford, Oxford University Press, 2020) 1.

that are linked together in the planning, production and distribution of products and services across international borders. It is important to emphasise that these networks are built upon a hierarchy of relationships that are defined by the ownership and/or control of IPRs.[80]

As we can infer from the content of the precedent lines, the economy of the DCS, including its monetary expressions, has to be analysed beyond popular approaches based on cybersecurity and personal data protection, and we have to start asking who controls the infrastructures and the transition rules that are being tested and deployed to allow innovations like stablecoins and CBDCs, and what are their contributions to the development of our dynamic social systems and their respective financial systems.

Chapter three provides a definition of electronic money, and from this it can be inferred that a basic element in finance is the representation and incorporation of 'value'. The latter can be represented by a writing, or more generally, through a 'data structure' fixed in a tangible medium as described by Floyd LJ in *Your Response Ltd. v Datateam Business Media Ltd*[81] and in the thesis of jurisprudence XVII.2o.C.T.23C[82] issued by the Supreme Court of Justice of Mexico. On this point, following the words of Lord Upjohn found in *Boardman v Phipps*,[83] the courts involved have held that information by itself cannot be considered property given that it relies on its external manifestation. However, these opinions have not stopped an increasing amount of references arguing that the legal notion of the *res* does not require physical objects of the real world, as in case of intangibles (eg electricity) and pure intangibles (eg IPRs).[84] Considering the characteristics of these innovations and the arguments presented by Stephen Morris QC in *Armstrong DLW GmbH v Winnington Networks Ltd*,[85] one can view a digital object as a definable, identifiable by third parties and a stable item within a network-based computer environment, which is structured around a set of sequences of bits or elements, each of which constitutes structured data interpretable by a computational facility.[86] Among these sequences, at least one has to denote a unique, persistent identifier for that object,[87] which in the case of digital payments will configure the basis for the principle of formality.

[80] RW Cox and. Wartembe, 'The Politics of Global Value Chains' in R Kiggins (ed), *The Political Economy of Robots. Prospects for Prosperity and Peace in the Automated 21st Century* (Cham, Palgrave Macmillan, 2018) 17–40, 17.

[81] [2015] QB 41 (UK), 56.

[82] *TRANSFERENCIAS ELECTRÓNICAS. NO Constituyen Documentos Privados, sino Elementos de Prueba Derivados de los Descubrimientos de la Ciencia, Cuya Valoración queda al Prudente Arbitrio del Juzgador* [2011] SCJN, Thesis of Jurisprudence XVII.2°.C.T.23.C. (MX).

[83] [1967] 2 AC 46 (UK), 127–28.

[84] A Rahmatian, 'Money as a Legally Enforceable Debt' (2018) 29 *European Business Law Review* 205, 210.

[85] [2012] EWHC 10 (Ch) (UK), 171.

[86] Kahn and Lyons (n 62) 193.

[87] ibid.

Now, in the DCS, electronic commerce allows us not only to create and transfer digital objects, but also to make payments. Trying to replicate the anonymity of cash in the decentralised structure that defines the very existence of the Internet, we witnessed how some of the first attempts to create digital cash failed or went nowhere, through the existence of projects like Ecash, Hashcash, BitGold, and patents, such as US6157920 A,[88] constituted and/or granted before 2008. Most of these projects were designed to achieve the anonymity and/or decentralisation associated with the 'cypherpunk' movement. So, it is not a complete surprise that some developers and proponents of our current cryptoassets were members of that movement.[89] Among them, Eric Hughes published 'A Chypherpunk's Manifesto' in which he stated that: 'We the cypherpunks are dedicated to building anonymous systems. We are defending our privacy with cryptography, with anonymous mail forwarding systems, with digital signatures, and with electronic money.'[90]

With these ideas in mind, it is possible to argue that all electronic payments have been dematerialised, and after the gradual centralisation verified through the emergence of intermediaries like VISA and Mastercard, electronic money has been defined following the content of normative instruments, such as, the Electronic Money Regulations 2011[91] in the UK and the 2EMD.[92] However, given this process of dematerialisation associated with the DCS, and the risks reflected in documents like the OECD Guidelines for Cryptography Policy[93] and the World Economic Forum's Global Risks Report 2023,[94] people around the world have been concerned about the integrity and security of the databases required to materialise our financial transactions, particularly, after the expansion of electronic commerce in the context of the COVID-19 crisis.

E. The Never-ending Task of Defining 'Money'

The lack of a uniform definition of 'money' has been identified in legal cases, such as *Perrin v Morgan*,[95] where Lord Chancellor Viscount Simon considered:

> [T]he word 'money' has not got one natural or usual meaning. It has several meanings, each of which in appropriate circumstances may be regarded as natural. In its original

[88] [1998]US6157920 A: 'Executable digital cash for electronic commerce'.

[89] Franco (n 14) 160–61.

[90] E. Hughes, 'A Chypherpunk's Manifesto' (1993), available at www.activism.net/cypherpunk/manifesto.html.

[91] The Electronic Money Regulations 2011, No 99, 19 January 2019.

[92] Directive 2009/110/EC of the European Parliament and of the Council on the taking up, pursuit and prudential supervision of the business of electronic money institutions amending Directives 2005/60/EC and 2006/48/EC and repealing Directive 2000/46/EC OJ L 267/7, 16 September 2009.

[93] Organization for Economic Cooperation and Development, 'OECD Guidelines for Cryptography Policy' (1997), available at www.oecd.org/sti/ieconomy/guidelinesforcryptographypolicy.htm.

[94] World Economic Forum, 'World Economic Forum's Global Risks Report 2023' (2023), available at www.weforum.org/reports/global-risks-report-2023.

[95] [1943] AC 399 HL (UK), 406–07.

> sense, which is also its narrowest sense, the word means 'coin.' Moneta was an appellation of Juno, and the Temple of Moneta at Rome was the mint. Phrases like 'false money' or 'clipped money' show the original use in English, but the conception very quickly broadens into the equivalent of 'cash' of any sort. The question: 'Have you any money in your purse?' refers presumably to bank notes or Treasury notes, as well as to shillings and pence. A further extension would include not only coin and currency in the possession of an individual, but debts owing to him, and cheques which he could pay into his banking account, or postal orders, or the like … Sums on deposit, whether with a bank or otherwise, may be included by a further extension, but this is by no means the limit to the senses in which the word 'money' is frequently and quite naturally used in English speech. The statement: 'I have my money invested on mortgage, or in debentures, or in stocks and shares, or in saving certificates,' is not an illegitimate use of the word 'money' on which the courts are bound to frown, though it is a great extension from its original meaning to interpret it as covering securities, and, in considering the various meanings of the word 'money' in common speech, one must go even further, as any dictionary will show …'

Certainly, if one selects the 'dictionary' definition, the issue could get a little out of hand.

Considering the complexities described above, is not surprising that authors such as Leland B Yeager[96] and Agustín Carstens[97] affirm that it is practically impossible to define and specify what now counts as money, given that any potential answer to this millenary question will depend on how deep and philosophical one wants to be. On this point, this book starts by acknowledging that, despite all the centuries of study and debate on this matter, and the temptation to join these efforts, 'money' has never been successfully defined – and probably never will be.[98] Consequently, the definitions that the reader will find in this work have been developed as secondary elements for practical reasons, and they do not constitute the primary aim of this effort. After all, even the very legislators who should provide us with these definitions are sometimes prepared to recognise that certain words, like 'money', fundamentally resist definition.[99]

This obstacle does not simplify our task. However, to address accurately the regulatory questions that are emerging about new monetary instruments introduced by the private sector in the DCS and the potential development of CBDCs, it is vital to change our approach. We must stop paying excessive attention to the technical structure of Bitcoin and focus our efforts instead on the material and the legally relevant effects of the distinguishing feature of these infrastructural assets

[96] LB Yeager, 'The Continuing Search for a Monetary Constitution' in LH White, VJ Vanberg and EA Köhler (eds), *Renewing the Search for a Monetary Constitution. Reforming Government's Role in the Monetary System* (Washington, Cato Institute, 2015) Kindle EBook Loc 229-550, Loc 250.

[97] A Carstens, 'Money in the Digital Age: What Role for Central Banks?' (2018), available at www.bis.org/speeches/sp180206.pdf.

[98] V Chick, 'Unresolved Questions in Monetary Theory: A Critical Review' (1978) 126 *De Economist* 37, 38.

[99] R Harris and C Hutton, *Definition in Theory and Practice: Language, Lexicography and the Law* (London, Continuum, 2007) 34; Goode (n 70) 22.

as means of payment. On this point, different authorities and institutions like the House of Commons in the UK[100] and the Bank for International Settlements (BIS)[101] have argued, taking as their starting points the sovereign prerogatives to create money known *as ius cudendae monetae/lex monetae*,[102] that cryptoassets do not have the characteristics nor perform the functions that traditionally help us to define money. We do not completely agree. We have to remember that practically any commodity may serve as a unit of account, even if the obligations are not paid in that referential unit, as explained by Lord Denning MR in *Woodhouse AC Israel Cocoa Limited v Nigerian Produce Marketing Ltd*,[103] and that every durable and resalable asset is, by its very nature, a potential store of value.[104] Furthermore, the value of these assets is generated by their use as medium of exchange,[105] as has been noted recently in *Wisconsin Central Ltd et al v United States*.[106] If cryptoassets do not fulfil these functions in an optimal way, that is matter for a different discussion. Of course, this is not a full departure from the state theory of money. However, we will argue that this theory of money is incomplete given that it is structured only around the characteristics of sovereign currencies, ignoring different expressions of 'inside money' that are created within the market, but tolerated and sanctioned by the state in exercise of its *ius cudendae monetae*.[107]

III. Regulating in the Fourth Industrial Revolution

The potential of cryptoassets is closely related to the technological environment, as a socio-evolutionary rather than revolutionary one. As we can see through the case of metallic coins, bills of exchange, banknotes and electronic money, each monetary instrument and institution that might be described in any banking law, economics or anthropology book has reflected the state of its own dynamic social system. Therefore, cryptoassets can be understood as an expression of what we call the Fourth Industrial Revolution (FIR).[108]

[100] House of Commons, 'Crypto-Assets. Twenty-Second Report of Session 2017–19' (2018), available at publications.parliament.uk/pa/cm201719/cmselect/cmtreasy/910/910.pdf, 4.

[101] Carstens (n 97).

[102] Generally, the *ius cudendae monetae/lex monetae* is understood as the sovereign power over the monetary system by which the state defines the unit of account, regulates the creation and circulation of currency within its territory, the right to determine and change the value of the currency, and its interaction with foreign currencies. See E Avgouleas and W Blair, 'The Concept of Money in the 4th Industrial Revolution. A Legal and Economic Analysis' (2020) *Singapore Journal of Legal Studies* 4, 25; K Byttebier, *Towards a New International Monetary Order* (Cham, Springer, 2017) 61.

[103] [1971] 2 QB 23 (CA) (UK), 54.

[104] R Clower, 'A Reconsideration of the Microfoundations of Monetary Theory' (1967) 6 *Western Economic Journal* 1, 3; J Hicks, *A Market Theory of Money* (Oxford, Oxford University Press, 1989) 42.

[105] M Aglietta, *Money. 5,000 Years of Debt and Power* (New York, Verso, 2018) 31–32.

[106] [2018] 138 S Ct 2067 (US), 6.

[107] FA Mann, *The Legal Aspect of Money* (London, Oxford University Press, 1938) 11–12.

[108] K Schwab, *The Fourth Industrial Revolution* (London, Portfolio Penguin, 2017) 6–7.

Of course, the FIR follows three other industrial revolutions. The First Industrial Revolution (1760–1840) was triggered by the use of water and steam power to mechanise production; thus, small home-based industries gradually gave way to larger-scale production projects.[109] The Second (late 19th century into the early 20th century) was structured around the development of electrical communications, and the use of electric power to create mass production through the advent of the assembly line.[110] Finally, the Third, popularised by Jeremy Rifkin,[111] started in the 1960s and was based on the use of electronics and information technology (IT) to process large volumes of data, automate production and improve decision-making.[112] One could argue that the FIR is an extension of the Third, based on its reliance on machine learning, open-source software, cloud computing and Big Data.[113] However, studies published by the World Intellectual Property Organization (WIPO)[114] and the European Patent Office (EPO), for example,[115] countries such as China and the USA are taking advantage of such technologies to reach consumers where they spend most of their time:[116] on their smartphones, tablets and laptops. Furthermore, the diffusion of these technologies is blurring the lines among the physical, digital and biological spheres,[117] and, consequently, are configuring Kevin Kelly's *technium*[118] and Roger Clark's *digital persona.*[119]

Through this Schumpeterian chain, it is possible to see how, through the fusion of these technologies, companies like Ripple, Harness, IBM and Facebook are

[109] DE Frederick, 'Libraries, Data and the Fourth Industrial Revolution' (2016) 33 *Library Hi Tech News* 9, 9; Schwab (n 108) 6–7.

[110] Schwab (n 108) 6–7.

[111] J Rifkin, *The Third Industrial Revolution. How Lateral Power is Transforming Energy, the Economy, and the World* (New York, St Martin's Press, 2011).

[112] J Téllez-Valdés, *Derecho Informático* (Mexico City, McGraw-Hill, 2008) 6; Frederick (n 52); Rifkin (n 111); Schwab (n 108).

[113] 'Big data is a large and complex collection of data sets, which is difficult to process using on-hand database management tools and traditional data processing applications.' See B Furht and F Villanustre, 'Introduction to Big Data' in B Furht and V Villanustre (eds), *Big Data Technologies and Applications* (Cham, Springer International Publishing, 2016) 3, 3.

[114] World Intellectual Property Organization, 'WIPO IP Facts and Figures 2018.' (2019), available at www.wipo.int/edocs/pubdocs/en/wipo_pub_943_2018.pdf.

[115] European Patent Office, 'Patents and the Fourth Industrial Revolution. The Inventions behind Digital Transformation.' (2017), available at documents.epo.org/projects/babylon/eponet.nsf/0/17FDB5538E87B4B9C12581EF0045762F/$FILE/fourth_industrial_revolution_2017__en.pdf.

[116] F Leibert, 'New Computing in Digital Marketplaces Unleashed' in C Linnhoff-Popien, R Schneider and M Zaddach (eds), *Digital Marketplaces Unleashed* (2018, Berlin, Springer-Verlag) 13–16, 14.

[117] K Schwab, 'The Fourth Industrial Revolution. What It Means and How to Respond' (2015), available at www.foreignaffairs.com/articles/2015-12-12/fourth-industrial-revolution.

[118] Kevin Kelly argues, under this term, that technological inventions and innovations have become so complex and interlinked with our lives that we are witnessing the emergence of a vast techno-social system. See K Kelly, *What Technology Wants* (2010, New York, Viking Press).

[119] Roger Clarke defines the digital persona as 'a model of an individual's public personality based on data and maintained by transactions, and intended for use as a proxy for the individual.' See R Clarke, 'The Digital Persona and Its Application to Data Surveillance.' (1994) 10 *The Information Society* 77, 77.

blurring the line between technology companies and financial intermediaries,[120] thereby changing the way we make payments and adding a new set of complexities to our regulatory challenge that go beyond the simple use of technology-neutral approaches to describe the new reality. Therefore, while banks and bank-based payment systems still dominate the financial landscape in most jurisdictions, in recent years we have witnessed the emergence of different service providers like Monzo[121] and TransferWise,[122] which Awrey and van Zwieten[123] include in what they call the 'shadow payments system'.

To participate in this 'financial arms race' fostered by the development of these technologies within GVCs, some of the finest minds are being employed by both traditional banks and other tech/financial institutions that one could currently classify as 'shadow banks'. The purpose of this trend is to develop new complex ways to create money, and improve the infrastructural pipelines required for that purpose, taking advantage of the absence of appropriate regulatory frameworks.[124] Accordingly, the development of new financial products and services have seduced not only graduates of elite business programmes, but also PhDs in fluid dynamics, astrophysics, cellular biology and computer engineering,[125] whom Larry Summers has described as 'good at solving very difficult mathematical problems'.[126] For example, in 2015, engineers comprised around one-third of Goldman Sachs' 33,000 staff.[127] Of course, transparency and explainability requirements needed to face operational risks that will derive from regulations such as Article 17 of the Markets in Financial Instruments Directive 2014/65/EU (MiFID II),[128] and the

[120] M Andreessen, 'Why Software is Eating the World' (2011), available at www.wsj.com/articles/SB10001424053111903480904576512250915629460.

[121] Monzo is an FCA-regulated non-bank that provides payment services. See Financial Conduct Authority (a), 'Monzo Bank Ltd.' (2016), available at register.fca.org.uk/ShPo_FirmDetailsPage?id=001b000002syvKiAAI.

[122] TransferWise is an FCA-regulated PSP that eases international transfers and now, since this recognition, has access to the Real-Time Gross Settlement system of the Bank of England. See Bank of England (a), 'First Non-Bank Payment Service Provider (PSP) Directly Accesses UK Payment System' (2018) available at www.bankofengland.co.uk/news/2018/april/non-bank-psp-access-to-the-payments-system-announcement.

[123] D Awrey and K van Zwieten, 'The Shadow Payment System.' (2018) 43 *The Journal of Corporation Law* 102–41, 103.

[124] M Haiven, 'The Creative and the Derivative.' (2014) 118 *Radical History Review* 113–38, 113.

[125] N Gupta and I Hacamo, 'Early Career Choices of Superstar Entrepreneurs' (2019), available at papers.ssrn.com/sol3/papers.cfm?abstract_id=3136751&download=yes; Haiven (n 124).

[126] L Summers, 'Fourth Annual Marshall J. Seidman Lecture on Health Policy' (2004), available at www.harvard.edu/president/speeches/summers_2004/seidman.php.

[127] Arner, Barberis and Buckley (n 2) 24.

[128] 'An investment firm that engages in algorithmic trading shall have in place effective systems and risk controls suitable to the business it operates to ensure that its trading systems are resilient and have sufficient capacity, are subject to appropriate trading thresholds and limits and prevent the sending of erroneous orders or the systems otherwise functioning in a way that may create or contribute to a disorderly market. Such a firm shall also have in place effective systems and risk controls to ensure the trading systems cannot be used for any purpose that is contrary to Regulation (EU) No 596/2014 or to the rules of a trading venue to which it is connected. The investment firm shall have in place effective business continuity arrangements to deal with any failure of its trading systems and shall ensure its

introduction of automated DevOps[129] pipelines, will lead to an increase in these numbers.

These innovations, on the one hand, offer borrowers, investors and financial intermediaries new and more flexible opportunities for increasing their liquidity and to provide the infrastructure required by these innovative efforts.[130] Unfortunately, on the other hand, the risks that result from these innovations have become too complex to understand, explain and manage.[131] Consequently, we are relying on the development and proliferation of new techniques, instruments and institutions like Computer Forensics, Regulatory Technology (RegTech) and safe spaces to test innovative products, services, business models and delivery mechanisms popularly known as regulatory sandboxes,[132] which, in turn, pose their own set of complexities. Given that this is a rather competitive business – and a lucrative one – this scenario raises a key question that we should answer before issuing any regulatory proposals: what kind of institutions do we want to be providing the legal and technological infrastrucutre required to develop and diffuse these innovations?

In the context of rapid social and technological transformation, answering this question is not an easy task. The increasing reliance on algorithmic codes and the idealisation of its neutral virtues to manage risks and foster processes of decentralisation/disintermediation obscures questionable assumptions on the nature of the innovations being offered.[133] At the same time, while the extraordinary changes relating to the FIR are taking place, legislators start to realise that some norms are obsolete and/or suboptimal to face these innovations, and try to work on a new set of guidelines to face the new conditions introduced by innovators. However, as one can see in legislative efforts like the Mexican Law to Regulate Financial Technology Institutions[134] and its normative 'patches' like that presented

systems are fully tested and properly monitored to ensure that they meet the requirements laid down in this paragraph'. See Directive 2014/65/EU of the European Parliament and of the Council on markets in financial instruments and amending Directive 2002/92/EC and Directive 2011/61/EU OJ L 173/149, 15 May 2014.

[129] DevOps represent a paradigm put in place by companies around the world where both the development and operation teams have independent tools, processes and knowledge bases that are mingled together within a pipeline with the aim to develop continuously in-house software. See M Akbar et al, 'Toward Successful DevSecOps in Software Development Organizations: A Decision-Making Framework' (2022) 147 *Information and Software Technology* 1.

[130] H Mayer and J Kneeshaw, 'Financial Market Structure and Regulatory Change' in A Heertje (ed), *Innovation, Technology, and Finance* (Oxford, European Investment Bank, 1988) 126–57, 126.

[131] Ford (n 46) 29.

[132] Financial Conduct Authority, 'Regulatory Sandbox' (2015), available at www.fca.org.uk/publication/research/regulatory-sandbox.pdf.

[133] Ford (n 46).

[134] This law, which was published on 9 March 2018 in the Official Journal of the Federation, regulates different issues relating to FinTech, but most of the issues covered are addressed as they were evolving in 2016; thus, it does not tackle the 'Too-Complex-To-Fail' problem and new innovations. In other words, this legislative exercise was conceived, in certain way, as an anachronism. See Law to Regulate Financial Technology Institutions DOF, 19 March 2018.

in Circular 4/2019 issued by the Mexican central bank (Banxico),[135] these changes tend to be materialised on a reactive basis, based on the elements in place when the norm is studied. As one would expect, the final product that emerges from these efforts tends to be a normative anachronism that does not address the needs/risks of the new scenario. Additionally, on many ocassions, one has to face an agency problem by which regulators may pursue their own objectives – or the objectives of specific sectors – to the detriment of the spirit of the norm as originally enacted by the legislature.[136] As a consequence, even the most informed regulatory response tends to be prone to error when the new set of rules come into force.[137]

Compounding this problem, legislators are humans too and are subject to the same behavioural biases that lead to overanalysed traders and IT developers, and tend not to rework financial regulatory frameworks, even when they become widely acknowledged as flawed or seriously deficient.[138] Consequently, we end up working with a set of very complex products and services that even those persons described by Summers,[139] cannot fully explain.

IV. The Structure of the Book

Nakamoto's white paper[140] presents a myriad of beautiful ideas on freedom, new digital social agreements and money that have been materialised through the referred asset, which, in turn, paradoxically, has acted as a digital *Bildungstrieb* that fosters the emergence and evolution of our FinTech dragon. Unfortunately, courts and authors tend to take the characteristics of Bitcoin to present us 'universal' theories that try – unsuccessfully – to cover every instrument in existence, ignoring the fact that each cryptoasset is deployed in different contexts following different designs.

With these experiences in mind, this book is not structured to offer a single unified regulatory theory of cryptoassets, but to analyse only those instruments that are used as means of payment and/or as infrastructural assets in new payment systems. For this purpose, the book has been structured around the efforts of the author to answer the following question: Do cryptoassets represent a monetary

[135] Circular 4/2019 addressed to Credit Institutions and Financial Technology Institutions related to the general provisions applicable to Credit Institutions and Financial Technology Institutions in the transactions conducted with virtual assets DOF, 8 March 2019.

[136] MD McCubbins, 'The Legislative Design of Regulatory Structure' (1985) 29 *American Journal of Political Science* 721–48; A Schleifer 'Understanding Regulation' (2005) 11 *European Financial Management* 439, 446.

[137] E Novoa, *El Derecho como Obstáculo al Cambio Social* (Mexico City, Siglo XXI Editores, 1980) 37.

[138] AW Lo, *Adaptative Markets. Financial Evolution at the Speed of Thought* (New Jersey: Princeton University Press, 2017) 368; R Romano, 'Regulating in the Dark and a Postscript Assessment of the Iron Law of Financial Regulation' (2015) 43 *Hofstra Law Review* 25, 27.

[139] Summers (n 126).

[140] Nakamoto (n 25).

revolution that needs a new body of regulations, or just another link of the evolutionary chain of money that can be addressed using current regulatory tools? To present a full and relevant answer, this book takes the following structure:

Chapter two is intended to provide a socio-legal analysis of 'money'. It opens with the question 'what is money?', which will be the *leitmotiv* of the entire book. To answer this question, this chapter provides a historical account of how money emerged in different parts of the world through the incorporation of different underlying social agreements/*res*, such as those related to different banker gods and digital fictions ruled by legal and algorithmic codes. This initial exercise is useful for our purposes given that it shows that the work of Satoshi Nakamoto[141] is not offering something radically new. We have had anonymous payment systems, as explained in *Carr v Carr*,[142] we have relied on P2P governance schemes like *lex mercatoria*, and the gradual sovereign recognition and incorporation of payment technologies as seen in *Suffel v Bank of England*.[143] On this point, this chapter shows how money evolves through cyclical patterns that involve the creation of 'inside monies', their diffusion, and their gradual sovereign recognition/adoption based on the exercise of the state's *lex monetae*, which evolved from an original 'sacred' source of liquidity. This has been verified through the recognition and adoption of metallic coins and paper money, and, in our context, through current efforts put in place by countries like Sweden,[144] China[145] and England[146] to design and issue CBDCs.

These examples reveal much about the nature of money and trust incorporated within it. Money, as a socio-economic technology, does not evolve in isolation or spontaneously through the will of a single person/entity. It relies on network effects and economies of scale that derive from social agreements incorporated in normative instruments and technological infrastructures. Illustrations of this infrastructural dependence can be found in the pre-capitalist merchant networks developed in Mesopotamia and Mesoamerica; in the international branch system put in place by Italian families like the Peruzzi, the Bardi, and the Frescobaldi during the Renaissance; and in the current networks of agreements and GVCs

[141] ibid.

[142] This case refers to the principle which states that 'money has no earmark'. See JH Merivale, *Reports of Cases Argued and Determined in the High Court of Chancery. Vol 1* (London, Joseph Butterworth and Son, 1817) 543.

[143] This case is interesting given that it highlights the difference between a banknote issued through the *lex monetae* and an ordinary promissory note. See [1882], 9 QBD 555 (UK), 563.

[144] Sveriges Riksbank, 'E-Krona' (2019), available at www.riksbank.se/en-gb/payments--cash/e-krona.

[145] The Digital Currency Institute of the People's Bank of China has filed several patent applications related to the development of CBDCs, among which we can find the following: [2016] Patent application CN107230077: 'Digital Currency Exchange Method, Digital Currency Payment Method and Digital Currency Systems'; and [2017] Patent application CN107358521: 'Method and System for Using Digital Currency to Exchange Deposit'.

[146] Bank of England, 'The digital pound: Technology Working Paper.' (2023), available at www.bankofengland.co.uk/paper/2023/the-digital-pound-technology-working-paper.

that allow us to use electronic money across the Internet.[147] Accordingly, special attention is paid to the emergence, evolution and regulation of payment systems beyond single instruments, and the emergence of central banking; an effort that is useful to understand who can create money.

From the lessons obtained from this socio-legal analysis, particularly after the analysis of cases like the *Case of Mixed Money in Ireland*[148] and the nature of the current fiat paradigm that emerged from the collapse of the Bretton Woods system, pure Mengerian theories are discarded. The chapter provides evidence that money relies not on the material content of the asset, but on the legal recognition of the *res* incorporated within it, which in the case of our national currencies is the very post-Westphalian social contract. On this basis, I will argue that both the Societary Theory and the State Theory of money are accurate but incomplete approaches that complement each other to configure a Socio-Legal theory of money. The development of this theory throughout the book will play a pivotal role in the analysis of the cryptoassets market and its evolution towards a fourth generation of payment instruments. At the end of this chapter, I present a first definition of 'money', which will be the basis for the analysis that is developed in chapter three.

Chapter three continues with the work developed in chapter two, and develops its definition of money into 'inside money' and 'outside money'. This aims to open the analysis on how the law has standardised the three main functions that tend to be employed to define money: money as unit of account, store of value and means of payment. For this purpose, I analyse cases such as *Deutsche Bank v Humphrey*,[149] *Banco de Portugal v Waterlow & Sons Ltd*,[150] and *White v Elmdene Estates Ltd*,[151] whose spirits can be found in normative instruments like the UK's Currency Act 1982[152] and Sale of Goods Act 1979,[153] among others. A notable finding from this legal analysis is that focusing our efforts only on the traditional functions of money to define it in law is an incomplete effort. The emergence of Bitcoin and the diffusion of DLT through projects like the JPM Coin, which are presenting more familiar paradigms related to the sovereign unit of reference, have posed the question 'who can create money?'

[147] For further information on the configuration of these networks, particularly in pre-capitalist societies, see CA Smith, 'Economics of Marketing Systems: Models from Economic Geography' (1974) 3 *Annual Review of Anthropology* 167; ME Smith, 'The Archaeology of Ancient State Economies' (2004) 33 *Annual Review of Anthropology* 73.

[148] In this case, the court stated that 'the king hath the same prerogative to give value to base metal by his impression or character, as he hath to give estimation to a mean person by imparting the character of honour to him.' *Gilbert v Brett (The Case of Mixed Money)* [1605] Cobb St Tr 114 (UK), 125–26.

[149] [1926] 272 U.S, 517 (US).

[150] [1932] All ER Rep 181 (UK).

[151] In this case, the court argued that the word 'payment' 'may cover many ways of discharging obligations', including a discharge by what is called 'payment in kind'. See *White v Elmdene States Ltd* [1959] 2 All ER 605 (US), 610–11.

[152] Currency Act 1982 c 3, 2 February 1982.

[153] 'A contract of sale of goods is a contract by which the seller transfers or agrees to transfer the property in goods to the buyer for a money consideration, called the price.' See Sale of Goods Act 1979 c 54, 6 December 1979.

With a view to answering this question, first, this book states that the legal definition of money relies on the exercise of the *ius cudendae monetae*. Initially, we could be tempted to infer that, under the Lockean Rule of Law,[154] there cannot be non-sovereign laws and, consequently, there cannot be private monies[155] – a fact that is highlighted by constitutions and constitutional conventions, which configure a 'fourth constitutional power' related to central banks' monopoly on money creation. Now, the *lex monetae*[156] tends to be analysed under these prerogatives related to the creation and the stability of sovereign currencies. However, we argue that a proper analysis of the *lex monetae* has to comprise the power of the state over the design and structure of the monetary system beyond the creation of national currencies, including the control over different expressions of 'inside money' and the infrastructures related to them. Through this new approach, we conclude that money is a social conception that can be created by different stakeholders but, just as in the case of *lex mercatoria*, new monetary instruments cannot be labelled as money if they – and their infrastructures – are not recognised as such and/or tolerated by law.

Now, in order for money to act as a means of payment to discharge contractual obligations there needs to be a secure way of transferring that incorporated value, or at least to transfer a message relating to that value: a payments system.[157] These systems tend to be structured around the constitutional objectives, functions and powers of central banks that follow the design of a Foucauldian 'panopticon',[158] by which sovereign entities tend to adopt new technologies to maximise their control and power, which, following historical patterns, is *reified* in our currencies and means of payment. However, their material operation usually relies on the infrastructure provided and controlled by the private sector, as can be seen in the case of the network of agreements and IPRs that configure electronic money. Based on the increasing infrastructural power held by the private sector, this chapter highlights how banks create digital purchasing power for their borrowers through a financing through money creation (FMC) model in stark contrast to the traditional view of these institutions as simple intermediaries of loanable funds.[159]

[154] J Locke, *Two Treatises of Government* (London, Whitmore and Fenn and C Brown, 1821), 300–12.

[155] N Dodd, *The Social Life of Money* (Princeton: Princeton University Press, 2014) 223.

[156] Avgouleas and Blair (n 102); Byttebier (n 102).

[157] R Ali et al, 'Innovation in Payment Technologies and the Emergence of Digital Currencies' (2014) 262, available at www.bankofengland.co.uk/-/media/boe/files/quarterly-bulletin/2014/innovations-in-payment-technologies-and-the-emergence-of-digital-currencies.pdf.

[158] Uta Kohl argues, building on the work of Bentham and Foucault, that technology can be employed as a regulatory 'panopticon' where sovereign control is pervasive and hidden in technological structures and designs. See U Kohl, 'The Rise of Online Intermediaries in the Governance of the Internet and Beyond' (2012) 26 *International Review of Law, Computers & Technology* 185, 187–88.

[159] Z Jakab and M Kumhof, 'Banks Are Not Intermediaries of Loanable Funds. Facts, Theory and Evidence' (2019), available at www.bankofengland.co.uk/-/media/boe/files/working-paper/2018/banks-are-not-intermediaries-of-loanable-funds-facts-theory-and-evidence.pdf?la=en&hash=5FCDED87A783AA0483319CD4351170DB94C8A771.

In this spirit, authors such as Nigel Dodd have argued, building upon the Societary theory of money, that 'the era in which money was defined by the State is coming to an end',[160] but is this possible and/or a new idea? Studies of non-sovereign means of payment show that throughout our history, people have constantly disrupted 'monetary uniformity' through the design of new complementary practices and the periodical introduction of different communitarian schemes by which they offer private means of payment that are sometimes adopted and integrated into the legal monetary infrastructure. The intended purpose of these schemes has had very different targets, ranging from meeting local credit demand and stimulating local economies, to achieving social and political reforms.[161] However, among the discussions relating to these complementary means of payment, this book pays attention to the new generation of cryptoassets, which is currently in the middle of a diffusion process through the efforts of central banks and regulated payment systems, thus replicating the behaviour that arose from the adoption of technologies such as those that currently support real-time gross settlement (RTGS) systems.[162]

With that private–public 'panopticon' in mind, two months after Lehman Brothers' failure, Bitcoin was announced, its creator claiming that it is possible to create and transfer money in the absence of a trusted third party.[163] With the aim of focusing our efforts only on the elements that define Bitcoin, chapter four offers a novel analysis of the cryptoassets market. For that purpose, it opens by building on the description of the technology presented above with the aim of defining cryptoassets in the light of our Socio-Legal theory of money. Additionally, this chapter will show how IPRs act as the conduits for the underlying *res* that is incorporated in the new generation of cryptographic instruments. Consequently, it is not surprising that DLT now counts major corporations like Facebook and JP Morgan as among its advocates. To highlight this trend, the chapter offers an account of the evolution of the cryptoassets market; which has been divided into three main generations based on the nature of their respective protocols, the characteristics of their stakeholders, and their underlying agreements: the first identified with Bitcoin supported by a decentralised network of verification and money creation; the second based on the value of GVCs, which allow companies like Ripple and Ethereum to provide relevant infrastructures to run smart contracts and design payment systems; and the third, which relies on traditional means of incorporation to present us instruments like 'stablecoins', tokenised deposits and CBDCs.

[160] N Dodd, 'Utopian Monies' in N Bandelj, FF Wherry and VA Zelizer (eds), *Money Talks. Explaining How Money Really Works* (Princeton, Princeton University Press, 2017) 230–47, 234.

[161] M Naqvi and J Southgate, 'Banknotes, Local Currencies and Central Bank Objectives' (2013), available at www.bankofengland.co.uk/publications/Documents/quarterlybulletin/2013/qb130403.pdf.

[162] ML Bech and B Hobjin, 'Technology Diffusion within Central Banking. The Case of Real-Time Gross Settlement' (2006) 260 *Federal Reserve Bank of New York Staff Reports* 1.

[163] S Nakamoto, 'Bitcoin Open Source Implementation of P2P Currency' (2009), available at p2pfoundation.ning.com/forum/topics/bitcoin-open-source.

Building on this segmentation and on the content of chapters two and three, I argue, first, that these instruments can be labelled as money and that, in some cases, regulated under the terms applicable to electronic money as defined by instruments like the Second Electronic Money Directive (2EMD).[164] Second, just as in the case of other innovations like paper money and electronic money, cryptoassets rely on a network of agreements to constitute payment systems and on the development of intermediaries, such as issuers, miners, exchanges and wallets, following the historical patterns found in chapter two.

In chapter five, my aim is to highlight how, after the GFC, several questions regarding fundamental issues on the exercise of *lex monetae* and the current paradigm of finance started to emerge in different forums. However, despite the numerous efforts put in place to answer these questions, scholars and regulators have failed to describe the world as it really is.[165] As a result of this unfortunate fact, in most of the cases, suboptimal regulatory answers have been put in place, focused mainly on old and rigid paradigms. Based on this rigidity, now we are not only facing the traditional textbook case of intermediaries TBTF, but also a new generation of evolving 'shadowy' players that could be considered TCTF, independently of their size. Furthermore, the innovative minds behind the unregulated innovations that are presented throughout this research are finding, in these suboptimal efforts, the perfect conduits to generate risky links with our regulated institutions.

As a response to this behaviour, chapter six does not present something radically new, and argues that the Internet offers not only a new space of interaction, but also a particular type of regulatory model where sovereign control is pervasive, and hidden in structures and designs.[166] Considering that the networks of agreements and the intermediaries that are emerging form the evolution of our cryptoassets market introduce several market imperfections, I argue that these infrastructures need to be analysed and regulated. For that purpose, I take the main arguments, lessons and discoveries found in the previous chapters to present a hypothetical fourth generation of cryptoassets structured around a payments system controlled by a central bank.

Accordingly, I start to develop a proposal that builds on the constitutional documents and conventions that are currently in force around the world, and their interactions with the increasing infrastructural power of the private sector.

[164] Art 2(2) of the 2EMD defines electronic money as 'electronically, including magnetically, stored monetary value as represented by a claim on the issuer which is issued on receipt of funds for the purpose of making payment transactions as defined in point 5 of Article 4 of Directive 2007/64/EC, and which is accepted by a natural or legal person other than the electronic money issuer.' See Directive 2009/110/EC of the European Parliament and of the Council on the taking up, pursuit and prudential supervision of the business of electronic money institutions amending Directives 2005/60/EC and 2006/48/EC and repealing Directive 2000/46/EC OJ L 267/7, 16 September 2009.

[165] G Calabresi, *The Future of Law & Economics. Essays in Reform and Recollection* (New Haven, Yale University Press, 2016) 3.

[166] Kohl (n 136) 188.

Building on this exercise, this book presents a two-front strategy that would allow the issuance of a fourth generation of cryptoassets and set the cornerstones for new payment systems founded on these interactions.

First, following the spirit of proposals like the Fedcoin, the CAD-coin and Project Aurum, I argue that central banks could act as stakeholders within publicly centralised DLT networks structured around PoA protocols following the gradual process of administrative centralisation found in PoW and proof-of-stake (PoS) protocols. Within these permissioned networks, regulated institutions would act as nodes with access to this sovereign blockchain and develop off-chain interactions with users following the paradigm currently in force applicable to banknotes and coins. Therefore, while the central bank controls the new payments system with its native CBDC, regulated institutions would act as delegated monitors for the on-chain and off-chain interactions related to this network.[167] Additionally, following the example of countries like Japan, where exchanges have been incorporated in Chapter III-2 of the Payment Services Act,[168] one could include some elements of the new generation of intermediaries as regulated nodes of this system.

The second stage of this proposal considers that, even if the supply of our CBDC is restricted, the Cambrian explosion related to DLT presents us with an unlimited supply of private cryptoassets. To face this challenge – or if one wants to foster the development of a free banking system – one can present a set of conditions for those potential issuers through a 'cryptocharter'. Within this instrument, one could include the obligation for potential issuers to back their instruments following the model set by the Scottish and Northern Ireland Banknote Regulations 2009,[169] paired with a scheme based on unlimited liabilities, the explainability of the agreements that are incorporated within algorithmic black boxes, among other operative requirements. Under Regulation 6(2), a bank that has been authorised by the Bank of England to issue notes within these jurisdictions must have backing assets like Bank of England banknotes and current coins of the UK. Under a variation of the referred regulation, we could witness the gradual emergence of a new generation of banks of issue, which could be empowered to offer different cryptoassets that exist alongside our CBDCs, just as current Scottish and Irish notes circulate alongside coins of the UK.

To close this chapter, it is argued – based on existent regulations – that the evolution of the cryptoassets market could be analysed not as a set of players that want to provide new forms of money, but as a set of players that want to provide the new infrastructure required to constitute a payments system as it is described in chapter three. This approach is developed considering that these cryptoassets could be understood as integral elements of the system following the ideas

[167] F Allen and E Carletti, 'The Roles of Banks in Financial Systems' in AN Berger, P Molyneux and JO Wilson (eds), *The Oxford Handbook of Banking* (Oxford, Oxford University Press, 2010) 37, 41; Freixas and Rochet (n 14) 29–30.

[168] Payment Services Act, Act No 59, 24 June,2009.

[169] Scottish and Northern Ireland Banknote Regulations 2009, No 3056, 23 November 2009.

set in cases such as *Diamond, Commissioner of Patents and Trademarks v Diehr et al*,[170] where the potential patentability of a piece of software relied on its secondary nature within a more complex invention. To support this argument, we show how current projects developed by institutions like Ripple and JP Morgan are pushing on this line through the protection of their IPRs and the development of their own network of agreements signed with different commercial banks around the world.

Finally, I present my conclusions through a brief discussion of the main findings of this research and the future work that can be developed from some of the ideas presented here based on the certainty that fourth generation of sovereign cryptoassets or CBDCs will not be the end of the story. Accordingly, the book closes arguing that these processes could be based on the interaction of technologies like Machine Learning, 5G and a new generation of DLT protocols, such as, Tangle,[171] by which new 'shadow banks' could foster the development of open banking models,[172] the active adoption of the Internet of Things (IoT) in the financial sector, and even the emergence of a new generation of payment instruments that could take the terms set in regulations, such as the Bills of Exchange Act 1882, to a new era.

[170] In this case, Rehnquist J argued that 'an application of a law of nature or mathematical formula to a known structure or process may well be deserving of patent protection.' See [1981] 450 US 175 (US), 187–88.

[171] S Popov, 'The Tangle' (2018), available at assets.ctfassets.net/r1dr6vzfxhev/2t4uxvsIqk0EUau6g2sw0g/45eae33637ca92f85dd9f4a3a218e1ec/iota1_4_3.pdf.

[172] Ana Badour and Domenic Presta define open banking as 'an emerging financial services business model that focuses on the portability and open availability of customer data, including transactional information. The core aim of open banking is to enable consumers to share their financial data between their financial institution and third party providers (and between financial institutions), typically through the use of application programming interfaces (APIs).' See. A Badour and D Presta, 'Open Banking: Canadian and International Developments' (2018) 34 *Banking and Finance Law Review* 41, 42.

1

Socio-economic Analysis of the Concept of Money

I. Introduction

It is common within the DCS for cryptoassets to be denominated as 'cryptocurrencies', implying similarities with established currencies issued by constitutional authorities in exercise of their *lex monetae*.[1] As a result of this abuse of language, practically every academic and regulatory effort related to these cryptographic innovations starts answering in positive or negative ways the question 'are cryptoassets money?' To offer an accurate answer to this question, first, we need to discuss and answer and older one: 'what is money?'

This chapter takes the definition of 'money' provided by Darling J in *Moss v Hancock*[2] and identifies the common elements that have configured monetary innovations throughout the financial history of the world, from pre-capitalist societies to our DCS. Among these elements, we identify the need for such innovations to face transaction costs within specific communities and their gradual adoption and/or regulation by a stakeholder. For this purpose, this socio-economic analysis of money will open with a starting time (t_0) following the Arrow-Debreu model,[3] which take us to the barter paradigm and the double coincidence of wants, which, in turn, will highlight the need for the first proto-monetary instruments to act as *reifiers* following socio-qualitative elements.[4]

From this point, among the leading money theories (the Mengerian/Metallist, the State/Chartalist and the Societary theories) I will discard the pure Mengerian/Metallist theory of money. To support this assertion, I will argue that money emerges, first, as a social conception whose gradual diffusion relies on the power of a sovereign stakeholder, particularly after taxation became organised and normalised.[5]

[1] G. Söderberg, 'Are Bitcoin and Other Crypto-Assets Money?' (2018), available at www.riksbank.se/globalassets/media/rapporter/ekonomiska-kommentarer/engelska/2018/are-bitcoin-and-other-crypto-assets-money.pdf.

[2] [1899], 2 QB 111 (UK), 116.

[3] KJ Arrow and G Debreu, 'Existence of an Equilibrium for a Competitive Economy' (1954) 22 *Econometrica* 265.

[4] L Walras, *Elements of Pure Economics* (Illinois, Richard D Irwin, 1926) 212.

[5] CAE Goodhart, 'The Two Concepts of Money. Implications for the Analysis of Optimal Currency Areas' (1998) 14 *European Journal of Political Economy* 407, 408.

Building on the work of Kiyotaki and Wright,[6] we will see how money *reifies* social relations, and how the emergence of stakeholders and the adoption of new legal-technological innovations will increase its acceptability through network effects. To have a better understanding of these processes, I will make an historical tracing of the development and evolution of these infrastructures and innovations from temples in Mesopotamia to the medieval *lex mercatoria*, and from the conception of central banking after the Peace of Westphalia to current post-Bretton Woods arrangements.

This will allow us to understand through cases, such as *Burton v Davy*,[7] the *Case of Mixed Money*,[8] *Miliangos v George Frank (Textiles) Ltd*,[9] among others, how the law engages with the initial uncertainty that characterises monetary innovation, and highlights the need for a Socio-Legal theory of money to understand that public–private Schumpeterian trends matter for the regulation of the early stages of monetary diffusion, independently in the case of coins, bills of exchange, banknotes or cryptoassets.

II. What is Money?

For most of us, the answer to this question will seem self-evident. After all, everybody understands money in relation to terms such as 'dollars', 'pesos', 'renmimbis' and 'pounds', which have become so familiar in our culture that their very existence and nature are taken for granted.[10] At the same time, anthropologists, economists and lawyers have sought a definition that can transcend specific institutional arrangements[11] and have reached partial consensus in definitions like that provided by Darling J in *Moss v Hancock*,[12] who defines money as:

> [T]hat which passes freely from hand to hand throughout the community in final discharge of debts and full payment for commodities, being accepted equally without

[6] N Kiyotaki and R Wright, 'On Money as a Medium of Exchange.' (1989) 97 *Journal of Political Economy* 927, 950.

[7] Tony Moore argues that there are only two surviving sources for *Burton v Davy* [1437]: 'The Calendar of Letter Books of the City of London K' and 'Select Cases Concerning the Law Merchant AD 1251–1779.' The latter has been used in this book. See H Hall, *Select Cases Concerning the Law Merchant AD 1251–1779. Vol III* (1932, London Selden Society), 117–19; T. Moore, ''According to the Law of Merchants and the Custom of the City of London': Burton v. Davy (1436) and the Negotiability of Credit Instruments in Medieval England' in M Allen and M Davies (eds), *Medieval Merchants and Money. Essays in Honour of James L Bolton* (London, University of London, 2016) 305–22, 308–09.

[8] *Gilbert v Brett (The Case of Mixed Money)* [1605] Cobb St Tr 114 (UK), 125–16.

[9] [1976] AC 443 (UK), 460–70.

[10] JJ Chung, 'Money as Simulacrum: The Legal Nature and Reality of Money' (2009) 64 *Roger Williams University Legal Studies Research Paper Series* 108–68, 109; R Kreitner, 'Legal History of Money' (2012) 8 *The Annual Review of Law and Social Science* 415, 417; H Withers, *The Meaning of Money* (London, John Murray, 1948) 2.

[11] B Geva, *The Payment Order of Antiquity and the Middle Ages. A Legal History* (Oxford, Hart Publishing, 2011) 18.

[12] [1899], 2 QBD 111 (UK), 116.

> reference to the character or credit of the person who offers it and without the intention of the person who receives it to consume it.

However, although the main socio-legal elements of this definition can be found in instruments such as Regulation 2(1) of the Electronic Money Regulations 2011,[13] there is a failure here to properly analyse these elements beyond the monetary functions found in every economics book.[14] Money was conceived as one of our essential social technologies – along with writing and the conception of numbers – that fostered the rationalisation and evolution of our social interactions.[15] It allowed the creation, incorporation and mobilisation of rights, introducing a new way to record and transfer information beyond our DNA.[16] Based on this, it should not be surprising, that, as a social invention, money adapts itself to new environments, recording and transferring data on social values and hierarchies based on the transition rules that define each dynamic social system.

The processes and the means to reach social aims within these systems have not always been uniform, as one could be tempted to conclude from some Mengerian/Metallist arguments, which are built upon the intrinsic value of certain circulating commodities and currencies.[17] Each social system has taken different objects to incorporate liquidity based on their respective cultural backgrounds to structure their acts of standardisation and payment.[18] If you visit a numismatic collection, the first and main objects that you will see are coins and notes, but, as was highlighted in *Wisconsin Central Ltd et al v United States*,[19] you will also find that:

> Cowrie shells once were such a medium but no longer are, see J. Weatherford, The History of Money 24 (1997); our currency originally included gold coins and bullion, but, after 1934, gold could not be used as a medium of exchange, see Gold Reserve Act of 1934, ch. 6, §2, 48 Stat. 337; perhaps one day employees will be paid in Bitcoin or some other type of cryptocurrency, see F. Martin, Money: The Unauthorized Biography – From Coinage to Cryptocurrencies 275–278 (1st Vintage Books ed. 2015). Nothing in the statute suggests the meaning of this provision should be trapped in a monetary time warp, forever limited to those forms of money commonly used in the 1930's.

[13] '"[E]lectronic money" means electronically (including magnetically) stored monetary value as represented by a claim on the electronic money issuer which a) is issued on receipt of funds for the purpose of making payment transactions; b) is accepted by a person other than the electronic money issuer; and c) is not excluded by regulation 3.' See *The Electronic Money Regulations 2011 (SI 2001, No 99).*

[14] Money as a medium of exchange, money as a unit of account, and money as a store of value.

[15] G Ingham, *The Nature of Money* (Cambridge, Polity Press, 2004) 3; V Zelizer, 'The Social Meaning of Money: "Special Monies"' (1989) 95 *American Journal of Sociology* 342, 342.

[16] S Hawking, *Brief Answers to the Big Questions* (London, John Murray, 2018) 78; M Monteagudo, 'Neutrality of Money and Central Bank Independence' in M Giovanoli and D Devos (eds), *International Monetary and Financial Law. The Global Crisis* (Oxford, Oxford University Press, 2010) 484–505, 485.

[17] Goodhart (n 5).

[18] B Maurer and L Swartz, 'Introduction. Curating Transactional Things' in B Maurer and L Swartz (eds), *Paid. Tales of Dongles, Checks, and Other Money Stuff* (2017, Massachusetts, The MIT Press) xv–xxv, xv.

[19] [2018] 138 S Ct 2067 (US), 6.

These rather interesting collections and opinions show how money – and the instruments and institutions relating to it – has evolved as an integral element of our dynamic social systems from one generation to the next, through a variety of different meanings and goods in different contexts and transition rules – from sacred objects related to different banker gods to digital fictions ruled by algorithmic codes.

A. Money and the Evolution of Liquidity Sources

When analysing money from a socio-economic approach, we find a myriad of interpretations that are focused exclusively either on its anthropological or economic aspects. Furthermore, most of the analyses that could be relevant to the legal studies of money argue that this social innovation must have started somewhere, but their authors simply cannot agree on exactly where and what money was originally.[20] Consequently, for most anthropologists, economists and jurists, the state that follows the Machiavellian tradition[21] is as 'ancient' as they are willing to study. As is evident in famous works such as Karl Menger's[22] *On the Origin of Money* and Moses I Finley's[23] *The Ancient Economy*, most of our monetary histories start with the conception of the Lydian *electrum* or any other metallic chattel, which are taken as the basis of our systems following the collision of the two predominant theories on the origin and the nature of money: the Mengerian/Metallist theory and the State/Chartalist theory.[24]

As discussed above, the Mengerian/Metallist theory argues that money emerged through the use of different commodities as means of exchange before their respective adoption and regulation,[25] while the Chartalist theory[26] states that money is a legal creation of a sovereign stakeholder. Regardless of their preferred theory, most works on money are structured around the three main monetary functions recognised by the economists, based on the characteristics of well-developed currencies

[20] N Dodd, *The Social Life of Money* (Princeton: Princeton University Press, 2014) 15.

[21] Niccolò Machiavelli in his works *The Prince* and the *Discourses on Livy*, tends to structure his arguments on the beginnings of the states and their laws around the examples of Rome and Greece, a practice that can be found in many (if not most) monetary studies. See N Machiavelli, *Escritos Políticos e Históricos. El Príncipe, Reforma de la Constitución de Florencia, Vida de Castruccio Castracani, Informe Sobre el Duque de Valentinois* (Barcelona, Librería Científico-Literaria de Toledano, López y Cía, 1900); N Machiavelli, *Discursos Sobre la Primera Década de Tito Livio* (Madrid, Alianza Editorial, 1900).

[22] K Menger, 'On the Origin of Money' (1892) 2 *The Economic Journal* 239, 239.

[23] MI Finley, *The Ancient Economy* (California, University of California Press, 1973) 166.

[24] S Gleeson, *The Legal Concept of Money* (New York, Oxford University Press, 2018) 28; Goodhart (n 5).

[25] This theory can be identified in the work of authors such as Marcel Mauss and Karl Menger. See M Mauss, *The Gift* (London, Routledge Classics, 2002); Menger (n 22).

[26] The spirit of the Chartalist theory can be found in the work of authors like Georg F Knapp and Christine A Desan. See CA Desan, 'Money as a Legal Institution' in D Fox and W Ernst (eds), *Money in the Western Legal Tradition. Middle Ages to Bretton Woods* (Oxford, Oxford University Press, 2016) 18–35; GF Knapp, *The State Theory of Money* (London, Macmillan & Company Limited, 1924).

like the *electrum*, and largely ignoring the traits of other proto-monetary units and transitional forms.

Therefore, in order to understand current and future monetary developments, we first have to tackle these academic anachronisms. For this purpose, it is worth starting the present socio-economic analysis with the promissory texts found on different banknotes around the globe, for example, those issued by institutions such as the Royal Bank of Scotland or the Bank of England, by which the banks promise to pay the bearer on demand a specific sum of money. Beyond the evolutionary analyses and the comparisons between these notes and instruments such as bills of exchange and promissory notes, it is possible to argue that these words are the remnants of proto-monetary forms used to *reify* claims and debts with different objects, which probably worked like the *vaygu'a* of the *kula* ring described by Bronislaw Malinowski.[27] These proto-monetary transactions depended on the level of commercialisation of every social dynamic system, the recognition of different political arrangements,[28] and the spiritual power that was incorporated in each transfer that underpinned the obligation to reciprocate.[29] For a proper legal analysis, this is rather important; it shows how fundamental legal relations are developed as 'opposites' and 'correlatives' designed around those rights recognised by a community in a specific context,[30] which in turn are incorporated in payment instruments. Within this is the first element that will complicate the very definition of money: What is the nature of the right incorporated? In *United States v Patrick; et al*[31] Justice Jackson argued that:

> The words 'rights' or 'privilege' have, of course, a variety of meanings, according to the connection or context in which they are used. Their definition, as given by standard lexicographers, include 'that which one has a legal claim to do,' 'legal power,' 'authority,' 'immunity granted by authority,' 'the investiture with special or peculiar rights.'

From these lines, we can infer that the relationship between the right and object or *res* within a specific context is highly significant.[32] We can say that the *reified* 'opposites' and 'correlatives' can be identified, on the active side, with the creditor, whose right will be called 'claim', and, on the passive side, we will find the debtor, whose obligation will be called 'debt'.[33] Consequently, we can argue that the idea of

[27] B Malinowski, *Argonauts of the Western Pacific. An Account of Native Enterprise and Adventure in the Archipelagos of Melanesian New Guinea* (London, Routledge & Kegan Paul, 1966).

[28] ME Smith, 'The Archaeology of Ancient State Economies' (2004) 33 *Annual Review of Anthropology* 73, 79.

[29] R Ziegler, 'What Makes the Kula Go Round? A Simulation Model of the Spontaneous Emergence of a Ceremonial Exchange System' (2008) 30 *Social Networks* 107, 107–08.

[30] W Hohfeld, 'Some Fundamental Legal Conceptions as Applied in Judicial Reasoning' (1914) 16 *Yale Law Journal* 16, 30.

[31] [1893] 54 F 338 (US), 348.

[32] A Rahmatian, 'Money as a Legally Enforceable Debt' (2018) 29 *European Business Law Review* 205, 209.

[33] ibid.

social debt must pre-date the idea of money and markets,[34] since these debts are the dematerialised property or *res* that will be incorporated in different monetary *reifiers* depending on the context.[35]

Now, to constitute this dematerialised *res* and incorporate it within certain goods, we first need to separate commodities from nature and/or create new goods through a process of manufacture; after all, a cacao seed or a piece of silver by itself cannot be considered money per se.[36] These commodities were adopted as proto-monetary forms by virtue of the real rights developed among persons with regard to these things and the abstract social obligations *reified* within them in a particular socio-economic context. Consequently, the nature of these first practices leads us to the conception of the Societary theory of money, which defines money based on the practices accepted *erga omnes* within a community in a specific context.[37]

However, Malinowski[38] warned us of the risks relating to the use of the words 'money' and 'currency' to describe or classify different objects and commodities that were used under certain exchange/gift schemes, such as the *kula* and the *potlatch*. For him, these goods were not used as means of exchange nor as denominators of value following the traditional economic theories. In response, Marcel Mauss,[39] in a long footnote, defended the applicability of the Societary theory of money to institutions like the *kula's vaygu'a* arguing that:

> These precious objects have the same function as money in our societies and consequently deserve at least to be placed in the same category. They have purchasing power, and this power has a figure set on it ... The idea of number is present, even if that number is fixed in a different way from the authority of the state, and varies during the succession of kula and potlatches. Moreover, this purchasing power does indeed discharge debts.

Consequently, to understand the nature of money, the original question ('what is money?') has to be refined; we must ask 'what does money do?'. We can argue that, following the Societary theory of money, cultural valuable substances and/or goods, such as, silver, whales' teeth or *vaygu'a* could have served, firstly, as commodities valuable for ornamental/ritual purposes, as the result of increases in population size, density and socialisation; secondly, as incorporated wealth that enhanced the prestige and influence of the holder; and thirdly, as a medium of

[34] S Eich, *The Currency of Politics. The Political Theory of Money from Aristotle to Keynes* (New Jersey, Princeton University Press, 2022) 5; Gleeson (n 24) 32.

[35] Rahmatian (n 32) 209.

[36] ibid.

[37] C Proctor and V Dixon, *Goode on Payment Obligations in Commercial and Financial Transactions* (London, Thomson Reuters, 2016) 5.

[38] Malinowski argued that the tokens of wealth relating to the *kula* were 'neither used nor regarded as money or currency, and they resemble these economic instruments very little, if indeed there is any resemblance at all, except that both money and *vaygu'a* represent condensed wealth. *Vaygu'a* is never used as medium of exchange or as measure of value, which are the two most important functions of currency or money.' For a deeper analysis of the *kula* see Malinowski (n 27) 511.

[39] Mauss (n 25) 127–28.

exchange; and finally, as a standard measure of value.[40] One can argue that these functions emerged following a different order, particularly between the third and fourth transition; however, we lack the proper legal-archaeological evidence to make a definite statement on a specific order.[41] Independently of this, it can be argued that the custom relating to the use of esteemed/sacred articles as store of value probably preceded their employment as medium of exchange; thus, pre-capitalist societies created a primitive source of socio-economic liquidity whose nature and processes of incorporation changed according to its cultural context. As can be seen in the cryptoassets market, value is not a natural property, such as colour, taste or smell, that belongs to an object. It is a third category that is incorporated into an asset through real rights, thereby creating a cultural link between the members of a community and the objects they use to transact and communicate with each other.[42]

B. Barter and the Emergence of Standardised Mediums of Exchange

Money, like other elements that have configured our civilisations, is a far more ancient institution than we were taught to believe. Its origins are lost in the 'mists of time', as Keynes noted, 'in the Islands of the Hesperides or Atlantis or some Eden of Central Asia'.[43] Consequently, today we fail to understand the transition between barter and the use of metallic coins as evidenced by the Roman Jurist Paul in the Book XVIII of the Justinian's *Corpus Iuris Civilis*,[44] even when we can argue that money did not suddenly appear in its finished form reflecting its pure concept as the ultimate means of payment.[45] This lack of understanding results from academic differences on the analyses of the history of particular monetary expressions – the classic example being metallic coins – and the history of money throughout different dynamic social systems and transition rules.[46]

Regardless of these differences, one can find a common argument among these analyses, which states that money emerged as a consequence of the needs of the

[40] WS Jevons, *Money and the Mechanism of Exchange* (New York, D Appleton and Company, 1975) 15–16; Kiyotaki and Wright (n 6).

[41] It could even be argued that climate change played a role on the evolution of socialisation and the development of social technologies, such as money. On this point, see P Frankopan, *The Earth Transformed. An Untold History* (London, Bloomsbury, 2023) 48–49.

[42] G Simmel, *The Philosophy of Money* (New York, Routledge Classics, 2004) 68; Rahmatian (n 32) 209.

[43] JM Keynes, *A Treatise on Money. Vol I* (London, MacMillan and Co, 1914) 13.

[44] Justinian I, 'Corpus Iuris Civilis (Volume 1).' (2015), available at www.heinonline.org.ezproxy.is.ed.ac.uk/HOL/Page?handle=hein.beal/corpscivls0001&id=1&size=2&collection=beal&index=beal/corpscivls.

[45] Simmel (n 42) 127.

[46] Dodd (n 20) 15.

Commercial Society[47] to face Jevons'[48] double coincidence of wants, the next step after the barter paradigm described in Walrasian models.[49] Thus, it is possible to say that the first trade – not the first transference[50] – was conducted via barter by means of which all goods were exchanged directly for all other goods based on the specialisation described by Adam Smith[51] in Chapter II of the *Wealth of Nations*, but in the absence of perfect information, these transactions were materialised at different exchange rates.[52]

For the purposes of my argument, it is possible to take a basic model of a barter paradigm in which each node represents a particular commodity. This barter–subsistence economy would have vectors among a wide variety of goods, one for each pair of goods representing an individual with a matching demand and supply on a single temporal line.[53]

Figure 3 Barter equilibrium in t1[54]

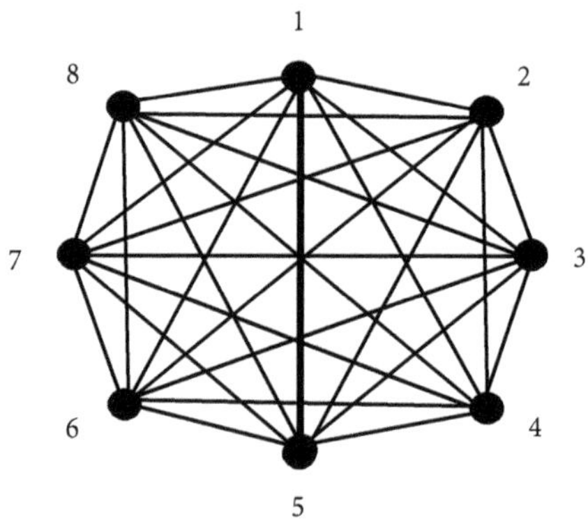

[47] Adam Smith highlights the relevance of human nature on the emergence of money and the Commercial Society arguing that 'nobody ever saw a dog make a fair and deliberate exchange of one bone for another with another dog.' See A Smith, *An Inquiry into the Nature and Causes of the Wealth of Nations* (Oxford, Oxford University Press, 2008) 36–39.

[48] Jevons (n 40).

[49] For an example of these models, see AV Banerjee and ES Maskin, 'A Walrasian Theory of Money and Barter' (1996) 111 *Quarterly Journal of Economics* 955.

[50] Authors like David Graeber state that most of the arguments relating to money start with a fantasy world of barter, considering the fact that no example of a barter economy has ever been described. See D Graeber, *Debt: The First 5,000 Years* (New York, Melville House, 2011) 21–29.

[51] At the end of chapter II of the *Wealth of Nations*, Smith argues that 'among men … the most dissimilar geniuses are of use to one another; the different produces of their respective talents, by the general disposition to truck, barter, and exchange, being brought, as it were, into a common stock, where every man may purchase whatever part of the produce of other men's talents he has occasion for.' Smith (n 47) 121.

[52] Banerjee and Maskin (n 49) 957–58.

[53] RM Starr, 'Why is there Money? Endogenous Derivation of "Money2 as the Most Liquid Asset: A Class of Examples' (2003) 21 *Economic Theory* 455, 459.

[54] ibid, 460.

In scenarios of two commodities (A and B) that are exchanged in the absence of externalities, marketplaces and innovation,[55] in contexts similar to those found approximately 70,000 years ago,[56] it is easy to claim that we do not need money. Yet, one can state accurately that barter was not a great system; and we could even argue that its existence in certain contexts did not go beyond a couple of exchanges. First, one or both goods involved can become useless or unlimited in quantity, something that would decrease their value in exchange, and, second, this becomes complicated when we introduce additional goods (C, D, E, etc). Consequently, in both scenarios – in the absence of money – we would obtain only imperfect equilibriums.

With this obstacle in mind, let us consider again the potential exchange between commodities A and B. One may be unable to find someone who wishes to make that the proposed deal at that same time, facing additionally a problem of what one could call a double coincidence of time – following George A Akerlof's[57] Lemons Principle, we have to consider that some commodities have different qualitative rates.[58] If the parties involved do not trust each other given these asymmetries, then the equilibrium solution is that neither party cooperates and no exchange takes place.[59] However, to avoid this problem, our counterpart could offer us a commodity that we probably do not desire at that moment and which was not originally exchanged in the marketplace, but which might have a high cultural value *reified* within it, so fulfilling the obligations related to our hypothetical transaction.

This hypothetical exchange shows how, as they evolved, proto-monetary forms could perform additional economic functions by serving as a means of exchange, acting as sources of social and 'sacred' liquidity, utilised to acquire or amend status, or to celebrate ritual events.[60] Thus, in this hypothetical scenario between commodities A and B, one of the parties would face credit risk that they may not be able to obtain the good they want, but once the qualitative characteristics of the commodity offered by the other party can be reasonably discerned by every trader, its general acceptance gradually becomes self-reinforcing, building upon

[55] Arrow and Debreu (n 3); Smith (n 28) 79.

[56] Evidence of the first processes of innovation and development of technologies can be found at Blombos Cave in South Africa, where beads made of estuarine mollusks were manufactured 70,000 years ago. See Frankopan (n 41).

[57] Akerlof argues that all the goods in a particular market present different qualitative characteristics that foster some negative behaviours, which require the emergence of counteracting institutions to face the uncertainty that is related to this diversity of qualities. See GA Akerlof, 'The Market for "Lemons": Quality Uncertainty and the Market Mechanism' (1970) 84 *The Quarterly Journal of Economics* 488.

[58] On this point CAE Goodhart argues that these informational difficulties are the main drawback found in the models that take metallic standards as their starting point. See Goodhart (n 5) 410.

[59] V Lehdonvirta, 'The Blockchain Paradox: Why Distributed Ledger Technologies May Do Little to Transform the Economy' (2016) available at www.oii.ox.ac.uk/blog/the-blockchain-paradox-why-distributed-ledger-technologies-may-do-little-to-transform-the-economy.

[60] Mauss (n 25) 5; Zelizer (n 15) 349.

network effects that support the Societary theory of money.[61] In other words, this acceptance became an integral part of these dynamic systems; thus, configuring a proto-*lex monetae.*

From that point, the parties involved in the creation, adoption and diffusion of monetary instruments, collectively – as one can read in the white papers of different 'stablecoins' and in the central banks' mandates – have had an interest in maintaining a stable and standardised reference. Here one can find a warning from history for our current regulators and innovators. Throughout the financial history of the world, people from different cultures and times have introduced dishonesty costs,[62] and have debased the money they use by paying with fake or inferior *reifiers*,[63] thus driving good money out of circulation[64] and fostering the emergence of financial crises.[65] As an illustration, Sahagun[66] described the existence of 'bad cacao sellers' who counterfeited cacao to deceive people throughout the Aztec markets system. With this trend in mind, the classic solution to this dilemma, described accurately by Aristophanes[67] in his work the *The Frogs* and popularly known as the law of Oresme, Copernicus and Gresham (Gresham's Law),[68] has been third-party monitoring and enforcement.[69] From this we can infer that these dishonesty costs set the basis for the emergence of the regulations that gradually configured the *lex monetae.*

During the first existential stages of our first monetary *reifiers*, merchants probably oversaw the referred proto-*lex monetae*, in a similar way to those DLT networks designed around a *crypto lex monetae* exercised through IPRs, which I will develop further in chapter four. As can be seen through the cases of Mesopotamia and Mesoamerica, sovereign entities did not initially concern themselves with the public supply of monetary commodities like silver and cacao, which, were at the time pure forms of 'inside money' based on debts *reified* within the private sector whose acceptability increased through network effects. However, the diversity of the goods used as a means of payment, and the qualitative asymmetries found

[61] JA Schumpeter, 'Money and Currency' (1991) 58 *Social Research* 499, 531; Dodd (n 20) 18–29; Banerjee and Maskin (n 49) 957.

[62] Akerlof (n 57) 495.

[63] Lehdonvirta (n 59).

[64] G Selgin, 'Gresham's Law' in S Battilossi et al (eds), *Handbook of the History of Money and Currency* (Singapore, Springer Nature, 2018) 2, 2.

[65] CM Reinhart and KS Rogoff, *This Time is Different. Eight Centuries of Financial Folly* (New Jersey, Princeton University Press, 2009) 6.

[66] B Sahagun, *Historia General de las Cosas de la Nueva España* (Madrid, Dastin, 2003) 791.

[67] 'It has often struck our notice that the course our city runs / Is the same towards men and money. She has true and worthy sons: / She has good and ancient silver, she has good and recent gold. / These are coins untouched with alloys; everywhere their fame is told; / Gold or silver, each well minted, tested each and ringing clear. / Yet, we never use them! Others always pass from hand to hand. / Sorry brass just struck last week and branded with a wretched brand.' See Aristophanes, *The Frogs* (London, George Allen & Sons, 1908) 56.

[68] TW Balch, 'The Law of Oresme, Copernicus and Gresham' (1908) 47 *Proceedings of the American Philosophical Society* 18; Selgin (n 64).

[69] Akerlof (n 57) 499; Lehdonvirta (n 59).

among them, were eventually seen as a problem when taxation became organised and normalised.[70] To face this practical obstacle, the sovereign recognition and/or the adoption of certain goods and social customs, as reflected in documents such as the Mendoza Codex, was set as the imposed standard of value, and independently regulated to some extent by kings and temples, as the goods involved were not directly provided by them.[71] It can be argued that standardisation in these contexts eased the creation of an external source of liquidity by grouping together all the heterogeneous items used as money and grading them in regimented ways under new transitional rules within the social system,[72] thus gradually transferring the control of the proto-*lex monetae* to a sovereign stakeholder.[73]

Once standardised *reifiers* started to circulate, these reduced the transaction costs of governments, *pari passu* with that of the private sector.[74] In other words, the state starved agents of alternatives to the new standard on the basis that every person who owed a contribution to the centre would be willing to take it in exchange for goods.[75] Accordingly, under this Chartalist account (from *charta*, the Latin word for 'token'), taxes exist because they allowed these sovereign stakeholders to create a demand for their own tokens.[76]

Consequently, if we want to define money in law – and determine if cryptoassets are money – we first need to acknowledge that both the State/Chartalist theory and the Societary theory of money are partially correct: they are accurate but incomplete approaches that complement each other to configure a Socio-Legal theory of money by which we argue that money emerges and evolves through different goods, typified as money by a sovereign stakeholder, that represent a *res* relevant to everyone in a particular society.[77] We can therefore discard purist Mengerian/Metallist approaches and deduce that money, including its regulation and standardisation, long predates the coinage of precious metals.[78]

C. Emergence of Monetary Institutions

As the use of well-defined instruments expands beyond tightly knit communities the development of institutions with power not only to apply the law to the

[70] Goodhart (n 5) 412.

[71] JP Baron, 'Making Money in Mesoamerica: Currency Production and Procurement in the Classic Maya Financial System' (2018) 5 *Economic Anthropology* 210, 213; C Eagleton and J Williams, *Money. A History* (London, The British Museum Press, 2013) 19; Goodhart (n 5) 412.

[72] Baron (n 71) 214.

[73] WJ Ashworth, 'Metrology and the State: Science, Revenue, and Commerce' (2004) 306 *Science* 1314, 1314; JA O'Keefe, *The Law of Weights and Measures* (London, Butterworths, 1966) 1–2.

[74] Goodhart (n 5) 416.

[75] N Kiyotaki and J Moore, 'Liquidity, Business Cycles, and Monetary Policy' (2008), available at www.princeton.edu/~kiyotaki/papers/ChiKM6-1.pdf, *Princeton University*; Desan (n 26) 25; Goodhart (n 5) 416.

[76] Eich (n 34) 5.

[77] Desan (n 26) 25; Rahmatian (n 32) 210.

[78] Smith (n 28) 91; Menger (n 22) 241.

settlement of disputes,[79] but also to regulate the *reifiers* and create new law if needed,[80] became increasingly necessary for our commercial societies.[81] Given these needs, and the ceremonial values that ruled the existence of the non-capitalist societies that conceived the first monetary *reifiers*,[82] the economic legal importance of the royal palaces and the sanctuaries of antiquity has long been recognised.[83] For instance, in financial transactions, the position of the Babylonian temples was not different from that of national banks,[84] and they – just as the Chief Executive of Goldman Sachs, Lloyd Blankfein,[85] stated in 2009 on the social functions of banking – did the work of God.

Initially, one can be tempted to infer that there was no formal financial system among non-capitalist societies, even when one can trace the evolution of certain payment mechanisms in those contexts. However, these mechanisms were initiated through the conversion of goods at a discount rate, and through the issue of payment orders,[86] which involved groups of merchants and private lenders, that on many occasions had their own gods, and, according to Goetzmann,[87] had the power to undermine the nascent *lex monetae*.[88] Accordingly, the inception of the first 'financial' institutions may be found in the sacred character of the laws and revenues found in places like the Babylonian sanctuaries and the Mesoamerican networks, and the cults relating to deities, such as Sămăs, the sun god and lord of justice and righteousness, at Sippar,[89] and Yacatecuhtli, the Aztec god of long-distance trade and cacao. Following the cults relating to these gods, it can be argued

[79] R Ali; et al, 'Innovation in Payment Technologies and the Emergence of Digital Currencies' (2014) 262, available at www.bankofengland.co.uk/-/media/boe/files/quarterly-bulletin/2014/innovations-in-payment-technologies-and-the-emergence-of-digital-currencies.pdf; Goodhart (n 5) 413.

[80] GW Paton, *A Text-Book of Jurisprudence* (London, Oxford University Press, 1964) 47.

[81] Gleeson (n 24) 10.

[82] G Papadopoulos, 'Blockchain and Digital Payments: An Institutional Analysis of Cryptocurrencies' in DL Kuo Chuen (ed), *Handbook of Digital Currency. Bitcoin, Innovation, Financial Instruments, and Big Data* (San Diego, Academic Press, 2015) 153–72, 163; M Sahlins, 'The original Political Society' in D Graeber and M Sahlins (eds), *On Kings* Chicago, Hau Books, 2017) 23–64, 24; P Sieghart, *The Lawful Rights of Mankind. An Introduction to the International Legal Code of Human Rights* (Oxford, Oxford University Press, 1985) 13.

[83] B Bromberg, 'The Origin of Banking: Religious Finance in Babylonia' (1942) 2 *The Journal of Economic History* 77, 77; C Davies, *A History of Money. From Ancient Times to the Present Day* (Cardiff: University of Wales Press, 1994) 49.

[84] Bromberg (n 83) 77.

[85] In the aftermath of the collapse of Lehman Brothers, Lloyd Blankfein was quoted as saying that he was 'doing God's work'. See J Gapper, 'Master of Risk Who did God's Work for Goldman Sachs but Won It Little Love' (2009), available at www.ft.com/content/479ac4ba-eb32-11de-bc99-00144feab49a.

[86] K Hirth, *The Aztec Economic World. Merchants and Markets in Ancient Mesoamerica* (New York, Cambridge University Press, 2016) 266; Geva (n 11) 118–19.

[87] WN Goetzmann, *Money Changes Everything. How Finance Made Civilization Possible* (New Jersey, Princeton University Press, 2016) 57.

[88] Just as Paul Sieghart notes, a breach of the law was not only a transgression against a socially accepted code, but was considered an affront to the sacred deity, in this case against a merchant god. See Sieghart (n 82) 13.

[89] Bromberg (n 83).

that the role of the oath in legal decisions played a decisive role in the definition of the 'opposites' and the 'correlatives' that constitute our monetary *res.*[90]

Ancient Mesopotamia has been identified as 'the cradle of banking';[91] however, lending, deposit-taking and payment services were carried out as secondary activities by temples, palaces, merchants and landowners.[92] Consequently, if one wants to find the source of regular income of the temples, the tithes payable not only by private individuals, but also by the Babylonian cities and the royal family as well are a good starting point.[93] Based on this income, the first financial transactions developed by temples, like the one found at Sippar,[94] relied on the incorporation of a source of sacred liquidity. As an illustration of this, we have a grain loan offered on behalf of the sun god who was the notional creditor in over 80 per cent of the temple loans from the Old Babylonian period[95] during the reign of Sin-muballit, Hammurabi's father:[96] '10 gur of grain-at the rate of 1/5th gur per gur- Minutum has borrowed from Sămăs. At harvest time he shall return it. 3 witnesses. Undated.' Furthermore, over time, receipt testifying deposits or tithes gradually led temples and depositors to convert their wealth into an income-earning asset by allowing the temple to convert the deposits and tithes into loans, perhaps as a way of temporarily managing shortages in the temple economy.[97]

D. The Development of Socio-Metallism

Temples also played a central role in what one could call Socio-Metallism, which can be considered a sub-nucleus of our Socio-Legal theory of money. Just as Aristotle[98] described, after our ancestors' skill as metallurgists allowed them to make a distinction between base and precious metals,[99] silver and gold started to be considered available, affordable, durable, fungible, portable and reliable means of fulfilling monetary functions. Consequently, under a *proto lex monetae*, these temples were probably the guardians of the official weights and were generally important in the regulation of the silver system closely related to the medium of exchange in circulation.[100] On this basis, it is not strange to find metallic loans that resemble to proto-promissory notes charged by the Sămăs temple, just as one

[90] W Hohfeld, 'Some Fundamental Legal Conceptions as Applied in Judicial Reasoning.' (1914) 16 *Yale Law Journal* 16, 30; ME Stevens, *Temples, Tithes, and Taxes. The Temple and Economic Life of Ancient Israel* (Massachusetts, Hendrickson Publishers, 2006) 139; Rahmatian (n 32) 209.

[91] Bromberg (n 83) 77; Geva (n 11) 119.

[92] ibid.

[93] Bromberg (n 83) 77.

[94] For authors like Bromberg, this temple could be acted as the first bank in the world. See ibid.

[95] Stevens (n 90) 151.

[96] Bromberg (n 83) 80.

[97] Davies (n 83) 49; Stevens (n 90) 142.

[98] Aristotle, *Politics* (Oxford, Clarendon Press, 1908) 42.

[99] Davies (n 83) 54.

[100] Eagleton and Williams (n 71) 19; Goodhart (n 5) 412.

can see in this extract from the Abi-Ešuh reign (1711–1684 BC):[101] '51/2 shekels of silver Idn-Šamaš. At harvest time he shall pay back to Sămăs the money and its interest. 2 witnesses. Date 20th of Šebat (January).'

In similar way, in Ancient Greece, the *hieropoipoi*[102] of Delos managed several lists with 'monetary' accounts, which included how many coins the *hieropoipoi* received assuming office, spent developing their functions and transmitted to the next manager. The other section showed an inventory of the temple, which listed mostly silver, the weight of was always recorded.[103]

From these practices one can argue that although metallurgical developments came initially from the private sector, governments, through a proto-*lex monetae*, paired with religious occasions and fiscal needs, made monetary processes into a pillar of what we would eventually identify as the Westphalian State,[104] particularly after the traditionally accepted sovereign transition materialised through the Lydian *electrum* apparently conceived between the late-seventh or early-sixth century BC.[105] However, one has to be cautious with this historical example found in most of the sources on economics history and banking law. If one looks for evidence regarding the transition between the first forms of money and the sovereign currencies, it is possible to find different sources like the Sennacherib's claim by which the Assyrian ruler declared in approximately 694 BC: 'I built forms of clay and poured bronze into them over and over again; I perfected their forms as in pouring into one-shekel pieces.'[106] Furthermore, during an auction held on 19 November 2019, a piece of silver from the fourteenth century BC with a seal of Tutankhamun – which identified him as the monetary stakeholder – went under the hammer as one of the first monetary expressions of the history of humankind.[107] Thus, on this evidence, one can conclude that, under the Western legal tradition, the first currency was probably created before the introduction of the Lydian coin, as a socio-legal expression that derived from the proto-*lex monetae* exercised by temples.

To close this section, it is important highlight an historical lesson that may feel rather familiar. These first forms of coinage, at their beginnings, may have been developed by merchants and/or proto-bankers as *reifiers* of their socio-legal

[101] Bromberg (n 83) 83.

[102] Temple managers.

[103] DM Schaps, 'What Was Money in Ancient Greece?' in WV Harris (ed), *The Monetary System of the Greeks and Romans* 39–48, 43.

[104] D Schoenmaker, *Governance of International Banking. The Financial Trilemma* (New York, Oxford University Press, 2013) 2–3; Goodhart (n 5) 413.

[105] This unit made of a natural alloy of gold and silver, which was found on Mount Tmolus and in the sands of the River Pactolus, containing approximately 73% gold and 27% silver. Consequently, based on practices of Asia Minor, the electrum was exchanged at the rate of 3:4 with pure gold, and 10:1 with silver. See FW Hirst, *Money. Gold, Silver & Paper* (London, Charles Scribner's Sons, 1932) 11; JK Galbraith, *Money. Whence It Came, Where It Went* (London, Andre Deutsch, 1975) 8; DM Schaps, *Invention of Coinage and the Monetization of Ancient Greece* (Michigan, The University of Michigan Press, 2013) 95.

[106] P Vargyas, 'Sennacherib's Alleged Half-Shekel Coins' (2002) 61 *Journal of Near Eastern Studies* 111.

[107] Numismatica Genevensis, 'Ancient and World Coin Auction. Lot 101' (2019) available at www.biddr.ch/auctions/ngsa/browse?a=791&l=831356.

relationships; however, just as we are witnessing in a myriad of regulatory debates on DLT innovations around the world, the state had to intervene in the creation of money for three main reasons. First, socio-metallic systems required inventories of precious metals that attracted opportunistic behaviours; thus, only those who wielded the force necessary to maintain law and order could extract the most value from the system.[108] Second, following the asymmetries described by Akerlof,[109] the costs of identifying the true qualitative value of the metals could, and did, lead to the debasement of the monetary asset.[110] Third, as the emergence of banking houses like the Grandsons of Egibi in Babylon[111] showed, private parties tend to obtain excessive infrastructural and political power, as Susan Strange[112] argued in her article on what she termed 'Westfailure'. Accordingly, this process of innovation, adoption and regulation that gives form to our *ius cudendae monetae* will be repeated every time a new form of money emerges through new technologies, usually developed by the private sector.

E. Religion and Money in the Western World

After the initial conception of coins, which can be defined as tokens 'issued by a taxing authority on the basis of a promise that it will be accepted in discharge of tax obligations',[113] coinage – as it is evidenced in documents like the *Athenian Constitution*[114] – was actively diffused in the key poleis of the Aegean (eg Aegina, Corinth and Athens) and along the main axes of Greek overseas migration.[115] Following the path set by every monetary innovation, Aristotle[116] noted how a new business model emerged through a new generation of intermediaries who took advantage of the wide offer of coins that circulated among the Greek states. These intermediaries were the first money-changers.[117] Eventually, secondary innovations, such as the *eranos*,[118] the *aes grave* (heavy bronze) and small commercial lenders like the *argentarii/trapezitae* inserted coinage into every level of the credit

[108] Goodhart (n 5) 412.
[109] Akerlof (n 57).
[110] Goodhart (n 5) 412–13.
[111] Davies (n 83) 50.
[112] S Strange, 'The Westfailure System' (1999) 25 *Review of International Studies* 345; Geva (n 11) 84–85.
[113] Gleeson (n 24) 35.
[114] Aristotle, *The Athenian Constitution, The Eudemian Ethics, and Virtues and Vices* (London, Harvard University Press, 1952) 33.
[115] W Scheidel, 'The Divergent Evolution of Coinage in Eastern and Western Eurasia' in WV Harris (ed), *The Monetary Systems of the Greeks and Romans* (Oxford, Oxford University Press, 2008) 268, 268; Galbraith (n 105) 8.
[116] Aristotle (n 98) 46.
[117] According to Schaps, 'no such a person is attested before the fifth century, and we may question whether there was any need for money changers in the early period.' See Schaps (n 105) 179.
[118] The *éranos* worked as a monetised *kula* by which a single borrower borrowed from personal friends and family. See ibid, 188.

structure, which would eventually reach Rome[119] to substitute the *ROMANORUM* (of the Romans) bronze bars stamped 'with the likeness of sheep and oxen'[120] (*aes signata*) described by Pliny and related to the standards found in the Twelve Tables of c 450 BC.[121]

Greek coins would eventually set the model for Rome which, building upon its economic predominance on the peninsula, would coin its own currencies and, with the production of the Campanian silver *stater*,[122] Roman coins acquired conclusively and irreversibly the form of standardised metallic chattels, issued by the state and stamped exercising its *lex monetae*.[123] The monetary system that emerged from the consolidation of the *ius cudendae monetae* was structured around three different metals – *aureus* (gold), *denarius* (silver) and *sestertius* (bronze) – all stamped with the image of a sovereign figure and/or a cultural element, such as flowers, animals, and gods,[124] thus acting as active means to transfer information relating to the social system.[125] However, with the fall of Rome in 476 CE, came the end of monetary antiquity and the beginning of the Middle Ages,[126] which introduced new ways to *reify* and transfer liquidity.

After Christianity conquered Rome, taking advantage of weakened imperial institutions, invading barbarian armies, punitive taxation and a tired and weary population,[127] the dominant view in Christendom was structured around a celestialisation of sovereignty as an ideological expression of the real political order.[128] From St Augustine's notion that 'a part of the earthly city was made an image of the heavenly',[129] to Carl Schmitt's assertion that 'all significant concepts of the modern theory of the State are secularized theological concepts',[130] it can be said that human institutions, including our *lex monetae*, were commonly considered to be modelled on the Kingdom of God.[131]

On this basis, the monetarisation of the European economy, which began in the late twelfth century during the so-called 'commercial revolution', became a

[119] BE Woytek, 'Monetary Innovation in Ancient Rome: The Republic and its Legacy' in P Bernholz and R Vaubel (eds), *Explaining Monetary and Financial Innovation. A Historical Analysis* (Cham, Springer, 2014) 197–226, 204; Schaps (n 105) 179.

[120] H Rackham, *Pliny. Natural History with an English Translation in Ten Volumes. Volume V* (Massachusetts, Harvard University Press, 1950) 196.

[121] 'Before the Empire' (2023) 18 *Coin Collector* 36, 36; Woytek (n 119) 200.

[122] Scheidel (n 115) 270–71.

[123] Geva (n 11) 87.

[124] R Doty, *Money of the World* (London, Ridge Press, 1978) 24; N Ferguson, *The Ascent of Money. A Financial History of the World* (New York, The Penguin Press, 2008) 24; Withers (n 10) 7.

[125] An interesting case of study of this function during this period can be found in the provincial coinage of Emperor Aemilian. G Watson, 'The Provincial Coinage of Aemilian: A Study in Imperial Communication' (2018) 178 *The Numismatic Chronicle* 184–212.

[126] Geva (n 11) 352.

[127] C Nixey, *The Darkening Age. The Christian Destruction of the Classical World* (London, Pan Books, 2018) 7.

[128] Sahlins (n 82) 23.

[129] St Agustine, *The City of God (De Civitate Dei)* (Edinburgh, John Grant, 1909) 56.

[130] C Schmitt, *Political Theology: Four Chapters on the Concept of Sovereignty* (Massachusetts, MIT Press, 1985) 36.

[131] Sahlins (n 82) 23.

matter of major concern for the Church and its law.[132] After all, as expressed by Eusebius of Caesarea in his *The Life of the Blessed Emperor Constantine*,[133] money reflected the influence of God over Constantine's reign. The spirit of these lines is verified in an interesting line found in the Gratian's[134] *decretum* which pointed to the general rule that '*solidus, qui non habet charagma Caesaris, reprobus est*'.[135] The reference to Caesar is based on the fact that Roman law assigned the prerogative to mint money to the emperor, and the glossators confirmed this expression of our *lex monetae*; consequently, this principle was generally accepted, as expressed in Petrus Ancharanus's[136] statement, '*ad reges spectat cudere monetam*'.[137]

Considering that the Gratinan's *decretum* recognised that the *ius cudendae monetae* continued to be bound to a 'sacred' source of liquidity, authors, such as Jean Bodin[138] and Thomas Hobbes[139] considered that princes were bound and had the right to intervene in monetary matters supported by the terms set by divine and natural law.[140] Following this interpretation, it should not surprise us that, citing a solemn oath took by Peter II, King of Spain, by which he would preserve unaltered the coins of his father, King Alphonse II, in 1199, Innocent III issued a decretal beginning with the words *Quanto personam tuam*:[141]

> We suggest and order that you demonetize that coinage, which has been defrauded from legitimate weight, and that you coin other mint under your father's name, which you bring back to its legitimate weight in that state, which it had during your father's reign at best, so that also the old coinage, which has not been defrauded at this state, is set in circulation; by this approach expenses can be avoided and the oath can be preserved.

As one would expect, this decretal had a strong impact on all later discussions of princes' entitlements to exercise the *lex monetae*,[142] and highlighted the fact that, before the consolidation of the Rule of Law and constitutionalism, royal power was fraught with paradoxes.[143] On the one hand, it was, in principle, absolute. Kings,

[132] A Thier, 'Money in Medieval Canon Law' in D Fox and W Ernst (eds), *Money in the Western Legal Tradition. Middle Ages to Bretton Woods* (Oxford, Oxford University Press, 2016) 136, 138.

[133] Eusebius, *The Life of the Blessed Emperor Constantine* (London, Samuel Bagster and Sons, 1845) 188.

[134] Gregory XIII, 'Corpus juris canonici emendatum et notis illustratum' (1582), available at digital.library.ucla.edu/canonlaw/librarian?ITEMBREAK=CJC1_0350&SIZE=1.2&INUM=0; Thier (n 132) 139.

[135] 'A solidus, which does not have the Caesar's stamp on it is false.'

[136] P de Ancharanus, 'Super secundo Decretalium facundissima commentaria.' (1581), available at digibug.ugr.es/handle/10481/9160.

[137] 'The right to mint money is with the kings.'

[138] J Bodin, 'Six Books of the Commonwealth' (2018), available at www.yorku.ca/comninel/courses/3020pdf/six_books.pdf, 47.

[139] T Hobbes, *Leviathan* (Oxford, Oxford University Press, 2008) 166–67.

[140] A Nussbaum, 'A Note on the Idea of World Money' (1949) 64 *Political Science Quarterly* 420, 423.

[141] Translation provided by Andreas Thier. See Thier (n 132) 164.

[142] ibid, 140.

[143] D Graeber, 'Notes on the Politics of Divine Kingship, or Elements for an Archaeology of Sovereignty' in D Graeber and M Sahlins (eds), *On Kings* (Chicago, Hau Books, 2017) 377–464, 378.

as we can see through the work of Hobbes[144] and the words of James VI and I,[145] tended to insist that they stood above the legal order, so this order couldn't be reliably enforced. This fostered the production of texts, such as *De Jure Regni apud Scotos Dialogus*,[146] and the creation of instruments like Magna Carta,[147] which, eventually, contributed to the emergence of the Rule of Law. On the other hand, as presented through Innocent III's words, by using the term *moneta legitimo pondere defraudata*,[148] holders of sovereign power often used to lead lives so circumscribed by custom and ceremony that they could barely do anything at all. What is more, this paradox can be seen today in the peculiar way we imagine the Westphalian state, where sovereignty has, in principle, transitioned from the king to an entity we refer to as 'the people'.[149] This abstraction is protected by sovereign immunity that derives from the English antecedent that presumed that 'the king can do no wrong' as described in cases such as *AINS, Inc v The United States*[150] on the nature of the US Mint. However, 'the people', as innovators and enthusiasts experience through different regulatory responses, are bound and constrained by the very laws of the realm.[151]

i. Before Nakamoto, We had the Medieval Merchant

In the early centuries of the Middle Ages, the economy collapsed, and there was a substantial reduction in trade.[152] The last Roman banks disappeared in the course of the sixth and seventh centuries, and, as seen through the numerous coin and hack-silver hoards found across Europe during this period, the financial infrastructure ceased to exist altogether.[153] As result, monetary institutions only survived in a rudimentary form until the twelfth century. From this point, in Italy, there was a gradual re-emergence of banks and, generally overlooked, the beginning of new

[144] Hobbes (n 139) 312–13.

[145] James VI and I argued in a speech to Parliament in 1610 that 'the state of monarchy is the supremest thing upon earth. For kings are not only God's lieutenants upon earth, and sit upon God's throne, but even by God himself they are called gods.' See R Griffith-Jones, *Magna Carta 1215–2015. London's Temple and the Road to the Rule of Law* (Gloucestershire, Pitkin Publishing, 2013) 28; University of Cambridge, 'King James VI and I, Speech to Parliament (1610)' (2023), available at www.hist.cam.ac.uk/divine-right-kings-4#:~:text=King%20James%20VI%20and%20I%2C%20Speech%20to%20Parliament%20(1610)&text=The%20state%20of%20monarchy%20is,himself%20they%20are%20called%20gods.

[146] G Buchanan. *De Jure Regni apud Scotos Dialogus* (Glasgow, Ronerti Urie,1750) 72–73.

[147] D Jones, *Magna Carta. The Making and Legacy of the Great Charter* (London, Head of Zeus, 2014); PT Leeson and PA Suarez, 'An Economic Analysis of Magna Carta' (2016) 47 *International Review of Law and Economics* 40, 41; Graeber (n 143) 378.

[148] 'Money forged in its legitimate weight.'

[149] Graeber (n 143) 378.

[150] [2002] 02-133C (US), 1–2.

[151] Graeber (n 143) 378.

[152] B Geva, 'The Order to Pay Money in Medieval Continental Europe' in D Fox and W Ernst (eds), *Money in the Western Legal Tradition. Middle Ages to Bretton Woods* (Oxford, Oxford University Press, 2016) 409–40, 409.

[153] ibid.

ways of liquidity incorporation that set the basis for our modern cashless payment system.[154] Notarial records dating from 1200 include descriptions of how Genoese bankers enabled their wealthy clients to make payments by means of transfers on the accounts of the bank.[155] Therefore, merchants could make payments by directing their banks, who acted as complete clearing systems, to debit their accounts and credit that of their creditors, assuming that both parties had accounts at the same bank.[156]

This reappearance was the result of common endogenous demands within dynamic social systems, which experienced an enormous expansion of trade that was made possible in cities like Genoa and Marseilles where new intermediaries emerged following some practices associated with the Roman *argentarii*, as we can see in this receipt for a deposit from a money-changer:[157]

> March twenty-eighth, in the year of the Incarnation of the Lord, 1248.
>
> I, Giraud Alaman, money-changer, citizen of Marseilles, confess and admit to you, Peter Mazele of Baza, that I have had and received from you by way of deposit ten pounds of mixed money now current in Marseilles, renouncing, etc.
>
> I have promised to give and pay to you these ten pounds or to a known messenger of yours or to any one whom you command to receive it, whenever it shall please you. Pledging all my goods, etc.; renouncing all delays of the law, etc.
>
> Witnesses, etc.

As we can conclude from the last lines of the receipt, these deposit bankers and merchant bankers discovered that gold and silver could be economised by the use of transcriptions in their account books and paper, which represented an underlying *res* by which they multiplied the metals. Consequently, instruments such as the *letters de foire* and the *instrumentum debiti ex causa cambii a scholaribus et clericis contracti*, would gradually evolve into what we know as the bill of exchange and its derivative instruments.[158]

ii. The Lex Mercatoria *and the New Diffusion of Innovations in Payments*

Additionally, these notes suggest the existence of informal governance arrangements, which current regulations like the ECB's Regulation 795/2014[159] classify as

[154] S Meder, 'Giro Payments and the Beginnings of the Modern Cashless Payment System' in D Fox and W Ernst (eds), *Money in the Western Legal Tradition. Middle Ages to Bretton Woods* (Oxford, Oxford University Press, 2016) 441–60, 441; Geva (n 152) 354.

[155] D Awrey and K van Zwieten, 'The Shadow Payment System.' (2018) 43 *The Journal of Corporation Law* 102–41, 110.

[156] Gleeson (n 24) 33.

[157] P Halsall, 'Medieval Sourcebook: Receipt of Deposit from a Money-Changer, 1248' (1998), available at sourcebooks.fordham.edu/source/1248moneychanger.asp.

[158] AP Usher, 'The Origin of the Bill of Exchange' (1914) 22 *Journal of Political Economy* 566, 566–69.

[159] Regulation of the European Central Bank 795/2014 on oversight requirements for systemically important payment systems OJ L 217/16, 3 July 2014.

payment systems. For instance, different banking families in Italy like the Peruzzi, the Bardi, and the Frescobaldi constituted and controlled a network of branches in different parts of Europe and facilitated payments among their accounts; an arrangement that was eventually diffused throughout much of Western Europe.[160] Furthermore, replicating the network effects that characterised the first proto-monetary goods, confidence in the infrastructural power of a banker became sufficiently established to induce the community to circulate and value fiat money[161] as seen in *Tassell and Lee v Lewis*.[162]

As is seen in the *Tassell* case, long before the consensus mechanism that enforced the sets of rules and incentives that characterise DLT protocols, the emergence of the medieval law merchant introduced a governance paradigm that for hundreds of years subsisted as a distinct source of rights and concepts, such as, 'just price' and *ex aequo et bono*.[163] These rights were administered, expeditiously and efficiently by courts set up on trade routes and at trade centres in which the merchants acted as judges, before ultimately becoming redundant because of the adaptation of the common law itself to commercial needs and usages.[164] Therefore, the maritime courts, the courts of the fairs and boroughs, the staple courts, and other commercial courts of the Middle Ages determined disputes involving foreigners and foreign payment instruments. Their decisions were not based on domestic law,[165] but according to a law uniform in nature and universal in application similar to *lex naturae*, based on mercantile codes and customs, such as the *Rolls of Oléron*, which reflected the international maritime and commercial practice.[166]

To these courts – as to their counterparts elsewhere in the Western world – came not only local merchants but foreign traders from across Europe, content to have their disputes resolved by P2P tribunals which, though located in countries like England, Italy and Spain, were required to have an equal number of foreign merchants and 'reputable and law-abiding men of the place where the lawsuit

[160] Awrey and van Zwieten (n 155) 110; Usher (n 158) 570.

[161] Kiyotaki and Wright take as their starting point a commodity money equilibrium in which fiat money does not circulate to demonstrate that confidence and preferences relating to other goods can influence in the gradual adoption of fiat money which could circulate in equilibrium as general medium of exchange. See Kiyotaki and Wright (n 6) 942–44.

[162] In this case, the court, following the custom of merchants stated that 'the notes of goldsmiths (whether they be payable to order or to bearer) are always accounted among merchants as ready cash, and not as bills of exchange.' [1695] 1 Ld Raym 743 (UK), 1398.

[163] LE Trakman, 'From the Medieval Law Merchant to E-Merchant Law' (2003) 53 *The University of Toronto Law Journal* 265–304, 268.

[164] R Goode, *Goode on Commercial Law* (London, LexisNexis, 2009) 3.

[165] The very term *lex mercatoria* (not *Ius Mercatorum)* evidenced how the authority of all kingdoms and commonwealths recognised the customary nature of this law that was not established by the sovereignty of any prince. However, authors like Francis A Mann argue the existence of a *lex mercatoria* per se is very doubtful based on the absence of the sovereign element. See FA Mann, 'The Proper Law in the Conflict of Laws' (1987) 36 *The International and Comparative Law Quarterly* 437–53, 448; Trakman (n 163) 271.

[166] JH Baker, 'The Law Merchant and the Common Law before 1700' (1979) 38 *Cambridge Law* Journal 295, 299; Goode (n 164) 3, Trakman (n 163) 271–72.

happens to takes place',[167] as one can see in the *Carta Mercatoria* of 1303. On monetary matters, from the recognition found in *Burton v Davy*,[168] it is possible to deduce that the adaptability of 'the law merchant and the custom of the city of London' were important in the evolution of money and payment mechanisms through the recognition of negotiability of credit instruments. This socio-legal recognition eventually covered bills of exchange and promissory notes, and would be incorporated into the Statute of Anne in 1704.[169] From this, one can infer that well before the birth of the English law of contract, the law merchant accepted that a right to a sum of money embodied in a bill of exchange or promissory note could be conferred even though the instrument was not under seal,[170] thus highlighting the increasing relevance of the trust on the constitution and the diffusion of payment instruments and practices, such as the indorsement and the protest.

In the context of cryptoassets, the diffusion of trust has been at the core of practically every effort to offer decentralised P2P alternatives and, for that purpose, developers rely on a *crypto lex mercatoria* that depends – paradoxically – on trust in a world of algorithmic 'black boxes'. Even, as it is verified through the case of OpenAI's boss Sam Altman and Worldcoin, the celebrity of certain technology in a specific context could invite particular stakeholders to propose multi-jurisdictional projects built on a set of rules developed by the private sector.[171] As will be seen in chapter four, this obfuscated trust relies on the exercise (or lack of exercise and understanding) of IPRs in the software industry, a fact that has been evidenced in *Google v Oracle*,[172] which confirmed the dynamics that define the practices accepted by the industry.

Another contribution of the Middle Ages to our Socio-Legal theory of money was the development of the philosophy of metallic money. In the Ancient era, the function of the sovereign seal was to certify the intrinsic value of the coins under the social agreement. However, in the Middle Ages, following the spirit of our 'sacred liquidity', the seal came to confer upon the unit its exchange value,[173] thus setting the basis for the Chartalist view of money.[174]

[167] Florilegium Urbanum, 'The Statute of New Custom (Commonly Known as Carta Mercatoria, 1303)' (2015), available at users.trytel.com/tristan/towns/florilegium/economy/eccom21.html.

[168] On the transfer of a bill of exchange issued by one John Audeley, who was factor and attorney of one Elias Davy, and claimed by one John Walden, the mayor of London, John Mitchell, recognised the transfer and the claims relating to it according to the law merchant and the custom of the city of London. See Hall (n 7) 117–19.

[169] M Dylag, 'The Negotiability of Promissory Notes and Bills of Exchange in the Time of Chief Justice Holt' (2010) 31 *The Journal of Legal History* 149, 165.

[170] Goode (n 164) 4.

[171] I Levingston and G Hammond, 'Open AI's Sam Altman Nears $100mn Funding for Worldcoin Crypto Project' (2023), available at www.ft.com/content/f1de2aee-ee13-45e1-bd61-0a269cd650d3.

[172] [2020] 18-956 SC (US).

[173] Geva (n 11) 89.

[174] CAE Goodhart, *Money, Information and Uncertainty* (Hong Kong: The Macmillan Press1975) 9–10.

III. Conclusion

Money is a dynamic institution, one that reflects the dynamism of our social systems. This chapter has shown that money and the institutions related to it reflect endogenous needs developed within each social system, in different times, which allow us to identify common evolutionary patterns. These patterns can help us to address current needs and challenges materialised through a new generation of financial innovation. Certainly, innovations like cryptoassets offer us new technological tools that could be employed to *reify* rights and claims, but they do not represent a new experience. Just as it was analysed throughout this chapter, particularly in the context of the invention of coinage and bills of exchange, the private sector tends to introduce new monetary practices and technologies, which have eased the transition from commodity money to our current fiat paradigms. To understand these dynamics, I introduced the Socio-Legal theory of money, which reflects the referred interactions between endogenous needs and transitional rules that have offered us different monetary outputs throughout the financial history of the world. Currently, these interactions configure our *lex monetae*.

Another key point that emerged from the analyses developed within this chapter is the need for legal-technological infrastructures to diffuse monetary innovations and ease the transition mentioned above. Coins, paper money, electronic money and even cryptoassets foster the emergence of intermediaries, such as bill brokers, banks, exchanges and clearing infrastructures. Building upon the Socio-Legal theory of money, the first forms of commodity money required the *potestas* of the temples to evolve into proper currencies in the Mediterranean. Bills of exchange and promissory notes evolved through the introduction of figures like the protest and the indorsement. As will be explored in the following chapter, paper money relied on the soundness of the banks to incorporate trust, as evidenced in *Tassell and Lee v Lewis*,[175] and eventually led to the consolidation and diffusion of the sovereign monopoly on money creation in the nineteenth century. It is even possible to argue that the diffusion of cryptoassets is at the centre of regulatory discussions as a result of the development of a new generation of shadow banks and, certainly, its consolidation will depend on the exercise of *lex monetae* to adopt and regulate, not cryptoassets by themselves, but the infrastructures involved and the new practices that could evolve from the use of DLT.

In the context of this book, it is possible to witness how the FIR is contributing not only to the evolution of the functions associated with money, but also to our broad social values and structures.[176] This change is relevant for the Socio-Legal theory of money given that they could change the very source of the liquidity that will be incorporated in the new generation of payment instruments. In other

[175] [1695] 1 Ld Raym 743 (UK), 1398.

[176] P Boucher, 'What if Blockchain Changed Social Values?' (2017), available at www.europarl.europa.eu/RegData/etudes/ATAG/2017/603176/EPRS_ATA%282017%29603176_EN.pdf.

words, the new underlying obligations that could result from the gradual adoption of technologies, such as DLT, could depend on a new set of social and private agreements and their respective stakeholders. After all, just because DLT enthusiasts and developers argue that this technology is decentralised and open to everyone, it does not mean that it is neutral. On the contrary, as it will be explored in chapter four, DLT, like all technologies, has values, politics, as well as legal regimes under which they operate that reflect the interests of their creators.[177] Therefore, just as we have seen in this chapter how the emergence of different monetary expressions took place, our 'sacred' source of liquidity keeps evolving to adapt itself to a new digitalised environment, in which, for monetary matters, it is possible to state that the trust in algorithmic codes could become the new source of this liquidity.

[177] K Werbach, *The Blockchain and the New Architecture of Trust* (Massachusetts, MIT Press, 2018) 11; Boucher (n 436).

2

Who Can Create Money?

I. Introduction

The definition and understanding of the term *lex monetae* are closely related to the answer to the question 'who can create money'? The most common answer found in many academic sources tends to be structured around the institution of central banking. This is not surprising; after all, monetary outputs that are familiar to us are created under the coordination and exercise of the objectives, functions and powers of institutions, such as the Federal Reserve, the Riksbank, and the Bank of England. Now, is this perception correct? The answer is, partially, yes. However, as this chapter will show, central banking represents only a relatively new view of the cathedral that constitutes our *ius cudendae monetae* and, certainly, it is not the only possible answer to the question posed above. In the context of dynamic social systems which are exposed to a continuous flow of inputs that force them to adjust their transitional rules with the aim of addressing endogenous needs in different scenarios, it is possible to find other solutions.

As noted in the conclusion of chapter one, money needs legal-technological infrastructures to support those acts of incorporation, increase the acceptability of new monetary technologies, and perform such functions appropriately. With that in mind, this chapter will focus on the design of payment systems as governance schemes, where central banks represent a fourth constitutional power with an underlying socio-legal contract that acts as the current source of liquidity. The introduction of this 'fourth power' highlights the harmonisation efforts that allow us to constitute international payment systems, which, independently of their reliance on infrastructures provided by the private sector, their very existence and diffusion depend on the passive/active sovereign exercise of *lex monetae.*

On the role of the private sector within these governance schemes, the chapter will highlight the FMC model by which, in opposition to the traditional conception of banks as mere intermediaries, institutions create money through the act of lending and their respective underlying obligations. Furthermore, we will evidence that the challenge posed by cryptoassets is not something new for our legal systems. After all, throughout our financial history different free banking systems have been designed to introduce complementary means of payment, as evidenced by the Scottish free banking system (1716–1845) and current communitarian monies. These experiences show how they have addressed the requirements of particular communities through the adoption of different monetary technologies and the constitution of regional social contracts. Consequently, it is not surprising that, at the margins of current analyses, heavily focused on Bitcoin, other monetary projects are using DLT to replicate historical patterns in new environments.

II. The *Lex Monetae*

The term *lex monetae* usually attracts arguments and discussions centred on the connections between money and sovereign stakeholders, eg monarchs and central banks.[1] At the cornerstone of these debates are the characteristics that define the post-Westphalian states whose sovereignty symbols are their flags, their military power and their currencies.[2] Consequently, the *lex monetae* tends to be defined as the prerogative of each nation to issue a particular currency and set its value as an integral part of its own monetary system,[3] as one can infer from cases such as those in the Permanent Court of International Justice on Serbian[4] and Brazilian[5] loans.

Of course, this definition provides a good starting point, but ignores a very important fact: money needs – in order to exist and circulate – infrastructures controlled by different stakeholders throughout GVCs. Accordingly, in exercise of the *lex monetae*, nations have selected commodities, such as gold and the best technologies available, like paper, to incorporate trust and constitute their monetary assets. Furthermore, under the the 'Mercury' and 'Mars' approaches,[6] the choice of these constitutive elements influences the value of the assets.

This book thus defines the *lex monetae* as the set of prerogatives by which each nation designs and puts in place, by itself or through a selection of stakeholders, the tangible and intangible infrastructure of its monetary system with the aim of creating, selecting, valueing, circulating, and even destroying a monetary asset. As will be seen in the case *Banco de Portugal v Waterlow & Sons Ltd*,[7] the selection of infrastructural stakeholders for the exercise of these prerogatives is not

[1] S. Gleeson, *The Legal Concept of Money* (New York, Oxford University Press, 2018) 28.

[2] D Schoenmaker, *Governance of International Banking. The Financial Trilemma* (New York, Oxford University Press, 2013) 3.

[3] K Sono, 'Legal Tender: A Notion Associated with Payment' in International Monetary Fund (ed), *Current Developments in Monetary and Financial Law* (Washington DC, IMF, 2003) 679–87, 679; H Syrstad, 'Introduction of Central Bank Digital Currency. Necessary Legislative Amendments' (2023) available at norges-bank.brage.unit.no/norges-bank-xmlui/bitstream/handle/11250/3058248/staff-memo-4-2023-cbdc-legislation.pdf?sequence=1&isAllowed=y.

[4] *The Government of the French Republic v The Government of the Kingdom of the Serbs, Croats and Slovenes* [1929] PCIJ (ser A) No 20 (NL), 33.

[5] *The Government of the French Republic v The Government of the Republic of the United States of Brazil* [1929] PCIJ (ser A) No 21 (NL), 116–17.

[6] E Avgouleas and W Blair, 'The Concept of Money in the 4th Industrial Revolution. A Legal and Economic Analysis' (2020) *Singapore Journal of Legal Studies* 4, 17; B Eichengreen, AJ Mehl and L Chitu, 'Mars or Mercury? The Geopolitics of International Currency Choice' (2017) 24145 *NBER Working Papers* 1, 2.

[7] *Banco de Portugal v Waterlow & Sons Ltd* [1932] All ER Rep 181 (UK).

something new nor exclusive of the DCS. Of course, the need for a definition like the one presented here is highlighted by the fact that our financial markets are based on interlocking systems of data transmission similar to those that define and give form to the internet.[8] Building on this definition, the following sections will show how the selection of commodities and technologies have set the bases and even given their name to different monetary policies and periods.

III. Paper Alchemy and the Emergence of Bank Money

Building on the commodity money equilibrium developed by Kiyotaki and Wright,[9] it can be said that a proper analysis of monetary matters from the Dark Ages to the current time must start with the coin[10] and evolve through its gradual *reification* through a new generation of payment instruments. Given that these units were the archetypical commodity money, coins issued under the authority of the sovereign emerged as the 'blood of a commonwealth'[11] between the twelfth and seventeenth centuries.[12] However, the blood of the commonwealth did not flow as freely as one would be tempted to think. Based on the work of authors such as Gasparo Scaruffi,[13] we know that in the Middle Ages European monetary systems were based on a complete decentralisation of power as part of the logic feudalism.[14] This paradigm posed problems to merchants and private persons who had to transact within the same markets with different currencies issued in different locations based on different metallic standards, which in turn reflected different underlying social agreements. Consequently, coinage could not provide an 'unambiguous and litigation-free means of settling debts'.[15]

[8] DC Donald, 'Information, and the Regulation of Inefficient Markets' in E Avgouleas and DC Donald (eds), *The Political Economy of Financial Regulation* (Cambridge: Cambridge University Press, 2002) 38, 41.

[9] N Kiyotaki and R Wright, 'On Money as a Medium of Exchange' (1989) 97 *Journal of Political Economy* 927, 942.

[10] CA Desan, 'Money as a Legal Institution' in D Fox and W Ernst (eds), *Money in the Western Legal Tradition. Middle Ages to Bretton Woods* (Oxford, Oxford University Press, 2016) 18–35, 9.

[11] T Hobbes, *Leviathan* (Oxford, Oxford University Press, 2008) 167.

[12] A Amend-Traut, 'Monetary and Currency Problems in the Light of Early Modern Litigation' in D Fox and W Ernst (eds), *Money in the Western Legal Tradition. Middle Ages to Bretton Woods* (Oxford, Oxford University Press, 2016) 295–316, 295.

[13] G Scaruffi, *L'alitinonfo* (Reggio, Hercoliano Bartoli, 1582).

[14] M Monteagudo, 'Neutrality of Money and Central Bank Independence' in M Giovanoli and D Devos (eds), *International Monetary and Financial Law. The Global Crisis* (Oxford, Oxford University Press, 2010) 484–505, 490.

[15] W Roberds and FR Velde, 'The Descent of Central Banks (1400–1815)' in MD Bordo; et al (eds), *Central Bans at a Crossroads* (New York, Cambridge University Press, 2016) 18–61, 21.

In reaction to the numerous complications of the feudal system, authors such as Jean Bodin[16] and Nicolas Copernicus[17] argued that money should be subject only to the royal authority. However, sovereign stakeholders imposed their sovereignty over money to project it within the international monetary system through the *lex monetae* for only a limited period of time. Initially, monetary issues were dealt with in political-theological pamphlets that analysed aspects of public policy. Only after the Peace of Westphalia in 1648 and the emergence of the nation-state was monetary stability considered as integral part of the 'good public order'.[18] The instruments to establish a stable monetary instrument were then put in place through sovereign acts, varying over time from bimetallism and trimetallism to the Bretton Woods system. As the analysis of these efforts show, the problem of monetary instability was not fully resolved until the Classical Gold Standard (CGS) of the late nineteenth century,[19] and it has not been solved again since.

Before the emergence of the nation-state and the Locke's idea of the Rule of Law,[20] sixteenth-century monarchs used their sovereign prerogatives to reverse the monetary decentralisation and gradually configure their monopoly over coinage,[21] which represented a source of revenue as result of the convenience that the public use of coins with a stated face value presented, rather than bullion, which was a form of inside money. As seen in documents such as An Act to Continue the Duties for Encouragement of the Coinage of Money of 1745, sovereign mints introduced a *seigniorage*[22] charge for providing this service. The Government's link to our sacred-sovereign source of liquidity gave it an advantage over private mints even when it did not prohibit them,[23] given that the private sector acted as a source of innovative power that in the future would give it an edge over the sovereign infrastructure; for example, the patent granted to David Ramsey in 1630[24] on a process for the separation of metals, and the patent granted to William Chamberlaine in 1673[25] related to a process of plating and tinning iron,

[16] J Bodin, 'Six Books of the Commonwealth' (2018) 47, available at www.yorku.ca/comninel/courses/3020pdf/six_books.pdf.

[17] N Copernicus, *On the Minting of Money* (New York. Laissez Faire Books, 2013) Kindle EBook, Loc 315.

[18] Amend-Traut (n 12) 298; Schoenmaker (n 2).

[19] R Edvinsson, T Jacobson and D Waldenström, 'Introduction' in R Edvinsson, T Jacobson and D Waldenström (eds), *Sveriges Riksbank and the History of Central Banking* (Cambridge: Cambridge University Press, 2018) 1–25, 8–17; Roberds and Velde (n 15).

[20] J Locke, *Two Treatises of Government* (London, Whitmore and Fenn and C Brown, 1821) 300–12.

[21] Monteagudo (n 14) 490.

[22] The difference between the value of the resources which could be obtained in exchange for the monetary asset and the cost of its production. See CAE Goodhart, *Money, Information and Uncertainty* (Hong Kong, The Macmillan Press, 1975) 10.

[23] M Friedman and AJ Schwartz, 'Has Government Any Role in Money?' in AJ Schwartz (ed), *Money in Historical Perspective* (Chicago, University of Chicago Press, 1987) 289–314, 295.

[24] [1630] UK No 53: 'Separating Metals.'

[25] [1673] UK No 171: 'Plating and Tinning Iron, Copper, &c.'

copper, and other metals.[26] These patents help us to identify some inventions that will allow us to create new monetary *reifiers* in which we can incorporate value, particularly when we are talking about the Gresham's Law, and consequently, to identify some FinTech developments centuries before the term had come into use.

Figure 4 Patents granted to David Ramsey and William Chamberlain related to the processing of metals

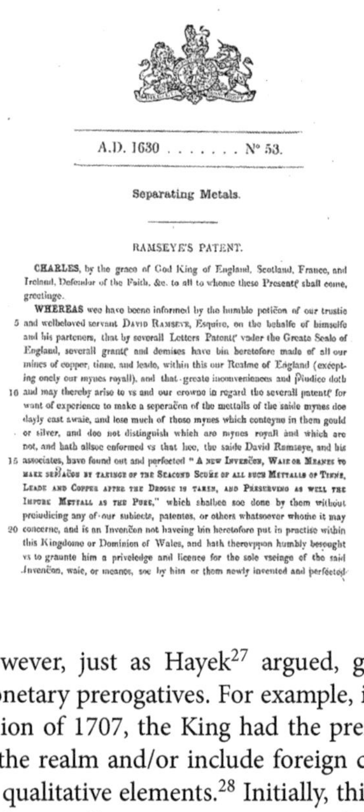

A.D. 1630 . . . . N° 53.

Separating Metals.

RAMSEYE'S PATENT.

CHARLES, by the grace of God King of England, Scotland, France, and Ireland, Defender of the Faith, &c. to all to whome these Presentę shall come, greetinge.

WHEREAS wee have beene informed by the humble petičon of our trustie and welbeloved servant DAVID RAMSEYE, Esquire, on the behalfe of himselfe and his parteners, that by severall Letters Patentę vnder the Greate Seale of England, severall grantę and demises have bin heretofore made of all our mines of copper, tinne, and leade, within this our Realme of England (excepting onely our mynes royall), and that greate inconveniences and ꝑiudice doth and may thereby arise to vs and our crowne in regard the severall patentę for want of experience to make a seperačon of the mettalls of the saide mynes doe dayly cast awaie, and lose much of those mynes which conteyne in them gould or silver, and doe not distinguish which are mynes royall and which are not, and hath allsoe enformed vs that hee, the saide David Ramseye, and his associates, have found out and perfected "A NEW INVENČON, WAIE OR MEANES TO MAKE SEPAČON BY TAKINGE OF THE SEACOND SCUÑE OF ALL SUCH METTALLS OF TINNE, LEADE AND COPPER AFTER THE DROSSE IS TAKEN, AND PRESERVING AS WELL THE IMPURE METTALL AS THE PURE," which shallbee soe done by them without preiudicing any of our subiects, patentes, or others whatsoever whome it may concerne, and is an Invenčon not haveing bin heretofore put in practise within this Kingdome or Dominion of Wales, and hath thervppon humbly besought vs to graunte him a priveledge and licence for the sole vseinge of the said Invenčon, waie, or meanes, soe by him or them newly invented and perfected

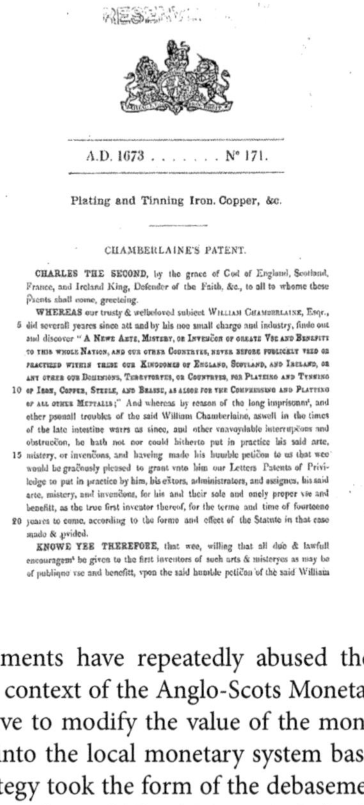

A.D. 1673 . . . . N° 171.

Plating and Tinning Iron. Copper, &c.

CHAMBERLAINE'S PATENT.

CHARLES THE SECOND, by the grace of God of England, Scotland, France, and Ireland King, Defender of the Faith, &c., to all to whome these ꝑsents shall come, greeteing.

WHEREAS our trusty & welbeloved subiect WILLIAM CHAMBERLAINE, Esqr., did severall yeares since att and by his noe small charge and industry, finde out and discover "A NEWE ARTE, MISTERY, OR INVENČON OF GREATE VSE AND BENEFITT TO THIS WHOLE NATION, AND OUR OTHER COUNTRYES, NEVER BEFORE PUBLICKLY VSED OR PRACTISED WITHIN THESE OUR KINGDOMES OF ENGLAND, SCOTLAND, AND IRELAND, OR ANY OTHER OUR DOMINIONS, TERRYTORYES, OR COUNTRYES, FOR PLATEING AND TYNNING OF IRON, COPPER, STEELE, AND BRASSE, AS ALSOE FOR THE COMPRESSING AND PLATTING OF ALL OTHER METTALLS;" And whereas by reason of the long imprisonmt, and other psonall troubles of the said William Chamberlaine, aswell in the times of the late intestine warrs as since, and other vnavoydable interrupčons and obstručon, he hath not nor could hitherto put in practice his said arte, mistery, or invenčons, and haveing made his humble petičon to us that wee would be gračously pleased to grant vnto him our Letters Patents of Priviledge to put in practice by him, his exⁱtors, administrators, and assignes, his said arte, mistery, and invenčons, for his and their sole and onely proper vse and benefitt, as the true first inventor thereof, for the terme and time of fourteene yeares to come, according to the forme and effect of the Statute in that case made & ꝓvided.

KNOWE YEE THEREFORE, that wee, willing that all due & lawfull encouragemt be given to the first inventors of such arts & misteryes as may be of publique vse and benefitt, vpon the said humble petičon of the said William

However, just as Hayek[27] argued, governments have repeatedly abused their monetary prerogatives. For example, in the context of the Anglo-Scots Monetary Union of 1707, the King had the prerogative to modify the value of the money of the realm and/or include foreign coins into the local monetary system based on qualitative elements.[28] Initially, this strategy took the form of the debasement of the metallic coinage, as seen in the famous *Case of Mixed Money in Ireland*,[29] which arose out of Elizabeth's debasement of the Irish currency in 1601,[30] so that

[26] Documents provided to the author by the British Library.

[27] FA Hayek, *Choice in Currency. A Way to Stop Inflation* (London, The Institute of Economic Affairs, 1976) 15.

[28] D Fox, 'The Anglo-Scots Monetary Union of 1707' (2018) 24 *Edinburgh School of Law Research Paper Series* 1, 6.

[29] In this case, the court stated that 'the king hath the same prerogative to give value to base metal by his impression or character, as he hath to give estimation to a mean person by imparting the character of honour to him.' *Gilbert* v *Brett (The Case of Mixed Money)* [1605] Cobb St Tr 114 (UK), 125–26.

[30] D Fox, 'The Case of Mixt Monies' in D Fox and W Ernst (eds), *Money in the Western Legal Tradition. Middle Ages to Bretton Woods* (Oxford, Oxford University Press, 2016) 224–243, 224.

the stated face value of the coins exceeded the market value of the precious metal they contained, just as in the case of Akerlof's[31] lemons.[32]

At this monetary stage, banking was not limited to financial intermediation, as it is understood today. Just as with the Roman *argentarii*, it was common that in large trading centres like Amsterdam and London, goldsmiths, who often had close associations with the crown, issued receipts that incorporated the gold or silver deposited with them as an underlying *res*. These instruments took the form of those promissory notes analysed by Lord Holt in cases such as *Clerke v Martin*[33] and *Buller v Crips*,[34] which resembled the banknotes issued by financial intermediaries like the Bank of England, following a 'closed bag' deposit model by which the depositary was obliged to return the identical metal or coins that had originally been entrusted to his care.[35] Furthermore, as described in *Tassell and Lee v Lewis*,[36] these receipts circulated and were gradually accepted by the public, which preferred to avoid handling metallic coins.[37] As an answer to this need, between the sixteenth and seventeenth century, some innovative minds started to pose challenges to our legal science that derive in the exceptions to the *nemo dat quod non habet*, which was accurately described by Lord Mansfield in *Miller v Race*:[38] a rule to ensure the transferability of these paper instruments. Consequently, a normative framework was required to regulate emerging free-banking models whose diffusion relied on the use of paper-based mediums of payment, which, as we have seen, unsettled the traditional conception of money.[39]

[31] GA Akerlof, '"The Market for "Lemons": Quality Uncertainty and the Market Mechanism.' (1970) 84 *The Quarterly Journal of Economics* 488.

[32] Friedman and Schwartz (n 23) 295.

[33] [1702] 2L d Raym. 758 KB (UK).

[34] [1703] 6 Mod 29 KB (UK).

[35] B Geva, 'The Order to Pay Money in Medieval Continental Europe' in D Fox and W Ernst (eds), *Money in the Western Legal Tradition. Middle Ages to Bretton Woods* (Oxford, Oxford University Press, 2016) 409, 411; H Siekmann, 'Deposit Banking and the Use of Monetary Instruments' in D Fox and W Ernst (eds), *Money in the Western Legal Tradition. Middle Ages to Bretton Woods* (Oxford, Oxford University Press, 2016) 489–531, 494; H Withers, *The Meaning of Money* (London, John Murray, 1948) 18.

[36] [1695] 1 Ld. Raym 743 (UK), 1398.

[37] N Shafer, 'Goldsmith Receipts Tell Interesting Tale' (2019), available at www.numismaticnews.net/article/goldsmith-receipts-tell-interesting-tale, *Numismatic News*.

[38] In this case, 'it was admitted and agreed, that, in the common and known course of trade, banknotes are paid by and received of the holder or possessor of them, as cash; and that in the usual way of negotiating banknotes, they pass from one person to another as cash, by delivery only and without any further inquiry or evidence of title, than what arises from the possession.' See [1758] 97 ER 398 (UK), 399. In the present this rule can be seen in Regulation 29 of the Bills of Exchange Act, which sets that 'A holder in due course is a holder who has taken a bill, complete and regular on the face of it, under the following conditions; namely … That he took the bill in good faith and for value, and that at the time the bill was negotiated to him he had no notice of any defect in the title of the person who negotiated it.'

[39] In that context, the legal nature of money was understood taking as basis the principles set in Roman law, which were structured around a Metallist argument. See S Meder, 'Giro Payments and the Beginnings of the Modern Cashless Payment System' in D Fox and W Ernst (eds), *Money in the Western Legal Tradition. Middle Ages to Bretton Woods* (Oxford, Oxford University Press, 2016) 441–40, 442.

A. Fiat Money

The use of written documents as means of payment was first reported in the seventh century during the Tang dynasty in China. Paper money per se, was in turn introduced in the Mongol Empire during the thirteenth century.[40] Following this monetary and technological innovation, Marco Polo described, with surprise, how the Grand Khan of the Mongols used paper money, noting that:[41]

> In this city of Kanbalu is the mint of the grand khan, who may truly be said to possess the secret of the alchemists, as he has the art of producing money by the following process. He causes the bark to be stripped from those mulberry-trees the laves of which are used for feeding silk-worms, and takes from it that thin inner rind which lies between the coarser bark and the wood of the tree. This being stepped, and afterwards pounded in a mortar, until reduced to a pulp, is made into paper … When ready to us, he has it cut into pieces of money of different sizes.

Paper clearly has no intrinsic value, so why accept it as payment? Building upon our Socio-Legal theory of money, we can say that paper is at the intersection of two concepts of money under this approach: as a monetary *reifier* and as a liability-*res*.[42] In this context, paper is just another *reifier* of the abstract underlying source of liquidity.[43] Consequently, the answer is that the Mongol regime, in exercise of its *lex monetae*, had decreed paper's use, so its value was equivalent to the citizens' belief in the stability of the governing regime[44] – thus creating fiat money. In other words, the state, replicating the adoption/standardisation witnessed in the context of proto-monetary goods and coins, evolved to become the absolute source of the liquidity incorporated in a new generation of payment instruments.

Just as other monetary innovations that have successfully emerged, in the beginning, banknotes were promissory notes payable on demand[45] issued by institutions that were more or less private, which were subject to experimentation and abuses. Among the successful cases, one can find the *assignaties* issued by the *kaissiers* in Amsterdam, which allowed the parties involved to transfer a negotiable instrument that, given the practices fostered by the commercial revolution,[46] raised the money supply.[47] As more banks issued promissory notes, the term

[40] Siekmann (n 35) 489.

[41] M Polo, *The Travels of Marco Polo the Venetian* (London, JM Dent & Sons, 1908) 202.

[42] A Rahmatian, 'Money as a Legally Enforceable Debt.' (2018) 29 *European Business Law Review* 205, 209–12; FR Velde, 'Experiments with Paper Money' in S Battilossi et al (eds), *Handbook of the History of Money and Currency* (Singapore, Springer Nature, 2018) 2–12, 2.

[43] Rahmatian (n 42) 212.

[44] JP Coggan, *Paper Promises. Money, Debt, and the New World Order* (London, Penguin, 2011) 33; Kiyotaki and Wright (n 9) 943.

[45] Rahmatian (n 42) 212.

[46] Initially, these instruments were issued as mere receipts, but, eventually, they were issued in absence of pre-existent deposits. See Siekmann (n 35) 489.

[47] Geva (n 35) 416.

'banknote' emerged and was employed to describe all payment instruments issued by a bank other than coins.[48]

Following the Genoese tradition, these banks kept ledgers of their customers' deposits, which enabled payments to be made by making changes in these ledgers rather than physically exchanging the physical assets. Each bank kept its own ledger and in the earliest days there was no interbank settlement, so notes could only be redeemed at the bank and the branch where they were issued. In other words, any payment requiring the transfer of money to a different bank would require the bearer of a note to first disincorporate the *res* and then to physically transport it to the new bank to have access to a new *reifier.*[49] Developments such a the *assignaties* can be labelled as successful financial innovations, but others offer us useful warnings.

B. Satoshi Nakamoto for the Twentieth Century

Satoshi Nakamoto's white paper and the software relating to it introduced a 'novel' way to create and transfer money, which has been subject to different analyses, processes of diffusion and regulatory proposals. Interestingly, we can find a rather similar document in the eighteenth century. Before the collapse of the Banque Royale and the Mississippi Company, John Law wrote his famous *Money and Trade Considered,*[50] on which he presented a proposal to introduce a scheme based on paper money managed by a commission, which would have the task to keep its acquisitive value beyond the traditional socio-metallic standards. After the rejection of his proposal in Edinburgh, Law presented it in France where it was enacted through the Banque Royale –originally constituted as the Banque Générale – which was licensed to issue notes payable *in specie*. However, this power was employed to expand the volume of paper money in circulation with the aim of fostering speculative behaviour that would end in the Mississippi Bubble, particularly after 1720 when the Mississippi Company acquired the bank and law fixed the exchange rate between the shares of the company and the banknotes – thus, turning the shares into currency[51] – similar to the model set by modern stablecoins. Of course, a fall in demand, paired with the increase in inflation that resulted from the banknotes and the shares in circulation, fostered a run on the notes and shares, and left behind a crisis that went unresolved during the reigns

[48] Siekmann (n 35) 490.

[49] R. Ali et al., 'Innovation in Payment Technologies and the Emergence of Digital Currencies' (2014) 264, available at www.bankofengland.co.uk/-/media/boe/files/quarterly-bulletin/2014/innovations-in-payment-technologies-and-the-emergence-of-digital-currencies.pdf.

[50] J Law, *Money and Trade Considered with a Proposal for Supplying the Nation with Money* (Glasgow, R. & A. Foulis, 1750).

[51] WN Goetzmann, *Money Changes Everything. How Finance Made Civilization Possible* (New Jersey, Princeton University Press, 2016) 357.

of Louis XV and Louis XVI.[52] This case highlights, first, the problem of over-issue based on vulnerable social agreements, and, second, the relevance and the risks associated with the selection of stakeholders with the aim to design a monetary system. Paper money is worthless in alternative contexts, and, consequently needs an alternative mechanism to ensure its value.[53] We will likely witness a similar scenario and face the same necessities within the cryptoassets market in the coming years.

IV. Free Banking Paradigms

The reliance on the infrastructural power of the private sector has led to a growing number of proposals that have been constituted around free banking models to challenge the role of the state on its exercise of the *lex monetae*. But, what is free banking? Just as in the case of money, defining 'free banking' is a challenging task. The more purist definitions state that this model can be defined simply as a banking system that works in absence of any sovereign intervention.[54] This basic definition has been very popular during the last 15 years, particularly after the emergence of Bitcoin and the decentralised design of its original structure based on a PoW protocol. Independently of this, in practice, most of the financial intermediaries that have operated in the systems denominated under this term have fulfilled different legal requirements ranging from the basic rules for their proper incorporation to the licences needed to issue money based on a sovereign unit of reference. In simpler terms, they have been subjected to the exercise of the *ius cudendae monetae*.

This first definition is rather useful given that it allows us to trace the origins of this model to the very conception of money and financial intermediation as developed in chapter one, when different expressions of 'inside money' appeared before their gradual sovereign adoption and regulation through the exercise of the *lex monetae*. In other words, one can say that this model represents the pure state of the functions developed by the financial sector.[55] However, for the purposes of our legal analysis, we define 'free banking' as a model in which duly constituted private intermediaries issue monetary instruments on receipt of funds based on a sovereign unit of reference, in the absence of a central bank, a central control of reserves, a public lender of last resort and/or a sovereign scheme of guarantees.

[52] N Ferguson, *The Ascent of Money. A Financial History of the World* (New York, The Penguin Press, 2018) 138–57; Goetzmann (n 51) 347–61.

[53] Velde (n 42) 15.

[54] K Dowd, 'Free Banking' in CJ Coyne and PJ Boettke (eds), *The Oxford Handbook of Austrian Economics* (Oxford, Oxford University Press, 2015) 215; K Schuler, 'The World History of Free Banking. An Overview' in K Dowd (ed), *The Experience of Free Banking* (London, Routledge, 1992) 7–47, 8; LH White, *Free Banking in Britain: Theory, Experience and Debate 1800–1845* (London, The Institute of Economic Affairs, 1995) 1.

[55] M Aglietta, *Money. 5,000 Years of Debt and Power* (New York, Verso, 2018) 137.

Of course, these institutions had to fulfil several legal requirements, such as putting in place an unlimited liabilities scheme and/or backing their monetary issuances with sovereign assets to constitute an underlying source of liquidity.

A. The 'Currency' and the 'Banking' Schools Controversy

The model developed under the definition presented above was at the centre of the famous 1820s–1840s controversies between the 'Currency School' led by Lord Overstone, George Norman and Robert Torrens, and the 'Banking School' represented by Thomas Tooke, John Fullarton and James Wilson.[56] The crux of these controversies lay, on the one hand, with whether money creation should be left to the state, given that – in the absence of a general consensus on the definition of money – the different sources of liquidity that emerge from the business habits and needs of a community would complicate the task of putting a line between what is money and what is not money.[57] On the other hand, it was argued that a single bank of issue would be subject to pressures that could bring catastrophe to the whole system, given that the exercise of the *lex monetae* would be subject to the human biases of the central banker;[58] therefore, it was suggested that this prerogative should be left to the private sector.[59] Eventually, the 'Currency' versus 'Banking School' controversy was settled with the Bank of England Act 1833 and the Bank Charter Act of 1844.[60] The former made banknotes issued by the Bank of England legal tender, while the latter established the central bank's monopoly of banknotes in England and Wales.[61]

Even though our current paradigms are structured around different expressions of 'outside monies' as result of the 'victory' of the 'Currency School', there are several arguments that maintain support for free banking models. The first is by analogy with the general case for free trade. If free trade and competition are beneficial in other economic activities, what is so special about banking that justifies imposing special controls, regulation and supervision?[62] This argument has had different supporters internationally. For instance, Walter Bagehot[63] argued that a natural system integrated by independent banks would perform better in the absence of sovereign intervention, given that these institutions would keep

[56] CAE Goodhart, *The Evolution of Central Banks* (Massachusetts, MIT Press, 1998, 1; J Huber, *Sovereign Money. Beyond Reserve Banking* (Cham, Palgrave Macmillan, 2017) 43; R Skidelsky, *Money and Government. A Challenge to Mainstream Economics* (London, Allen Lane, 2018) 49.

[57] RS Sayers, *Central Banking After Bagehot* (London, The Clarendon Press, 1957) 5.

[58] ibid.

[59] Huber (n 56) 42.

[60] Bank Charter Act 1844 c 32.

[61] Skidelsky (n 56) 50; Huber (n 56) 47.

[62] Goodhart (n 56) 13.

[63] W Bagehot, *Lombard Street. A Description of the Money Market* (London, Henry S King & Co, 1973) 103–04.

sufficient reserves because their own existence and credibility would depend on it. In other words, the creation of money could be 'safer under Adam Smith's Invisible Hand than under the hand of the Old Lady of Threadneedle Street'.[64]

In the Americas, the same spirit can be found in the words of José Yves Limantour who, in the exposition of motives of the General Law of Credit Institutions of 1897 of Mexico, developed and explained a model to exercise the *lex monetae* (the 'Limantour model') by which he rejected the monopoly on the creation of money and supported free competition among different banks of issue, authorised by the state for that purpose.[65] His argument was based on the plurality of banks of issue that emerged from pre-existent concessions – many of them traced back to the conflict of the Commercial Code – which were structured around the idea that regional banks can address more efficiently the needs of 'inside monies' of those territories in which they are located.[66]

B. The Scottish Experience

In addition, authors like Hayek,[67] Sargent and Wallace[68] argued that it does not make sense to assign to the state the monopoly of money creation as the private sector could, following our definition of 'free banking', issue means of payment previously determined and approved by the state more efficiently than by the latter based on its own infrastructural power. Empirical studies relating to certain periods of free banking between the eighteenth and nineteenth century in countries like Scotland[69] seem to confirm this idea. Largely unaffected by the Royal Exchange and London Assurance Corporation Act 1719, commonly known as the Bubble Act, and exempt from the Bank of England Act of 1708, which had extended the central bank's monopoly on note issuance in England, Scotland from 1716 to 1845 is widely considered by financial historians to have been one of the closest ever historic approximations to the ideal exercise of 'free banking', through the operations developed by institutions like the Bank of Scotland and Royal Bank of Scotland,[70] which continue to issue notes under a variation of this paradigm today.

[64] Sayers (n 57) 2.

[65] E Turrent, *Historia del Banco de México. Antecedentes, Fundación y Despegue. Volumen I* (Mexico City, Banco de México, 2015) 50–52.

[66] JY Limantour, *Apuntes Sobre Mi Vida Política* (Mexico City, Editorial Porrúa, 1965) 57–58.

[67] FA Hayek, *Denationalisation of Money. The Argument Refined* (London, Institute of Economic Affairs, 1978) 41.

[68] T Sargent and N Wallace, 'The Real Bills Doctrine versus the Quantity Theory. A Reconsideration' (1982) 90 *The Journal of Political Economy* 1212.

[69] White (n 54).

[70] TB Goodspeed, *Legislating Instability. Adam Smith, Free Banking, and the Financial Crisis of 1772* (Cambridge, Harvard University Press, 2016) 7; R Perman, *The Rise and Fall of the City of Money. A Financial History of Edinburgh* (Edinburgh. Birlinn, 2020); LH White, 'The World History of Free Banking. An Overview' in K Dowd (ed), *The Experience of Free Banking* (London, Routledge, 1992) 157–86, 157.

Consequently, there is a uniform criterion that from the expiration of the Bank of Scotland's monopoly charter in 1716 to the passage of the Peel's Banking Act of 1844[71] and the Bank Notes (Scotland) Act of 1845,[72] the Scottish financial system worked successfully with no official central bank or lender of last resort – aside from the fact that the Bank of Scotland and Royal Bank of Scotland exercised a form of *lex monetae* through their interaction with smaller banks – no public or private monopolies on currency issuance, and no legal restrictions on entry, among other favourable conditions that differed from those restrictions set in England.[73] Furthermore, the Scottish economy during that period saw faster growth and greater financial stability than England, or subsequently in Scotland itself.[74] This fact was echoed by an anonymous bank manager who argued that the free reception of notes issued by Scottish banks, as result of public confidence in the infrastructure provided by the private sector, prevented the local circulation of gold that was subject to an expensive deterioration.[75] Therefore, studies relating to this period conclude that free banking systems can function reasonably well; the only serious failure in Scotland was the Douglas, Heron & Co collapse.[76] Furthermore, authors such as Randall Kroszner[77] argue that the Scottish experience may provide a model for financial reform in emerging economies today.

V. The Conception of Central Banking

As one can see in some of the resolutions issued by the senate of Venice between 1593 and 1607 – and as seen through the Byzantine Generals Problem in the Introduction to this book – the need to make payments among banks led to the emergence of a 'central counterpart' at which all the member banks could hold accounts, making interbank payments simpler.[78] Additionally, merchants complained that they used to receive bills with as many as 10 or 20 signatures, which reflected an overuse of endorsement.[79] But, can we label these counterparts as central banks? Or can we define central banking building upon their functions? The answer is not an easy one. In the Anglophone world, central banking is sometimes represented as a spontaneous, late-seventeenth-century

[71] Bank Charter Act 1844 c 32.

[72] Bank Notes (Scotland) Act of 1845 c 38.

[73] V Smith, *The Rationale of Central Banking and the Free Banking Alternative* (Indianapolis, Liberty Fund, 1990) 167–96; Perman (n 70) 158; White (n 54).

[74] Goodspeed (n 70).

[75] A Bank Manager, *Papers on Banking & Finance* (London, Bemrose and Sons, 1871) 70.

[76] F Brady, 'So Fast to Ruin. The Ayr Bank Crash' (1973) 11 *Ayrshire Collection* 27; Smith (n 73) 26.

[77] RS Kroszner, 'Free Banking. The Scottish Experience as a Model for Emerging Economies' (1995) 1536 *World Bank's Policy Research Working Papers* 1.

[78] Ali et al (n 49) 263.

[79] Roberds and Velde (n 15) 22.

invention of the Bank of England.[80] However, authors such as Edvinsson, Jacobson and Waldenström[81] argue that, just as in the case of proto-monetary expressions, it is possible to find proto-central banks such as the Casa di San Giorgio in Genoa, the Banco della Piazza di Rialto in Venice, the Taula de Canvi of Barcelona, among others, which performed some functions traditionally associated with modern central banking, among which we can highlight the creation of more stable and liquid claims.[82]

However, it was in Amsterdam where the first effective solution arose; one that, fascinatingly, reflects the spirit of the arguments of DLT innovators like those behind projects, such as Ripple where a central party introduces an asset to uniform monetary interactions through different jurisdictions. On 31 January 1609, the Amsterdamsche Wisselbank was founded to solve the problems described by Scaruffi[83] and Fox[84] relating to the circulation of multiple currencies coined by no fewer than 14 different mints and copious amounts of foreign coins which had different denominations and varying degrees of debasement.[85] To face this challenge, the Dutch Bank's guilder/florin was conceived not as a traditional coin, but as legal fiction, similar to a modern stablecoin,[86] designed to set a fiat benchmark based on a fixed exchange ratio to silver by which an amount denominated in this unit would be credited to an account, and the balance of this account could easily, practically cost-free, be transferred to a different account, in part or whole.[87] Additionally, the Wisselbank played an important role in the development of banknotes through the practice of issuing written receipts on the counter-value of the coins submitted in exchange. Money orders and *recipis* issued by the bank could also be used to fulfil contractual obligations based on the underlying obligations incorporated in them.[88] For a very long period of time, the bank money of the Wisselbank was stable, but confidence in the bank eroded in the late eighteenth century as result of the pressures that derived from the Fourth Anglo–Dutch War and the French Revolution. It was liquidated in 1821, its stock of silver and gold depleted.[89]

After the emergence of the Wisselbank, the Stockholms Banco was founded in 1658 by the merchant Johan Palmstruch, who conceived the epoch-making

[80] W Roberds and FR Velde, 'Early Public Banks' in D Fox and W Ernst (eds), *Money in the Western Legal Tradition. Middle Ages to Bretton Woods* (Oxford, Oxford University Press, 2016) 321–55, 321.

[81] Edvinsson, Jacobson and Waldenström (n 19) 9.

[82] Roberds and Velde (n 15) 23.

[83] Scaruffi (n 13).

[84] Fox (n 28).

[85] LP Rochon and M Vernengo, 'State Money and the Real World: Or Chartalism and Its Discontents' (2003) 26 *Journal of Post Keynesian Economics* 57, 59; Ferguson (n 52) 48; Siekmann (n 35) 493.

[86] J Frost, HS Shin and P Wierts, 'An Early Stablecoin? The Bank of Amsterdam and the Governance of Money' (2020), available at www.bis.org/publ/work902.pdf.

[87] S Quinn and W Roberds, 'Death of a Reserve Currency' (2016) 12 *International Journal of Central Banking* 63, 64; Siekmann (n 35) 494.

[88] ibid.

[89] Edvinsson, Jacobson and Waldenström (n 19) 4; Frost, Shin and Wierts (n 86); Quinn and Roberds (n 87).

notion of giving notes not only to those who had deposited metal, but also to those who came to borrow them, thus creating modern fractional reserve banking.[90] In essence, it was now possible to create non-metallic 'inside money' that was independent of deposits given that loans could be provided for as much as the bank was prepared to issue notes, relying not only on the underlying obligations, but also on the bank's credibility.[91] Unfortunately, the Stockholms Banco closed in 1666 as result of a panic related to an over-issue of notes.[92] Interestingly, the Parliament identified three flaws that could be used to define certain DLT projects today: 1) its governance by a private owner; 2) its note issue; and 3) the instability of the underlying source of liquidity.[93] After the Peace of Westphalia, and the diffusion of modern constitutionalism that emerged from it, in 1668, the Sveriges Riksbank was founded as a solution to the problems mentioned above; an institution with a constitutional mandate that is considered to be the oldest central bank in Europe.[94]

The third great innovation that led us to our modern understanding of central banking was an outcome of the Glorious Revolution.[95] When King William arrived from the Dutch provinces, he introduced a number of monetary practices from his native country, which in 1694 configured the Bank of England.[96] This institution was constituted on the basis of a *quid pro quo* as a private joint stock, limited liability company with King William and Queen Mary among the first subscribers, with a Charter subject to periodic renewal and renegotiation.[97]

In exchange for financing the national debt and the war with France, in the form of bond purchases with notes, the Bank of England was given distinctive privileges, in particular a commitment not to charter another bank and the partial monopoly on note issue in England. This eventually evolved into a full monopoly as result of the victory of the 'Currency School' that arose as a result of the Bank Charter Act 1844.[98] With these elements in mind, the traditional perception of the *lex montae* emerged, which stated that, in order to control the banking system, central banks controlled the supply of cash.[99]

[90] K Fregert, 'Sveriges Riksbank: 350 Years in the Making' in R Edvinsson, T Jacobson and D Waldenström (eds), *Sveriges Riksbank and the History of Central Banking* (Cambridge, Cambridge University Press, 2018) 90–142, 95–96; Ferguson (n 52) 49; Withers (n 35) 18.

[91] G Wetterberg, *Money and Power. From Stockholms Banco 1656 to Sveriges Riksbank Today* (Stockholm, Atlantis, 2009) 39; Siekmann (n 35) 496.

[92] Fregert (n 90) 96.

[93] ibid.

[94] The constitutional status of the *Riksbank* was set by a royal decree from 1668 and ratified by the Instruments of Government of 1772, 1809 and 1974. See ibid, 91.

[95] Roberds and Velde (n 15) 35.

[96] Perman (n 70) 6.

[97] CAE Goodhart, 'The Bank of England, 1694–2017' in R Edvinsson, T Jacobson and D Waldenström (eds), *Sveriges Riksbank and the History of Central Banking* (Cambridge, Cambridge University Press, 2018) 143–71, 144; Perman (n 70) 16.

[98] Roberds and Velde (n 15) 35; Perman (n 70) 16–17.

[99] Sayers (n 57) 38.

On this basis, it is possible to see how the emergence of banknotes and free banking models fostered the evolution of our *ius cudendae monetae* in a new environment; an evolutionary process that is evident in our context through the discussions and proposals related to the creation of CBDCs. As consequence of these innovations, the stock of money in each country included not only coins, but also paper money based on sovereign underlying obligations. Of course, as seen through John Law's experience, this model would not be free of problems.

Returning to the *Case of Mixed Money*[100] and the words of Innocent III, one could see how governments and monarchs tended to finance their projects through debasements. However, the development of the banking system enabled them to reach the same aim through depreciation and printing money building upon only on the 'strength' of the social contract.[101] Based on this behaviour, it should not be surprising that during the last decades of the eighteenth century and the first decades of the nineteenth century, political and monetary instability was a common trait, and that many countries experienced very high inflation rates. For instance, the Danish–Norwegian monetary unit, the Riksdaler courant, was devalued by 90 per cent in 1813 against silver,[102] while 1866 saw the collapse of *Overend, Gurney & Co*, which, it has been said, inspired through the work of Walter Bagehot,[103] the function of central banks as lenders of last resort.[104] This instability, just as one can see in our context post-Lehman Brothers, also generated great political and monetary innovations.

It was during this period that many of our central banks were constituted, including the Banco Nacional de San Carlos created in 1782, the Banque de France in 1800, the Finlands Bank in 1811, the Nederalandsche Bank in 1814, the Norges Bank and the Österreichische Nationalbank in 1816, and the Danmarks Nationalbank in 1818.[105] Accordingly, by 1850 the principle that the monetary unit should not be arbitrarily redefined was accepted, and paper money constituted beyond the underlying obligations that defined bills of exchange and promissory notes was widely used. However, in contrast to the referred payment instruments, its issue was not independent of the state.[106] Consequently, we can define central banking as the provision of standardised monetary *res* and public policies aimed at fostering monetary and financial stability through the

[100] *Gilbert* v *Brett (The Case of Mixed Money)* [1605] Cobb St Tr 114 (UK), 125–26.

[101] M Bordo and A Redish, 'Putting the "System" in the International Monetary System' in D Fox and W Ernst (eds), *Money in the Western Legal Tradition. Middle Ages to Bretton Woods* (Oxford, Oxford University Press, 2016) 595–610, 611.

[102] Edvinsson, Jacobson and Waldenström (n 19) 13.

[103] Bagehot (n 63) 103–04.

[104] It is possible to argue that this distinctive function of central banking is a constitutive element of our *ius cudendae monetae*, given that one of its main functions is to preserve the payments infrastructure that runs throughout the banking system and by which monetary assets circulate throughout the economy.

[105] Edvinsson, Jacobson and Waldenström (n 19) 13.

[106] Bordo and Redish (n 101) 599.

definition of constitutional objectives, and normative functions and powers focused on those aims.[107]

A. Rise and Collapse of the Gold Standard

While in the early nineteenth century most countries' monetary systems were designed around a bimetallic standard based on a 1:15.5 ratio of exchange between gold and silver, a new evolutionary transition was taking form, building upon the legal standards that were part of our *lex monetae*.[108] Pure bimetallism works in closed economies where an absolute value ratio can be maintained between the two metals.[109] However, in an open economy where there are external factors driving the price of the two metals, a country, in practice, relies either on an effective gold or effective silver monometallic standard depending on the country's 'mint-price ratio'.[110] Following a Wallersteinian[111] trend, 'core countries' such as France, Germany and the USA started a gradual demonetisation of silver in favour of a full gold standard between 1880 and 1913.[112] This standard, which relied on banks of issue like the Riksbank and the Bank of England,[113] linked the volume of a nation's currency to its gold stock based on fixed exchange rates set by each state, which, in absence of a formal international coordination effort, has led to its description as a 'spontaneous order'.[114] Although we are talking about a Wallersteinian Financial World System (FWS), the CGS is identified as a single regime, mainly because it succeeded in providing the two essential public goods that define any post-Westphalian international monetary system: well-defined international currencies; and external stability.[115]

The stability of the system relied on the diffusion of trust within the FWS. The cornerstone of this diffusion process was a context of international peace

[107] S Ugolini, 'The Historical Evolution of Central Banking' in S Battilossi et al (eds), *Handbook of the History of Money and Currency* (Singapore, Springer Nature, 2018) 1–22, 1.

[108] B Eichengreen, 'Introduction' in B Eichengreen (ed), *The Gold Standard in Theory and History* (New York, Methuen, 1985) 1–35, 5; LH Officer, 'International Monetary Regimes: The Gold Standard' in S Battilossi et al (eds), *Handbook of the History of Money and Currency* (Singapore, Springer Nature, 2018) 1–33, 3; C Schenk and T Straumann, 'Central Banks and the Stability of the International Monetary Regime' in MD Bordo et al (eds), *Central Banks at a Crossroads* (New York, Cambridge University Press, 2016) 319–55, 326; Skidelsky (n 56) 50.

[109] Gleeson (n 1) 43.

[110] ibid; Officer (n 108) 3.

[111] Immanuel Wallerstein argued that Financial World Systems are constituted by the interaction of nuclear, semi-nuclear and peripheral elements which, through conflicts and innovation, seek eternally to remould them to their own advantage. See I Wallerstein, *World-Systems Analysis. An Introduction* (Durham, Duke University Press, 2004).

[112] Bordo and Redish (n 101) 599; Edvinsson, Jacobson and Waldenström (n 19) 13; Officer (n 108) 3; Skidelsky (n 56).

[113] Schenk and Straumann (n 108) 324.

[114] Bordo and Redish (n 101) 599; Skidelsky (n 56) 52.

[115] Schenk and Straumann (n 108) 326.

and domestic calm in which the ideology and practice of Socio-Metallism was widespread and shielded from domestic politics, and fostered the independence of central banks, who were able to contain financial panics.[116] Furthermore, contracts were expressed in gold; if convertibility were abandoned, contracts would inevitably be violated[117] in the absence of the post-Bretton Woods fiat flexibility found in the words of Lord Wilberforce in *Miliangos v George Frank (Textiles) Ltd*.[118]

The CGS was suspended by most countries at the outbreak of the First World War, and, during the interwar period, central banks struggled to restore the gold-based FWS that emerged from a 'spontaneous Socio-Metallist order'.[119] The outcome of these interwar efforts was the Gold Exchange Standard (GES). This standard was based on legal definitions of central banks' reserve requirements and the introduction of a legal cover ratio based on the sum of banknotes in circulation and sight liabilities of the central bank that the issuing institution had to cover with international reserves.[120] Unfortunately, the crisis of 1931–33 resulted in the widespread abandonment of the GES, and the convertibility of banknotes ceased to exist; thus, dynamic social systems – addresing endogenous needs – eliminated the underlying obligation between the issuer of money and its holder.[121] Under these arrangements, certain practices like the insertion of a gold clause in a contract, which indexed the amount to be paid to the amount of gold which was obtainable at the time of the accrual of the monetary obligation, was regarded as an unacceptable challenge to the legal tender rule[122] as it was put in place through the House Joint Resolution 192, which set the Gold Clause Ban in the US in 1933. Finally, during the second half of the twentieth century, even the measurement of the unit of account by reference to a specified quantity of a given precious metal was abolished. Therefore, the external value of the standard sovereign unit of reference is now determined by the exercise of *lex monetae* in international financial markets building on the characteristics that define each social dynamic system and their interoperability.[123]

Immediately after the Second World War, a new system was created around a distinctive specialist international monetary institution: the International Monetary Fund (IMF). Under the so-called Bretton Woods System, all other currencies were pegged to the US dollar at a fixed rate while, in turn, the dollar was

[116] Officer (n 108) 21; Schenk and Straumann (n 108) 329.

[117] Officer (n 108) 21.

[118] [1976] AC 443 (UK), 460–70.

[119] Bordo and Redish (n 101) 603; Edvinsson, Jacobson and Waldenström (n 19) 15.

[120] Accominotti, 'International Monetary Regimes: The Interwar Gold Exchange Standard' in S Battilossi et al (eds), *Handbook of the History of Money and Currency* (Singapore, Springer Nature, 2018) 1–32, 11–12, 20.

[121] Accominotti (n 120) 20; Monteagudo (n 14) 491.

[122] K Sono, 'The Changing Role of Currency. Toward a Catastrophe or a New System?' (1995) 38 *The Japanese Annual of International Law* 83, 86.

[123] B Geva, *The Payment Order of Antiquity and the Middle Ages. A Legal History* (Oxford, Hart Publishing, 2011) 23.

pegged to gold at a fixed price of $32 per ounce. An extensive system of exchange controls paired with tight banking regulations kept this effort to put a Socio-Metallist system in place, valuing stability above competitive efficiency.[124]

Finally, the Socio-Metallist paradigm disappeared with the collapse of the Bretton Woods system between 1971, when the USA notified the IMF that it would no longer buy or sell gold for the settlement of international transactions, and 1973, when President Nixon announced that the US dollar would no longer be redeemable in gold.[125] To face these developments, a de facto floating exchange rate system was put in place in early March 1973 after the failed attempts by monetary authorities to keep a fixed-rate system to face a wave of chaotic monetary market movements.[126] Consequently, currencies were allowed to float freely against one another in contradiction of the Articles of the Agreement of the IMF, with their value determined by political and economic forces which configure the 'Mercury' and 'Mars' approaches,[127] in absence of a currency of the n-1 status at the core of the system.[128]

After the fall of the Bretton Woods system, the last vestiges of commodity money disappeared, and a system in which essentially every currency in the world is based on a pure fiat standard emerged.[129] There was no longer a link between the value of money and precious metal, taking the function of money as an abstract unit of account to its extreme, thus opening the door to innovations with which we are concerned. The role of central banks and the nature of the *ius cudendae monetae* changed from monopolisation of the main means of payment, to upholding the value of the unit of account and the standard of deferred payment,[130] as one can see in different constitutional documents around the world.[131]

The details of the context, the spirit of the Agreement, the execution of the 'par values' principle, and the palliatives devised to minimise the effects of Nixon's decision are lucidly described in *Lively Ltd and Another v City of Munich*.[132] In this case, there is a clear differentiation between sovereign obligations to the IMF and the rate exchange applicable to a commercial transaction. Thus, on this basis, the court concluded that the plaintiffs were right to submit that the middle market

[124] HM Schooner and MW Taylor, *Global Bank Regulation. Principles and Policies* (London, Academic Press, 2010) 8.

[125] *Lively Ltd and Another v City of Munich* [1976] WLR 1004 (UK), 1011; Schooner and Taylor (n 123) 8.

[126] Sono (n 122) 87.

[127] These approaches are discussed with more detail in ch 3. See Avgouleas and Blair (n 6) 17; Eichengreen, Mehl and Chitu (n 6) 2.

[128] FA Mann, *The Legal Aspect of Money* (London, Oxford University Press, 1938) 36; Schooner and Taylor (n 124) 9, Sono (n 122) 87.

[129] Friedman and Schwartz (n 23) 290.

[130] Edvinsson, Jacobson and Waldenström (n 19) 15–16.

[131] K Sono and H Kanda, 'In Search of Order in the World Monetary System: State Intervention after the Decline of the Lex Monetae' in M Giovanoli and D Devos (eds), *International Monetary and Financial Law. The Global Crisis* (Oxford, Oxford University Press, 2010) 506–16, 510.

[132] [1976] WLR 1004, QBD (UK).

rate on 1 December 1973 applied by virtue of article 13(c) of the Agreement on German External Debts of 27 February 1953.[133]

Under the float system, a visible trend emerged in international cases toward the abolition of the home currency rule in the courts of major countries. For example, in *Miliangos v George Frank (Textiles) Ltd*,[134] Lord Wilberforce stated that:

> The situation as regards currency stability has substantially changed even since 1961. Instead of the main world currencies being fixed and fairly stable in value, subject to the risk of periodic re- or devaluations, many of them are now 'floating,' i.e., they have no fixed exchange value even from day to day. This is true of sterling. This means that, instead of a situation in which changes of relative value occurred between the 'breach date' and the date of judgement or payment being the exception, so that a rule which did not provide for this case could be generally fair, this situation is now the rule. So the search for a formula to deal with it becomes urgent in the interest of justice.

Exchange controls were also dismantled, leaving capital free to flow to the highest returns. These flows were accompanied by other measures to deregulate the economy, particularly banking and finance, which were a core component of the free market policies pursued in the 1980s.[135]

B. Reconfiguring the 'Fourth Power'

After the emergence of the nation-state in the seventeenth century, governments started to rely on strategies built upon standardisation with the aim of obtaining the mutual recognition of their respective social contracts in international interactions. One of these strategies can be found in the traditional division of the state into legislative, executive and judicial branches; however, substantive policy demands have led to secondary institutional arrangements that have been materialised as independent regulatory institutions,[136] many of them as unelected powers, such as the military, the judiciary and even the Church.[137] Within these powers can be found the 'fourth constitutional power',[138] which arose through the constitution of central banks under the terms set in the Genoa Financial Commission Report of 20 April 1922. It stated that: 'Banks, and especially banks of issue, should be free from political pressure, and should be conducted solely on

[133] Article 13(c) of the Agreement 'provided that if neither par values nor rates in bilateral payments agreements were in force on the appropriate date, the middle rate of exchange generally applicable for transactions ruling for cable transfers in the currency of the country in which payment was to be made on the principal exchange market of the other country on that date, should apply.' See *Lively Ltd and Another v City of Munich* [1976] WLR. 1004, QBD (UK), 1004.

[134] [1976] AC 443 (UK), 463.

[135] Schooner and Taylor (n 124) 9.

[136] S Rose-Ackerman, 'The Regulatory State' in M Rosenfeld and A Sajo (eds), *The Oxford Handbook of Comparative Constitutional Law* (Oxford, Oxford University Press, 2012) 671–85, 676.

[137] P Tucker, *Unelected Power. The Quest for Legitimacy in Central Banking and the Regulatory State* (New Jersey, Princeton University Press, 2018) 3.

[138] Within this book, the 'fourth power' is a constitutional expression of monetary sovereignty, which generally is organised as an independent element of the three traditional powers.

lines of prudent finance. In countries where there'-is no central bank of issue one should be established.'[139]

Accordingly, from this point, common trends can be found in constitutional instruments and/or in special laws that have emerged from original sovereign prerogatives, such as the one found in *Gilbert v Brett.*[140] Among the common elements that allow a central bank to represent the monetary sovereignty of its social dynamic system before other nations within our FWS, the most well-known is the monopoly on national currency creation. In fact, these institutions 'were not initially called central banks but rather banks of issue'[141] based on the emergence of this quasi-universal prerogative. Today, this monopoly can be found in normative instruments, such as Article 128(1) of the Treaty on the Functioning of the European Union:[142]

> The European Central Bank shall have the exclusive right to authorise the issue of euro banknotes within the Union. The European Central Bank and the national central banks may issue such notes. The banknotes issued by the European Central Bank and the national central banks shall be the only such notes to have the status of legal tender within the Union.

Another example is Regulation XXVII of the Bank Charter Act 1844[143] of the UK:

> That the said Governor and Company of the Bank of England, shall have and enjoy such exclusive Privilege of Banking as is given by this Act, upon such Terms and Conditions, and subject to the Termination thereof at such Time and in such Manner, as is by this Act provided and specified.

And another is Article 28 of the Constitution of the United Mexican States,[144] which establishes that:

> In the United Mexican States there shall be no monopolies or estancos of any kind … excepting only those relating to the coinage of money, … to the issuance of paper money by a single bank to be controlled by the Federal Government.

We find these monopolistic prerogatives at the top of Kelsen's[145] hierarchical structure of legal systems, which are materialised through constitutional documents whose function consists of governing the organs and the processes of law creation that configure the *ius cudendae monetae.* From the top of this hierarchy, nation-states exercise their *lex monetae* on two fronts. The internal front empowers states to determine how their currencies will be issued, including the prerogatives to select

[139] Genoa Financial Commission, 'Genoa Financial Commission Report.' (1922), available at fraser.stlouisfed.org/files/docs/publications/FRB/pages/1920-1924/26565_1920-1924.pdf.

[140] [1605] Cobb St Tr 114 (UK).

[141] MD Bordo and PL Siklos, 'Central Banks. Evolution and Innovation in Historical Perspective' in R Edvinsson, T Jacobson and D Waldenström (eds), *Sveriges Riksbank and the History of Central Banking* (Cambridge, Cambridge University Press, 2018) 26–89, 26.

[142] Treaty on the Functioning of the European Union OJ C 326/47, 26 October 2012.

[143] Bank Charter Act 1844 c 32.

[144] Political Constitution of the United Mexican States DOF.

[145] H Kelsen, *Introduction to the Problems of Legal Theory* (tr BL Paulson and SL Paulson (New York, Oxford University Press, 2002) 64.

providers of infrastructure, and tolerate or forbid individual states, municipalities, local governments and/or private parties to create complementary instruments. The external front permits states to project the soundness of their institutions in the FWS, and determine the rules under which their currencies will interact with others within the referred system.

The spirit of these prerogatives is truly global and can be perceived beyond the law. Building on the work of Billio et al,[146] Michael D Bordo and Pierre L Siklos,[147] they demonstrate how central banks behave as if they were part of a related network, at least in so far as inflation differentials are concerned. Hence, the existence of a network of this nature does not imply how integrated dynamic social systems are, but highlights that there are links built upon the recognition of their respective monetary sovereignties. Furthermore, it considers that in order for central bank money to act as a means of payment to discharge contractual obligations beyond the traditional textbook examples related to spot transactions, there needs to be a secure way of transferring that asset, or at least to transfer a message relating to the asset's value by reducing uncertainties and increasing the probability of certain outcomes.[148] The answer to this is a payments system, which will be analysed in the following chapter.[149] Accordingly, central banks coordinate their efforts –and even select common infrastructural providers – to innovate their payment systems, as in the case of CBDCs in cross-border payments, such as Projects Jura, Dunbar and mBridge.[150]

Of course, just as in the case of the judicial power, the 'fourth power' represents a case of *auctoritas*, which relies on the executive's *potestas*.[151] As seen above, the cornerstone of this *auctoritas* was set during the course of the nineteenth century, when our financial *Bildungstrieb* led to the monopolisation of note issue.[152]

Susan Strange[153] explains that this 'fourth power' within the post-Westfalian system has failed, given that nation-states are unable 'to govern and control the institutions and markets that create and trade the credit instruments essential to the "real economy".'[154] Consequently, she labels this the 'Westfailure' system. Her argument is interesting. She argues that, throughout our history, we have witnessed different forms of symbiosis between the sovereign political system and the market system – as we saw through the case of John Law – that one would

[146] M Billio et al, 'Econometric Measures of Connectedness and Systemic Risk in the Finance and Insurance Sectors' (2012) 104 *Journal of Financial Economics* 535.

[147] Bordo and Siklos (n 141) 79.

[148] Gleeson (n 1) 10.

[149] Ali et al (n 49).

[150] Bank for International Settlements, 'Lessons Learnt on CBDCs. Report submitted to the G20 Finance Ministers and Central Bank Governors' (2023), available at www.bis.org/publ/othp73.htm.

[151] AC Pereira, *Lecciones de Teoría Constitucional* (Porrúa. Mexico City, 2018) 289.

[152] R Edvinsson, T Jacobson and D Waldenström, 'Introduction' in R Edvinsson, T Jacobson and D Waldenström (eds), *Sveriges Riksbank and the History of Central Banking* (Cambridge: Cambridge University Press, 2018) 1–25, 14–15.

[153] S Strange, 'The Westfailure System' (1999) 25 *Review of International Studies* 345.

[154] ibid, 346.

be tempted to classify as governance paradigms. Therefore, on the one hand, the market economy requires the sovereign infrastructure that constitutes the *lex monetae*, while, on the other, the state depends on the financial technology developed around innovations introduced by the private sector (as we are witnessing today) to support its own infrastructure and even to create complementary 'inside monies'.[155] As result of this symbiosis, and although most monetary legislations are designed around the sovereign monopoly on the creation of 'outside money', the state has lost the control of the creation of money through practices that go beyond the simple acceptance and relending of deposits.[156]

C. The Role of Financial Intermediaries Beyond the Classic View of Financial Intermediation

Banking law textbooks tend to use the intermediation of loanable funds (ILF) model to analyse and define banking, which harks back to the original functions of banking as storehouses and mere intermediaries.[157] Under the ILF model, it is argued that commercial banks produce credit and provide liquidity through a process that 'involves channelling resources from entities with excess of funds (savers) to entities with a scarcity of funds (investors).'[158] Furthermore, many orthodox policy prescriptions and even banking regulations currently in force are designed around this, in particular the view that money's value is linked to its scarcity.[159] For instance, Article 2 of the Mexican Credit Institutions Law[160] states that:

> For purposes of the provisions of this Law, it shall be considered as banking and credit service the raising of funds from the public within the domestic market for their placement among the public, through acts resulting in direct or contingent liabilities, being the intermediary bound to cover the principal and, as the case may be, the financial ancillaries of the funds raised.

[155] ibid, 348.

[156] C Proctor and V Dixon, *Goode on Payment Obligations in Commercial and Financial Transactions* (London, Thomson Reuters, 2016) 3.

[157] X Freixas and JC Rochet, *Microeconomics of Banking* (Cambridge, MIT Press, 2008) 1; M McLeay, A Radia and R Thomas, 'Money Creation in the Modern Economy' (2014), available at www.bankofengland.co.uk/publications/Documents/quarterlybulletin/2014/qb14q1prereleasemoneycreation.pdf; Z Jakab and M Kumhof, 'Banks Are Not Intermediaries of Loanable Funds. Facts, Theory and Evidence' (2019), available at www.bankofengland.co.uk/-/media/boe/files/working-paper/2018/banks-are-not-intermediaries-of-loanable-funds-facts-theory-and-evidence.pdf?la=en&hash=5FCDED87A783AA0483319CD4351170DB94C8A771.

[158] PE Strahan, 'Liquidity Production in Twenty-First-Century Banking' in AN Berger, P Molyneux and JO Wilson (eds), *The Oxford Handbook of Banking* (Oxford, Oxford University Press, 2010) 112–45, 112.

[159] LR Wray, 'From the State Theory of Money to Modern Money' in D Fox and W Ernst (eds), *Money in the Western Legal Tradition. Middle Ages to Bretton Woods* (Oxford, Oxford University Press, 2016) 631–52, 631.

[160] Credit Institutions Law DOF.

The advantage of the CGS was precisely the imposed scarcity; however, after the collapse of the Bretton Woods system, the problem with fiat money is that it can be 'dropped by helicopters' as in Friedman's[161] famous analogy, in absence of the assumption that it would be 'a unique event which will never be repeated'.

In opposition to this academic anachronism, Zoltan Jakab and Michael Kumhof[162] present the 'financing through money creation' (FMC) model, which is structured around the fact that the amount of money in our economies is determined less by the need to buy things – or pay taxes – and more by the supply of credit created by the private sector banks responding to the endogenous demand from borrowers.[163] This builds on the spirit of the resolutions found in cases such as *Carr v Carr*,[164] *Folley v Hill*[165] and *Libyan Arab Foreign Bank v Bankers Trust Co*,[166] in which it is made clear that when a customer gives money to a bank, that money becomes the property of the bank, and the bank 'is liable merely to answer the drafts of his customer to that amount'.[167] Consequently, commercial bank money is a *res* claim on a commercial bank for an abstract unit of account that is separated by the means of payment as described by Lord MacMillan in *Banco de Portugal v Waterlow & Sons Ltd*.[168]

Thus, one cannot say that saving, by itself, creates funds available for banks to lend.[169] When a bank receives a loan application, it does not peer into its vault to determine the quantity of depositors' funds are on hand to lend to third parties, as described in *United Dominions Trust v Kirkwood*,[170] and it does not typically do so by giving them thousands of pounds', dollars' or pesos' worth of banknotes.[171] In practice, banks hold only cash enough to process their legal obligations – eg those that derive from the Basel Accords – and, under a FMC model, they fund new loans by creating new ledger-entry deposits for their borrowers, through 'transactions that involve a single-cum-depositor and no saver'.[172] For this reason, James Tobin[173] put the 'money created by bankers' fountain pens' and the 'money created by public printing presses' at the same level. Through this new lending, the balance

[161] M Friedman, *The Optimum Quantity of Money and Other Essays* (New York, Macmillan, 1969) 4.
[162] Jakab and Kumhof (n 157).
[163] M King, *The End of Alchemy. Money, Banking and the Future of the Global Economy* (London, Little, Brown, 2016) 61–63.
[164] JH Merivale, *Reports of Cases Argued and Determined in the High Court of Chancery. Vol 1* (London, Joseph Butterworth and Son, 1817) 541.
[165] [1848] 2 HLC 28 (UK), 36.
[166] [1989] QB 728 (UK), 748.
[167] Merivale (n 164).
[168] [1932] AC 452 (UK), 459, 482, 485, 503.
[169] McLeay, Radia and Thomas (n 157).
[170] 'An establishment for the custody of money received from, or on behalf of, its customers. Its essential duty is to pay their drafts on it: its profits arise from the use of money left unemployed by them.' See [1966] 2 QB 431 (UK), 447.
[171] C Morgan-Webb, *The Money Revolution* (New York, Economic Forum Inc, 1935) 19–20.
[172] Jakab and Kumhof (n 157).
[173] J Tobin, 'Commercial Banks as Creators of Money.' (1963), available at cowles.yale.edu/sites/default/files/files/pub/d01/d0159.pdf.

sheets of different sectors of the economy are affected. In the books, this transaction appears as an asset and a liability of the bank as described with detail in *Folley v Hill*,[174] on the one hand, and an asset and a liability of the borrower, on the other.[175]

Figure 5 Balance sheet of commercial banks and consumers during the process of broad money creation[176]

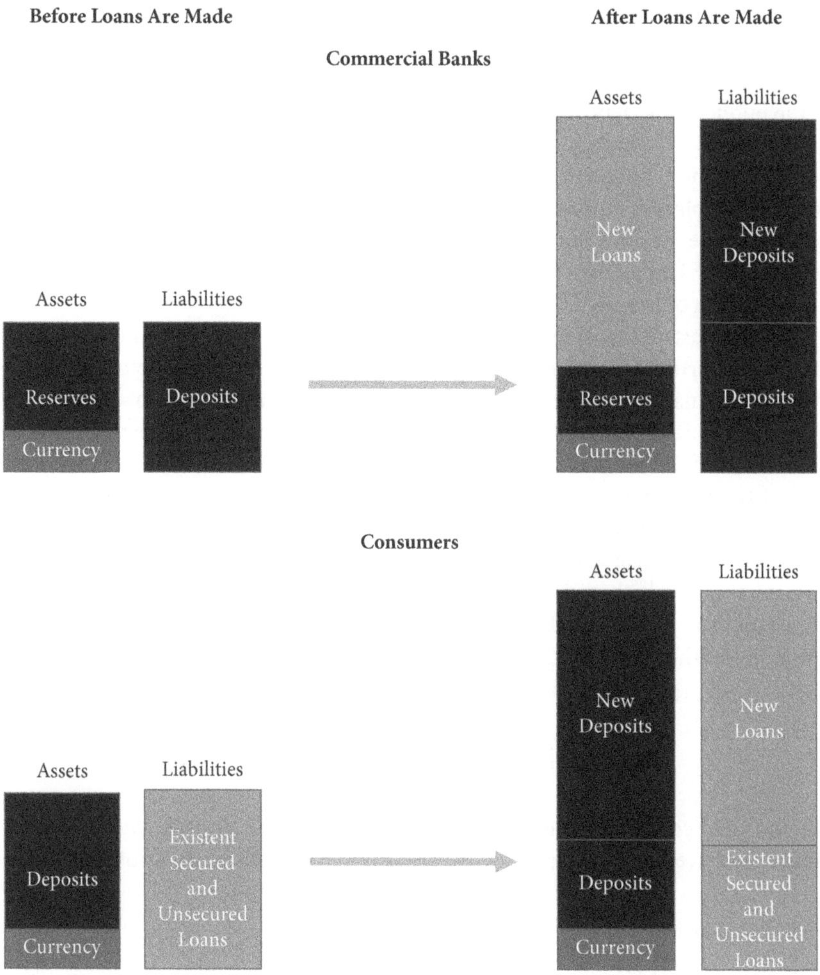

Figure 5 shows us how, in principle, banks create their own funding in the act of lending. No real resources are diverted from other uses in order to be able to lend

[174] [1848] 2 HLC 28 (UK), 36.
[175] McLeay, Radia and Thomas (n 157).
[176] ibid.

to a new customer. This purchasing power is injected into the economy independently of the economy's pre-loan income flow.[177] In simpler terms, what is needed in an FMC model from third parties is not a deposit of tangible assets, but the acceptance of the new dematerialised purchasing power in payment for physical resources.[178]

When governments allowed the creation of money to become a by-product of the expansion of banks' balance sheets, they lost the power to limit expenditures from banks and enterprises, and they do not fully understand their behaviour effectively to the point that we are witnessing quasi-theological debates within regulatory bodies and central banks.[179] While this happens, from the perspective of the public, bank deposits are practically indistinguishable from 'outside money', despite Goode[180] warning us that it is important to avoid confusion on this matter. For him, money created under an FMC model lacks at least most of the legal characteristic of physical money: it is not issued under the authority of the state, it is no legal tender, it does not serve as a universal medium of exchange, and it is not negotiable.[181] Under this approach, bank credit money would be excluded from the definition of money.[182]

On this last point, Friedman and Schwartz[183] note that with the suspension of the convertibility and the recognition of currencies as key symbols of the Westphalian nation-state, by means of which now we take pure fiat standards as the cornerstones of our financial systems, we no longer need to make these distinctions. Thus, if the state does not have a monopoly over the creation of money, can central banks survive an IT revolution? For Charles Goodhart[184] the answer is positive: central banks are unlikely to be sidelined by the FIR and the FMC model given that they will at least retain a monopoly over the design and structure of the monetary system[185] based on the social contract, independently that the material infrastructural power is held by the private sector – a power that is evident when one analyses the risks associated to the TBTF and the TCTF problems.

VI. Facing Free Banking in the FIR

Beyond the Scottish experience after the collapse of the Bretton Woods System, regulators have been very permissive regarding the establishment of alternatives

[177] Jakab and Kumhof (n 157).
[178] ibid.
[179] N Kiyotaki and J Moore, 'Liquidity, Business Cycles, and Monetary Policy' (2001), available at www.princeton.edu/~kiyotaki/papers/ClarendonLec2.pdf; Coggan (n 44) 39.
[180] R Goode, *Goode on Commercial Law* (London, LexisNexis, 2009) 489.
[181] ibid.
[182] Gleeson (n 1) 118.
[183] Friedman and Schwartz (n 23) 296.
[184] CAE Goodhart, 'Can Central Banking Survive the IT Revolution?' (2000) 3 *International Finance* 189, 190, 207.
[185] Proctor and Dixon (n 156) 6.

to traditional intermediaries, as seen through the gradual conception of decentralised finance (DeFi) as an integral part of the 'shadow banking system'. In the context of the FIR, where the digital divide is decreasing and where policymakers around the world are working to make access to the internet a fundamental right, a major concern for our financial regulators should be the generation of unregulated intermediaries. This new generation of shadow banks could be empowered – by normative/regulatory omission – to issue excessive quantities of rather volatile 'inside monies' that eventually, through secondary innovations, could delude the original *res* incorporated in the instruments and influence negatively the real economy.

It is suggested that this behaviour is an important argument against the private issuance of money or, at least, against its unregulated status.[186] In the absence of this sovereign intervention, it is very likely that we would witness different scenarios that would follow the example set by Johan Palmstruch's *Stockholms Banco* (as explored in section V of chapter two). Such scenarios provide sovereign entities with the rationale to usurp private forms of money through the exercise of *lex monetae*; after all, governments can have debt crises, but they are far less vulnerable to runs than are private institutions.[187]

It is possible to say – and see, through the case of the 'stablecoins' and CBDCs – that each currency needs a sound underlying agreement supported by a strong institutional–sovereign backstop to be credible.[188] As will be explored further in chapter six, in addition to the sovereign adoption and issuance of complementary payment schemes, if we want to support current DLT projects under a free banking paradigm, we should create a sound regulatory framework for the constitution, incorporation and transfer of liquidity sources. This framework should be based on clear definitions and 'moral' incentives, similar to those conceived in eighteenth-century Scotland where the unlimited liability of shareholders in bankrupt banks sequestrated their personal estates.[189] Under this paradigm, the Scottish financial system mitigated counterparty risk and moral hazard, thus giving the monetary instruments a credible underlying backstop that would increase the diffusion of the network effects, and creating an effective set of stablecoins.

Furthermore, it is important to consider in our efforts that all free banking experiences have relied on effectively working clearing arrangements.[190] During the first stages of these paradigms, bilateral and multilateral clearing agreements emerged given the low number of players during the first stages; after all, there is no evident need of clearing houses in cities with two or three banks.[191] Following

[186] M Friedman, *A Program for Monetary Stability* (New York, Fordham University Press, 1960).
[187] ibid, 25–26.
[188] D Schoenmaker, *Governance of International Banking. The Financial Trilemma* (New York, Oxford University Press, 2013) 3.
[189] Goodspeed (n 70) 26.
[190] Goodhart (n 56) 29.
[191] JTP Knight, *Canadian Banking Practice* (Montreal, F Wilson-Smith, 1908) 137.

the definitions of payment systems, clearing houses under this model were developed beyond their initial role as money exchanges and became the cornerstone of different governance schemes.[192] As an illustration of this, we have the case of the Banco Central Mexicano, which was constituted in 1899 by a group of Mexican free banks to act as a clearing house and a lender of last resort to banks facing local panics.[193] Based on these experiences, it is possible to see how some of the first cryptoasset exchanges like Coinbase and the Mexican Bitso are evolving and extending their services to cover necessities closely related to the traditional functions developed by regulated payment systems.

A. The GFC and the Emergence of New Challengers

Wang Zhenying[194] accurately stated that 'crises destroy, but crises also create'. Financial crises unleashed by our financial *Bildungstrieb* tend to trigger changes in economic thinking as well as in our monetary arrangements. These changes were witnessed during the First World War when gold convertibility was abandoned. The Great Depression made possible the rise of Keynesian economics, while countries gradually abandoned the CGS. The Bretton Woods System collapse raised the stature of monetarist and New Classical approaches, thus configuring the New International Financial Architecture (NIFA).[195] And it happened again in September 2008, following the GFC, which posed different questions relating to the benefits and risks of free banking models and the nature of money in the FIR.

Following the GFC, Nigel Dodd argued that 'the era in which money was defined by the State is coming to an end'.[196] But, is this possible and/or is this a new idea? Studies of non-sovereign means of payment show that throughout history, people constantly disrupt 'monetary uniformity' through the design and periodical introduction of different schemes by which they offer private and semi-private means of payment that, on some occasions, are adopted and integrated into the legal monetary infrastructure. The intended purpose of these 'inside monies' has had very different targets, ranging from meeting local credit demand and stimulating local economies, to achieving social and political reforms.[197]

[192] Schuler (n 54) 17–18.
[193] ibid.
[194] W Zhenying, 'Trading Economies: A New Theoretical System' (2017), available at ftalphaville.ft.com/2017/11/06/2195583/guest-post-trading-economics-a-new-theoretical-system.
[195] FH Rogers, 'The Global Financial Crisis and Development Thinking' (2010), available at documents.worldbank.org/curated/en/312881468161350853/pdf/WPS5353.pdf; Coggan (n 44) 256.
[196] N Dodd, *The Social Life of Money* (Princeton, Princeton University Press, 2014) 234.
[197] M Naqvi and J Southgate, 'Banknotes, Local Currencies and Central Bank Objectives.' (2013), available at www.bankofengland.co.uk/publications/Documents/quarterlybulletin/2013/qb130403.pdf.

These complementary means of payment *reified* within the private sector can be broadly categorised into three groups: 1) backed tokens; 2) un-backed tokens; and 3) mutual credit system tokens.[198] The first is backed by commodities for which they can be exchanged at a fixed fee.[199] Although among these asset-backed tokens we find some of the earliest examples of incorporation of assets/rights, as we can verify through the tokens of Mureybet,[200] today we are witnessing the emergence of digital versions, such as, those 'stablecoins' propounded by companies like IBM and Celo who rely on their IPRs and/or the nature of the assets incorporated within their cryptoassets to create trust. Unbacked tokens are typically tied to the provision of some services or simply one hour of labour as it can be seen through the case of the Ithaca Hours,[201] used in Ithaca, New York. Finally, mutual credit systems work through networks like the Edinburgh Local Exchange Trading System (LETS)[202] that can be considered a form of payment club by which, after paying a fee, its users transform working time, products and/or services into an underlying obligation that will give form to an alternative monetary unit.[203] In Edinburgh, the LETS is the Reekie.

B. Incorporation and Recognition of 'Stablecoins' in the Past

Just as we are witnessing through the utility tokens issued as integral parts of some ICOs, which one could argue are commercial expressions as defined in cases such as *Securities and Exchange Commission v Wall Street Publishing Institute Inc dba Stock Market Magazine*,[204] the regular issue of tokens by general stores, bakers, barbers, hoteliers, transportation, etc has been a common practice. These chattels are useful for merchants given that they are designed as forms of inexpensive advertising, schemes to receive money in advance to face scenarios like that by COVID-19, alternative means of payment for small purchases, and a customer loyalty practice considering that these tokens can be redeemed only at the establishment of the issuing merchant. As examples of these tokens we can find the 'tlacos'[205] put in circulation by the Guild of Bakers in Mexico in 1793,[206] the dairy tokens issued by Clark Dairy Ltd and National Milk Co in Canada during the

[198] D Pfajfar, G Sgro and W Wagner, 'Are Alternative Currencies a Substitute or Complement to Fiat Money? Evidence form Cross-Country Data' (2012) 16 *International Journal of Community Currency Research* 46–56, 48.

[199] ibid.

[200] D Schmandt-Besserat, 'The Invention of Tokens' in A Crisà, M Grikaki and C Rowan (eds), *Tokens. Culture, Connections, Communities* (London, Royal Numismatic Society, 2–19) 11–18, 11.

[201] See ithacahours.com.

[202] See www.letsedinburgh.org.uk/.

[203] Pfajfar, Sgro and Wagner (n 198) 48.

[204] [1988] 851 F.2d 365 (US), 372.

[205] Private issued tokens.

[206] ML Muñoz, *Tlacos y Pilones. La Moneda del Pueblo de México* (Mexico City, Fomento Cultural Banamex, 1976) 49.

nineteenth century,[207] and some DLT utility tokens that are designed to act as means of payment on the issuer's platform, which cannot exist and/or be used outside it.[208] Therefore, one could argue that these instruments could be subject to existent regulations, such as Schedule 10A, Regulation 1(1) of the Value Added Tax Act 1994[209] of the UK, which defines 'face value vouchers' as 'a token, stamp or voucher (whether in physical or electronic form) that represents a right to receive goods or services to the value of an amount stated on it or recorded in it'.

On monetary matters, the state – in exercise of its *jus cudendae monetae* – has shown a dual approach towards these alternative means of payment. In most cases, the state decides to stamp them out, but, occasionally, it may decide to enable the use of these *reifiers*,[210] depending on their potential to disrupt its ability to meet monetary and financial stability objectives.[211] Now, can we say that these tokens are money? From a legal perspective, our answer will depend on the nature of the instruments. If a person other than the issuer of the token accepts them as a means of payment, we could say that these complementary instruments are money. If only the issuer accepts them, they could be labelled as simple vouchers.

Following this line, one can argue that these instruments also act as cornerstones for the development of governance paradigms based on our Socio-Legal Theory of money by means of which sovereign entities and private sector parties agree to introduce a monetary instrument, structured around a sovereign unit of reference, to fulfil social and/or political goals in different administrative levels. An example of this can be found in municipal complementary monies, such as the programme developed by the Government of Ichikawa, Japan designed around a local monetary unit to promote generalised trust among citizens by rewarding civic engagement and encouraging social interaction.[212] In this case, again, we can see that a social contract is incorporated within a payment instrument. After the GFC, in countries like France, the spirit of these efforts can be found in new legislation, such as the French Law No 2014-856 of 31 July 2014,[213] whose Section V, Article 16[214] established that only those legal persons referred in Article 1 of the

[207] PS Berry and K Bevan, 'Ottawa Dairy Tokens. An Overview of the Dairy Tokens of Ottawa and Their Issuers' (2008), available at www.bankofcanadamuseum.ca/wp-content/uploads/2014/07/ottawa-dairy-tokens.pdf.

[208] J Li and W Mann, 'Initial Coin Offering and Platform Building' (2018) 15, available at www.jbs.cam.ac.uk/fileadmin/user_upload/research/centres/alternative-finance/downloads/2018-af-conference/paper-li.pdf.

[209] Schedule added through Schedule 1 of the Finance Act 2003 c 14. See Value Added Tax Act 1994 c 23.

[210] K Dowd, 'Contemporary Private Monetary Systems' in LH White, VJ Vanberg and EA Köhler (eds), *Renewing the Search for a Monetary Constitution. Reforming Government's Role in the Monetary System* (Washington, Cato Institute, 2015) Kindle EBook Loc 3442–4029, Loc 3457.

[211] Naqvi and Southgate (n 197).

[212] S Richey, 'Manufacturing Trust: Community Currencies and the Creation of Social Capital.' (2007) 29 *Political Behavior* 69, 70.

[213] LOI n° 2014-856 du 31 juillet 2014 relative à l'économie sociale et solidaire JORF 12666, 31 July 2014.

[214] Currently the terms of this article are found in Article L311-5 of the French Monetary and Financial Code.

that law can issue local forms of money to promote the development of social and solidary economies.

VII. Conclusion

Complementing these policy changes, rapid advances in data-processing – paired with substantial falls in the cost of information and communication – and intensified use of global computer/payment networks, led to the integration of our WFS through innovations, such as RTGSs and electronic money.[215] Without the innovative use of computers and codes, the present set of intangible innovations would not exist. Probably we would keep using physical chattels as described by Sir Francis Mann,[216] that is, notes issued by the central bank and coins distributed by the Mint, when transferred as currency, not as a numismatic curiosity or other commodity. On this, Goode[217] argues that money should not include bank money or electronic money. However, as seen in the *Miliangos*[218] case, and as it will be analysed in chapter three, these and other instruments can be treated as money following the spirit of their respective *Bildungstrieb*.

Returning to the banknotes issued in Scotland and England, in this new scenario post-Bretton Woods one question emerges: 'five pounds of what?'[219] As seen in section III.A above, paper clearly has no intrinsic value and, if we want to present and protest this note, we will discover that there is no gold or silver incorporated within it, so why accept it as the final means of payment?[220] Initially, one could argue that banknotes are promissory notes within the meaning of Regulation 83 of the Bills of Exchange Act 1882,[221] which states that:

> A promissory note is an unconditional promise in writing made by one person to another signed by the maker, engaging to pay, on demand or at a fixed or determinable future time, a sum certain in money, to, or to the order of a specified person or to the bearer.

However, it is important to not overlook the criteria set in cases, such as, *Suffel v Bank of England*,[222] in which Sir George Jessel MR clearly stated that:

> A Bank of England note is not an ordinary commercial contract to pay money. It is in one sense a promissory note in terms, but no one can describe it as simply a promissory

[215] J Kay et al, 'Regulatory Reform in Britain' (1988) 3 *Economic Policy* 285, 296; Sono (n 123) 92.
[216] FA Mann, *The Legal Aspect of Money* (London, Oxford University Press, 1938) 8.
[217] Goode (n 180) 486.
[218] [1976] AC 443 (UK), 463.
[219] J Lanchester, 'When Bitcoin Grows Up' (2016), available at www.lrb.co.uk/v38/n08/john-lanchester/when-bitcoin-grows-up.
[220] Coggan (n 44) 33; Lanchester (n 219).
[221] Bills of Exchange Act 1882 c 61.
[222] [1882] 9 QBD 555 (UK), 563.

> note. It is part of the currency of the country … It is protected in a way no other instrument is protected, against alteration or mutilation, and its preservation in a pure state, to use a term as applied to deeds by some learned judges, is certainly a matter of the utmost importance.

In other words, the underlying obligation that gives form to current banknotes is closely related to the social contract. Of course, the disappearance of commodity standards and the gradual emergence of electronic-fiat standards within a FWS ruled by Wallersteinian rules, has generated alarmist reactions, such as, the cypherpunk movement, which claimed that this model configures a 'panopticon' by which the state violates the terms of the referred social contract while, at the same time, generating endless inflationary cycles.[223]

Even though most of our money is *reified* through electrons, instead of *electrum*, nations around the world, through their respective legal tender laws, had decreed its use following a Socio-Legal approach, so its value is equivalent to our belief in the stability of the governing regime and/or its financial intermediaries.[224] Therefore, we can say that money, independently of its post-Bretton Woods dematerialisation, is constituted around trust in a stakeholder, whether a bank or a government. However, it must be acknowledged that this trust ultimately results from a lack of information.[225] On this point, the particular case of Bitcoin is rather interesting. Despite Alan Greenspan[226] comparing Bitcoin to 1775 continental currency, the former, during its first stages, introduced the first asset that does not present an underlying obligation, and which is not backed by any well-defined authority. In other words, a digital commodity that has been recognised as such in cases like *Commodity Futures Trading Commission v Patrick K McDonnell and Cabbagetech, Corp d/b/a Coin Drop Markets.*[227] Interestingly, even when everyone recognised this fact, companies like PwC Hong Kong[228]

[223] The core of this argument can be found in E. Hughes, 'A Chypherpunk's Manifiesto' (1993), available at www.activism.net/cypherpunk/manifesto.html.

[224] D Orrell and R Chlupatý, *The Evolution of Money* (New York, Columbia University Press, 2016) 176; LR Wray, 'From the State Theory of Money to Modern Money' in D Fox and W Ernst (eds), *Money in the Western Legal Tradition. Middle Ages to Bretton Woods* (Oxford, Oxford University Press, 2016) 631–52, 631; Coggan (n 44) 33; Lanchester (n 219).

[225] According to François R Velde, if one party knows everything about his/her counterparty's motives and circumstances, he/she could predict the future actions within the interaction and choose his/hers accordingly, without having to trust in his/her counterparty. Consequently, technological developments that improve our ability to collect and use data can change both the degree to which money is useful and the form that useful money can take. See FR Velde, 'Technological Change and the Future of Cash' (2017) 15 *SUERF Policy Note* 1.

[226] L Moyer, 'Greenspan Compares Bitcoin to Colonial America Currency that Eventually Became Worthless.' (2017), available at www.cnbc.com/2017/12/06/greenspan-compares-bitcoin-to-colonial-america-currency-that-eventually-became-worthless.html.

[227] [2018] 18-CV-361 (US), 17–20.

[228] D McCance, 'PwC Hong Kong First Big Four Firm to Accept Bitcoin' (2017), available at economia.icaew.com/en/news/december-2017/pwc-hong-kong-first-big-four-firm-to-accept-bitcoin.

and Brewdog[229] have accepted it as a means of payment following the Societary Theory of Money.[230]

As will be developed in chapter four, Bitcoin and other cryptographic instruments of first generation – just as other monetary innovations in the past – have required the emergence of new stakeholders and intermediaries to boost their acceptance. With this in mind, building upon the Socio-Legal theory of money, it is possible to define money as a set of uniformed social conventions incorporated within a *reifier* whose characteristics are determined by a stakeholder by which the members of a community, other than the issuer, store value and discharge social obligations based on the practices, technologies and norms in force in each dynamic social system.

[229] Brewdog, 'Equity for Punks Accepts Cryptocurrency' (2019), available at efp.brewdog.com/equityforpunks/cryptocurrency?fbclid=IwAR1MaWR0VR9bG3J40BAyt_53B3bBFpZrFRiPMfwKhktUOB3S4O9OS4VETPA.

[230] This theory argues that we can define money based on what in practice is widely accepted as such, independently of the legal framework for its issue and use. See Proctor and Dixon (n 156) 5.

3

Legal Analysis of the Concept of Money

I. Introduction

As one can infer from the preceding chapters, it is possible to argue that money is one of the most fascinating institutions in the legal, economic and social history of human civilisation, taking many forms and fulfilling different functions that go beyond the economic descriptions given in most works on the subject. Additionally, it can be incorporated into social, legal and algorithmic codes. The evolutionary dynamics behind these qualitative elements have fostered the emergence of different categories of socioeconomic interactions that have relied in different means of exchange, monies and currencies whose source of liquidity can be found within and outside the market, which often tend to be labelled together under the generic terms 'money' and 'currency'.

Accordingly, this chapter will show how states, in exercise of their *ius cudendae monetae*, have faced such interactions standardising and stabilising the three traditional monetary functions, independently if we are talking about 'inside' and/or 'outside' monies. This chapter therefore opens with an analysis of these functions from a legal perspective structured around the constitutional elements introduced by the Peace of Westphalia. It takes as its starting point the function of money as an ideal and abstract unit of reference defined under a nominalist approach in laws, such as the Coinage Act of the United States,[1] the Monetary Law of the United Mexican States[2] and the Currency Act 1982[3] of the United Kingdom, among others, whose interactions tend to foster phenomena, such as currency wars by which states aim to secure an economic advantage following the Wallersteinian trends described chapter two.[4]

The analysis of this first function will show that the socio-qualitative element that was relevant in the configuration of the first monetary systems is still present today – seen in the 'Mercury' and 'Mars' approaches[5] – despite the common belief that, in the context of post-Bretton Woods fiat money, it has disappeared.

[1] An Act establishing a Mint, and regulating the Coins of the United States 1 Stat 246.

[2] Monetary Law of the United Mexican States DOF.

[3] Currency Act 1982.

[4] C Herrman and C Dornacher, *International and European Monetary Law* (Cham, Springer Nature, 2017) 13–14.

[5] E Avgouleas and W Blair, 'The Concept of Money in the 4th Industrial Revolution. A Legal and Economic Analysis' (2020) *Singapore Journal of Legal Studies* 4, 17; B Eichengreen, A. Mehl and

To highlight this fact, it shows how the material element that inspired the Socio-Metallist arguments has been displaced by the underlying socio-legal obligations recognised by each state that currently configures our money in both public and private spheres. Consequently, the functions of money can be seen as a store of value and means of payment that relies on socio-legal relationships and will be *reified* in instruments, such as banknotes, as described by Lord Macmillan in *Banco de Portugal v Waterlow & Sons Ltd.*[6]

The third function of money relates to the satisfaction of contractual obligations materialised through the act of payment, which tend to be described and illustrated through the exchange of commodities, coins, notes and other monetary *reifiers*. Again, this is an incomplete perception of the legal nature of this function. As will be developed in this chapter, a proper legal analysis of money needs to consider the extended ecosystem of infrastructural providers and dynamic systems that support the creation, circulation and even destruction of monetary assets. No legal analysis without consideration of the legal analysis of payment systems and their value chains. This chapter will analyse the process of payment through different instruments and infrastructures, highlighting the role of different stakeholders and governance paradigms in the materialisation of our financial transactions.

II. 'Inside' and 'Outside' Money

John C Gurley and Edward S Shaw, in their book *Money in a Theory of Finance*,[7] use the terms 'outside money' and 'inside money' to illustrate the different acts of incorporation explained in chapter two, and the different sources of liquidity that derive from the classification of rights described in *United States v Patrick; et al.*[8] The former is identified with our traditional coins and notes, and it is defined as 'money that is backed by foreign or government securities or gold; or fiat money issued by the government.'[9] This means that the money supply is an exogenous economic variable that is set independently of the market forces by a sovereign entity such as a central bank.[10] On the other hand, 'inside money' can be defined as privately issued assets and liabilities that respond to the behaviour of regulated and non-regulated intermediaries, individuals and companies as result of endogenous factors within the market.[11]

L Chitu, 'Mars or Mercury? The Geopolitics of International Currency Choice' (2017) 24145 *NBER Working Papers* 1, 2.

[6] *Banco de Portugal v Waterlow & Sons Ltd* [1932] AC 452 (UK), at 459, 482, 485, 503.

[7] JG Gurley and ES Shaw, *Money in a Theory of Finance* (Washington DC, The Brookings Institution, 1960) 364.

[8] [1893] 54 F 338 (US), at 348.

[9] Gurley and Shaw (n 7).

[10] S Gleeson, *The Legal Concept of Money* (New York, Oxford University Press, 2018) 97; L Wu et al, 'Electronic Payment Instruments and Endogenous Money Supply' (2009), available at ieeexplore.ieee.org.ezproxy.is.ed.ac.uk/stamp/stamp.jsp?arnumber=5279897.

[11] RP Falkner, 'The Currency Law of 1900' (1900) 16 *Annals of the American Academy of Political and Social Science* 33, 47; R. Lagos, 'Inside and Outside Money' (2006) 374 *Federal Reserve Bank of*

However, as has previously been seen in relation to the term 'money', its derivatives 'inside' and 'outside' money are generally defined according to the definition of 'money' adopted by the author who is proposing the definition, and/or the *res* incorporated within the monetary instrument under analysis. Hence, when one tries to analyse the evolution and nature of money on the basis of these monetary categories, textbooks and academic journals focus all their attention on scenarios without frictions, imaginary countries, economies without external influences or innovation processes, spontaneous transitions between barter and fiat money, among others. Of course, these efforts are not very helpful.

To face these challenges, in chapter two a first effort was introduced to define money as an instrument by which one can incorporate a source of social liquidity to discharge social obligations according to the practices and norms in force in each dynamic social system. Consequently, once the standardised conditions of incorporation have been determined by a stakeholder, the functions traditionally associated with money as unit of account, store of value and medium of exchange tend to be introduced in the market as a form of outside money.[12] Therefore, after an analysis of the socio-economic element that constitutes our Socio-Legal theory of money, the Legal/Chartalist element builds upon the arguments of authors such as Aristotle[13] and George Friedrich Knapp,[14] arguing that money is a creature of law – in other words, a form of outside money. As a consequence, its complement, inside money, emerges: 1) as contractual innovations developed periodically by the private sector to provide complementary sources of liquidity in different sociocultural contexts; and/or 2) as different conduits to transfer and multiply outside money under the conditions set by the state in the exercise of its sovereign prerogatives.

Based on this, is it possible to say that new cryptoassets are a form of inside money? Or can it be said that these innovations are evolving towards new expressions of outside money? To answer these questions, it is first necessary to understand the legal nature of money, its functions and the institutions that are closely related to it.

III. Money as a Common Denominator of Value

Chapters one and two examined how different monetary orders were designed around different governance paradigms, that went from the practices developed by temples and merchant networks to the gradual transfer of prerogatives in favour

Minneapolis Research Department Staff Report 1; C Sissoko, 'Why Inside Money Matters?' (2007) 39 *Journal of Money, Credit and Banking* 2097, 2097; Gleeson (n 10) 97; Wu et al (n 10).

[12] CAE Goodhart, 'The Two Concepts of Money. Implications for the Analysis of Optimal Currency Areas' (1998) 14 *European Journal of Political Economy* 407, 408; N Kiyotaki and R Wright, 'On Money as a Medium of Exchange' (1989) 97 *Journal of Political Economy* 927, 950.

[13] Aristotle, *Nicomachean Ethics* (London, Kegan Paul, Trench, Trübner & Co, 1906) 156.

[14] GF Knapp, *The State Theory of Money* (London Macmillan & Company Limited, 1924) 1.

of sovereign stakeholders, to configure our *lex monetae*. This transfer was consolidatated after the Peace of Westphalia of 1648, which brought new possibilities of self-determination in identity and government through the institutionalisation of state law.[15] Through this institutionalisation, sovereign states claimed supreme lawmaking and law-enforcing authority, and, consequently, eased and regularised domestic and transnational interactions by providing standardisation around legal and property rights.[16] Now, how does the law address monetary standardisation in a world of different dynamic social systems based on different legal traditions and liquidity sources?

Originally, as seen in the case of Mesopotamian and Greek temples, liquidity was incorporated and represented in valuable commodities such as gold and silver that were eventually adjusted to sovereign measures in terms that described a certain weight/value in a specific context. Therefore, the notion that a single coin had as much value as the quantity of silver it contained (*tantum valet unus nummus quantum argenti tantundem in massa*) was to become a key reference for the glossators' and the post-glossators' approach to currency policies.[17] From these Socio-Metallist approaches, coins were understood in many parts of the world as publicly certified pieces of silver or gold, as one can see in cases such as *St Pierre and Others v South American Stores (Gath & Chaves) Ltd and Chilean Stores (Gath & Chaves) Ltd*,[18] where MacKinnon LJ explained that:

> The word 'peso' in Spanish has a double meaning, as our word 'pound' has in English. It may mean weight, as I think 'peso' does in Italian, or it may mean a Chilean or an Argentine coin; it is the equivalent of the peseta in Spain, the franc in France, or the lira in Italy. If one knew only that much, the meaning of this sentence might be doubtful. It might be a promise to pay 93500 gold coins of a certain gold content or value, or it might mean a promise to hand over a certain weight of the commodity gold.

This means that money has been created through the normative standardisation of words to foster a behaviour 'that creates the concept it purportedly gives effect to'.[19] In a certain way, we can argue that this 'concept' is the basis for our constitutional monetary conventions that act as the transition rules that give form to our *lex monetae*.

This work has left behind the Socio-Metallist paradigms, and it is possible to argue that the substance of the *reifier* is legally irrelevant[20] and, in order to function, money relies on the abstraction of the *res* of money, which can be

[15] PA Hayman and J Williams, 'Westphalian Sovereignty. Rights, Intervention, Meaning and Context' (2006) 20 *Global Society* 521, 522; T Kayaoglu, 'The Extension of Westphalian Sovereignty. State Building and the Abolition of Extraterritoriality' (2007) 51 *International Studies Quarterly* 649, 651.

[16] Kayaoglu (n 15) 652.

[17] W Ernst, 'The Legists' Doctrines on Money and the Law from the Eleventh to the Fifteenth Centuries' in D Fox and W Ernst (eds), *Money in the Western Legal Tradition. Middle Ages to Bretton Woods* (Oxford, Oxford University Press, 2016) 110, 115.

[18] [1937] 3 All ER 349 (UK), at 357.

[19] A Rahmatian, 'Money as a Normative Text' (2014) 13 *Journal of International Business and Law* 221, 225.

[20] A Nussbaum, 'Basic Monetary Conceptions in Law' (1937) 35 *Michigan Law Review* 865, 870.

incorporated within a tangible object such as a banknote or within an intangible form of property that is 'definable, identifiable by third parties, capable in their nature of assumption by third parties, and having some degree of permanence'.[21] Courts have recognised, through cases like the famous *Legal Tender* cases[22] in the USA or *Gilbert v Brett*[23] in the UK, that money is transferred and accepted not for what it represents in tangible gold or silver, but as a fraction, equivalent or multiple of the ideal monetary unit.[24] Therefore, from an initial point of view, courts have stated that the unit of account prescribed by the state in exercise of its *lex monetae* must be treated as a measure of things within its boundaries not as the thing itself,[25] even if this measure has different values at different times.[26]

If money were regarded as a specific quantity of metal, in practice, there would not be a proper post-Bretton Woods unit of account, because the basis of practically every currency in the world would not be an independent abstract and ideal unit of reference, but a concrete and real unit of metal.[27] The abstraction requirement is needed given that when a price is named, it is named in abstract rather that concrete units, and when it is discharged the units to be used are accepted in payment by tale and not by weight.[28] This means that the state has the power to incorporate a sovereign source of liquidity, and set an ideal and abstract unit that could be made of lead or leather as standard to discharge contractual debts and to perform strategic asset allocations (SAA), even if the original transactions/allocations were materialised using gold coins.[29]

Today, the spirit of these arguments can be found in most of the monetary legislations in force around the world, which are designed under a nominalist approach,[30] taking as their starting point the constitutional values and the prerogatives that configure social contracts around the world. Illustrations of these values and prerogatives can be seen in the legislation of countries such as:

[21] Building on the Ainsworth test developed by Lord Wilberforce in *National Provincial Bank v Ainsworth*, Bryan J has stated that 'Bitcoins constitute property' based on these characteristics. See *AA v Persons Unknown & Ors, Re Bitcoin* [2019] EWHC 3556 (Comm) (UK), at 28.

[22] The cases *Hepburn v Griswold* [1870] 75 US, 603, 622–23 (US); *Knox v Lee* [1871] 79 US 457 (US); and *Juilliard v Greenman* [1884] 110 US 421 (US), popularly known as the *Legal Tender* cases, set the constitutionality of paper money beyond the original Mengerian interpretations of the sovereign power to coin metallic currency.

[23] [1605] Cobb St Tr 114 (UK), at 125–26.

[24] Nussbaum (n 20).

[25] *France v Kingdom of the Serbs, Croats and Slovenes* [1929] PCIJ (ser A) No 20 (NL), at 44, 72, 73; *National Bank of Australasia LTD v Scottish Union and National Insurance Co* [1952] 86 CLR 110 (AU), at 121–22; Gleeson (n 10) 80.

[26] *Deutsche Bank v Humphrey* [1926] 272 US, 517 (US), at 519.

[27] FA Mann, *The Legal Aspect of Money* (London, Oxford University Press, 1938) 32.

[28] Gleeson (n 10) 82; Mann (n 27) 464.

[29] A Joia and J Coche, 'Framework and Process for Strategic Asset Allocation in Central Bank Foreign Exchange Reserves Management' in AB Berkelaar, J Coche and K Nyholm (eds), *Central Bank Reserves and Sovereign Wealth Managment* (Hampshire, Palgrave Macmillan, 2010) 41–72, 47–48.

[30] D Fox, 'The Case of Mixt Monies: Confirming Nominalism in the Common Law of Monetary Obligations' (2011) 70 *Cambridge Law Journal* 144, 146.

(1) The United States (Section 20 of the Coinage Act of 1792):[31]

> And be if further enacted, that the money of account of the United States shall be expressed in dollars, or units, dismes or tenths, cents or hundredths, and the milles or thousandths, a disme being the tenth part of a dollar, a cent the hundredth part of a dollar, a mille the thousandth part of a dollar, and that all accounts in the public offices and all proceedings in the courts of the United States shall be kept and had in conformity to this regulation.

(2) Mexico (Article 1 of the Monetary Law of the United Mexican States):[32]

> 'The unit of the monetary system in the United Mexican States is the peso, with the equivalence that the law shall set forth afterwards.'

(3) The United Kingdom (Regulation 1 of the Currency Act 1982):[33]

> The denominations of money in the currency of the United Kingdom shall be the pound sterling and the penny or new penny, being one hundredth part of a pound sterling.

Therefore, under these legislative expressions, only those units defined and enforced by the state in terms of the social contract, and denominated under that terms, can legally be considered units of wealth. When multiplied or divided, they can be used to fulfil contractual obligations structured around the unit of reference described in the respective contract within a given geographical area.[34] Consequently, if a contract states that one party has to deliver pounds at a point in the future, and the UK Government decides – in exercise of its *lex monetae* – to change the definition of the pound at some point prior the obligation falling due, the obligation has to be fulfilled based on whatever the UK Government chooses to define as a pound.[35] Authors such as Cristoph Herrman, Corina Dornacher,[36] Kazuaki Sono and Hideki Kanda[37] have argued that one has to be careful when referring to the stability and territoriality requirements often found in the descriptions of this function, given that today most of major currencies are delocalised and traded in similar way to securities and commodities. Furthermore, they venture to say that the role of the *ius cudendae monetae* has been eroded by the technological preferences of the private sector. An interesting argument, but does it truly represent a new challenge? The answer is negative.

In chapter two, it was shown that the medium of exchange function can tolerate more than one currency without major trouble; however, can the same be said of the unit of account function? Authors, such as Charles Kindleberger[38] would

[31] An Act establishing a Mint, and regulating the Coins of the United States 1 Stat 246.

[32] Monetary Law of the United Mexican States DOF.

[33] Currency Act 1982.

[34] JM Keynes, *A Treatise on Money. Vol I* (London, MacMillan and Co, 1914) 13; T Parks, *Medici Money. Banking Metaphysics and Art in the Fifteenth-Century Florence* (London, Profile Books, 2006) 32.

[35] Gleeson (n 10) 113.

[36] Herrman and Dornacher (n 4) 14.

[37] K. Sono and H. Kanda, 'In Search of Order in the World Monetary System: State Intervention after the Decline of the Lex Monetae.' in M. Giovanoli and D. Devos (eds), *International Monetary and Financial Law. The Global Crisis* (2010, Oxford, Oxford University Press) 506–516, 507.

[38] C Kindleberger, *A Financial History of Western Europe* (London, Routledge, 1984) 55.

argue that it cannot tolerate more than one unit of reference. This is correct in relation to the standard set for a national currency within its territory. However, after the Anglo-Scots Monetary Union of 1707 assimilated the monetary system of Scotland with that of England and Wales, household accounts were still kept in pounds Scots[39] thus, highlighting how 'endogenous' and 'exogenous' units of reference, based on national and regional social contracts, can interact at the same time within a same context. Figure 6 shows how this was set out in a letter dated 1717 containing the terms of a contract between several private parties.

Figure 6 Letter (1717) which mentions the conditions of a contract set in pounds Scots after the Act of Union of 1707. Personal collection of the author and kept at Sala de Archivos y Colecciones Especiales at UDLAP

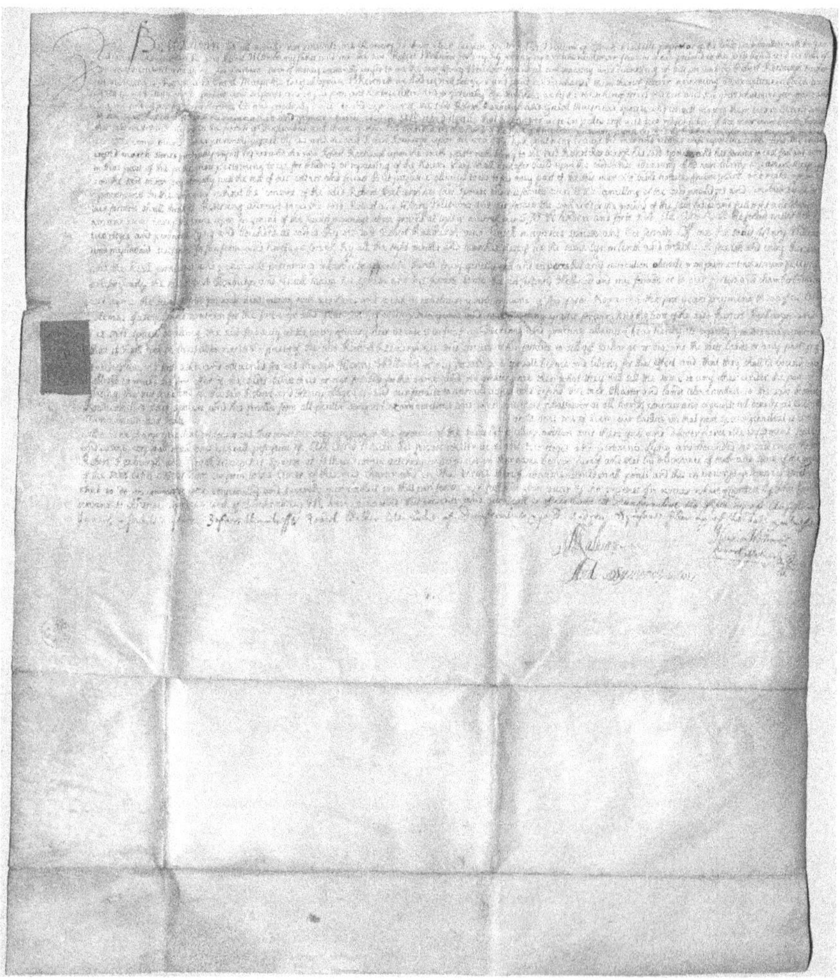

[39] D Fox, 'The Anglo-Scots Monetary Union of 1707' (2018) 24 *Edinburgh School of Law Research Paper Series* 1, 27.

It can even be said that this function can tolerate alternative private and public artificial monetary units. For instance, after the GFC, it was argued that one solution to improve understanding of economic systems and to prevent human error in economic thinking was to introduce new systems of economic units of measurement,[40] such as, the Investment Units (UDIs) found in Mexico, the European Unit of Account introduced in 1950 and the Barclays Unit (B-Unit).[41] However, despite their usefulness in protecting contracts against inflation, these units foster other misinterpretations based on functionalist analyses of money. For instance, through the thesis of jurisprudence 1a./J.16/2012 (9a) issued by the First Chamber of the Supreme Court of Justice of Mexico,[42] the Supreme Court argued that although these units can act as units of reference under *lex contractus*, they cannot stand alone as monetary units under *lex monetae*.

Furthermore, despite the apparent novelty of proposals such as XRP and Sam Altman's WorldCoin, the control of the fluctuation among different monetary systems has fostered, throughout the financial history of the world, several attempts to create a universal standard unit.[43] For instance, in the sixteenth century, Gasparo Scaruffi[44] propounded a global standard structured around the *moneta imaginaria* relation among gold, silver and copper, which would be permanently 1:12:120,[45] considering that the gold–silver ratio (1:12) was stable.[46] In recent times, other proposals for 'universal' standards have been made, such as the International Clearing Union proposed by Keynes, structured around an international bank money, called *Bancor*, which would be fixed in terms of gold, and accepted as the equivalent of gold by the British Commonwealth, the United States and all members of the International Clearing Union for settling international balances.[47] Unfortunately, given that there is no universal underlying social contract for all of our dynamic social systems – not even a universal set of terms and conditions for projects such as Facebook's LIBRA/DIEM – for now, under the Socio-Legal theory of money, it is impossible to materialise a global unit of reference.

[40] RJ Shiller, *The Subprime Solution. How Today's Global Financial Crisis Happened, and What to Do about It* (Princeton, Princeton University Press, 2008) 140–41.

[41] J. Aschheim and YS Park, 'Artificial Currency Units: The Formation of Functional Currency Areas' (1976) 114 *Essays in International Finance* 1, 6, 13.

[42] *UNIDADES DE INVERSIÓN (UDIS). Son Una Unidad de Cuenta y No Monetaria* [2012, SCJN, Thesis of Jurisprudence, 1a./J.16/2012 (9a), (MX).

[43] A Nussbaum, 'A Note on the Idea of World Money' (1949) 64 *Political Science Quarterly* 420, 423.

[44] G Scaruffi, *L'alitinonfo* (Reggio, Hercoliano Bartoli, 1582).

[45] W Ernst, 'Mensura et mensuratum: money as measure and measure for money' in J von Hagen and M Welker (eds), *Money as God? The Monetization of the Market and its Impact on Religion, Politics, Law, and Ethics* (Cambridge, Cambridge University Press, 2014) 60, 66; Nussbaum (n 43).

[46] Numismatic evidence shows that this ratio was recognised in many parts of Europe. An illustration of this is that James VI and Charles I applied it in London and Edinburgh for the sterling pound and the 'scot'. See AL Murray, 'Sir Isaac Newton and the Scottish Recoinage, 1707–1710' (1997) 127 *Proceedings of the Society of Antiquaries of Scotland* 921, 921.

[47] JM Keynes, 'Propuestas para un Fondo de Compensación Internacional' (1985) 44 *Investigación Económica* 21.

IV. Money as a Store of Value

From a legal perspective, most of the analyses on money are heavily focused on its functions as a means of payment and unit of account. The few lines spent on the function of money as store of value tend to follow the same path. The reader is invited to imagine different scenarios in which he/she has to spend his/her money as soon as it has been earned, or conversely, if he/she had to earn money immediately before purchasing any product and/or service.[48] After this exercise, authors explain how, to avoid these suboptimal scenarios, people incorporate their property in a financial instrument so that they may carry it with them on a long journey or transmit it to different counterparts in a distant country and in different temporal lines.[49] These arguments are not incorrect. However, as it was explained in chapter one, this process of incorporation goes beyond the solution of a practical problem. Through the act of incorporation, communities have transferred not only commodities, but also cultural traits that have configured real rights, SAAs, international relations and our sovereign currencies.

Furthermore, it is possible to state that different monetary expressions can circulate within a complex social economy that remains hidden from traditional scholarship. For example, under the term 'special monies' Vivian Zelizer[50] highlights that our money is subject to extra-economic influences that add incorporated value in isolated contexts, as in the case of domestic and charitable money, which invite us to ask to ourselves certain questions, such as 'under what conditions did money acquire sacred religious or moral value?' and 'how should money be allocated, regulated, and defined in the separate social world of a prison, a mental asylum, or an orphanage?' As one can infer, the potential answers to these questions take us to the impossibility described by Lord Viscount Simon.[51]

Despite the existence of an array of special monies', authors such as Niall Ferguson[52] and Voltaire[53] have argued that, as a direct consequence of the nature of our current bills and coins 'that are literally made from junk', it is not possible to say that money currently fulfils this function. From a legal perspective, building upon post-Westphalian standardisation, it is possible to argue that money does not become valueless merely because its tangible composition has been

[48] JP Coggan, *Paper Promises. Money, Debt, and the New World Order* (London, Penguin, 2011) 25.

[49] CA Desan, 'Money as a Legal Institution' in D Fox and W Ernst (eds), *Money in the Western Legal Tradition. Middle Ages to Bretton Woods* (Oxford, Oxford University Press, 2016) 18–35, 18.

[50] V Zelizer, 'The Social Meaning of Money: "Special Monies"' (1989) 95 *American Journal of Sociology* 342, 354, 370–71.

[51] *Perrin v Morgan* [1943] AC 399 HL (UK), at 406–07.

[52] N Ferguson, *The Ascent of Money. A Financial History of the World* (New York, The Penguin Press, 2008) 29.

[53] J Parton, *Life of Voltaire*. Vol.1 (Cambridge, The Riverside Press, 1881) 134.

substantially reduced, as explored through the *Case of Mixed Money in Ireland*.[54] On the contrary, following theSocio-Legal theory of money, it can be said that the value of money is socially determined through network effects.[55] This point is rather important. To harmonise the transferability of money through these effects, we need standardised instruments with strict formal requirements, such as *reified* promises and instructions to pay[56] that evolve on the promises analysed in the context of non-capitalist societies, which represent the abstract underlying *res* incorporated within the instruments that act as *reifiers*, to make them recognisable and enforceable against third parties.[57]

Chapter two analysed the origin of this function and its relevance for the origin and the evolution of money through the incorporation of a 'sacred' *res*, which has evolved into our post-Westphalian rules of transition identified with the social contract. With that in mind, the purpose of this section is to present several arguments relating to how this function depends on the credit of the sovereign stakeholder,[58] and even on its selection of infrastructure providers in a world of GVCs, through decisions relating to cases such as *Banco de Portugal v Waterlow & Sons Ltd*.[59] In this case, the central bank of Portugal commissioned, through a contract dated 27 November 1922, the defendant printers to produce 600,000 Vasco da Gama 500-escudo notes. However, Messrs Waterlow delivered 580,000 notes printed from the original plates to one Marang van Ysselvere, who, as an active member of a group of criminals, put the notes into circulation. Because these notes were not distinguishable from the original set, Banco de Portugal had to withdraw the entire issue from circulation and replace both the genuine and fraudulent notes.[60]

The main issue here regarding the function of money as store of value can be found in the determination of the court regarding: a) whether Banco de Portugal was empowered to reclaim damages based on the face value of the notes; or, building on Ferguson'[61] s words, b) whether it was it entitled to recover only the cost of the physical materials used to print and produce the notes. In this sense, the majority in both the Court of Appeal (Greer and Slesser LJJ) and the House of Lords (Viscount Sankey, Lord Atkin and Lord MacMillan) did not agree with Ferguson's perception.[62] Thus, building on

[54] [1605] Cobb St Tr 114 (UK), at 125–26.

[55] Gleeson (n 10) 66.

[56] For an illustration of these formality requirements see Reg 3(2) of the Bills of Exchange Act, which states that 'An instrument which does not comply with these conditions, or which orders any act to be done in addition to the payment of money, is not a bill of exchange.'

[57] A Rahmatian, 'Money as a Legally Enforceable Debt' (2018) 29 *European Business Law Review* 205, 212.

[58] Kiyotaki and Wright (n 12).

[59] *Banco de Portugal v Waterlow & Sons Ltd* [1932] All ER Rep 181 (UK).

[60] C Proctor, *Mann on the Legal Aspect of Money* (Oxford, Oxford University Press, 2012) 35.

[61] N Ferguson, *The Ascent of Money. A Financial History of the World* (New York, The Penguin Press, 2008) 29.

[62] *Banco de Portugal v Waterlow & Sons Ltd* [1932] AC 452 (UK), at 459, 482, 485, 503.

the words of Lord MacMillan, the bank recovered damages based on the face value given that 'a note when issued by the Bank of Portugal becomes by the mere fact of its issue legal tender for the sum which it bears on its face', independently of the 'trivial cost of printing new notes'.[63] After all – and as seen in Chapter 2 – the selection of the providers of infrastructure is integral part of the exercise of the *lex moneate*.

The most important issue to highlight within the words of Lord MacMillan is: 'a note when issued'. On the one hand, if the notes are not issued, or if they are destroyed before issue, they do not have legal effects as special promissory notes whose preservation 'is certainly a matter of the utmost importance' as described by Sir George Jessel MR in *Suffel v Bank of England*,[64] and, consequently, the liability for damages would be restricted to the costs of the paper and the printing of the notes.[65] However, after issue, the notes start to circulate with an underlying obligation that is denoted by the face value of the notes, which, in this case, is the proper measure of the damages.[66] In simpler terms, this means that, just as in the case of a cryptoasset like Bitcoin,[67] the mere printed paper represents the personal property-*res*, while the face value on the banknote represents the debt/money-*res* that relies 'on the power of the issuing Nation to incorporate trust'.[68] This point will be applicable to the incorporation of CBDCs and the nature of the algorithms and value chains involved.

In the context of post-Westphalian states, another expression of this function can be found in the so-called reserve currencies.[69] These expressions of *lex monetae* are used actively in international payments and as integral elements of SAAs developed by central banks considering the privileged positions that certain currencies like the US dollar have within the Wallersteinian system that has evolved from the 'spontaneous order', which, in turn, derived from the CGS.[70] The selection of these currencies and the evolution of the referred system tend to be described under either the 'Mercury approach' or the 'Mars approach'.[71] The Mercury approach – inspired by the Roman god of commerce – is focused on pecuniary motives, and emphasises the importance of safety, liquidity, network effects, trade links and financial connections in determining a currency's role as a reserve currency. The 'Mars approach' – inspired by the Roman god of war – is mainly applied to the choice of a reserve currency based on strategic, diplomatic and military inducements. It is also possible to argue for a third approach: the

[63] ibid, at 508.
[64] [1882], 9 QBD 555 (UK), at 563.
[65] Rahmatian (n 57) 213.
[66] ibid.
[67] Bryan J has stated that 'Bitcoins constitute property'. See *AA v Persons Unknown & Ors, Re Bitcoin* [2019] EWHC 3556 (Comm) (UK), at 28.
[68] *Banco de Portugal v Waterlow & Sons Ltd* [1932] AC 452 (UK), at 509; Rahmatian (n 19) 213.
[69] Avgouleas and Blair (n 5) 16–17.
[70] ibid.
[71] Avgouleas and Blair (n 5) 17; Eichengreen, Mehl and Chitu (n 5).

'Yacatecuhtli approach'. Inspired by the Aztec god of trade, war and cacao, this proposed line of analysis could be structured around pecuniary, technological and political elements that could help a currency to reach a privileged position within the evolving FWS. A good case to analyse under this approach could be the CBDCs and the increasing role of infrastructure providers such as R3 in these projects.

What the case of *Banco de Portugal*[72] and the Mercury/Mars/Yacatecuhtli approaches show is how important the unquestioned belief in the stakeholder, and on the underlying obligations and infrastructures, is in monetary matters. As Milton Friedman[73] stated in his work *The Island of Stone Money*, some monies have been designed to appear 'real' and 'rational' to us, while the money of other peripheral countries/communities often seems to us like paper, worthless metal or giant stones, even when the purchasing power and the value stored within them is high in relation to their cultural traits.

V. Money as a Standard for Discharge or Satisfaction of Contractual Obligations

When the first cryptoassets were conceived, the main idea was to offer a means of payment for goods and services that would be outside the influence of the sovereign prerogatives that give form to our *ius cudendae monetae*. Today, most have become speculative commodities, but some are accepted as means of exchange in certain contexts under the *lex contractus*. However, before claiming that these units are the means of payment of the future, it is important to analyse what payment amounts to in law.

In legal sense, payment is understood in the same terms that fostered the emergence of our primitive liquidity and the first exchange transactions. Sir Roy Goode[74] defines it as 'a gift or loan of money or any act offered and accepted in performance of a monetary obligation' following the Roman maxim, *omins condemnation est pecuniaria*.[75] Consequently, a monetary *res* must be present in some way: either because payment is in physical sovereign chattels,[76] or because the obligation is discharged 'by some other operation which the creditor demands and which the debtor is either obliged or is content to perform'.[77]

[72] [1932] AC 452 (UK).
[73] M Friedman, 'The Island of Stone Money' (1991) 91 *Hoover Institution Working Papers* 1, 5.
[74] R Goode, *Goode on Commercial Law* (London, LexisNexis, 2009) 498.
[75] Mann (n 27) 65.
[76] ibid, 14.
[77] See *Libyan Arab Foreign Bank v Bankers Trust Co.* [1989] QB 728 (UK), at 764.

It is possible to argue that, based on the normative spirit of the Sales of Goods Act 1893,[78] which can also be found in the content of Regulation 2(1) of the Sale of Goods Act 1979[79] of the UK, Article 2248 of the Federal Civil Code[80] of Mexico, and cases such *Moss v Hancock*,[81] that 'payment is a concept peculiar to money, and differs from the delivery of specific goods'.[82] This is an important point. It is true that certain obligations can be fulfilled through the transfer of certain goods in isolated contexts; however, these transactions can be classified as barter agreements where the concept of uniform universal valuation is absent.[83] This was the reason behind the removal of barter transactions from the Sales of Goods Act 1893.[84] After all, money has to be structured around a uniform set of formal requirements that will be incorporated into the means of payment to be accepted universally within a community that shares common traits.

Consequently, building on these descriptions, within the universe of commodities and goods that one can find in markets around the world, two sub-universes can be identified that will constitute our means of payment. As Figure 7 shows the main universe represents all the goods and commodities that can act as means of exchange (no means of payment) in different transactions and in different markets. From this universe, market participants – as integral parts of dynamic social systems – will take some of these goods as inputs that will be processed with the aim of obtaining the rules of standardisation required to foster universal acceptance, as described by Darling J,[85] which in turn will act as the bases for the development and diffusion of inside and outside monies. Based on this, the first sub-universe can be related to the endogenous adoption of some commodities and manufactured goods as standardised means of payment that, on many occasions, will be gradually adopted, regulated and issued by a sovereign stakeholder, thus, introducing to the social dynamic system an outside money commonly identified with national currencies.

[78] Sale of Goods Act 1893.

[79] 'A contract of sale of goods is a contract by which the seller transfers or agrees to transfer the property in goods to the buyer for a money consideration, called the price.' See Sale of Goods Act 1979.

[80] 'There is a sale of goods contract when one of the parties is bound to transfer the property of a thing or a right, and in turn the other party is bound to pay for them a fixed price in money.' See Federal Civil Code DOF.

[81] [1899], 2 QB 111 (UK), at 116.

[82] M Brindle and R Cox, 'Introduction' in M Brindle and R Cox (eds), *Law of Bank Payments* (London, FT Law & Tax, 1996) 1–23, 1.

[83] See the use of 'World Cup Coins' in *Esso Petroleum Co Ltd v Customs and Excise Commissioners* [1976] 1 All ER 117 (UK); S Green, 'It's Virtually Money' in D Fox and S Green (eds), *Cryptocurrencies in Public and Private Law* (Oxford, Oxford University Press, 2019) 13–31, 20.

[84] Sale of Goods Act 1893.

[85] *Moss v Hancock* [1899], 2 QB 111 (UK), at 116.

Figure 7 Universe of means of exchange

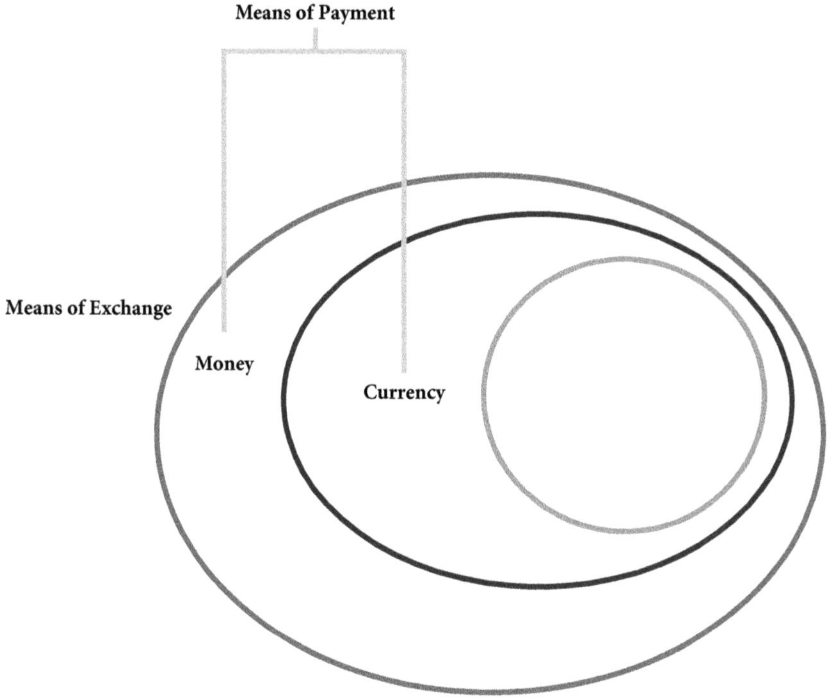

Following the definition of payment, it can be argued that the means of payment is an integral aspect of a process divisible into three parts.[86] The first is the agreement between the parties, consisting of a promise to deliver and another to pay within a stipulated period[87] 'for a money consideration called the price'.[88] After all, as is evident in the explanation provided by Hobhouse J, who quotes Francis Mann in *TSB Bank of Scotland Limited v Welwyn Hatfield District Council and Council of the London Borough of Brent*,[89] 'no payee is under legal obligation to accept any payment and no debtor can enforce any payment that has not been agreed between the parties.'

The second and the third consist of the actual delivery of goods and money by both parties involved, based on the contract description and building upon

[86] B Geva, 'The Concept of Payment Mechanism' (1986) 24 *Osgoode Hall Law Journal* 1, 5; J Hicks, *A Market Theory of Money* (Oxford, Oxford University Press, 1989) 42.

[87] J Hicks, *A Market Theory of Money* (Oxford, Oxford University Press, 1989) 42; C Proctor and V Dixon, *Goode on Payment Obligations in Commercial and Financial Transactions* (London, Thomson Reuters, 2016) 52.

[88] Introduced in Art 1 of the Sale of Goods Act 1893 and currently found within the Sale of Goods Act 1979, s. 2(1).

[89] [1993] 2 Bank LR 267 (UK), at 6.

the contents of the Sale of Goods Acts 1893[90] and 1979.[91] In the case of spot transactions that involve cash, the satisfaction of obligations occurs simultaneously, culminating in the payee's assent upon the delivery of money.[92] In this process, the payer and the payee, respectively, are in the position of a seller and buyer of money, following the spirit of the original medium of exchange function identified in Figure 7.[93] Furthermore, beyond the description found in the *Esso*[94] case, as seen in the case *Burton v* Davy,[95] it is possible to face scenarios where we can find instruments like bills of exchange and cheques, which are not legal tender but are recognised as cash by endogenous commercial practices and courts.

Kiyotaki and Moore[96] argue against analysing the means of payment involved in the satisfaction of these transactions under a primitive approach,[97] consistent in restricting the act of payment to a mere transfer of sovereign chattels. Most of the models used to explain the functions performed by money depicted it as a finite resource in form of cash bound to paradigms that resemble some of the arrangements that were in force before 1973, or even in pre-Westphalian arrangements. Accordingly, it is rather common to find in many academic sources the description of the act of payment as a set of individual interactions that involve the transference of tangible chattels.[98] Of course, it can be argued that spot payment with cash is by no means the only way of conducting our everyday transactions. While the number of transactions which are settled in cash are still relevant, particularly in economic interactions of low value or in regions where a large part of the population can be considered as unbanked, the vast majority of transactions are completed by the transfer of some kind of 'bank money' through the infrastructure provided by banks and shadow banks.[99]

As analysed in chapters one and two, throughout history, innovators have introduced different practices and instruments to ease the transfer of money

[90] Sale of Goods Act 1893.

[91] 'A contract of sale of goods is a contract by which the seller transfers or agrees to transfer the property in goods to the buyer for a money consideration, called the price.' See Sale of Goods Act 1979.

[92] B Geva, *The Payment Order of Antiquity and the Middle Ages. A Legal History* (Oxford, Hart Publishing, 2011) 32; Hicks (n 87) 42.

[93] V. Chick, 'Unresolved Questions in Monetary Theory: A Critical Review' (1978) 126 *De Economist* 37, 40; Geva (n 92) 33.

[94] *Esso Petroleum Co Ltd v Customs and Excise Commissioners* [1976] 1 All ER 117 (UK).

[95] H Hall, *Select Cases Concerning the Law Merchant AD 1251–1779. Vol III* (London, Selden Society, 1932) 117–19.

[96] N Kiyotaki and J Moore, 'Liquidity, Business Cycles, and Monetary Policy' (2001), available at www.princeton.edu/~kiyotaki/papers/ClarendonLec2.pdf, *Princeton University*.

[97] Despite the use of the term 'primitive' in different works relating to this approach, it is important to note that, for example, the Roman concept of money was not confined to coins. As one can see in texts of the Justinianic compilations, credit and credit money played an important role in Roman economy. See T Rüfner, 'Money in the Roman Law Texts' in D Fox and W Ernst (eds), *Money in the Western Legal Tradition. Middle Ages to Bretton Woods* (Oxford, Oxford University Press, 2016) 93–109, 94.

[98] See L Walras, *Elements of Pure Economics* (Illinois, Richard D Irwin, 1926); Kiyotaki and Wright (n 12).

[99] Mann (n 27) 6; Proctor and Dixon (n 87) 222.

beyond the simple use of cash. In our context, the development of electronic fund transfers has revolutionised and taken to the next level these means of discharging monetary obligations and has created the perception that current practices are closely associated to the twentieth and twenty-first centuries. However, as seen through the Genoese case presented in section V.B of chapter two,[100] the physical tender of a sum of money became an obsolete practice in business transactions during the Middle Ages. It has become outine for a creditor to designate his/her bank account to which crediting may be effected, and it is a common practice that parties in a transaction agree that this scheme is the only way of discharging the monetary obligation.[101]

Developed around the principles of legal standardisation that emerged at the end of the Thirty Years' War, cases such as, *Barclays Bank International v Levin Brothers*[102] recognise the option to be paid in a foreign currency in which the parties have more confidence[103] and/or in a large variety of assets and commodities, as in cases such as *Vick v Howard*,[104] *White v Elmdene Estates Ltd*[105] and decision SCR 100 of the Supreme Court of Canada in the Matter of Three Bills Passed by the Legislative Assembly of the Province of Alberta at the 1937 (Third Session).[106] Furthermore, if there is a need to reduce transaction costs as evidenced by Staughton J in *Libyan Arab Foreign Bank v Bankers Trust Co*,[107] it is possible to materialise payments through the infrastructure provided by the private sector using different financial instruments, such as cheques or debit cards that represent titles to money,[108] which could include interests, rents, dividends or similar.[109]

[100] D Awrey and K van Zwieten, 'The Shadow Payment System' (2018) 43 *The Journal of Corporation Law* 102–41, 110.

[101] K Sono, 'The Changing Role of Currency. Toward a Catastrophe or a New System?' (1995) 38 *The Japanese Annual of International Law* 83, 93.

[102] [1976] 3 WLR 852 (UK), 865.

[103] Mann (n 27) 145.

[104] This case presents us with a rather interesting principle: 'all money is not legal tender, though all legal tender is money'. See [1923] 116 SE 465 (US), 214.

[105] In this case, the Court argued that the word 'payment' 'may cover many ways of discharging obligations', including a discharge by what is called 'payment in kind'. See *White v Elmdene States Ltd* [1959] 2 All ER 605 (US), at 610–11. The same spirit can be found in § 2-304 (1) of the Uniform Commercial Code of the USA, which states that 'the price can be made payable in money or otherwise. If it is payable in whole or in part in goods each party is a seller of the goods which he is to transfer.'

[106] 'But money as commonly understood is not necessarily legal tender. Any medium which by practice fulfils the function of money and which everybody will accept in payment of debt is money in the ordinary sense of the words even although it may not be legal tender.' See [1938] *RE Alberta Statutes* SCR 100 (CA), at 116.

[107] [1989] QB 728 (UK), at 750–51.

[108] Goode (n 74) 513.

[109] G Papadopoulos, 'Between Rules and Power: Money as an Institution Sanctioned by Political Authority' (2009) XLIII *Journal of Economic Issues* 951, 951; BZ Yang, 'What is (not) Money? Medium of Exchange ≠ Means of Payment.' (2007) 51 *The American Economist* 101; Proctor (n 60) 34.

Even though instruments such as cheques and bills of exchange are regarded as equivalents to cash,[110] following the spirit of the *lex mercatoria*,[111] or that credit/debit cards are labelled as 'plastic money,' they are not money *per se*, even if they are sometimes referred to as such.[112] In *Ward v Evans*[113] and the thesis of jurisprudence 343,361 issued by the Third Chamber of the Supreme Court of Justice of Mexico[114] one can find that a cheque is an instrument that 'is independent relating to the original obligation'. Therefore, if a party X orders goods/services from party Y and pays the price using an instrument, such as a cheque or a bill of exchange, the obligation contained in the main contract is suspended and revives only if the referred instrument is dishonoured by non-acceptance or by non-payment at maturity.[115] Therefore, it can be said that the transfer of the piece of paper passes with it the right to enforce the obligation *reified* within it, and may confer on the transferee a better right over the transferor, thus constituting a 'documentary intangible'.[116]

Since this documentary intangible itself constitutes a separate contract, the obligations relating to the sale agreement are not fully discharged until the recipient has finally received the final settlement asset issued by the competent sovereign authority (or under its instruction), as shown in Figure 8,[117] and accurately explained by Dixon CJ of the High Court of Australia in Tilley v Official Receiver:[118]

> Prima facie when a cheque is taken for the price of goods, or for that matter in respect of any other debt contracted, it operates as conditional payment. The condition is that the cheque be paid on presentation: if it is dishonoured the debt upon the original consideration revives. The rule is, of course, an old one and the presumption applies to other negotiable instruments as well as to cheques, although perhaps not necessarily with the same strength.

[110] See *Davies v Customs and Excise Commissioners* [1975] 1 WLR 204 (UK); *The Brimnes: Tenax Steamship Co Ltd v The Brimnes (Owners)* [1974] 3 All ER 88 (UK); *Oxigen Evironmental Ltd v Mullan* [2012] NIQB 17 (UK); *CHEQUE. Su Naturaleza como Instrumento de Pago o Forma de Extinción de las Obligaciones* [2004], SCJN, Thesis of Jurisprudence III.1°.A.112 A (MX).

[111] See *Cebora SNC v SIP (Industrial Products)* [1976] 1 Lloyd's Rep 271 (UK), 278–79. In this case the Court of Appeal argued that 'Any erosion of the certainties by our Courts of the law merchant relating to bills of exchange is likely to work to the detriment of this country, which depends on international trade to a degree the needs no emphasis.'

[112] Goode (n 74) 499.

[113] Independently of the custom of the merchants, in this case, Lord Holt argued that the acceptance of a note issued by a goldsmith was not actual payment. See *Ward v Evans* [1662] 2 Ld Raym 928 (UK), at 121.

[114] *CHEQUE. Naturaleza Jurídica del* [1950], SCJN, Thesis of Jurisprudence No 343,361 (MX).

[115] R Cranston et al, *Principles of Banking Law* (Oxford, Oxford University Press, 2017) 345; Goode (n 74) 517.

[116] B Geva and S Peari, *International Negotiable Instruments* (Oxford, Oxford University Press, 2020) 6–10.

[117] These instruments have to be structured around a sovereign unit of reference, given that they are not negotiable if they are structured around other goods, such as 'good merchantable whiskey'. See *Rhodes v Lindly* [1827] 3 OH 51 (US).

[118] [1960] 103 CLR 529 HC (AU) at 532.

In other words, just as Lord Holt stated in *Ward v Evans*,[119] the acceptance of these instruments does not represent an actual payment. A payment is to be understood as a discharge of an obligation and not as an intermediate step in the exchange;[120] thus, the payee does not receive money, but something of equivalent monetary value[121] that eases the transfer of 'liquid' money from one party to another, without being themselves the final means of payment.[122] Again, we find the relevance of the words of Lord MacMillan[123] by which he made the simple distinction between the monetary *res*, and payment instruments, which represent the *reifiers* of the claim.[124]

Figure 8 Cheque as a means of payment but not a medium of exchange

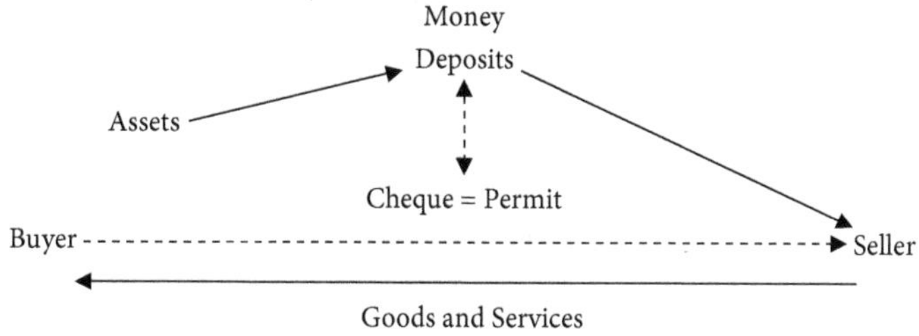

A. From Paper Instruments to Electronic Money

Paper instruments emerged as an innovation to ease the processing of money in the pre-FinTech 1.0 era.[125] They were very useful to incorporate, transport, transfer, and even to create fiat money through legal fictions. Their diffusion eventually required the development of standardised infrastructures and legal instruments, such as the *Ordonnace de Commerce* of 1673, the Bills of Exchange Act 1882, the United Nations Convention Providing a Uniform Law for Bills of Exchange and Promissory Notes and the Convention Providing a Uniform Law for Cheques, among others,[126] to foster their acceptance through the interaction between international soft law and national hard law. Certainly, paper-based instruments brought many benefits for national and international trade, but

[119] [1702] Ld Raym, 929, at 121.
[120] Papadopoulos (n 109) 958.
[121] J Huber, *Sovereign Money. Beyond Reserve Banking* (Cham, Palgrave Macmillan, 2017) 11.
[122] Proctor and Dixon (n 87) 225; Yang (n 109) 103.
[123] *Banco de Portugal v Waterlow & Sons Ltd* [1932] AC 452 (UK), at 459, 482, 485, 503.
[124] Gleeson (n 10) 15.
[125] Arner, Barberis and Buckley divide FinTech developments into three main periods: FinTech 1.0 (1866–1967), FinTech 2.0 (1967–2008) and FinTech 3.0 (2008–present). These periods are individualised based on the technological developments that have been introduced in the financial industry the last 150 years. See DW Arner, J.= Barberis and RP Buckley, '150 Years of Fintech. An Evolutionary Analysis' (2016) 3 *The Finsia Journal of Applied Finance* 22.
[126] Geva and Peari (n 116) 12–14.

also gave rise to legal challenges. For instance, as seen in cases such as *Banco de Portugal v Waterlow & Sons Ltd*[127] and *Middle Temple v Lloyds Bank*,[128] paper money is subject to forgery or mistakes without negligence during its analogical processing.

The emergence and diffusion of Informatics, allowed the automatic process of elarge volumes of data, improved decision-making, and the development of infrastructures to diffuse the acceptance of new instruments to incorporate our monetary *res*. However, despite these technological benefits, these innovations pose legal challenges. For instance, what are the legal implications of a payment materialised using other forms of money transfer such as a payment card? And, are these cards and cheques analogous modes of payment under the technology neutrality principle? In cases such as *Commissioner of Police for the Metropolis Respondent and Charles Appellant*[129] and the thesis of jurisprudence I.3o.C. 161 C (10a) issued by the Third Collegiate Tribunal on Civil Matters of the First Circuit of Mexico,[130] it can be argued, on the one hand, that cheques – just as the original bills of exchange – are no more than instructions by the drawer to the bank to pay the amount stated to the payee; thus 'if one has funds in one's current account at a bank, then one is entitled to draw on them. The bank does not give authority for a cheque to be drawn.'[131]

B. Card-Based Systems

In the case of modern card-based systems, there is a set of innovations that do not constitute legal instruments in the sense in which a bill or check are.[132] They can be defined as sets of personal data that indicate that the holder has been granted a line of credit, which in turn configures a mechanism that enables the holder to make purchases and/or withdraw cash up to a prearranged limit.[133] Consequently, the acceptance of some payment cards, such as credit cards, constitutes an unconditional discharge of the debtor, given that the card:[134]

> [I]s the representation by the drawer's production of the card that he has that authority that creates such contractual relationship and estops the bank from refusing to honour

[127] [1932] AC 452 (UK).

[128] [1999] 1 All ER Comm. 193 (UK).

[129] [1977] AC 177 (UK), at 185.

[130] *CHEQUE. Es un instrumento de pago, no de crédito por lo que es improcedente la excepción de causalidad opuesta, cuando se exige en la vía judicial* [2015] TCTCMFC, Thesis of Jurisprudence No. I.3o.C. 161 C (10a), (MX).

[131] *Commissioner of Police for the Metropolis Respondent and Charles Appellant* [1977] AC 177 (UK), at 185.

[132] T Russell, *The Economics of Bank Credit Cards* (New York, Praeger Publishers, 1975) 1.

[133] Bank for International Settlements, 'A Glossary of Terms Used in Payments and Settlement Systems' (2003), available at www.bis.org/cpmi/glossary_030301.pdf; Circular 34/2010 on the Rules for Credit Cards DOF 12 November 2010.

[134] *Commissioner of Police for the Metropolis Respondent and Charles Appellant* [1977] AC 177 (UK), at 191.

> the cheque. By drawing the cheque the accused represented that it would be met, and by producing the card so that the number thereon could be endorsed on the cheque he in effect represented, 'I am authorised by the bank to show this to you and so create a direct contractual relationship between the bank and you that they will honour this cheque.' The production of the card was the badge of the accused's ostensible authority to make such a representation on the bank's behalf.

Therefore, the cardholder becomes liable to make full payment to the issuing company following receipt of his/her statement that includes commissions and charges set by the issuer.[135] As will be see in section VI.A below, these payment cards can be considered as an underlying contractual basis within a network constituted by the participants that take part in each transaction.[136]

Based on these commercially accepted practices and the list of instruments available (that Goode[137] considers is not closed), one can argue that judgments and opinions such as the one issued by Teresa Pooler[138] relating to the nature of cryptoassets like Bitcoin, are erroneous.[139] Even though legal tender plays a major role in facilitating our monetary interactions, there exists a large variety of contracts and claims[140] such as demand deposits and checkable mutual funds, and commodities,[141] such as gold and silver, which are accepted as means of payment.[142] Consequently, building upon the words of Lord Denning MR in *Woodhouse AC Israel Cocoa Limited v Nigerian Produce Marketing Ltd*,[143] one can infer that if one pays for a coffee with Bitcoin, the unit of account will tell us *how much* we have to pay, while the money of payment tells us *by what means* we have to pay.

VI. Central Banks and Payment Infrastructures

Within today's DCS, we are witnessing and participating in different debates on the development of CBDCs. This should not be surprising; after all, central banks tend to act as settlement agents within payment systems, and they are responsible for their oversight,[144] as verified by Part 1A (Financial Stability)

[135] Proctor and Dixon (n 87) 229.

[136] Cranston, et al (n 115) 394.

[137] Goode (n 74) 513.

[138] *The State of Florida v Michelle Abner Espinoza* [2014] F14-2923 FL (US), at 5–6.

[139] PJ Eder, 'Legal Theories of Money' (1934) 20 *Cornell Law Review* 52, 69.

[140] W Hohfeld, 'Some Fundamental Legal Conceptions as Applied in Judicial Reasoning' (1914) 16 *Yale Law Journal* 16–59, 30; Rahmatian (n 57).

[141] On this point, is interesting to note that, following the criteria set on *A Ltd v B Bank* [1997] 6 Bank LR 85 CA (US), foreign currencies 'are not regarded as legal tender, but commodities or objects of commerce'.

[142] E Nosal and G Rocheteau, *Money, Payments, and Liquidity* (Massachusetts, The MIT Press, 2011) 251.

[143] [1971] 2 QB 23 (CA) (UK), at 54.

[144] R Gogoski, 'Payment Systems in Economy. Present and Future Tendencies' (2012) 44 *Procedia – Social and Behavioral Sciences* 436, 439.

of the Bank of England Act 1998 and in the CHAPS Reference Manual.[145] As chapter two showed, through the case of proto-central banks, the evolution of payment systems has been closely related to the diffusion of central banking[146] through governance paradigms, such as clearing houses, interbank settlement arrangements[147] and the selection of infrastructural providers as presented in the *Banco de Portugal*[148] case.

Generally, it is argued that, as an integral part of the sovereign exercise of the *lex monetae*, central banks support the evolution of our payment systems through clearing, settlement and lending services,[149] and, of course, through regulation, particularly after the collapse of the NIFA framework. On this last point, one function is very important for the development of payment systems, but is unfortunately under-studied: the selection of and the interaction with operators of payment systems. For instance, the Bank of England, building on the content of sections 184, 188, 189 and 206A of the Banking Act 2009,[150] is empowered to issue codes and publish principles applicable to different stakeholders throughout payment systems; instruments that are interoperable with principles like those published by the BIS[151] on operational resilience.

On these roles, we are witnessing how central banks are becoming more involved on the DevOps culture[152] related to the development and testing of new payment systems such as Helvetia,[153] Polaris[154] and Icebreaker.[155] But before discussing the role of central banks in the development and regulation of new payment systems based on DLT, we first have to understand what a payments system is.

[145] See www.bankofengland.co.uk/-/media/boe/files/payments/chaps/chaps-reference-manual.pdf.

[146] C Kahn, S Quinn and W Roberds, 'Central Banks and Payment Systems: The Evolving Trade-off between Cost and Risk' (2014), available at www.norges-bank.no/contentassets/3fba8b3a3432407d929ae9218db1ffc4/10_kahn_quinn_roberds2014.pdf.

[147] B Norman, R Shaw and G Speight, 'The history of interbank settlement arrangements: exploring central banks' role in the payment system' (2011), available at www.bankofengland.co.uk/working-paper/2011/the-history-of-interbank-settlement-arrangements-exploring-central-banks-role-in-the-payment-system.

[148] *Banco de Portugal v Waterlow & Sons Ltd* [1932] AC 452 (UK).

[149] JM Lacker, 'Payment Economics and the Role of Central Banks' (2005), available at www.richmondfed.org/-/media/RichmondFedOrg/press_room/speeches/president_jeff_lacker/2005/pdf/lacker_speech_20050520.pdf.

[150] Banking Act 2009.

[151] Bank for International Settlements. 'Principles for Operational Resilience' (2021), available at www.bis.org/bcbs/publ/d516.htm.

[152] For instance, we can access some public repositories in GitHub related to data and software developed by central banks such as the Bank of England. See github.com/orgs/bank-of-england/repositories.

[153] Bank for International Settlements. 'Project Helvetia: A Multi-Phase Investigation on the Settlement of Tokenised Assets in Central Bank Money' (2022), available at www.bis.org/about/bisih/topics/cbdc/helvetia.htm.

[154] Bank for International Settlements. 'Project Polaris: Handbook for offline payments with CBDC' (2023), available at www.bis.org/publ/othp64.htm.

[155] Bank for International Settlements. 'Project Icebreaker concludes experiment for a new architecture for cross-border retail CBDCs' (2023), available at www.bis.org/about/bisih/topics/cbdc/icebreaker.htm.

A. Payment Systems

Collectively, payment systems around the world facilitate over US $400 trillion in non-cash transactions per year, approximately five times the total value of the global gross domestic product.[156] But, what is a payments system? Following legislation such as Article 2(1) of the ECB's regulation 795/2014[157] and Article 4(7) of the Directive 2015/2366,[158] commonly known as the Payment Services Directive 2 (PSD2), a payments system can be defined as a funds transfer system based on formal and standardised arrangements among three or more participants, with common rules for the processing, clearing and/or settlement of payment transactions. However, the spirit of this definition could be seen as being structured to describe the interactions developed by banks, as normative instruments like Regulation 182(2) of the Banking Act 2009[159] of the UK and the PSD2 exhort us to take into consideration a new generation of digital shadow banks in this definition.[160]

As shown in current analyses relating to the potential creation of CBDCs, the institutional arrangements that configure our payment systems fall into two categories: wholesale payment systems; and retail payment systems.[161] The first category is composed by those systems with a high volume of value transfer, typically used by financial institutions to settle mutual obligations and, in some cases, between these institutions and their large commercial clients.[162] The second category is comprised of retail payment systems that facilitate the flow of funds among and between businesses, households and governments. Retail payment systems include those facilitating the use of debit and credit cards, automated teller machines (ATMs), cheques and electronic fund transfers (EFT). While conceptually distinct, wholesale and retail payment systems are often highly interconnected from an operational perspective.[163]

[156] Awrey and van Zwieten (n 100) 102.

[157] Regulation of the European Central Bank 795/2014 on oversight requirements for systemically important payment systems OJ L 217/16, 3 July 2014.

[158] Directive 2015/2366 of the European Parliament and of the Council on payment services in the internal market, amending Directives 2002/65/EC, 2009/110/EC and 2013/36/EU and Regulation (EU) No 1093/2010, and repealing Directive 2007/64/EC OJ L 337/35, 25 November 2015.

[159] Regulation 182(2) states that 'the fact that persons other than financial institutions can participate does not prevent arrangements from being an inter-bank payment system.' See Banking Act 2009.

[160] PSD2 pays particular attention to 'payment initiation service', which is defined in Art 4(15) as 'means a service to initiate a payment order at the request of the payment service user with respect to a payment account held at another payment service provider.'

[161] M Bech and R Garratt, 'Central Bank Cryptocurrencies' (2017), available at www.bis.org/publ/qtrpdf/r_qt1709f.htm.

[162] H Scott, 'The Importance of the Retail Payment System' (2015), available at dash.harvard.edu/bitstream/handle/1/16883011/hal-scott---mastercard-retail-payment-systems.pdf?sequence=1; Awrey and van Zwieten (n 100) 107–08.

[163] Awrey and van Zwieten (n 100) 107–08.

At its simplest, as evident in Article 3(3) of the Settlement Finality Directive 98/26/EC,[164] and in cases such as *Dubai Islamic Bank PJSC v Paymentech Merchant Services INC*,[165] the transfers of funds among different financial institutions is not controlled by substantive law, but by governance arrangements. When thinking of governance, there is a notion that good governance model has to be provided by the state. This would sound logical following the sovereign exercise of the *lex monetae* that acts as the cornerstone of our monetary systems. However, governance and government should not be regarded as synonymous. To understand the difference between these two terms, Avinash Dixit[166] defines governance, following the spirit of our Socio-Legal approach, as: 'the structure and functioning of the legal and social institutions that support economic activity and economic transactions by protecting property rights, enforcing contracts, and taking collective action to provide physical and organizational infrastructure.'

Following this definition, as seen in *Ohio, et al v American Express Company, et al*,[167] these transactions rely on networks of contracts that set the rules of interaction based on the particular set of circumstances that each system has to face. Non-compliance, just as it was seen through the hypothetical origin of money in chapter 1 section II.B, could result in a disciplinary action, and, ultimately, in the exclusion from the payments system.[168]

Again, while one might be tempted to think of money as a set of physical sovereign chattels, most payment systems today transfer money following two models: 1) a credit transfer system, generally slower and cheaper; and 2) wires, which are faster and more expensive.[169] Typically, a non-cash payment transaction between a payer and a payee presupposes both to have accounts with financial institutions, usually deposit-taking institutions, as described in Regulation 2(1) of the Banking Act 2009[170] of the UK and Article 2 of the Mexican Credit

[164] 'The moment of entry of a transfer order into a system shall be defined by the rules of that system. If there are conditions laid down in the national law governing the system as to the moment of entry, the rules of that system must be in accordance with such conditions.' See Directive 98/26/EC of the European Parliament and of the Council on settlement finality in payment and securities settlement systems OJ L 166/45, 19 May 1998.

[165] On this point, Aikens J describes the relevance of the Visa International Operating Regulations in the development of the interactions within the VISA network. See [2001] 1 Lloyd's Rep. 65 (UK), at 517–18.

[166] A Dixit, 'Governance Institutions and Economic Activity' (2009) 99 *The American Economic Review* 3, 5.

[167] [2018] 16-1454 (US), at 2.

[168] Cranston et al (n 115) 353.

[169] E McCune, 'There Is No Such Thing as an International Wire' (2014), available at pv.glenbrook.com/there-is-no-such-thing-as-an-international-wire; MT Rosner and A Kang, 'Understanding and Regulating Twenty-First Century Payment Systems: The Ripple Case Study' (2016) 114 *Michigan Law Review* 650–81, 652.

[170] 'In this Part "bank" means a UK institution which has permission under [F1Part 4A] of the Financial Services and Markets Act 2000 to carry on the regulated activity of accepting deposits (within the meaning of Regulation 22 of that Act, taken with Schedule 2 and any order under Regulation 22).' See Banking Act 2009.

Institutions Law,[171] or as explained by Lord Denning and Harman LJ in *United Dominions Trust v Kirkwood.*[172] These transactions can be divided into credit and debit transfers according to the constitution of their underlying obligations and the way the payment instruction is communicated to the payer's bank.[173] In a credit transfer, the payer instructs his/her bank to pay; thus, the bank responds by debiting his/her account, and the account of the payee, at the same or other bank, is credited within a two-sided market.[174] On the other hand, in a debit transfer, the sequence begins with the payer authorising his/her bank to pay, but actual payment is initiated when the payee conveys a payment instruction to his/her own bank to collect money from the payer's bank.[175]

The payments through the banking system are made by reducing the balance in a customer's account and increasing the balance in the recipient's account by an equivalent amount, a process that barely has changed since the sixteenth century.[176] The difference lies in the technology employed to record the balances and the transfers materialised among different banks.[177] Debiting the debtor's bank account and crediting the creditor's bank account are accounting techniques, which are similar to the disposition in which a company that holds two accounts in separate branches of a bank instructs the bank to debit one for the credit of the other for a specific amount. As seen in *Joachimson v Swiss Bank Corporation,*[178] *Royal Products Ltd v Midland Bank Ltd*[179] and *Dovey v Bank of New Zealand,*[180] the execution of payments through the banking system relies on four integrated elements: the availability of funds; the payment order; the movements on accounts; and the processes of clearing and settlement.[181]

It is therefore inaccurate to speak of the 'transfer of funds' as there is no actual transfer of money from the payer to the payee and no assignment of the debt owed to the payer by his/her own bank, as observed in *Libyan Arab Foreign Bank v Bankers Trust Co,*[182] where Staughton J observed that: '"Transfer" may be a somewhat misleading word, since the original obligation is not assigned

[171] 'For purposes of the provisions of this Law, it shall be considered as banking and credit service the raising of funds from the public within the domestic market for their placement among the public, through acts resulting in direct or contingent liabilities, being the intermediary bound to cover the principal and, as the case may be, the financial ancillaries of the funds raised.' See Credit Institutions Law DOF.

[172] See [1966] 2 QB 431 (UK), at 447, 465.

[173] R Hooley and JC Taylor, 'Payment by Funds Transfer' in M Brindle and R Cox (eds), *Law of Bank Payments* (London FT Law & Tax, 1996) 25–142, 26.

[174] *Ohio, et al v American Express Company, et al* [2018] 16-1454 (US), at 2.

[175] Cranston et al (n 115) 338; Hooley and Taylor (n 173) 27–28.

[176] R Ali et al, 'Innovation in Payment Technologies and the Emergence of Digital Currencies' (2014) 263, available at www.bankofengland.co.uk/-/media/boe/files/quarterly-bulletin/2014/innovations-in-payment-technologies-and-the-emergence-of-digital-currencies.pdf.

[177] ibid.

[178] [1921] 3 KB 110 (UK).

[179] [1981] Lloyd's Rep 194 (UK).

[180] [2000] 3 NZLR 641 (UK).

[181] Cranston et al (n 115) 337.

[182] [1989] QB 728 (UK), at 750.

(notwithstanding dicta in one American case which speaks of assignment); a new obligation by a new debtor is created.'

On this point, it could be argued that it does not consider the existence of an international wire. However, one can soundly affirm that there is no international wire;[183] a fact that has fostered the development of several DLT projects, such as Ripple and JPM Coin. Building upon the definition provided by Dixit,[184] payment systems are governance paradigms in which participant intermediaries agree to cooperate with each other with the aim to transfer messages of economic and legal value. Within the practice of international transfers, there is a decentralised network of agreements among different institutions in different jurisdictions fulfilling the payment orders through domestic transactions as seen in cases such as *Dubai Islamic Bank PJSC v Paymentech Merchant Services INC.*[185] In other words, it is an illusion that money moves freely beyond national borders via different transfers.

The language sometimes used, such as 'funds transfer', conjures up an image of the tangible transferences of funds or property, such as those developed in chapter one. Legal analyses that cover the payments system, like the one relating to the English doctrine of tracing, have been bewitched in the past by this image of money or property moving along a chain. This image has been analysed by Lord Millet, who highlighted in *Foskett v McKeown and Others*[186] that:

> We speak of tracing money into and out of the account, but there is no money in the account. There is merely a single debt of an amount equal to the final balance standing to the credit of the account. No money passes from paying bank to receiving bank or through the clearing system.

Furthermore, in *R v Preddy*,[187] Lord Jauncey of Tullichettle stated the use of the word 'money' in these contexts is used for convenience, 'but it is of course simply a sum entered into the books of the bank' with nothing really being transferred.[188] Consequently, it can be inferred, based on the analysis of the first acts of *reification* in chapter one, that money is a form of dematerialised property.[189]

B. Payment Orders, Clearing Arrangements and Interbank Settlements

Following the practices introduced by the bill of exchange, payment orders can be defined as unconditional instructions to effect payments in favour of a payee,

[183] McCune (n 169).
[184] Dixit (n 166) 5.
[185] [2001] 1 Lloyd's Rep. 65 (UK).
[186] [2001] 1 AC 102 (UK), at 127–28.
[187] [1996] AC 815 (UK), at 17.
[188] Cranston et al. (n 115) 338; Gleeson (n 10) 168.
[189] Gleeson (n 10) 14.

which will be divided among the customer's mandate to its bank – who acts as the original drawee – to pay, the instruction, which that bank then sends to another bank, and so on. Traditionally, these orders were paper-based, but outside the realm of cheques and bills of exchange, they are now conveyed electronically, through the use of payment cards, debit cards, credit and charge cards, prepaid cards, and the providers of payment initiation services described in the PSD2.[190] For such payment orders, where the payer and the payee have accounts in different banks, interbank clearing is required. Clearing is the process of transmitting, reconciling, and, on some occasions, confirming payment transactions prior to settlement based on the nature of the payment order employed or the existent agreements among the banks involved.[191] It may include the netting of transactions and the establishment of final positions for settlement,[192] and it takes place in clearing houses, or otherwise over clearing facilities that are specialised according to the instrument employed.[193]

On this point, as a result of the introduction of algorithmic automation in the financial industry during the 1960s[194] and the analyses issued in the 1980s by working groups, such as that chaired by Dennis M Child, three groups of clearings can be identified: 1) bulk paper clearings (cheques and paper credit clearing); 2) high-value clearing (CHAPS); and 3) electronic bulk clearings (BACS).[195] The Child report recommended that membership to these governance arrangements be open to all appropriately regulated institutions.[196] For example, given this specialisation, if a cheque is involved in a transaction materialised in the UK, the Cheque and Credit Clearing Company will manage the interaction.[197] Clearing is followed by interbank settlement that, in the case of transactions that involve two or more domestic large banks, is typically carried out over the books of the domestic central bank.[198]

Settlement can be defined as the transfer of value to discharge a payment obligation.[199] As one can infer from the descriptions found in *United Dominions Trust v Kirkwood*,[200] the process starts when a customer creates an underlying *res* that acts as source of liquidity through a deposit balance into his/her account. If this customer needs to discharge a payment obligation, the bank, acting as an intermediary drawee in the payment process, uses these deposits to 'transfer' money from

[190] Bank for International Settlements, 'Payment, Clearing and Settlement Systems in the United Kingdom' (2012), available at www.bis.org/cpmi/publ/d105_uk.pdf; Cranston et al (n 115) 337.
[191] Cranston et al (n 115) 349.
[192] ibid.
[193] A Arora, *Electronic Banking and the Law* (London, Banking Technology, 1993) 9.
[194] A Sweetman. *Cyber and the City. Securing London's Banks in the Computer Age* (Cham, Springer Nature, 2002) 13.
[195] Arora (n 193).
[196] ibid.
[197] Bank for International Settlements (n 190).
[198] Geva (n 92) 24.
[199] Cranston et al (n 115) 349.
[200] See [1966] 2 QB 431 (UK), at 447, 465.

the payer's account to the payee's bank account by decreasing the payer's deposit balance account and increasing the payee's deposit balance account.[201]

Despite the application of new technology over the past 60 years, the *lex monetae* sets the constitutional framework for a hierarchy of paymasters.[202] At the heart lies the central bank, which acts as paymaster to commercial banks and payment service providers, and these intermediaries act as paymasters to the rest of the economy.[203] For instance, the Bank of England currently supports four settlement models for payment systems: 1) real-time gross settlement (RTGS); 2) delivery versus payment; 3) prefunded; and 4) unfunded models for deferred net settlements.[204] Each participant, typically a commercial bank, holds a balance – constituted independently of the legal reserves – at the central bank, which is recorded in the ledger, but also reflected in the participant bank's own ledger. Individual customers, branches, or even smaller intermediaries would then hold balances at the participant bank, which would, again, be reflected in its own ledger.[205]

Historically, given that these arrangements can be classified as governance models, the operation of payment systems has not been subject to the same supervision as banks. The systemic consequences of large-value payment system failures have been the main element in the calls issued for greater action given that the intermediaries that participate in these systems incur serious intraday credit exposure, which, in turn, gives rise to settlement failures and, consequently, systemic risk.[206] It could also result in calls on the central bank to provide liquidity through lender-of-last-resort facilities,[207] even if the respective normative contains terms against it.

C. Electronic Fund Transfers (EFTs)

With the emergence of the internet and its principles of decentralisation, self-financing and local/institutional management,[208] electronic money emerged as the third great monetary *Bildungstrieb* following coins and paper-based money. This process relied on the Lancasterian theory, which states that when there are changes in the environment, such as the introduction of new technologies, one can witness the emergence or the increase of a demand for new financial products.[209]

[201] Cranston et al (n 115) 349; Rosner and Kang (n 169) 652.

[202] A paymaster can be defined as 'a person who provides payment services'. See Gleeson (n 10) 94.

[203] ibid.

[204] Bank of England, 'RTGS Renewal Programme Proof of Concept: Supporting DLT Settlement Models' (2018), available at www.bankofengland.co.uk/news/2018/july/rtgs-renewal-programme-proof-of-concept-supporting-dlt-settlement-models.

[205] Ali et al (n 176) 263.

[206] K Alexander, R Dhumale and J Eatwell, *Global Governance of Financial Systems. The International Regulation of Systemic Risk* (New York, Oxford University Press, 2006) 184.

[207] Cranston et al (n 115) 354.

[208] M Becerra-Ramírez, *La Propiedad Intelectual en Transformación* (Porrúa, Mexico City, 2009) 128.

[209] P Artus and C de Boissieu, 'The Process of Financial Innovation: Causes, Forms, and Consequences' in A Heertje (ed), *Innovation, Technology, and Finance* (Oxford, European Investment Bank, 1988) 101–26, 110; Arora (n 193) 1–2.

As seen in the explanation provided by Davies LJ in *The Brimnes: Tenax Steamship Co Ltd v The Brimnes (Owners)*,[210] during the transitions between the FinTech 1.0 and FinTech 2.0 eras,[211] the transfer of money employing technologies like telex, and long before it, the telephone, familiarised bankers with paperless transfers.[212] At present, there are EFT networks such as BACS and CHAPS in the UK, FEDNow and FEDWire in the USA, and SPEI and CoDi in Mexico,[213] that just as in the case of cryptoassets in our context post-NIFA, reflect a set of changing social and economic expectations.

Electronic money differs from other existing means of payment in several ways. First, in comparison with cash, which uses only physical security features, electronic money products depend on smartcard- and software-based systems whose execution is structured around symmetric and asymmetric cryptographic codes to authenticate transactions, and to protect the confidentiality and the integrity of data.[214] Secondly, in contrast to DLT, an EFT relies on a string of contracts, none of which brings into existence a negotiable instrument, as explained by Lord Millet in *Foskett v McKeown and Others*.[215] Thirdly, a negotiable instrument is payable to the payee's order; however, an EFT does not assume on its face the form of an unconditional order.[216] Fourthly, while a negotiable instrument is in itself the subject of transfer and/or negotiation, and EFT is created in order to be redeemed.[217] Finally, cash represents an anonymous means of exchange in stark contrast to EFTs, which are based on non-anonymous record-keeping devices and acts of processing among controllers and processors.[218]

Based on these characteristics, and building upon normative instruments, such as section 2(1) of the Electronic Money Regulations 2011[219] of the UK, and Article 2(2) of the 2EMD,[220] electronic money can be defined as monetary value represented by a claim and stored electronically in a device, such as a chip on a plastic card or a hard drive in a personal computer, that is issued on receipt

[210] [1974] 3 All ER 88 (UK), at 623.

[211] Arner, Barberis and Buckley (n 125) 22–23.

[212] E Smart, 'Electronic Banking. An Overview of the Legal Implications' in RM Goode (ed), *Electronic Banking. The Legal Implications* (London, The Institute of Bankers, 1985) 1–4, 1.

[213] P Ellinger, 'Electronic Funds Transfer as a Deferred Settlement System' in RM Goode (ed), *Electronic Banking. The Legal Implications* (London, The Institute of Bankers, 1985) 29–44, 30.

[214] L Edgar, 'Electronic Money' in C Reed, I Walden and L Edgar (eds), *Cross-Border Electronic Banking. Challenges and Opportunities* (London, LLP Professional Publishing, 2000) 201–21, 202; J Téllez-Valdés, *Derecho Informático* (Mexico City, McGraw-Hill, 2008) 112–13.

[215] [2001] 1 AC 102 (UK), at 127–28.

[216] Edgar (n 214) 202; Ellinger (n 213) 34.

[217] C Reed, *Electronic Finance Law* (Cambridge, Woodhead-Faulkner, 1991) 2; Ellinger (n 213) 34–35; Gleeson (n 10) 97.

[218] CM Kahn, J McAndrews and W Roberds, 'Money Is Privacy' (2005) 46 *International Economic Review* 377, 378.

[219] The Electronic Money Regulations 2011 (SI 2011/99).

[220] Directive 2009/110/EC of the European Parliament and of the Council on the taking up, pursuit and prudential supervision of the business of electronic money institutions amending Directives 2005/60/EC and 2006/48/EC and repealing Directive 2000/46/EC OJ L 267/7, 16 September 2009.

of funds and accepted as a means of payment by a person other than the electronic money issuer.[221] Thus, electronic money is basically a claim-*res* on an issuer stored in electronic form[222] that shares common elements with other definitions of 'money', such as the one provided in *Moss v Hancock*.[223] For that very reason, and because electronic money is issued on receipt of funds, its balances are usually denominated in the same referential unit as central bank money, and can easily be exchanged at par value for them or redeemed in cash.[224]

Given the wide offer of electronic payment services available in the market, we could be tempted to identify two categories of electronic money. The first tends to be identified with electronic purses or digital wallets, which work around pre-loaded monetary value in cards or devices that can be used to acquire low-value goods and services from retailers.[225] The second form is digital cash, which enables a person to upload funds from a bank account or credit card to an internet-based account that may be used to pay for goods and services as one can verify through payment systems like *PayPal*.[226] However, although both electronic representations are usually exchanged in centralised infrastructures, where a trusted entity sets the rules of interaction, clears and settles transactions,[227] the first category cannot be defined as electronic money given that in order to be labelled as such, a product must be capable of being used to make payments to persons other than the issuer.[228]

Certainly, electronic money eases our interactions in digital environments; however, its use is not free of difficulties. The use of EFTs introduces high transaction costs, new forms of fraudulent activity and – as seen in *Ohio, et al v American Express Company, et al* and *Dubai Islamic Bank PJSC v Paymentech Merchant Services INC*[229] – complexities related to the intervention of multiple parties and technologies in the processing of a single payment throughout a global decentralised network of payments services providers.[230] Accordingly, banks and the referred services providers are considered the most exposed to cyber threats due to the relative ease with which the end user – typically the weakest link in the security chain – can be attacked.[231] The set of risks that our payment systems face are classified into three categories: 1) card-related; 2) merchant-related; and 3)

[221] Bank for International Settlements, 'Digital Currencies' (2015), available at www.bis.org/cpmi/publ/d137.pdf; Huber (n 121) 12.

[222] Gleeson (n 10) 205.

[223] [1899] 2 QB 111 (UK), at 116.

[224] Bank for International Settlements (n 221).

[225] Cranston, et al (n 10) 366.

[226] ibid.

[227] Bech and Garratt (n 161); Bank for International Settlements (n 221).

[228] Gleeson (n 10) 205.

[229] [2018] 16-1454 (US).

[230] D Abrazhevich, 'Classification and Characteristics of Electronic Payment Systems' in K Bauknecht, S Kumar Madria and G Pernul (eds), *Electronic Commerce and Web Technologies* (Berlin, Springer-Verlag, 2001) 81–90, 81.

[231] A Fazio and F Zuffranieri, 'Interbank Payment System Architecture from a Cyber Security Perspective' (2018) 418 *Questioni di Economia e Finanza* 1–19, 5.

internet-related, which in turn are addressed through the use of cryptography.[232] To address these risks, and considering the emergence of new technologies, such as DLT, AI and 5G, financial regulators are launching several initiatives to enhance cyber resilience of our financial systems,[233] among which we find the interoperability among different regulatory frameworks on incident reporting and operational resilience, such as the NIS2 Directive, Article 32(c) of the GDPR,[234] Article 96 of the PSD2,[235] among others.

With the elements that define electronic money in mind, some institutions, such as the FCA,[236] have posed the following question: can we regulate cryptoassets under the existent normative applied to electronic money? The answer for now is no. At least, not under the present conditions of the cryptoassets market. As expressed by the Court of Justice of the European Union (EU) in *Skatteverket v Hedqvist*:[237]

> Virtual currencies differ from electronic money, as defined in Directive 2009/110/EC of the European Parliament and the Council of 16 September 2009 on the taking up, pursuit and prudential supervision of the business of electronic money institutions amending Directives 2005/60/EC and 2006/48/EC and repealing Directive 2000/46/EC (OJ 2009 L 267, p. 7), in so far as, unlike that money, for virtual currencies the funds are not expressed in traditional accounting units, such as in euro, but in virtual accounting units, such as the 'bitcoin'.

Furthermore, most cryptoassets do not fit in that definition because they are not 'issued on receipt of funds' and, as one can see in the case of Bitcoin, some of them lack an 'electronic money issuer' against which users of the unit can exercise a claim,[238] thus fostering discussions that invoke the classification of property developed by Sir William Blackstone. Of course, as it will be developed in chapters four and five, the evolution of DLT in favour of more centralised models and the emergence of stablecoins backed by sovereign currencies could foster the gradual emergence of instruments that could fit in the legal definition of electronic money.

[232] M Ndaw, G Mendy and S Ouya, 'Modelling the Effect of Security Measures on Electronic Payment Risks' in A Abraham et al (eds), *Innovations in Bio-Inspired Computing and Applications* (Cham, Springer, 2017) 255–65, 256.

[233] Fazio and Zuffranieri (n 231).

[234] '1. Taking into account the state of the art, the costs of implementation and the nature, scope, context and purposes of processing as well as the risk of varying likelihood and severity for the rights and freedoms of natural persons, the controller and the processor shall implement appropriate technical and organisational measures to ensure a level of security appropriate to the risk, including inter alia as appropriate: … (c) the ability to restore the availability and access to personal data in a timely manner in the event of a physical or technical incident.'

[235] In the case of a major operational or security incident, payment service providers shall, without undue delay, notify the competent authority in the home Member State of the payment service provider.

[236] Financial Conduct Authority, 'Guidance on Cryptoassets' (2019), available at www.fca.org.uk/publication/consultation/cp19-03.pdf.

[237] [2015] C-264/14 (EU).

[238] Proctor and Dixon (n 87) 269.

Despite the existence of the sovereign elements mentioned above, and the opinion of Friedman and Schwartz[239] on the irrelevance of the terms 'inside money' and 'outside money', several authors[240] argue that money is a creation of private commerce; thus, we can identify two basic kinds of money that have derived from the *jus cundendae monetae*. The first represents sovereign money generated by an empowered authority, including coins minted by treasuries and notes issued by central banks, while the second represents bank money on account and as electronic money in mobile sub-accounts, introduced through different governance arrangements.

VII. Conclusion

This chapter has illustrated how the figure of the stakeholder analysed in chapter two and introduced in our first definition of 'money', is identified with the post-Westphalian state and its exercise of *lex monetae*. The relevance of this sovereign prerogative was highlighted across this chapter to foster its proper understanding beyond the simple constitution of monopolies in the supply of currency, given that it influences the existence and the design of both 'inside money' and 'outside money'. Accordingly, the three main functions employed to define 'money' are standardised, although that does not mean that the law does not allow them to be separated or for them to be used together according to the context of each transaction, as can be inferred from the words of Mocatta J in *Barclays Bank International v Levin Brothers*.[241]

Following the definition of 'money' presented in chapter two, and the elements that configure monetary functions in law under the light of this chapter, one could define money, from a legal perspective, as those monetary *reifiers* defined by a sovereign stakeholder, which are structured around a sovereign unit of reference by which members of a community, other than the same stakeholder, can discharge private and public obligations, according to the practices and technologies recognised in the transaction's socio-legal context. The use of this definition is not restricted to 'outside monies'; however, independently of the *reifier* employed to fulfil the respective obligations, the underlying social contract is present through the unit of account.

The identity of each system is related to the function of money as unit of account, which in our post-Bretton Woods models is an abstract and ideal unit of reference independent from the other two functions, as seen in the words

[239] M Friedman and AJ Schwartz, 'Has Government Any Role in Money?' in AJ Schwartz (ed), *Money in Historical Perspective* (Chicago, University of Chicago Press, 1987) 289–314, 295.

[240] See A Pettifor, *The Production of Money. How to Break the Power of Bankers* (London, Verso, 2017); Huber (n 121) 39–42.

[241] [1976] 3 WLR 852 (UK), at 865.

of Lord MacMillan[242] in *Banco de Portugal v Waterlow & Sons Ltd*, and even from other alternative units that are subject to the *lex contractus.* Some innovators and enthusiasts argue that cryptoassets like Bitcoin, LIBRA or XRP could foster the creation of a universal unit of reference; unfortunately, an effort of that nature would need a universal underlying social contract. The closest thing that we have to that aim is related to the function of money as store of value following the socioeconomic, diplomatic and military inducements that define the positions of reserve currencies within our FWS building upon the Mercury/Mars/Yacatecuhtli approaches.

In stark contrast to the common views of money as chattels that circulate within our economies, cases such as *Carr v Carr*,[243] *Folley v Hill*[244] and *Libyan Arab Foreign Bank v Bankers Trust Co*,[245] highlight the fact that money keeps evolving as a *reified* claim throughout a set of infrastructures known as payment systems. As can be verified through the cases of RTGSs, EFTs and cryptoassets, the private sector tends to provide the technological infrastructure for the development of these governance arrangements; however, at the core of these there is still a *lex monetae.* Sovereign institutions such as central banks act as the anchors of these infrastructures –which allow private parties to process payment orders and settle obligations – while they fulfil their constitutional mandates related to the stability of the sovereign unit of reference. Do they exercise their constitutional power without frictions? The answer is no.

Throughout history, different paradigms have emerged by which the private sector creates money under the conditions set by the state, which tolerates and/or adopts them. Among these models is the FMC model described by Jakab and Kumhof,[246] which evidences the anachronistic nature of the ILF model, and free-banking models structured around regional social contracts. On this point, some communities are taking advantage of new technologies like DLT to incorporate the referred agreements. During the Monetary Innovation and Complementary Currencies Researcher Symposium held on 25 October 2018 in Geneva, different and interesting presentations relating to certain 'community currencies' developed in Portugal, Spain and Switzerland were highlighted as making the transition from paper-based instruments to digital representations of these latter using DLT and protocols such Proof-of-Location (PoL). Illustrations of these projects are the *léman* and its crypto-wallet *Biletujo.* According to the General

[242] [1932] AC 452 (UK), at 459, 482, 485, 503.

[243] JH Merivale, *Reports of Cases Argued and Determined in the High Court of Chancery. Vol 1* (London, Joseph Butterworth and Son, 1817) 541.

[244] [1848] 2 HLC 28 (UK), at 36.

[245] [1989] QB 728 (UK), at 748.

[246] Z Jakab and M Kumhof, 'Banks Are Not Intermediaries of Loanable Funds. Facts, Theory and Evidence' (2019), available at www.bankofengland.co.uk/-/media/boe/files/working-paper/2018/banks-are-not-intermediaries-of-loanable-funds-facts-theory-and-evidence.pdf?la=en&hash=5FCDED87A783AA0483319CD4351170DB94C8A771.

Secretary of the project, Antonin Calderon, this unit was introduced in Geneva in 2015 and was used to acquire products and services in 550 local shops and businesses within the city, thus reflecting a social contract within it that acts as its source of liquidity. However, the biggest debate regarding this technology starts with a particular unit, the one that introduced the use of DLT for monetary applications: Bitcoin.

4

Legal-Economic Analysis of Cryptoassets

I. Introduction

Throughout history, many different decentralised and anonymous payment systems have been utilised, cash being the system that most of us use. Banknotes and coins – in contrast to nominative negotiable instruments, such as cheques and promissory notes – are instruments that can be used by anyone, but they do not carry any information other than 'value', and so information attached to payment activities such as who pays whom and when, is not managed by any commercial and/or central bank.[1] In other words, these transactions are anonymous following the old doctrine of the Common Law found in cases such as *Carr v Carr*[2] and *Moss v Hancock*,[3] which states that 'money has no earmark'. Consequently, one can infer that new arguments in favour of decentralisation and anonymisation of money are the result of the evolution of our payment systems, which currently rely on two inventions that highlight the dematerialised nature of our monetary *res* while, at the same time, have provided new tools to constitute new digital 'panopticons':[4] computer-based money and the internet.

Based on these inventions and their respective processes of innovation and diffusion, our dynamic social systems and their respective markets have been subject to a continuous evolution towards digitalisation, as evidenced by, for example, the increasing role of third-party online marke places, which witnessed escalations in sales between 10 and 50 per cent after the outbreak of the COVID-19 crisis.[5] However, while these technologies offer us instant gratification and a means to transmit information to materialise these transactions, concerns

[1] H Nakaso, 'Future of Central Bank Payment and Settlement Systems under Economic Globalization and Technological Innovation' (2017), available at www.bis.org/review/r170425h.pdf.

[2] JH Merivale, *Reports of Cases Argued and Determined in the High Court of Chancery. Vol 1* (London, Joseph Butterworth and Son, 1817) 541.

[3] [1899], 2 QB 111 (UK), at 114.

[4] See U Kohl, 'The Rise of Online Intermediaries in the Governance of the Internet and Beyond' (2012) 26 *International Review of Law, Computers & Technology* 185, 187–88.

[5] United Nations Conference on Trade and Development, 'COVID-19 and E-Commerce. Impact on Businesses and Policy Responses.' (2020), available at unctad.org/system/files/official-document/dtlstictinf2020d2_en.pdf.

about operational resilience[6] have given rise to governance paradigms and international standards, such as the NIST framework,[7] the ISO 20022[8] and the CPMI-IOSCO guidance for cyber-resilience of financial market infrastructures.[9] With these concerns in mind, Bitcoin was launched on an internet mailing list for cryptographers on 1 November 2008 by an individual or group named Satoshi Nakamoto.[10] In this email, Nakamoto announced that they had 'been working on a new electronic cash system that's fully peer-to-peer, with no trusted third party'.[11]

The authors of the first generation of academic scholarship on the internet argued that, considering its transnational nature, commercial activities developed online cannot be regulated through individual efforts, and so should be governed by a new *lex mercatoria*[12] or even by a constitution for cyberspace.[13] Regarding the creation of means of payment in this new environment, in the 1990s, authors such as Chris Reed[14] recognised that dematerialised financial instruments did not exist, although the technology required to create them was theoretically available in processes and infrastructures such as those that support electronic data interchange (EDI) systems. Consequently, in theory, one could evidence the *res* incorporated in these instruments and the chain of transfers to the current holder by encrypting the instrument using some form of symmetric cryptosystem[15] based on standards, such as the Data Encryption Standard (DES), the Triple-DES (three DES devices in a row), the Advanced Encryption Standard (AES), or a proprietary algorithm developed using DevOps.[16]

Certainly, Bitcoin is an interesting project that gave rise to a new *crypto lex mercatoria*, which, in turn, has been the aim of practically every academic and

[6] According to a survey developed for the World Economic Forum's Global Risks Report 2023, most of the respondents expect that the risks related to cybercrime and cyber insecurity will be constant for the next two years. See World Economic Forum, 'The Global Risks Report 2023' (2023), available at www3.weforum.org/docs/WEF_Global_Risks_Report_2023.pdf.

[7] See www.nist.gov/cyberframework.

[8] See www.iso20022.org.

[9] Bank for International Settlements and International Organization of Securities Commissions, 'Guidance for Cyber-Resilience of Financial Market Infrastructures' (2016), available at www.bis.org/cpmi/publ/d146.pdf.

[10] BP Eha, *How Money Got Free. Bitcoin and the Fight for the Future of Finance* (London, Oneworld Publications, 2017) 11.

[11] S Nakamoto, 'Bitcoin Open Source Implementation of P2P Currency' (2009), available at p2pfoundation.ning.com/forum/topics/bitcoin-open-source.

[12] F Marrella and CS Yoo, 'Is Open Source Software the New Lex Mercatoria' (2007) 47 *Virginia Journal of International Law* 808, 808.

[13] E Suñé Llinás (ed), *La Constitución del Ciberespacio* (Mexico City, Porrúa, 2015).

[14] P Ellinger, 'Electronic Funds Transfer as a Deferred Settlement System' in RM Goode (ed), *Electronic Banking. The Legal Implications* (London, The Institute of Bankers, 1985) 29–44, 34–35; S Gleeson, *The Legal Concept of Money* (New York, Oxford University Press 2018) 118; C Reed, *Electronic Finance Law* (Cambridge, Woodhead-Faulkner, 1991) 2.

[15] They are called symmetric cryptosystems given that the parties involved share the same common key.

[16] B Schoenmakers and HCA van Tilborg, 'What Cryptology Can Mean for Electronic Commerce' in JEJ Prins et al (eds), *Trust in Electronic Commerce. The Role of Trust from a Legal, and Organizational and a Technical Point of View* (The Hague, Kluwer Law International, 2002) 45–54, 46.

regulatory effort to find a solution to the challenges posed by this innovation. However, this book will offer an analysis of the evolution of the cryptoassets market beyond this first-generation asset with the aim to provide a sound basis for the analyses and proposals that will be developed in the following chapters, and in the context of the development of regulated stablecoins and CBDCs.

II. Defining Cryptoassets

The standard analysis on cryptoassets starts by arguing that Bitcoin emerged as an endogenous social answer to the externalities faced by social systems in the DCS in the post-NIFA environment, and – as verified in *AA v Persons Unknown & Ors, Re Bitcoin*[17] – tries to allocate it to one of the two categories of property described by Sir William Blackstone, who, in the chapter on *Property in Things Personal* of his famous *Commentaries*[18] stated that:

> PROPERTY in chattels personal may be either in possession: which is where a man hath not only the right to enjoy, but hath the actual enjoyment of the thing: or else it is in action; where a man hath only a bare right, without any occupation or enjoyment. And of these the former, or property in possession, is divided into sorts, an absolute and a qualified property.

Unfortunately, these efforts do not adequately describe these innovations beyond the first generation. So, how can we define cryptoassets? First, it is important to understand that digital monetary expressions are not a new trend that emerged with Bitcoin. If one follows the discussions held around the world regarding the regulation of cryptoassets it is possible to see how they follow a rather familiar path. Back in 1994, the Working Group on EU Payment Systems[19] argued that new developments, such as prepaid cards, could 'become a direct competitor not only to cashless payment instruments already in existence, but also to banknotes and coins issued by central banks and national authorities'. Consequently, in August 1998, the ECB[20] issued a report on the issuance of electronic money in which one can find analyses and proposals relating to the risks to the *lex monetae*, particularly those associated with the mass production of transactional information and its processing.[21] After all, banks cannot tolerate a reputation for insecurity, whether in relation to the management of paper stacks or

[17] [2019] EWHC 3556 (Comm).

[18] W Blackstone, *Commentaries on the Laws of England. Book the Second* (London, A Strahan, 1827) 389.

[19] Working Group on EU payment Systems, 'Report to the Council of the European Monetary Institute on Prepaid Cards' (1994), available at www.ecb.europa.eu/pub/pdf/other/prepaidcards1994en.pdf?9fc7b56c72b0b1a42eb60ad5f97fb7d3.

[20] European Central Bank, 'Report on Electronic Money' (1998), available at www.ecb.europa.eu/pub/pdf/other/emoneyen.pdf.

[21] EH Solomon, *Virtual Money. Understanding the Power and Risks of Money's High-Speed Journey into Electronic Space* (New York, Oxford University Press, 1997) 220.

computational systems.[22] These concerns sound rather similar – if not the same – to those published since the emergence of Bitcoin, as evident in the following from the report:[23]

> The question of overissue of electronic money is also related to the question of whether electronic money could endanger the unit-of-account role as incorporated in central bank money. If, in the absence of any regulation, certain electronic money products were to spread at a rapid rate, market views about the creditworthiness of issuers could be affected and electronic money products from different issuers could start to be traded at varying exchange rates. Therefore, the need to preserve the unit-of-account function of money is another argument for imposing a redeemability requirement on electronic money. Such a requirement would guarantee that the role of money in providing a common financial denominator for the whole economy will be maintained.

Furthermore, digital economies and the means of payment employed within them have been the subject of interest for researchers and regulators, even before the emergence of cryptoassets. For example the monies employed in virtual worlds, which are in turn in the middle of new discussions in the context of the wide offer of metaverses and paradigms based on digital twins. Authors such as Edward Castronova[24] found that each 'world, game or platform has its own form of money that one obtains swapping real currency for these digital assets or accumulating coins and credits by taking part in different activities based on the rules set for each digital environment.

Taking these experiences as their starting point, institutions such as the ECB initially tried to define DLT innovations as if they were 'virtual currencies' and put them in the same category of the Linden Dollars used in the Second Life platform.[25] Therefore, the ECB[26] initially defined these assets as 'a type of unregulated, digital money, which is issued and usually controlled by its developers, and used and accepted among the members of a specific virtual community.' However, three years later, the same ECB[27] presented a new definition and stated that an instrument of this nature can be understood as 'a digital representation of value, not issued by a central bank, credit institution or e-money institution, which in some circumstances can be used as an alternative to money.' As one can see, these definitions have been refined to address issues that were far beyond the practices developed by the gamers and developers who inspired the first efforts on this matter.

[22] A Sweetman, *Cyber and the City. Securing London's Banks in the Computer Age* (Cham, Springer Nature, 2022) 11.

[23] ECB (n 20).

[24] E Castronova, 'On the Research Value of Large Games: Natural Experiments in Norrath and Camelot' (2005) 1621 *CESifo Working Papers* 1.

[25] D Campbell, 'Virtual Economics: Economists Explore the Research Value of Virtual Worlds' (2008) 12 *Region Focus* 18.

[26] European Central Bank, 'Virtual Currency Schemes' (2012), available at www.ecb.europa.eu/pub/pdf/other/virtualcurrencyschemes201210en.pdf.

[27] European Central Bank, 'Virtual Currency Schemes. A Further Analysis' (2015), available at www.ecb.europa.eu/pub/pdf/other/virtualcurrencyschemesen.pdf.

Currently, as result of the evolution of these technologies, the ECB[28] and institutions such as the FCA[29] define these assets under the term 'cryptoassets' and describe them as cryptographically secured digital representations of value that can be stored, transferred or traded electronically even when some of these assets do not represent a claim on the issuer. Accordingly, although these definitions have been refined, for now, cryptoassets are not considered or defined as forms of electronic money. With that in mind, how can these cryptographic instruments be legally recognised as electronic money or as a new payment instrument? To answer this question, we first need to understand the evolution of the cryptoassets market.

III. Bitcoin and the First Generation of Cryptoassets

Over the last 60 years, computers, algorithms and the internet have configured our third monetary *Bildungstrieb*. Accordingly, a myriad of projects have tried to dematerialise money and address the imperfections that these technologies and innovations introduce to their respective markets through private and public efforts. Certainly, this Cambrian explosion that has been built on the referred *Bildungstrieb* could offer us a substantial number of stages of monetary evolution, whose analysis could get out of hand. Consequently, the starting point of the present analysis of the cryptoassets market for the purpose of this book can be found in the unit by which one or several innovators – depending on your theory regarding the identity of Satoshi Nakamoto – looked to solve the Byzantine Generals problem: Bitcoin.

To face the problems that define dynamic social systems in the Black Box Society described by Frank Pasquale,[30] the famous white paper, 'Bitcoin: A Peer-to-Peer Electronic Cash System'[31] presents a distributed ledger, which, following Article 3(2) of MiCA[32] can be understood as 'an information repository that keeps records of transactions and that is shared across, and synchronised between, a set of DLT network nodes using a consensus mechanism.' In the context of Bitcoin, this ledger, commonly denominated as the blockchain, is, in turn, defined as a 'distributed ledger with confirmed blocks organised in an append-only, sequential chain using cryptographic links'.[33] In the case of Bitcoin, its ledger

[28] European Central Bank, 'Crypto-Assets: Implications for Financial Stability, Monetary Policy, and Payments and Market Infrastructures' (2019), available at www.ecb.europa.eu/pub/pdf/scpops/ecb.op223~3ce14e986c.en.pdf.

[29] Financial Conduct Authority (c), 'Guidance on Cryptoassets' (2019), available at www.fca.org.uk/publication/consultation/cp19-03.pdf.

[30] F Pasquale, *The Black Box Society. The Secret Algorithms that Control Money and information* (Massachusetts, Harvard University Press, 2015).

[31] S Nakamoto, 'Bitcoin: A Peer-to-Peer Electronic Cash System' (2008), available at bitcoin.org/bitcoin.pdf.

[32] Regulation 2023/1114 OJ L 150/40, 31 May 2023.

[33] A. 3.6. of ISO 22739:2020 (en) Blockchain and distributed ledger technologies – Vocabulary.

relies on a 'cryptographic proof instead of trust' known as the PoW consensus mechanism.[34] Through these rules and procedures, DLT nodes can transfer information over the network through a 'work' aimed to solve a mathematical problem denominated hash puzzle.[35]

Figure 9 Proof-of-Work model

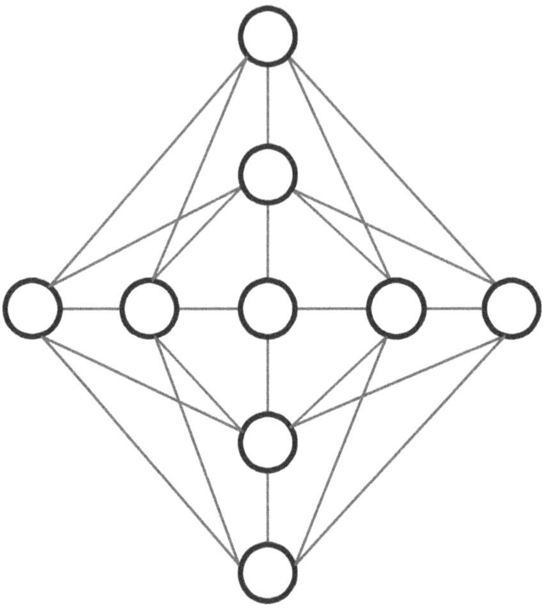

Under a PoW mechanism (Figure 9), the developer(s) aim to put in practice the principles of decentralisation and disintermediation found in Nakamoto's white paper.[36] Accordingly, in stark contrast to centralised verifications covered by normative instruments such as Article 34 of the Commission Delegated Regulation (EU) 2018/389,[37] this consensus mechanism offers an entirely decentralised

[34] Nakamoto (n 31).

[35] JJ Doguet, 'The Nature of the Form: Legal and Regulatory Issues Surrounding the Bitcoin Digital Currency System' (2013) 73 *Lousiana Law Review* 1119, 1125; S Green, 'Cryptocurrencies: The Underlying Technology' in D Fox and S Green (eds), *Cryptocurrencies in Public and Private Law* (Oxford, Oxford University Press, 2019) 1–12, 3; LP Nian and DL Kuo Chuen, 'Introduction to Bitcoin' in DL Kuo Chuen (ed), *Handbook of Digital Currency. Bitcoin, Innovation, Financial Instruments, and Big Data* (San Diego, Academic Press, 2015) 6–29, 15; A Wright and P De Filippi, 'Decentralized Blockchain Technology and the Rise of Lex Cryptographia' (2015) available at papers.ssrn.com/sol3/papers.cfm?abstract_id=2580664.

[36] Nakamoto (n 31).

[37] 'For the purpose of identification, as referred to in Article 30(1)(a), payment service providers shall rely on qualified certificates for electronic seals as referred to in Article 3(30) of Regulation (EU) No 910/2014 or for website authentication as referred to in Article 3(39) of that Regulation.' See Commission Delegated Regulation (EU) 2018/389 of 27 November 2017 supplementing Directive

identity management scheme, which includes two reward mechanisms to invite potential DLT nodes to download the OS software to take part of the verification process. The first incentive is based on the solution to the hash puzzles by which DLT nodes within the network add blocks to the chain with the aim of 'mining' new Bitcoins. The second incentive takes the form of those transaction fees that are obtained each time a transaction is validated by those DLT nodes distributed throughout the network.[38]

If we return to the analyses developed in chapters two and three, is it possible to identify the figure of the stakeholder and the underlying obligation to define these instruments as money? The main stakeholder would be the author of the source code, who – despite the claims of authors such as Craig Wright – is currently unknown, leading courts to argue that Bitcoin is a digital commodity/property.[39] In other words, Bitcoin is like paper. We can have a specific amount of paper to sell as a commodity for different purposes across different industries; however, if we insert the monetary *res*, the commodity becomes a *reifier* of the socio-legal source of liquidity. From this *reification*, one could argue that – following the blueprint set by Malinowski's[40] *Kula* ring – the incorporated obligation is a digital social contract subscribed by the developers and users of the asset by which each Bitcoin incorporates the obfuscated terms of the social agreement. It could be inferred that the volatility of the asset is based on the obfuscated nature of the interactions among the members of the Bitcoin community.

The ledger at the core of this digital social contract is a record of every transaction made using the asset from the Genesis Block created on 3 January 2009 to the current block.[41] To reach this aim, each blockchain is encrypted and organised into smaller datasets referred to as 'blocks' which are grouped almost every ten minutes, and then recorded one after the other on a chain.[42] Through this process, the protocol aggregates all valid changes of ownership to a unified ledger of which many copies are distributed across the network through a block that contains a certain number of transactions, a reference to the preceding block in the blockchain, as well as an answer to a hash puzzle.[43] Based on this riddle, the network validates and broadcasts the data associated with that block and assures that all of

(EU) 2015/2366 of the European Parliament and of the Council with regard to regulatory technical standards for strong customer authentication and common and secure open standards of communication OJ L 69/23, 13 March 2018.

[38] P Bains, 'Blockchain Consensus Mechanisms: A Primer for Supervisors' (2022), available at www.imf.org/en/Publications/fintech-notes/Issues/2022/01/25/Blockchain-Consensus-Mechanisms-511769.

[39] See *AA v Persons Unknown & Ors, Re Bitcoin* [2019] EWHC 3556 (Comm) (UK); *Commodity Futures Trading Commission v Patrick K McDonnell and Cabbagetech, Corp d/b/a Coin Drop Markets* [2018] 18-CV-361 (US).

[40] B Malinowski, *Argonauts of the Western Pacific. An Account of Native Enterprise and Adventure in the Archipelagos of Melanesian New Guinea* (London, Routledge & Kegan Paul, 1966).

[41] Green (n 35).

[42] Bank for International Settlements, 'Digital Currencies' (2015), available at www.bis.org/cpmi/publ/d137.pdf; FR Velde, 'Technological Change and the Future of Cash' (2017) 15 *SUERF Policy Note* 1; Green (n 35) 2; Wright and De Filippi (n 35).

[43] ibid.

its nodes have access to the full history of transactions.[44] Of course, access in an obfuscated environment does not necessarily translate in a useful way to verify the social obligations incorporated in the transaction.

If a node wants to modify the content of any given block after it has been added to the blockchain, it would also have to all of blocks which follow it, and compete to persuade all nodes that the new reality is the right one.[45] This process is rather difficult to execute, particularly in terms of computational power, so, in practice, the referred block can no longer be deleted and/or modified, and the transactions it contains can be accessed and – in theory– verified by everyone in the network.[46] In other words, each block becomes a permanent record that all nodes on the network can use to coordinate an action or verify an event.[47] Consequently, those nodes who invest substantial computer resources to this verification process and solve the respective puzzles receive, as an incentive, new Bitcoins every time a group of blocks is recorded on the chain.[48]

Therefore, this mechanism solves the double-spending problem by maintaining a ledger of balances that, rather than being centralised within a single certifier, decentralises the responsibilities to the entire network of computers that communicate with each other via the internet.[49] When a node distributes a message to the rest of the network, he/she does not think if the other nodes are trusted, as we should do in the case of the generals described in the Byzantine Generals Problem. Each node relies only on the incentive mentioned above and the code-based governance paradigm, which ensure that all copies of the ledger are updated appropriately.[50]

Unsurprisingly, the purist enthusiasts of this innovation claim that we are witnessing a revolution that offers an alternative to existing payment systems and which would eliminate the need for banks and other financial intermediaries to form bonds of trust on our behalf. Therefore, it would, in theory, enable us to create and move money almost instantaneously from one side of the planet to the other without the interference of sovereign entities, and without alleged exploitation by traditional intermediaries in exercise of their infrastructural power.[51] This takes into consideration that the OS software required to execute on-chain transactions could act as a *crypto lex mercatoria*.

[44] ibid.

[45] Green (n 35) 4.

[46] ibid; Wright and De Filippi (n 35).

[47] ibid.

[48] I Cedillo, 'A New Approach for 'Cryptoassets' Regulation' (2019) 35 *Banking & Finance Law Review* 37, 42.

[49] Bank for International Settlements (n 42); Green (n 35) 2; Velde (n 42); Wright and De Filippi (n 35).

[50] S. Cohney, et al, 'Coin-Operated Capitalism.' (2018) 12, available at papers.ssrn.com/sol3/papers.cfm?abstract_id=3215345; G Huberman, JD Leshno and C Moallemi, 'Monopoly without a Monopolist: An Economic Analysis of the Bitcoin Payment System' (2017), available at helda.helsinki.fi/bof/handle/123456789/14912.

[51] S Lo and JC Wang, 'Bitcoin as Money?' (2014), available at www.bostonfed.org/publications/current-policy-perspectives/2014/bitcoin-as-money.aspx; Eha (n 10) 2.

A. The Role of Intellectual Property Rights (IPRs)

Such is the fascination with the idea that a piece of software can act as the basis for Bitcoin's crypto *lex mercatoria* that most of the works on the cryptoasssets market tend to forget that, in essence, the proposal found in Nakamoto's white paper[52] is a payments system designed around an algorithmic *lex monetae*. In other words, these cryptoassets do not exist as isolated golden 'coins' that one frequently sees in different media around the world,[53] but as integral parts of a multi-layered system of stakeholders. When one changes the approach from the asset to this system under a functional approach, it is possible to find more interesting challenges and solutions in other elements closely related to DLT innovations that go beyond Bitcoin itself. These elements are IPRs and GVCs.[54]

Most discussions around IPRs and money relate to the role of copyright in the elaboration of the designs that define and identify banknotes and coins, or to the patents that support the security features of banknotes and the use of computer-based money. Of course, it is possible to argue that IPRs play a more critical role in the context of the DCS, which, as seen in the introductory part of this work, builds on the collective and distributed efforts that emerge from paradigms, such as open-sourced software and cloud computing.

Most of the software created in the second half of the twentieth century was 'open' in the sense that it was developed by academics and institutional researchers who, based on a cooperation model structured around transparency and sharing, fostered the development of the industry. Of course, given that software not was included in the original instruments (the Berne and the Paris Conventions) they had to rely on a mingle of *lex contractus* principles and the copyright system relying on the Kantian element to align its protection to that offered to literary works.[55] However, the interoperable model that emerged from the characteristics of software accurately described in *Apple Computer v Franklin Computer*,[56] fostered the constitution of the Free Software Foundation, whose efforts led to a new generation of licences that have configured the DCS, as seen in *Google v Oracle*[57] and the increasing reliance on open-source software by companies and even by central banks through the diffusion and evolution of development paradigms such as DevOps and DevSecOps.

[52] Nakamoto (n 31).

[53] The FCA has found that some people believe that, as result of the use of the terms 'mining' and 'coins', they are investing in tangible assets. See Financial Conduct Authority, 'Guidance on Cryptoassets' (2019), available at www.fca.org.uk/publication/consultation/cp19-03.pdf.

[54] Cedillo (n 48) 42.

[55] C Maracke, 'Free and Open Source Software and FRAND-Based Patent Licenses. How to Mediate Between Standard Essential Patent and Free and Open Source Software' (2019) 22 *The Journal of World Intellectual Property* 78, 80.

[56] [1983] 714 F.2d 1240 (US).

[57] [2020] 18-956 SC (US).

Building upon the free software movement and distribution licences, such as the Berkeley Software Distribution (BSD) licence,[58] the Bitcoin system runs using an OS software over a decentralised and 'permissionless' network of computers that belongs to the people around the world who download the software under the terms of its licence.[59] This is a rather simple process:[60]

> Permission is hereby granted, free of charge, to any person obtaining a copy of this software and associated documentation files (the 'Software'), to deal in the Software without restriction, including without limitation the rights to use, copy, modify, merge, publish, distribute, sublicense, and/or sell copies of the Software, and to permit persons to whom the Software is furnished to do so, subject to the following conditions:
>
> The above copyright notice and this permission notice shall be included in all copies or substantial portions of the Software.
>
> THE SOFTWARE IS PROVIDED 'AS IS', WITHOUT WARRANTY OF ANY KIND, EXPRESS OR IMPLIED, INCLUDING BUT NOT LIMITED TO THE WARRANTIES OF MERCHANTABILITY, FITNESS FOR A PARTICULAR PURPOSE AND NONINFRINGEMENT. IN NO EVENT SHALL THE AUTHORS OR COPYRIGHT HOLDERS BE LIABLE FOR ANY CLAIM, DAMAGES OR OTHER LIABILITY, WHETHER IN AN ACTION OF CONTRACT, TORT OR OTHERWISE, ARISING FROM, OUT OF OR IN CONNECTION WITH THE SOFTWARE OR THE USE OR OTHER DEALINGS IN THE SOFTWARE.

B. The Relevance of Moral and Economic Control of Infrastructures

Independently of the charm of this copyleft[61] licence, and as seen in *Jacobsen v Katzer*,[62] 'copyright holders who engage in open source licensing have the moral right to control the modification and distribution of copyrighted material' following the contents of Article 2(1) of the Berne Convention, not only under industrial property rights as under instruments such as Article 1(1) of the Directive 2009/24/EC[63] of the European Parliament and of the Council of 23 April 2009, which states the following:

[58] D Rowland, U Kohl and A Charlesworth, *Information Technology Law* (bingdon, Routledge, 2017) 518–21.

[59] P Vigna and MJ Casey, *Cryptocurrency. The Future of Money?* (London, Vintage, 2015) 65; Doguet (n 35) 1125; Nian and Kuo Chuen (n 35).

[60] The Bitcoin Core Developers and Bitcoin Developers, 'The MIT License' (2009), available at github.com/bitcoin/bitcoin/blob/master/COPYING.

[61] Through a copyleft licence, the copyright holder prevents someone from turning free or open-source software into proprietary software. See MA Lemley et al, *Software and Internet Law* (New York, Walters Lower Law & Business, 2011) 301.

[62] [2008] 535 F.3d 1373 (US), at 1381.

[63] Directive 2009/24/EC of the European Parliament and of the Council on the legal protection of computer programs OJ L 111/16, 23 April,2009.

> In accordance with the provisions of this Directive, Member States shall protect computer programs, by copyright, as literary works within the meaning of the Berne Convention for the Protection of Literary and Artistic Works. For the purposes of this Directive, the term 'computer programs' shall include their preparatory design material.

Although the software is protected in similar ways to literary works, it is not subject to figures such as the first sale doctrine, as evidenced in cases such as *Microsoft Corp v Harmony Computers & Electronics, Inc*,[64] given that a licence does not represent a sale. Therefore, cryptoassets is a distribution model by which DLT nodes and secondary developers receive a non-negotiated licence to work on the code in absence of those economic rights that would be applicable to other creations.

On this point, it is one thing to have the right to develop derivative works based on the source code provided by the original developer under a copyleft licence, and a very different things to develop the infrastructure for a new payments system through patents. As is evident in Directive 2007/64/EC[65] of the European Parliament and the Council, the Banking Act 2009[66] or PSD2,[67] payment systems are subject to network effects. These effects have two implications related to potential strategies based on patent applications. First, they are an illustration of complementary assets that permit financial intermediaries to protect their inventions and innovations.[68] Second, networks are vulnerable to patent trolling by which: 1) third parties who own patents are suddenly in strong bargaining positions in licensing negotiations;[69] or 2) different stakeholders introduce knowledge to the state of the art[70] with the aim of blocking future patent applications by potential competitors. Consequently, we can be sure that a light will be shone on this networked vulnerability within the next five years.

With these effects in mind, institutions such as the People's Bank of China, Ripple and JP Morgan have filled patent applications related to the inventions that support the copyright elements mentioned above as interrelated elements, but clearly separated one from the other. As seen in recent cases such as *Nasdaq*,

[64] [1994] 846 F Supp 208 NY (US).

[65] Directive 2007/64/EC of the European Parliament and of the Council on payment services in the internal market amending Directives 97/7/EC, 2002/65/EC, 2005/60/EC and 2006/48/EC and repealing Directive 97/5/EC OJ L 319/1, 13 November 2007.

[66] Banking Act 2009.

[67] Directive 2015/2366 of the European Parliament and of the Council on payment services in the internal market, amending Directives 2002/65/EC, 2009/110/EC and 2013/36/EU and Regulation (EU) No 1093/2010, and repealing Directive 2007/64/EC OJ L 337/35, 25 November 2015.

[68] RM Hunt, 'Ten Years After: What Are the Effects of Business Method Patents in Financial Services?' (2008) 3 *Business Review* 21, 25.

[69] ibid.

[70] Section 2(2) of the Patents Act 1977 sets that the state of the art 'comprises all matter (whether a product, a process, information about either, or anything else) which has at any time before the priority date of that invention been made available to the public (whether in the United Kingdom or elsewhere) by written or oral description, by use or in any other way.'

Inc; Nasdaq Technology AB v IEX Group, Inc; Investors Exchange LLC,[71] the proper understanding of these differences will play a significant role in the development of new technologies and financial infrastructures. On this basis, the next patent war within the financial sector will not be centred on who will create the 'GlobalCoin', but on who will provide – and control – the new payments infrastructure for the DCS. Therefore, it is not surprising that software developers around the world have realised the real potential for DLT and have started to use this technology to create other infrastructural cryptoassets that can be classified as units of second and third generation, and foster the emergence of new intermediaries and technological infrastructures, which could be integral part of the exercise of the *lex monetae*. Of course – in exercise of these prerogatives – we have to be very careful not to introduce imperfections that could led us to a crisis based on an algorithmic Waterlow & Sons.[72]

IV. From Individual Users to Corporative Second Generation of Cryptoassets

The expiration in 1999 of the patent US4309569A that supported the Merkle hash-tree pattern, and the dissemination of free and OS licence models and public repositories have fostered a diffusion process by which the new techno-economic model is spreading from the initial users or areas of application to a much wider range of industries and services.[73] As illustrated above, to diffuse and consolidate an innovation, firms need high amounts of managerial, technological and entrepreneurial skill, and financial support. Consequently, successful projects relating to DLT innovations are associated with big firms such as JP Morgan and OpenAI,[74] which act as the stakeholders and the sources of liquidity of their respective networks.[75]

Furthermore, in practice, given that the creation of markets involves the development and use of GVCs based on hierarchical power and infrastructures, these protocols have allowed the referred big players to foster a gradual process of cartelisation that has inspired the development of new options. Among these options are protocols such as Proof-of-Stake (PoS) by which players that have invested certain amount of time and resources in the network increase their opportunities to obtain cryptoassets.

[71] In this case, Nasdaq claims that IEX has incurred in patent infringement relating to the US patent Nos: 7,647,264; 7,933,827; 8,117,609; 8,244,622; 8,280,797; and 8,386,362. See [2019] 3:18 CV 03014 (US).

[72] *Banco de Portugal v Waterlow & Sons Ltd* [1932] All ER Rep 181 (UK).

[73] C Freeman, 'Diffusion: The Spread of New Technology to Firms, Sectors and Nations' in A Heertje (ed), *Innovation, Technology, and Finance* (Oxford, European Investment Bank, 1988) 38–70, 53.

[74] C Ford, *Innovation and the State. Finance, Regulation and Justice* (New York, Cambridge University Press, 2017) 171.

[75] Cedillo (n 48) 44.

Figure 10 Proof-of-Stake model

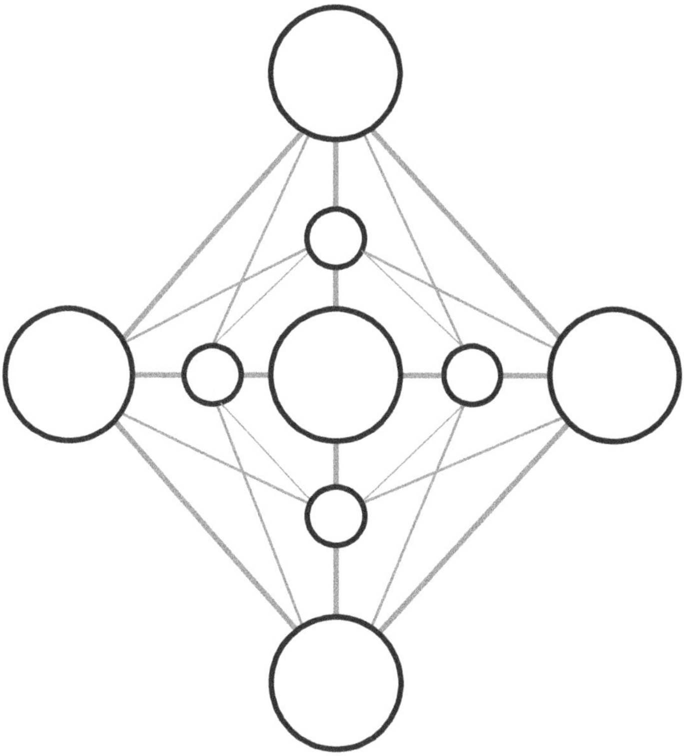

Following the development of the *proto-lex monetae* shown in chapter one, PoS protocols leverage digital assets based on the 'stake' of each validator node to solve a computation problem. The stakes of these protocols make reference to the number of cryptoassets owned by each node. Consequently, the opportunities to find a solution to the problem will depend on the number of cryptoassets a node has.[76] Although the original intentions of the first developers were aimed at solving problems that characterise PoW protocols, such as the increasing influence of big players known as 'whales' and the excessive consumption of energy, ironically, these paradigms introduce an inducement that, again, fosters a process of cartelisation within global value chains in which certain nodes influence the interactions developed within the network, thus introducing a source of market imperfections that justify sovereign intervention.

[76] W Li et al, 'Securing Proof-of-Stake Blockchain Protocols' in J García-Alfaro et al (eds), *Data Privacy Management, Cryptocurrencies and Blockchain Technology* (Cham, Springer International Publishing, 2017) 297–315, 300; D Karakostas et al, 'Cryptocurrency Egalitarianism. A Quantitative Approach' (2009), available at arxiv.org/abs/1907.02434#:~:text=A%20core%20criticism%20of%20proof,according%20to%20their%20computational%20power.

However, before reaching this point, transitional projects have been developed by organisations who rely on copies of other projects structured around programming languages, such as, C++. C++ has been used actively in the financial sector to develop applications that demand efficient memory management, speed and reliability, considering, for example, that many central bank-operated wholesale payment systems are programmed on current and future legacy systems that are no longer fit for their current purpose and markets, and whose modernisation costs are difficult to maintain.[77]

A. Ripple and DLT Solutions for the Financial Sector

As was argued in the introduction of this work, DLTs were introduced to the financial world as an alternative paradigm designed to compete with regulated commercial banks, which were considered responsible for the negative outcomes that defined the GFC. However, as has been seen in the introduction of expert systems and computer-based money to the financial industry, financial intermediaries tend to incorporate novel inventions and innovations in their operations and infrastructures. Accordingly, in the context of DLT, there are some projects whose aim is to improve existing regulated infrastructures, among which Ripple has received some attention.[78] Its inventors, Stefan Thomas and Robert D Way, developed in the description and claims of their patent application[79] some of the principles related to transaction validation that gave form to the initial enthusiasm for Bitcoin as the payments system of the future. Considering the elements relating to good faith and no negligence relating to cheques, analysed in cases such as *Middle Temple v Lloyds Bank*,[80] they argue that this technology could be useful to avoid 'situations where money, perhaps illegitimate money, is attempted to be transferred to a party not wanting to be involved in the transaction'.[81]

The charm of Ripple can be found in its own cryptoasset known as XRP, which, in contrast to the open mining model employed by Bitcoin, relies on a distributed network of trusted validators found in the Ripple Unique Node List, which is based on a source code developed between 2011 and 2012 by Arthur Britto, Jed McCaleb and David Schwartz for a cryptographically secured ledger[82]

[77] M Bech and R Garratt, 'Central Bank Cryptocurrencies' (2017), available at www.bis.org/publ/qtrpdf/r_qt1709f.htm; Deloitte, 'Modernizing Legacy Banking Systems. Practical Advice to Help Banks Succeed at Core and Application Modernization' (2020), available at www2.deloitte.com/us/en/pages/financial-services/articles/modernizing-legacy-systems-in-banking.html.

[78] Cedillo (n 48) 44–45.

[79] [2015] Patent application US20160224949 A1: 'Temporary consensus subnetwork in a distributed network for payment processing'.

[80] [1999] 1 All ER Comm 193 (UK).

[81] [2015] Patent application US20160224949 A1: 'Temporary consensus subnetwork in a distributed network for payment processing' 1.

[82] *SEC v Ripple Labs* [2023] 1:20-cv-10832-AT (US), at 2.

known as the XRP Ledger.[83] Furthermore, in clear opposition to the aversion that fostered the creation of Bitcoin, XRP was designed to attract financial institutions, and to improve their existent infrastructure,[84] which is evident in how the company has tried to promote agreements with different financial intermediaries.[85] However, its implementation has not been free of obstacles. For instance, regulated banks working in different projects that involve DLT are not sure if they can materialise them appropriately as they need to hold a certain amount of cryptoassets,[86] whose legal nature is still in doubt after the argument presented by Analisa Torres DJ, in *SEC v Ripple*.[87] As one can infer, following the recommendations issued by institutions such as the European Banking Authority[88] and the potential content of new regulations, such as MiCA, these intermediaries could face problems relating to the possession of these infrastructural assets independently of their final use. With these issues in mind, in Mexico, for example, the central bank, through Article 3 of the Circular 4/2019,[89] states that commercial banks can take part on cryptoassets transactions only to conduct their internal operations as infrastructural elements.[90]

Following that trend, Ripple has protected its own infrastructural power through three conduits. First, the company owns and controls key validator nodes and 61 per cent of the entire supply of 100 billion XRP[91] generated by the source code.[92] This is a powerful strategy considering the asset is required to materialise transactions throughout the network. Second, it has applied for protections for the inventions that support the software, such as in patent application US20160224949 A1. As seen above, it is one thing having the right to develop derivative works of the code, and another to develop the infrastructure to offer it to the financial sector. Third, it protects the identity of the company and the unit using trademarks such as Ripple and XRP, as seen in *Ripple Labs INC v Kefi Labs LLC, Paul Stavropoulos, Dean Stavropoulos and Brandon Ong*.[93]

[83] A Dickinson, 'Cryptocurrencies and the Conflict of Laws' in D Fox and S Green (eds), *Cryptocurrencies in Public and Private Law* (Oxford, Oxford University Press, 2019) 93–137, 103.

[84] S Leonard, '10 Things You Need to Know about XRP' (2017), available at ripple.com/insights/10-things-need-know-xrp.

[85] One has to be careful with the reports published by Ripple. For example, the company published on its website that it had more than 200 users within its RippleNet; however, searching for them often resulted in error messages such as '404 Not Found' or 'The resource you are looking for has been removed, had its name changed, or is temporarily unavailable'.

[86] I Allison, 'BBVA Can't Hold Cryptocurrency – and That's A Problem' (2018), available at www.coindesk.com/bbva-bank-cant-hold-crypto-problem.

[87] [2023] 1:20-cv-10832-AT (US).

[88] European Banking Authority, 'EBA Opinion on "Virtual Currencies"' (2014), available at www.eba.europa.eu/documents/10180/657547/EBA-Op-2014-08+Opinion+on+Virtual+Currencies.pdf.

[89] Circular 4/2019 addressed to Credit Institutions and Financial Technology Institutions related to the general provisions applicable to Credit Institutions and Financial Technology Institutions in the transactions conducted with virtual assets DOF 8 March 2019.

[90] Cedillo (n 48) 45.

[91] M del Castillo and B Reutzel, '$100 Billion Controversy: XRP's Surge Raises Hard Questions for Ripple' (2018), available at www.coindesk.com/100-billion-controversy-xrps-surge-raises-hard-questions-ripple.

[92] *SEC v Ripple Labs* [2023] 1:20-cv-10832-AT (US), at 2.

[93] [2015] 3:15-cv-04565 MEJ (US).

As one would expect, this strategy has been under attack. For example, in *Ryan Coffey v Ripple Labs INC*,[94] the plaintiff argued that, unlike other cryptoassets such as Bitcoin and Ethereum, which can be mined using protocols such as PoW by those who download the software for that purpose, all 100 billion of the XRP in existence were created 'out of thin air' by Ripple Labs in 2013. Consequently, the plaintiff argued that Ripple has offered securities unlawfully without the proper registration. On these arguments, Ripple's lawyers warned Ripple that XRP could be considered an 'investment contract' under the federal securities laws, and that XRP was unlikely to be considered a form of currency.[95] The Securities and Exchange Commission subsequently filed an action on 22 December 2020 in which it argued that Ripple's Offering of XRP represented an 'unlawful offer and sale of securities in violation of Sections 5(a) and 5(c) of the Securities Act 1933',[96] an argument that has not been clearly settled, particularly after the analysis presented by Analisa Torres DJ in 2023 under the *Howey* case, which centred on the relationship between the issuer and the investment contract.[97]

On proper monetary matters, institutions such as the Bank of England have carried out tests using the XRP Ledger to synchronise payments between two central banks.[98] However, central banks around the globe have already concluded that, for now, this protocol is not sufficiently mature given the existent frictions between the centralised structure of interbank payment system and the decentralised elements of the protocol,[99] a fact that has pushed central banks to work with centralised and permissioned protocols developed by companies such as R3.[100] These companies develop their solutions on smart contracts that are closely related to another unit of second generation that is preferred by innovators, entrepreneurs and even central banks for the exercise of a *crypto lex monetae*: Ether.

B. Ethereum and Smart Contracts

The other famous second-generation cryptoasset is Ether. Ethereum was developed to be much more than a payments system, building upon the ideas published by Vitalik Buterin[101] and the infrastructures and interactions enabled

[94] [2018] CGC-18-566271 (US), at 1–2.

[95] *SEC v Ripple Labs* [2020] 1:20-cv-10832 (US), at 10.

[96] *Ryan Coffey v Ripple Labs INC.* [2018] CGC-18-566271 (US), at 1–2.

[97] *SEC v Ripple Labs* [2023] 1:20-cv-10832-AT (US).

[98] Bank of England, FinTech Accelerator Proof of Concept (2017), available at www.bankofengland.co.uk/Documents/fintech/ripplepoc.pdf.

[99] S Ho, 'Bank of Canada says won't use Blockchain for Interbank Payment System' (2017), available at ca.investing.com/news/stock-market-news/bank-of-canada-says-won't-use-blockchain-for-interbank-payment-system-126381.

[100] The platform CORDA developed by R3 has been employed as one of the infrastructural cornerstones for the development of CBDC pilots around the world.

[101] As an interesting note, everyone can work on the Ethereum's white paper through the GitHub platform. See github.com/ethereum/wiki/wiki/White-Paper.

by cloud computing, and was launched on 30 July 2015[102] as a decentralised system that, besides transferring cryptoassets enables users to create and run smart contracts[103] on a distribution model known as Infrastructure as a Service (IaaS).[104] For this purpose, Ethereum extends the original Bitcoin's Turing incomplete Script language and develops a new blockchain to support the development of virtualisation technologies through the Ethereum Virtual Machine (EVM). This virtual machine, hosted within a computer, operates as a virtual server, executing bytecode smart contracts within an international network of public nodes.[105] Once a smart contract is compiled to EVM bytecode, it can be deployed to the Ethereum blockchain, thus making the instrument available to others.[106]

Although there is not a single and universal definition of smart contracts, these innovations have been defined in instruments such as the Act presented by the Legislature of the State of Wyoming[107] on the formation and management of decentralized autonomous organisations, as

> an automated transaction, as defined in W.S. 40-21-102(a)(ii),[108] or any substantially similar analogue, which is comprised of code, script or programming language that executes the terms of an agreement and which may include taking custody of and transferring an asset, administrating membership interest votes with respect to a decentralized autonomous organization or issuing executable instructions for these actions, based on the occurrence or nonoccurrence of specified conditions.

In theory, the performance and enforcement of the referred actions occur automatically, without the need for human or third-party intervention, acting – again – as a *crypto lex mercatoria*.

[102] Ethereum Foundation, 'History of Ethereum' (2016), available at www.ethdocs.org/en/latest/introduction/history-of-ethereum.html; J Harm, J Obregon and J Stubbendick, 'Ethereum vs. Bitcoin' (2016), available at www.economist.com/sites/default/files/creighton_university_kraken_case_study.pdf.

[103] In fact, one of the Ether denominations is known as Szabo. One Ether is composed by 1,000,000 Szabos. See M Fröwis and R Böhme, 'In Code We Trust? Measuring the Control Flow Immutability of All Smart Contracts Deployed on Ethereum' in J Garcia-Alfaro et al (eds), *Data Privacy Management, Cryptocurrencies and Blockchain Technology* (Cham, Springer International Publishing, 2017) 357–72, 358.

[104] This cloud computing service model is presented to users with the aim of offering raw computing resources, such as processing power and storage. See A Sweetman. *Cyber and the City. Securing London's Banks in the Computer Age* (Cham, Springer Nature, 2022) 6.

[105] J Li and W Mann, 'Initial Coin Offering and Platform Building' (2018) 11, available at www.jbs.cam.ac.uk/fileadmin/user_upload/research/centres/alternative-finance/downloads/2018-af-conference/paper-li.pdf; Cohney et al (n 50) 26; Fröwis and Böhme (n 103) 361.

[106] Fröwis and Böhme (n 103) 361.

[107] An Act relating to corporations; providing for the formation and management of decentralized autonomous organizations; providing definitions, Senate File No SF0038, 7 January 2021.

[108] '"Automated transaction" means a transaction conducted or performed, in whole or in part, by electronic means or electronic records, in which the acts or records of one (1) or both parties are not reviewed by an individual in the ordinary course in forming a contract, performing under an existing contract or fulfilling an obligation required by the transaction'.

Following Article 9 of the Directive 2000/31/EC[109] on Electronic Commerce and Article 89 of the Commercial Code[110] of Mexico, to be legally recognised, these instruments have to reflect technological neutrality, autonomy of the will, international compatibility and functional equivalency. Of course, as seen in *State of Wisconsin v Eric L. Loomis*,[111] in a context of obfuscated codes and trade secrets this could become difficult to verify. Furthermore, there might always be a risk that the performance of the contract is affected by an event external to the code and that, in such cases, one could take the issue to court[112] following the jurisdiction test found in *Zippo Manufacturing Co v Zippo Dot Com, Inc*[113] based on the nature and intensity of the interaction that a party conducts over the internet.

To resolve these issues, it has been argued that Ethereum's Turing-Complete language –which includes seven different programming languages – can, in theory, solve any computational problem, allowing for an even greater level of certainty across the entire computational architecture.[114] However, if these contracts become the underlying source of liquidity for new payment infrastructures, courts will need to consider a range of questions related to the explainability of the obligations incorporated: who is the audience for the explanation? How simple or complex should the explanation be? What structure or form should the explanation take: lines of code, visual presentations? More generally, what will constitute a meaningful explanation?[115]

Just as in the case of XRP, Ether is the native cryptoasset of the Ethereum network, which is released through a PoW mining process similar to Bitcoin's, but the reward per block of five Ether remains constant and does not halve. Furthermore, although in different academic forums presenters tend to attribute some virtues of Ether to Bitcoin, Ethereum differentiates from the first generation of cryptoassets for its ability to leverage the application of smart contracts within its code[116] to act as a source of liquidity just as commercial contracts would act as the source of liquidity for a bill of exchange or a promissory note.

[109] Directive 2000/31/EC of the European Parliament and of the Council on certain legal aspects of information society services, in particular electronic commerce, in the Internal Market (Directive on electronic commerce) OJ L 178/1, 8 June 2000.

[110] Commercial Code DOF.

[111] In this case, Eric Loomis argued that the use of obfuscated algorithms that are protected as trade secrets to guide a risk assessment at sentencing violated his right to due process. See [2016] 881 N.W.2d 749 (US).

[112] UK Jurisdiction Taskforce, 'Legal Statement on Cryptoassets and Smart Contracts' (2019), available at technation.io/about-us/lawtech-panel/#gf_41.

[113] [1997] 952 F Supp 1119 (US), at 1124.

[114] A D'Alfonso, P Langer and Z Vandelis, 'The Future of Cryptocurrency. An Investor's Comparison of Bitcoin and Ethereum' (2016), available at www.economist.com/sites/default/files/the_future_of_cryptocurrency.pdf; Harm, Obregon and Stubbendick (n 102).

[115] A. Deeks, 'The Judicial Demand for Explainable Artificial Intelligence' (2019) 119 *Columbia Law Review* 1829, 1837–38.

[116] P McCorry, E Heilman and A Miller, 'Atomically Trading with Roger. Gambling on the Success of a Hardfork' in J Garcia-Alfaro, et al (eds), *Data Privacy Management, Cryptocurrencies and Blockchain Technology* (Cham, Springer International Publishing, 2017) 334–53, 336; D'Alfonso, Langer and Vandelis (n 114).

One industry that is developing different uses for Ethereum is the IoT. This can be understood as a global information network where billions of networked internet-enabled devices become active participants in business processes.[117] However, just as in the case of the Byzantine Generals problem, none of these smart devices can be individually trusted. Consequently, these devices need a central reference point that can ease private and secure machine-to-machine (M2M) coordination.[118] At a time when over a billion devices could be connected to the internet, a universal digital ledger could store the relationship between internet-enabled machines at any given moment, and smart contracts can allocate corresponding rights and obligations of connected devices in electronic commerce environments.[119]

Ethereum also has many potential uses in the financial sector. Nearly every bank currently uses SWIFT messaging to securely process transactions, but Ethereum smart contracts could eventually challenge its market power.[120] For example, an initiative has been put in place by the Monetary Authority of Singapore (MAS), known as Project Ubin: SGD on Distributed Ledger. Ubin is a digital cash-on-ledger project run through a global value chain constituted by a myriad of institutions selected by the MAS – in exercise of its *lex monetae* – including Bank of America Merrill Lynch, R3, JP Morgan, Singapore Exchange and BCS Information Systems as a technology provider.[121] This project is structured around two targets developed around five phases:[122]

(1) Tokenise the Singapore Dollar (SGD)
(2) Reimagine the RTGS and develop the infrastructural source codes[123]
(3) Develop Delivery versus Payment (DvP) capabilities
(4) Develop analyses on the potential development of cross-border payments and settlements paradigms with the collaboration of stakeholders, such as the Bank of Canada and the Bank of England
(5) Foster broad ecosystem collaboration.

[117] RH Weber and R Weber, *Internet of Things. Legal Perspectives* (Heidelberg, Springer, 2010) 1.
[118] Wright and De Filippi (n 35).
[119] P Brody and V Pureswaran, 'Device Democracy. Saving the Future of the Internet of Things' (2014), available at www-03.ibm.com/press/de/de/attachment/45893.wss?fileId=ATTACH_FILE2&fileName=Device%20democracy-%20Saving%20the%20future%20of%20the%20Internet%20of%20Things.pdf.
[120] To face this challenge, SWIFT has developed an application programming interface (API) that allows participant banks to access their respective databases and verify the validity of bank account numbers when a payment order is issued. See L Noonan, 'SWIFT Takes on FinTechs with New Payment System' (2018), available at www.ft.com/content/05d41660-f7c8-11e8-af46-2022a0b02a6c.
[121] Deloitte and Monetary Authority of Singapore, 'The Future is here. Project Ubin: SGD on Distributed Ledger' (2017), available at www.mas.gov.sg/~/media/ProjectUbin/Project%20Ubin%20%20SGD%20on%20Distributed%20Ledger.pdf.
[122] Monetary Authority of Singapore, 'Project Ubin: Central Bank Digital Money using Distributed Ledger Technology' (2020), available at www.mas.gov.sg/schemes-and-initiatives/Project-Ubin.
[123] The source codes are available in the following GitHub repository: github.com/project-ubin.

Based on these objectives, a continuous depository receipt model was selected to run this project with the aim of creating the source of liquidity. Building upon this *res*, its receipts were designed to represent a claim on central bank reserves held in a segregated account against which the central bank issues digital units on an Ethereum-based distributed ledger provided by JP Morgan (Quorum), thus allowing two separate systems to be linked to increase money transfer efficiency between different accounts.[124] The second target aimed to build on the potential success of commercial experiences to conduct cross-border payments using central bank cryptoassets issued through the architecture of Ubin V.[125]

Following Scarufi's vision, and building on Ubin V and Project Dunbar, the MAS presented in November 2022 the project Ubin+ by which it will foster further collaborative efforts with different stakeholders to enhance connectivity with wholesale CBDCs.[126]

V. ICOs: The Third Generation of *Cryptoreifiers*

During the Schumpeterian process of diffusion, between the second and the third generation of cryptoassets, many readers probably found different sources stating that there were differences between cryptocurrencies and virtual tokens, as the two terms (among others) are often interchanged in media coverage, and even in some regulatory discussions. For example, the Malta Financial Services Authority[127] defines a cryptocurrency as a unit used as a digital medium of exchange, unit of account and/or store of value native to a blockchain such as Bitcoin, XRP and Ether. Conversely, these sources tend to argue that when one creates a token through an ICO in an existing platform, it is created as a smart contract, with each token being governed by a single, unique governing agreement as a source of underlying liquidity.[128] This distinction can be seen in Regulation 1 of the Virtual Financial Assets Act,[129] which under the denomination of 'DLT asset' covers '(a) a virtual token; (b) a virtual financial asset; (c) electronic money; or (d) a financial instrument.' In opposition to this trend, this book follows the example set by the FCA[130]

[124] Bech and Garratt (n 77); Deloitte and Monetary Authority of Singapore (n 121).

[125] Monetary Authority of Singapore, 'Project Ubin Phase 5. Enabling Broad Ecosystem Opportunities' (2017), available at www.mas.gov.sg/-/media/MAS/ProjectUbin/Project-Ubin-Phase-5-Enabling-Broad-Ecosystem-Opportunities.pdf?la=en&hash=91091CAD39265C03FF7A4253E70FBEE6D1177714.

[126] Monetary Authority of Singapore, 'MAS Launches Expanded Initiative to Advance Cross-Border Connectivity in Wholesale CBDCs' (2022), available at www.mas.gov.sg/news/media-releases/2022/mas-launches-expanded-initiative-to-advance-cross-border-connectivity-in-wholesale-cbdcs.

[127] Malta Financial Services Authority, 'Consultation Paper on the Financial Instrument Test' (2018), available at www.mfsa.com.mt.

[128] C Wermers; J Haust and K Bruinsma, 'Initial Coin Offerings in the Netherlands. An Overview of the Regulatory Environment' (2018) 6, available at cms.law/en/NLD/Publication/Initial-Coin-Offerings-in-the-Netherlands.

[129] Virtual Financial Assets Act 2018.

[130] Financial Conduct Authority (n 29).

and Article 3(5) of MiCA,[131] and analyses those assets used as means of payment under the term 'cryptoassets' independently of their design, thereby avoiding the mistake found in many sources that pay excessive attention to the technological characteristics of these innovations and forget to focus their efforts on the material effects that are legally relevant.

Unlike its namesake, the Initial Public Offering (IPO), ICOs are digital representations of value offered to investors and users by auction or through subscription, using DLT platforms such as Neo, Waves or Ethereum,[132] and generated using technical standards such as ERC-20, ERC-777, and ERC-721, which establish common sets of rules and keep track of ownership using P2P networks of computers.[133] In most cases, these innovations represent one of three types of instruments: 1) payment tokens, which act as means of exchange that do not give rise to claims on their issuers; 2) prepaid utility tokens to make payments on the platform of the issuer, generally a service that has not yet been significantly designed, built or tested; and 3) securities-like instruments related to rights on governance and revenue sharing in the project or a part of the expected return.[134] As result of the over-emphasis and idealisation of the technology, and the reactive and innovative nature of this new market, the legal status of ICOs is unclear, with regulators enquiring about the nature of this process and the instruments they issue.[135] Part of this problem can be found in the diversity of the instruments issued, which may give rise to wide variety of governance or financial rights depending on how the ICO is structured, thus, complicating their definition and inclusion within specific legal frameworks.

Building on the content of documents such as the SEC's[136] Framework for 'Investment Contract' Analysis of Digital Assets, the FCA's[137] Guidance on Cryptoassets, and the analysis found in *Commodity Futures Trading*

[131] Regulation 2023/1114 OJ L 150/40, 31 May 2023.

[132] Cohney et al (n 50) 2; Wermers, Haust and Bruinsma (n 128) 6.

[133] V Dhillon, D Metcalf and M Hooper, *Blockchain Enabled Applications. Understand the Blockchain Ecosystem and How to Make It Work for You* (California, APress Media, 2017) 80; A Gurrea-Martínez and N Remolina, 'The Law and Finance of Initial Coin Offerings' in C Brummer (ed), *Cryptoassets. Legal, Regulatory and Monetary Perspectives* (New York, Oxford University Press, 2019) 117–56, 118; International Organization of Securities Commissions, 'IOSCO Board Communication on Concerns Related to Initial Coin Offerings (ICOs)' (2018), available at www.iosco.org/news/pdf/IOSCONEWS485.pdf; Cohney et al (n 50) 2.

[134] S Das and A Majumdar, 'A Regulatory Outlook on Initial Coin Offerings' (2017), available at www.law.ox.ac.uk/business-law-blog/blog/2017/08/regulatory-outlook-initial-coin-offerings; Dutch Authority for the Financial Markets, 'AFM Warns of Serious Risks Associated with Initial Coin Offerings' (2017), available at www.afm.nl/en/professionals/nieuws/2017/nov/risico-ico; Gibraltar Financial Services Commission, 'Statement on Initial Coin Offerings' (2017), available at www.gfsc.gi/news/statement-on-initial-coin-offerings-250; Financial Conduct Authority (n 29); Wermers, Haust and Bruinsma (n 128) 7.

[135] Das and Majumdar (n 134).

[136] Securities and Exchange Commission, 'Framework for 'Investment Contract' Analysis of Digital Assets' (2019), available at www.sec.gov/files/dlt-framework.pdf.

[137] Financial Conduct Authority, 'Guidance on Cryptoassets. Feedback and Final Guidance' (2019), available at www.fca.org.uk/publication/policy/ps19-22.pdf.

Commission v Patrick K McDonnell and Cabbagetech, Corp d/b/a Coin Drop Markets,[138] the first group (payment tokens) can be classified as commodities that, under the Socio-Legal theory, could act as monetary *reifiers* based on digital social contracts. The second category (prepaid utility tokens) are closer to payment instruments, such as cheques and bills of exchange; however, as seen in chapter three, they cannot be labelled as money as they are not accepted by any person than the issuer.[139]

However, based on a technology-neutral approach, although we can represent the signatures and the instructions of these agreements in digital mediums, for now, actions such as the presentation of and the noting or protest set in documents such as the Regulation 51 of the Bills of Exchange Act 1882,[140] cannot be properly exercised in the case of these assets,[141] a fact that takes us to the main argument of this work, which states that – independently of their potential to act as the basis for new payment instruments – cryptoassets can be defined as infrastructural elements after current definitions applicable to electronic money and the qualified certificates related to it as defined in Article 3 (15) of Regulation 910/2014[142] of the European Parliament and of the Council if they are tolerated by the state in exercise of its *lex monetae*, and accepted by persons other than the issuer.

Finally, the third group (securities-like instruments) can be considered securities when, having a well-defined central third party, there is 'a contract, transaction or scheme whereby a person invests his money in a common enterprise and is led to expect profits solely from the efforts of the promoter or a third party'.[143] Of course, the analysis provided in the *Howey* case – and recently put into practice in *SEC v Telegram Group*[144] and *SEC v Ripple Labs*[145] – does not restrict other non-security cryptoassets from being packaged and sold as a security.[146] However, this book will focus on those cryptographic instruments designed to be employed as monetary *reifiers* and/or infrastructural assets within payment systems.

Unfortunately, as was seen in the case of the instruments of second generation, this classification is not stable given that some ICOs have retained the power to

[138] [2018] 18-CV-361 (US), at 128.

[139] Gleeson (n 14) 205.

[140] Bills of Exchange Act 1882.

[141] Regulation 89A of the Bills of Exchange Act and the Electronic Presentment of Instruments (Evidence of Payment and Compensation for Loss) Regulations 2018 allows us to present electronic images of a pre-existent tangible instruments, such as cheques and bills of exchange, for payment and compensation. Given that cryptoassets do not have a pre-existent tangible expression, they are not subject to these regulations.

[142] Regulation 910/2014 of the European Parliament and of the Council on electronic identification and trust services for electronic transactions in the internal market and repealing Directive 1999/93/EC OJ L 257/73, 23 July 2014.

[143] *SEC v WJ Howey Co et al* [1946] 328 US 293 (US), at 299.

[144] [2020] 19-cv-9439 (PKC) (US).

[145] [2023] 1:20-cv-10832-AT (US).

[146] W Hinman, 'Digital Asset Transactions: When Howey Met Gary (Plastic)' (2018), available at www.sec.gov/news/speech/speech-hinman-061418.

modify the rights associated with their instruments without disclosing that ability in simple terms, a strategy that is easy to implement given the lack of explainability of the algorithmic black boxes that configure the DLT protocols, the cloud services, and the smart contracts involved in the constitution, offering and diffusion of these cryptoassets.[147]

A. Designing Stable Reifiers: The Case of Stablecoins

The incorporation of non-standardised socio-legal sources of liquidity in assets that are inherently illiquid, and their rapid growth in adoption and diffusion, results in uncertainty that creates volatility within the cryptoassets market.[148] This volatility diminishes the market's ability to fulfil the expectations of those enthusiasts that claim that these instruments will act as the unit of account, means of payment and/or store of value of the DCS.[149] With this obstacle in mind, some developers have decided to attract new investors and users to their projects through the third generation of cryptoassets consistent in more centralised DLT protocols and ICOs commonly known as stablecoins. Ellen Gesmer J defines a stablecoin as a 'type of virtual currency that is designed to minimise price volatility'[150] by offering more familiar forms of incorporation of trust, which can be characterised as 1) asset-backed or 2) algorithmic.[151]

Within these categories is an evolutionary trend that started with the emergence of on-chain and off-chain collateralised projects that acted like digital versions of the Roman *aes signata*, linking the value of their instruments with a *res* identified with an asset or a pool of assets.[152] An illustration of these projects is Agrocoin.[153] Agrocoin started as an ICO – and currently offers different products as IEOs – and selected habanero peppers as the underlying source of liquidity for its asset, considering this crop's international prices, the favourable environment of the Yucatan Peninsula and increasing demand in foreign markets for

[147] Cohney et al (n 50) 6.

[148] Financial Stability Board, 'Decentralised Financial Technologies. Report on Financial Stability, Regulatory and Governance Applications' (2019) 15, available at www.fsb.org/wp-content/uploads/P060619.pdf.

[149] M Dell'Erba, 'Stablecoins in Cryptoeconomics: From Initial Coin Offerings to Central Bank Digital Currencies' (2019) 22 *Legislation and Public Policy* 1, 4–5.

[150] *Letitia James v iFinex Inc* [2020] 450545/19 (US), at 2.

[151] G Hileman et al, '2019 State of Stablecoins' (2019), available at www.blockchain.com/research; Financial Action Task Force (a), 'FATF Report to the G20 Finance Ministers and Central Bank Governors on So-Called Stablecoins' (2020), available at www.fatf-gafi.org/media/fatf/documents/recommendations/Virtual-Assets-FATF-Report-G20-So-Called-Stablecoins.pdf.

[152] G7 Working Group on Stablecoins, 'Investigating the Impact of Global Stablecoins' (2019), available at www.bis.org/cpmi/publ/d187.pdf; A Lipton, 'Toward a Stable Tokenized Medium of Exchange' in C Brummer (ed), *Cryptoassets. Legal, Regulatory and Monetary Perspectives* (New York, Oxford University Press, 2019) 89–115, 105–06; Dell'Erba (n 149) 10.

[153] Agrocoin, 'Agrocoin Whitepaper' (2018), available at agrocoin.com.mx/static/website/images/hidroponia/whitepaper.pdf; J Villamil, 'Cryptocurrency Backed with Habanero Peppers is a Thing in Mexico' (2018), available at www.bloomberg.com/news/articles/2018-03-22/crytpocurrency-backed-by-habanero-peppers-is-a-thing-in-mexico.

these peppers. Just as many other projects of this generation, the first version of Agrocoin was structured around a smart contract generated using an Ethereum standard such as ERC-20, and, in contrast with most of popular cryptoassets, each Agrocoin was backed by a square meter of a habanero pepper crop.[154] At first sight, this scheme could take our minds back to socio-Mengerian arrangements; however, this was only the first stage of a more complex incorporation process.[155]

From a monetary perspective, the circulation of these assets tends to be restricted to certain projects and platforms, similar to those tokens and vouchers described in Schedule 10A, Regulation 1(1) of the Finance Act 2003[156] of the UK. Furthermore, in the case of Agrocoin, one could easily argue that it was a security-like instrument given that, originally, it was a scheme by which people interested in investing their money were led, by a promoter/third party, to expect profits as described in *SEC v WJ Howey Co et al.*[157] After all, just as its white paper highlighted, the developers of this unit allowed 'investors to participate in the profit sharing of producing and commercialization (sic) habanero pepper'.[158] With that in mind, the market has required the gradual emergence of some hybrid projects that one could argue are ICOs given their design; however, their objective is to become global stable currencies. For this purpose, these cryptographic instruments are designed around different stabilisation mechanisms to be used outside their respective platforms by different persons other than the issuer, and backed (off-chain) by commodities such as oil, national currencies and (on-chain) by other cryptoassets.[159]

Within the first subgroup are projects that *reify* commodities and which are offered as ideal instruments to store value and to engage in commercial transactions outside their respective platforms, thus emerging as a key element of the decentralised finance (DeFi) ecosystem. An example of these instruments is OilCoin,[160] which was structured around the value of a reserve barrel of crude oil, just as Agrocoin backed its assets with habanero peppers. However, in the case of OilCoin, there is a transition that goes beyond its use in a specific platform or network. Oilcoin aimed to create a stablecoin that could be used widely in commercial transactions, changing the historical example of gold for oil as a source of underlying liquidity. Based on the characteristics of these innovations, Katherine Polk Failla DJ, has defined stablecoins as those assets that 'are designed

[154] Agrocoin (n 153).
[155] Cedillo (n 48) 48.
[156] Finance Act 2003.
[157] [1946] 328 US 293 (US), at 299.
[158] Agrocoin (n 153).
[159] G Baughman et al, 'The stable in stablecoins' (2022), available at www.federalreserve.gov/econres/notes/feds-notes/the-stable-in-stablecoins-20221216.html; Lipton (n 152) 103–05.
[160] We accessed the white paper on 6 January 2017; however, apparently, the website has ceased to exist. OilCoin, 'The OilCoin White Paper. A U.S. Based, Regulatory Compliant, Digital Reserve Currency' (2017), available at oilcoin.io/whitepaper/OilCoin_White_Paper.pdf.

to maintain a consistent value relative to non-digital assets such as gold or fiat currency, and for this reason they are neither decentralized nor mined.'[161]

However, during the development of this book, rather interesting project emerged within this subgroup; one that actually worked with an underlying digital social contract based on a set of terms and conditions that reproduced the contractual wording of the original USA source,[162] which, in turn, highlighted the relevance of the decisions taken within the referred jurisdiction for the global adoption of the project.[163] This project was Facebook's LIBRA/DIEM.

LIBRA/DIEM was presented through two white papers issued by the Libra Association, the first in June 2019[164] and the second in April 2020. The original proposal relied on the incorporation of a fully backed deposit within each Libra token as a *reifier* for a basket of major government-issued currencies, which would act as its trusted source of liquidity.[165] In practice, it would be designed as those artificial units of reference described in section III.A of chapter three. However, after the testimony of Mark Zuckerberg[166] before the US House of Representatives Committee on Financial Services, regulators from across the world argued that LIBRA/DIEM represented an infrastructural challenge to their *lex monetae* and issued some decisions, among which it is worth highlighting legislative drafts, such as A Bill to Prohibit Large Platform Utilities from Being a Financial Institution or Being Affiliated with a Person that Is a Financial Institution, and for Other Purposes.[167]

Following the structure of projects sponsored by large technology and/or financial firms, partially and fully collateralised with fiat money such as Tether,[168] Circle USD Coin,[169] Stronghold USD[170] or JPM Coin,[171] the second version

[161] *IN RE: Tether and Bitfinex Crypto Asset Litigation* [2021] 576 F.Supp.3d 55 (US), at 74.

[162] GN La Diega and I Walden, 'Contracting for the 'Internet of Things': Looking into the Nest' (2016) 7 *European Journal of Law and Technology* 1, 2.

[163] To illustrate this point, Mark Zuckerberg stated in a hearing that 'Facebook will not be a part of launching the Libra payments system anywhere in the world unless all US regulators approve it'. See M Zuckerberg, 'Hearing before the United States House of Representatives Committee on Financial Services' (2019), available at docs.house.gov/meetings/BA/BA00/20191023/110136/HHRG-116-BA00-Wstate-ZuckerbergM-20191023-U1.pdf.

[164] Libra Association, 'White Paper' (2019), available at libra.org/en-US/white-paper.

[165] DA Zetzsche, RP Buckley and DW Arner, 'Regulating Libra. The Transformative Potential of Facebook's Cryptocurrency and Possible Regulatory Responses' (2019) 47 *University of New South Wales Law Research Series* 1, 4; Zuckerberg (n 163).

[166] Zuckerberg (n 163).

[167] J García, 'A Bill to Prohibit Large Platform Utilities from Being a Financial Institution or Being Affiliated with a Person that Is a Financial Institution, and for Other Purposes' (2019), available at docs.house.gov/meetings/BA/BA00/20191023/110136/BILLS-116pih-KBTOFA.pdf.

[168] See tether.to.

[169] See www.circle.com/en-gb.

[170] See stronghold.co/stronghold-usd.

[171] JP Morgan, 'Digital solutions enabling instant transfer and clearing of multi-bank, multi-currency assets on a permissioned distributed ledger' (2023), available at www.jpmorgan.com/onyx/coin-system.htm#; H Son, 'JP Morgan Is Rolling out the First US Bank-Backed Cryptocurrency to Transform Payment Business' (2019), available at www.cnbc.com/2019/02/13/jp-morgan-is-rolling-out-the-first-us-bank-backed-cryptocurrency-to-transform-payments--.html.

of LIBRA/DIEM was closer to a fourth generation of cryptoassets that will be developed in the following chapters. This version, which bears similarities to the *recipis* system of the *Wisselbank*, added a single-currency model, that, according to the LIBRA Association, would be backed with sovereign currencies with a parity set 1:1, with the aim to create Libra dollars, Libra pounds, Libra euros, etc.[172] However, it is not certain that this parity will be stable in different scenarios and before certain externalities such as those introduced by the failure of Sillicon Valley Bank. To face this obstacle, some projects have incorporated a complementary set of rules known as Proof-of-Reserves (PoR) provided by companies such as Chainlink,[173] by which developers and centralised exchanges in DLT ecosystems are subject to independent audits in order to publicly verify the value of their reserves and prove their solvency.

B. Regulating Stablecoins in the Past, in the Present and in the Future

From an initial analysis, and from the experiences of Tether[174] and Circle's USDC,[175] which did not appropriately back their cryptoassets on the referred parity, a question emerges: if you are neither mining nor speculating on the value of the asset, what is the revenue model and/or the incentives that foster the creation of a cryptographic *reifier* of these characteristics? It is possible to argue that there is an historical inducement. For instance, IBM is working closely with projects such as Stronghold USD, aiming to create a new version of the current world wire: the IBM World Wire.[176] Furthermore, following the words of IBM's senior vice president of global industries, platforms and blockchain, Bridget van Kralingen, these efforts could be the cornerstone for a governance paradigm that would allow governments to issue CBDCs,[177] building upon instruments such as Article 11 of the 2EMD.[178] Of course, just as one can read between the lines of the second version of the LIBRA[179] white paper, these projects would allow

[172] Libra Association, 'Libra Whitepaper v 2.0' (2020), available at libra.org/en-US/white-paper/?noredirect=en-US.

[173] See chain.link/proof-of-reserve.

[174] NY Attorney General, 'Attorney General James Announces Court Order Against "Crypto" Currency Company Under Investigation for Fraud' (2019), available at ag.ny.gov/press-release/attorney-general-james-announces-court-order-against-crypto-currency-company-under.

[175] VG Huang, H Miao and C Ostroff, 'Circle's USDC Stablecoin Breaks Peg With $3.3 Billion Stuck at Silicon Valley Bank' (2023), available at www.wsj.com/articles/crypto-investors-cash-out-2-billion-in-usd-coin-after-bank-collapse-1338a80f.

[176] See stronghold.co/stronghold-usd.

[177] J Wieczner, 'IBM Is Working with A "Crypto-Dollar" Stablecoin.' (2018), available at fortune.com/2018/07/17/ibm-stablecoin-cryptocurrency-stellar.

[178] Directive 2009/110/EC of the European Parliament and of the Council on the taking up, pursuit and prudential supervision of the business of electronic money institutions amending Directives 2005/60/EC and 2006/48/EC and repealing Directive 2000/46/EC OJ L 267/7.

[179] Libra Association (n 164).

private parties to obtain lucrative contracts as infrastructural stakeholders and play a significant role in the organisation of new payment systems, and even in the design of CBDCs.[180]

These cases are rather interesting and bring to mind an existent model that *reifies* sovereign currencies that could ease the transition towards that aim: the Scottish and Northern Ireland banknotes.[181] Under Regulation 127 of the Banking Act 2009[182] and the Scottish and Northern Ireland Banknote Regulations 2009,[183] particularly Regulation 6(2), a bank that has been authorised by the Bank of England to issue notes within these jurisdictions must constitute an underlying source of liquidity through the following backing assets:

> (a) Bank of England banknotes of such denominations and series as are specified in the rules;
> (b) current coins of the United Kingdom; and
> (c) funds placed on deposit in sterling in an account held by the Bank of England and designated by the Bank of England for the purposes of this regulation.

To complement this model – or as an alternative – a scheme similar to the one developed by Limantour for the General Law of Credit Institutions of 1897[184] of Mexico, which was challenged with stabilising the value of the inside monies created by the banks of issue referred in its Article 15 around the monetary reference set by the state. For that purpose, Article 16 states that:

> The issue of notes shall not exceed three times the paid-up capital, nor shall it, together with deposits payable on demand or subject to withdrawal at not more than three days' notice, exceed twice the holdings of the bank in cash and gold and silver bullion.

Considering these elements, it would be interesting to see if the institutions – particularly commercial banks – that act as stakeholders in these stablecoin projects could, eventually, obtain a licence to issue regulated cryptographic *reifiers* backed by central bank money, under a variation of the Scottish and/or Mexican regulations. Under this arrangement, it would be possible to constitute public reserve-backed models that would complement those private stablecoins (known as tokenised deposits) employed by companies such as JP Morgan in order to ease wholesale transactions between financial intermediaries and their clients.[185]

Finally, at the end of this trend one can find algorithmic stablecoins, such as Basis,[186] which are not collateralised. These assets depend on an algorithmic *lex*

[180] Libra Association, 'Economics and the Libra Reserve' (2020), available at libra.org/en-US/economics-and-the-reserve/?noredirect=en-US#overview.
[181] Cedillo (n 48) 48.
[182] Banking Act 2009.
[183] Scottish and Northern Ireland Banknote Regulations 2009 (SI 2009/3056).
[184] Memoria Política de México, 'Ley General de Instituciones de Crédito, de Porfirio Díaz' (2023), available at www.memoriapoliticademexico.org/Textos/5RepDictadura/1897LGD.html.
[185] GY Liao and J Caramichael, 'Stablecoins. Growth Potential and Impact on Banking' (2022) 1334 *International Finance Discussion Papers* 1, 5.
[186] This project was not successful based on the conflicts of the secondary instruments required to run the protocol with some securities regulations currently in force in the US. See www.basis.io.

monetae expressed in software code by which their developers aim to maintain exchange rate stability through the interaction of different digital instruments.[187] The theory behind them sounds rather interesting and familiar, but the codes required for the operation of the smart contracts involved are designed by humans, *ergo* subject to key omissions, failures and biases. Furthermore, to avoid the introduction of black boxes with systemic relevance within our financial systems, the proper coding required by this model –and the challenge posed by the frictions between AI and Legisprudence[188] – would have to rely on a proper understanding of the socio-legal nature of money, which is one of the biggest challenges to have characterised our financial history.

VI. Are Cryptoassets Money?

During an interview on 25 June 2018, Agustín Carstens, the former governor of Banxico and current General Manager for the Bank for International Settlements, stated that cryptoassets 'are not money'.[189] This has been repeated by several central bankers around the world, such as the Governor of the Sveriges Riksbank, Stefan Ingves,[190] and inserted in the Directive (EU) 2018/843[191] of the European Parliament and the Council, popularly known as 5MLD,[192] and in Article 30 of the Law for the Regulation of Financial Technology Institutions of Mexico (FinTech Law).[193]

Following the same spirit, in its early stages, this work was structured around an aversion against the use of the term 'cryptocurrency' to define those cryptoassets used as means of payment, such as Bitcoin, Ether and XRP. This was supported by Betts J in *O'Dea v Merchants Trade Expansion Group Ltd*,[194] who stated that they could not be considered money at all based on the absence of a claim-*res*. Building Figure 7, one could argue that, under *lex contractus*, an agreement by which the parties involved agree on an exchange of goods for anything other than money can be treated as a barter instead of a sale. On this we can argue that contracts of

[187] Hileman at al (n 151).

[188] For an interesting discussion on this tension, see E Täks, et al, 'Creating CoReO, the Computer Assisted Copyright Reform Observatory' in M Araszkiewicz and K Płeszka (eds), *Logic in the Theory and Practice of Lawmaking* (Cham, Springer, 2015) 479–512.

[189] C Egli and C Hirter, 'My Message to Young People: Stop Trying to Create Money' (2018), available at www.bis.org/speeches/sp180704a.htm.

[190] S Ingves, 'Going Cashless' (2018) 55 *Finance & Development* 11, 12.

[191] Directive 2018/843 of the European Parliament and of the Council amending Directive (EU) 2015/849 on the prevention of the use of the financial system for the purposes of money laundering or terrorist financing, and amending Directives 2009/138/EC and 2013/36/EU OJ L 156/43, 30 May 2018.

[192] Article 2(d) defines 'virtual currencies' as 'digital representation of value that is not issued or guaranteed by a central bank or a public authority, is not necessarily attached to a legally established currency and does not possess a legal status of currency or money, but is accepted by natural or legal persons as a means of exchange and which can be transferred, stored and traded electronically.'

[193] Law for the Regulation of Financial Technology Institutions of Mexico DOF.

[194] [1938] 37 AR NSW (AU), at 417.

barter differ significantly from those transactions materialised using non-sovereign means of exchange as in *Wisconsin Central Ltd et al v United States*,[195] where the parties, following the words of Lord MacMillan,[196] assign monetary values to certain goods – separating the unit of account and the means of payment – and thus retaining their ultimate right to be paid on a sovereign currency.[197]

On this basis it can be argued that if it is possible to standardise and incorporate an underlying obligation that is accepted *erga omnes* within a community, these instruments could be considered money. For example, in *United States of America v Faiella*[198] the defendant, Robert Faiella, who operated on the now infamous Silk Road website, argued that Bitcoin did not qualify as money under Section 1960 of the US.Code;[199] however, Michael H Dolinger MJ, following Alison Nathan J did in *US v Murgio et al*,[200] rejected this argument, stating that:

> First, 'money' in ordinary parlance means 'something generally accepted as a medium of exchange, a measure of value, or a means of payment.' MERRIAM-WEBSTER ONLINE, http://www.merriam-webster.com/dictionary/money (last visited Aug. 18, 2014). As examples of this, Merriam-Webster Online includes 'officially coined or stamped metal currency,' 'paper money,' and 'money of account' – the latter defined as 'a denominator of value or basis of exchange which is used in keeping accounts and for which there may or may not be an equivalent coin or denomination of paper money' Id. Further, the text of Section 1960 refers not simply to 'money,' but to 'funds.' In particular, Section 1960 defines 'money transmitting' as 'transferring funds on behalf of the public by any and all means.' 18 U.S.C. § 1960(b)(2) (emphasis added). Merriam-Webster Online defines 'funds' as 'available money' or 'an amount of something that is available for use: a supply of something.' MERRIAM-WEBSTER ONLINE, http://www. merriam-webster.com/dictionary/fund (last visited Aug. 18, 2014).

So, when answering the question 'are cryptoassets money?' the first thing that one will find in academic sources relating to economics and banking law is the statement that money is an instrument that has to act as medium of exchange, unit of account and store of value. As developed in chapter two, these elements by themselves are not enough to define money in law. Despite the quasi-universal adoption of this definition, this is only a partial answer. Looking back at the definitions of money developed in chapters two and three, and that provided in cases such as *Moss v Hancock*[201] and *Miller v Race*,[202] the answer lies on the elements identified

[195] [2018] 138 S Ct 2067 (US), at 6.

[196] *Banco de Portugal v Waterlow & Sons Ltd* [1932] AC 452 (UK), at 459, 482, 485, 503.

[197] S Green, 'It's Virtually Money' in D Fox and S Green (eds), *Cryptocurrencies in Public and Private Law* (Oxford, Oxford University Press, 2019) 13–31, 20.

[198] [2013] 14-cr-243 JSR NY (US), at 545.

[199] Code of Laws of the United States of America (US Code) 44 Stat 778.

[200] [2015], 15-cr-00769 AJN (US), at 5–6.

[201] [1899], 2 QB 111 (UK), at 116.

[202] Lord Mansfield argued on the Bank of England notes that 'they are not goods, not securities, nor documents for debts, nor are so esteemed: but are treated as money, as cash, in the ordinary course and transaction of business, by the general consent of mankind; which gives them the credit and currency of money, to all intents and purposes.' See [1758] 97 ER 398 (UK), at 401.

by the Socio-Legal theory of money: the definition and standardisation of the underlying source of liquidity set by a stakeholder, the dynamic social system in which the new monetary instrument will circulate, and the necessities and oddities of this social system.

On this point, in the different academic forums where the Socio-Legal approach has been presented, some people have argued that one cannot use any available good to act as money, and in certain way, they are right. If one desires to fulfil certain obligations using artworks, as set out in the Decree of 31 October 1994[203] by which certain artists can pay their taxes in Mexico with their work, one could do it, but under exceptional circumstances, and these goods would not be considered as money per se. These goods and transactions are unique, and they do not represent the standardised practices recognised by a particular community. They represent an agreement between two parties, which is isolated from the remaining uniformed interactions: goods cannot buy goods.[204]

Therefore, just as in the case of complementary monies analysed in section VI.A of chapter two, cryptoassets depend on different sets of underlying obligations, stakeholders, governance arrangements based on computational codes and private entities that currently are not backed by any sovereign entity. So, in order to serve as means of payment, these units have to rely solely on the expectation on the part of private agents that they will be accepted following extrinsic beliefs, social customs, and/ technology preferences.[205] After all, as seen in cases such as *White v Elmdene Estates Ltd*[206] and decision SCR 100 of the Supreme Court of Canada in the Matter of Three Bills Passed by the Legislative Assembly of the Province of Alberta at the 1937 (Third Session),[207] it is possible to say that not being a liability of a central bank does not prevent cryptoassets from being used as money,[208] under the Socio-Legal theory of money.

First, as explored in chapters two and three, money has to act as store of value, means of payment and/or unit of account. If it does not fulfil one or all of these functions in an optimal way at the same time, that is matter for a different discussion. Following *Miliangos v George Frank (Textiles) Ltd*,[209] it is possible to argue that different assets may, in different contexts, play some or all of these roles,[210] and they may offer them for some people, but not for others, as seen under the

[203] Decree that partially forgives income tax liabilities of individuals engaged in the production of plastic works of art, and facilitates the payment of taxes for the sale of artistic works and antiques owned by such individuals DOF.

[204] LR Wray, 'Money' in GC Harcourt and P Kriesler (eds), *Oxford Handbook of Post-Keynesian Economics, Volume 1: Theory and Origins* (Oxford, Oxford University Press, 2013) 139–51, 139.

[205] N Kiyotaki and R Wright, 'On Money as a Medium of Exchange' (1989) 97 *Journal of Political Economy* 927–54, 928; Lo and Wang (n 51).

[206] [1959] 2 All ER 605 (US), at 610–11.

[207] [1938] *RE Alberta Statutes* SCR 100 (CA), at 116.

[208] R Ali et al, 'The Economics of Digital Currencies' (2014), available at www.bankofengland.co.uk/-/media/boe/files/digital-currencies/the-economics-of-digital-currencies.

[209] [1976] AC 443 (UK), at 460–70.

[210] R Ali et al (n 208).

Mercury/Mars/Yacatecuhtli approaches. Second, again, the argument against classifying cryptoassets as money is based on the unsupported assumption that all the instruments that constitute this market work using PoW protocols and follow Bitcoin's design, thus ignoring the existence and the potential of protocols, such as PoS, PoL and PoA to create permissioned networks with regulated and well-defined categories of nodes that could act as issuers/payers, payees, beneficiaries, etc. And third, it is possible to say that these arguments tend to ignore the potential evolution of these instruments and their gradual definition under existent regulations applicable to payment systems and electronic money.

Relatedly, although most DLT units are not restricted to geographical areas, it is evident that they are integral parts of digital communities structured around their own social agreements and networks in which *digital personas*, as described by Roger Clarke,[211] interact with each other using the technologies developed in the FIR. This argument can be taken further. Most of the analyses are focused on the role of cryptoassets as money, putting them at the same level as sovereign currencies; however, we see these innovations are money for Darwinian reasons, following the diffusion process that is taking us to the fourth generation of cryptoassets that will be introduced in chapter six.

Currently, cryptoassets can follow two paths. First, they can evolve and become a form of electronic money as defined in Regulation 2(1) of the Electronic Money Regulations 2011[212] of the UK and Article 2(2) of the 2EMD,[213] which can be used to make payments to different persons beyond the issuer.[214] This transition, in turn, would be the cornerstone for: a) a new payment system structured around governance paradigms, as described by Aikens J;[215] and/or b) set in place a free banking model designed around regulations, such as the Scottish and Northern Ireland Banknote Regulations 2009,[216] which could be the next step in the development of the stablecoins.

Second, following the spirit of cases, such as *Oxigen Evironmental Ltd v Mullan*,[217] these instruments could be considered *reifiers* equivalent to cash just other instruments such as cheques and bills of exchange are. Following the spirit of the *lex mercatoria* and the words of Lord Wilberforce in *Miliangos v George Frank (Textiles) Ltd*,[218] one can argue that money adapts itself to the necessities of trade. For

[211] R Clarke, 'The Digital Persona and Its Application to Data Surveillance' (1994) 10 *The Information Society* 77–92, 77.

[212] The Electronic Money Regulations 2011 (SI 2011/99).

[213] Directive 2009/110/EC of the European Parliament and of the Council on the taking up, pursuit and prudential supervision of the business of electronic money institutions amending Directives 2005/60/EC and 2006/48/EC and repealing Directive 2000/46/EC OJ L 267/7, 16 September 2009.

[214] Gleeson (n 14) 205.

[215] *Dubai Islamic Bank PJSC v Paymentech Merchant Services INC* [2001] 1 Lloyd's Rep 65 (UK), at 517–18.

[216] Scottish and Northern Ireland Banknote Regulations 2009 (SI 2009/3056).

[217] [2012] NIQB 17 (IRL).

[218] [1976] AC 443 (UK), at 460–70.

example, the JPM Coin and the other cryptographic *reifiers* that will follow it, could, in simpler terms, be designed to act as encrypted electronic cheques.

Some purists might argue that these projections go against the spirit of the Bitcoin white paper.[219] However, in practice, most of the parties involved in cryptoassets transactions do not accept cryptoasset payments through on-chain interactions. To conduct their activities, they employ the off-chain services offered by payment processors such as Coinbase, Binance or Bitso, which absorb all the liquidity and exchange risk in these transactions.[220] So, through this scheme, users receive currencies such as dollars, pounds and pesos, as in any ordinary monetary transaction, based on the exchange rate applicable at the moment of the operation[221] following the descriptions related to the *ius cudendae monetae* found in *Barclays Bank International v Levin Brothers*.[222]

VII. Conclusion

The aim of this chapter was to break with the trend found in academic and regulatory sources that rely heavily on Bitcoin and its characteristics to describe the cryptoassets market, and to offer solution to its imperfections. It presented a general introduction to DLT and the relevance of technology and service neutrality principles, as described in Article 9 of the Directive 2000/31/EC[223] on Electronic Commerce and Article 89 of the Mexican Commercial Code,[224] for the proper diffusion and gradual legal recognition of these cryptographic *reifiers*. This is not an easy process and, just as other monetary innovations have experienced in the past, these instruments require the development of new socio-legal infrastructures.

The cryptoassets market was analysed as three main generations that reflect perfectly a Schumpeterian trend. The first, represented by Bitcoin, introduced the DLT known as blockchain as the invention/commodity to be diffused. The second generation offers a transitional set of innovations materialised by projects such as Ripple and Ethereum, which started the diffusion process through global value chains and the creation of smart contracts to configure new payment systems. Finally, in the third generation can be seen the emergence of 'perfected' ICOs

[219] Nakamoto (n 31).

[220] T Durden, 'Cryptocurrency Concentration. Just 4% Own Over 95% of Bitcoin' (2017), available at www.zerohedge.com/news/2017-09-19/cryptocurrency-concentration-just-4-own-over-95-bitcoin.

[221] A Kroeger and A Sarkar, 'Is Bitcoin Really Frictionless' (2016), available at libertystreeteconomics.newyorkfed.org/2016/03/is-bitcoin-really-frictionless.html.

[222] [1976] 3 WLR 852 (UK).

[223] Directive 2000/31/EC of the European Parliament and of the Council on certain legal aspects of information society services, in particular electronic commerce, in the Internal Market (Directive on electronic commerce) OJ L 178/1, 8 June 2000.

[224] Commercial Code DOF.

known as stablecoins by which developers look to stabilise the value of the assets, backing them with sovereign currencies and/or algorithmic formulas. As one would expect, this diffusion process has caught the attention of central banks and big tech companies such as OpenAI, which are analysing whether cryptoassets are money and the potential of DLT to offer a fourth generation of these instruments under the label of CBDCs.

5

Shadow Banking and a New Generation of Intermediaries

I. Introduction

Bank business models are not static, and nor do they emerge spontaneously. They evolve over time and under the influence of a *Bildungstrieb* that in the financial world we know as 'shadow banking', which can be understood as the set of institutions and contracts that are designed and are legal outside the regulatory framework put in place by nations in a particular context to offer assets and liabilities that are accepted as substitutes of money. Consequently, the constitutive and operative elements of a shadow banking system do not have access to sovereign reserves and/or guarantees. However, such systems have fostered the evolution of our financial systems following a complex mix of exogenous and endogenous pressures, including: the structural evolution and internationalisation of the financial system; the regulatory framework; the competitive environment in banking markets; and the impact of new technologies.[1] Unfortunately, as seen through the lack of uniformity found in the definitions of 'money' and 'free banking' 'shadow banking tends to be described in the context of the GFC.

After the collapse of Lehman Brothers in 2008, authors such as Gary Gorton and Andrew Metrick[2] presented definitions of 'shadow banking' based on the structural changes of our FWS after the collapse of the Bretton Woods system; changes that resulted in the development of the financial landscape, which, in turn, fostered the fall of Lehman.[3] Therefore, they argue that private innovation, the global wave of financial deregulation, and the falling communications costs of the last 30–40 years helped to develop the *Bildungstrieb* referred to above.[4] Based on these developments, the very term 'shadow banking' has

[1] DT Llewellyn, 'Fifty Years in the Evolution of Bank Business Models' in M Balling and E Gnan (eds), *50 Years of Money and Finance. Lessons and Challenges* (Brussels, Larcier, 2013) 319–54, 319.

[2] G Gorton and A Metrick, 'Regulating the Shadow Banking System' Brookings Papers on Economic Activity (2010) available at muse.jhu.edu/article/420644/summary.

[3] HM Schooner and MW Taylor, *Global Bank Regulation. Principles and Policies* (London, Academic Press, 2010) 9–16.

[4] PR Lane and GM Milesi-Ferretti, 'The Drivers of Financial Globalization' (2008) 98 *American Economic Review* 327–32, 327.

been attributed to the economist and money manager Paul McCulley[5] who, in 2007, defined it as 'a large segment of financial intermediation that is routed outside the balance sheets of regulated commercial banks and other depositary institutions'.

However, before accepting these rather popular definitions, one has to question and understand how shadow banking is conceived. One problem is that, despite recognising that innovation and suboptimal regulations are behind these institutions and the crises relating to them, we keep working with models structured around the existence of a set of defined, unchanging, institutions, instruments and forms of money.[6] In opposition to this view, it is important to note that the history of shadow banking is one of shifts in the type of not only institutions, but also of contracts involved in the evolution of our financial systems.[7] So, can we say that shadow banking is a new phenomenon? Certainly, the answer is no.

Almost every year, even before the period of stability that came with the Bretton Woods system, a myriad of authors, including Hammond Chubb[8] and James Meigs,[9] claimed that we were living in the middle of periods of financial innovation that change the existing paradigm at the time they were writing. From their works, we will note, on the one hand, that these changes have their genesis in the introduction of new practices, flawed regulations, and pseudo-banking institutions that, in words of Chubb, 'are prepared to give effect to … false principles of banking'.[10] On the other hand, through these changes, it has been possible to introduce novel financial products and processes to improve the allocation of capital and risk management, such as in the case of bills of exchange and algorithmic trading.[11]

Now, can we say that new FinTech intermediaries and technology companies are shadow banks? The answer is yes. Furthermore, just as in the case of shadow banking, one can argue that FinTech is not a new phenomenon. If we understand this term as the use of technology to deliver financial solutions, there are many older examples, such as money itself, which is a technology created to *reify* socio-legal interactions, and the laying of transatlantic telegraph cable that, in 1866, provided the fundamental infrastructure for the period of strong financial

[5] P McCulley, 'Teton Reflections' (2007), available at www.pimco.com/en-us/insights/economic-and-market-commentary/global-central-bank-focus/teton-reflections.

[6] This view also is behind the development of certain elements of the Efficient Market Theory by means of which authors such as Eugene Fama argue that information about individual securities is practically freely available to all participants. See EF Fama, 'Mandelbrot and the Stable Paretian Hypothesis' (1963) 36 *Journal of Business* 420–29.

[7] P Jackson, 'Shadow Banking and New Lending Channels. Past and Future' in M Balling and E Gnan (eds), *50 Years of Money and Finance. Lessons and Challenges* (Brussels, Larcier, 2013) 377–414, 377.

[8] H Chubb, 'The Bank Act and the Crisis of 1866' (1872) 35 *Journal of the Statistical Society of London* 179.

[9] J. Meigs, 'Recent Innovations in the Functions of Banks' (1966) 56 *The American Economic Review* 167.

[10] Chubb (n 8) 179.

[11] E Avgouleas, 'Regulating Financial Innovation' in N Moloney, E Ferran and J Payne (eds), *Oxford Handbook of Financial Regulation* (Oxford, Oxford University Press, 2017) 660–92, 660.

globalisation from 1866 to 1913.[12] Even the origins of the term 'FinTech' can be traced back to the early 1990s and the Financial Services Technology Consortium initiated by Citigroup.[13] Currently, institutions like the Financial Stability Board (FSB) define FinTech as 'technology-enabled innovation in financial services that could result in new business models, applications, processes, or products with an associated material effect on financial markets and institutions and the provision of financial services.'[14] If we look again at our definition of shadow banking, it is easy to infer that FinTech innovations developed during the last 15 years have been created by entities that offer products and services, which, without being illegal in most cases, they are currently sub-optimally regulated. In the case of cryptoassets, we could even argue that they are subject to a sub-optimal exercise of *lex monetae*.

II. The Cryptoparadox

In May 2018, the author attended an academic event at a well-reputed business school where different presenters argued about the state of the cryptoassets market and the potential of its related innovations. Among the referred presenters was an IT expert who was very excited about the virtues of decentralisation and disintermediation. However, at the end of his defence of such virtues, he asked the audience: 'Who among you own Bitcoins?' After only few of us raised our hands, he announced to the rest of the auditorium: 'All of you have to open an account at CoinBase and spent at least £10, once you have left this room.'

Common among definitions of 'cryptoassets', such as that offered by the Treasury Committee of the House of Commons of the UK,[15] the FCA,[16] and the Law Commission,[17] is the notion that these instruments do not require the involvement of intermediaries. However, can we say that the evolution of this market and the institutions relating to it follows a decentralised/disintermediated paradigm? This book has emphasised that money needs infrastructures and social agreements for its optimal diffusion. However, just as was witnessed in the 1990s, during the early days of electronic commerce, the term

[12] DW Arner, J Barberis and RP Buckley, '150 Years of Fintech. An Evolutionary Analysis' (2016) 3 *The Finsia Journal of Applied Finance* 22–29, 22.

[13] DW Arner, J Barberis and RP Buckley, 'The Evolution of FinTech: A New Post-Crisis Paradigm?' (2016) 47 *Georgetown Journal of International Law* 1271–319, 1272.

[14] Financial Stability Board, 'Decentralised Financial Technologies. Report on Financial Stability, Regulatory and Governance Applications' (2019) 15, available at www.fsb.org/wp-content/uploads/P060619.pdf.

[15] House of Commons, 'Crypto-Assets. Twenty-Second Report of Session 2017–19' (2018) 4, available at publications.parliament.uk/pa/cm201719/cmselect/cmtreasy/910/910.pdf.

[16] Financial Conduct Authority, 'Guidance on Cryptoassets' (2019), available at www.fca.org.uk/publication/consultation/cp19-03.pdf.

[17] Law Commission, 'Digital Assets. Final Report' (2023), available at www.lawcom.gov.uk/project/digital-assets.

'disintermediation' plays a significant role in academic and regulatory discussions around the world.[18]

It can be argued that an intermediary is not required where a DLT node takes part in the interactions developed within certain blockchains, or works on copies of different source codes to create new sources of liquidity. However, the DCS has not only fostered the gradual replacement of traditional intermediaries by business models, such as Open Banking, but also the emergence of new intermediaries like cryptoassets miners. Now, although developers and enthusiasts like Vitalik Buterin – following the example set by Aristotle in his *Politics*[19] – actively attack the emergence of this new generation of intermediaries,[20] the cryptoassets market demands, following the Lancasterian hypothesis, the creation of these institutions to serve it.[21] Furthermore, it must also be highlighted that a rising number of cryptoasset transactions are not performed 'on-chain' (directly on the respective DLT network), but 'off-chain' via internal accounting systems operated by centralised exchanges, wallets and payment companies. Consequently, although most 'coiners' argue that they are DLT 'experts' because they make transactions every day through different exchanges, these 'off-chain' transactions do not appear on the decentralised public ledgers.[22]

A. Issuers

The most shadowy element of the cryptoasset ecosystem, and even within the organic elements of our FinTech dragon, is the cryptoassets issuer, particularly the unbacked cryptoassets issuer. In exercise of this *crypto lex monetae*, during a 2018 meeting held with innovators, and staff of the FCA and the Bank of England, the leader of one DLT project stated that he 'acted as a central banker'. Nobody discussed this point further, and this was not surprising. Most of the recent cases[23] that involve cryptoassets issuers mention section 5(a) and (c) of the Securities Act, which requires issuers of securities to register their offerings of securities

[18] D Rowland, U Kohl and A Charlesworth, *Information Technology Law* (Abingdon, Routledge, 2017) 73.

[19] Aristotle argued that those intermediaries that emerged to create money from money, developed 'unnatural' and 'hated' activities. See Aristotle, *Politics* (Oxford, Clarendon Press, 1908) 46.

[20] R Dillet, 'Vitalik Buterin: "I Definitely Hope Centralized Exchanges Go Burn in Hell as Much as Possible"' (2018), available at techcrunch.com/2018/07/06/vitalik-buterin-i-definitely-hope-centralized-exchanges-go-burn-in-hell-as-much-as-possible/?guccounter=1.

[21] P Artus and C de Boissieu, 'The Process of Financial Innovation: Causes, Forms, and Consequences' in A Heertje (ed), *Innovation, Technology, and Finance* (Oxford, European Investment Bank, 1988) 101–26, 110.

[22] G Hileman and M Rauchs, 'Global Cryptocurrency Benchmarking Study' (2017), available at www.jbs.cam.ac.uk/fileadmin/user_upload/research/centres/alternative-finance/downloads/2017-global-cryptocurrency-benchmarking-study.pdf.

[23] See *SEC v Sun, et al. and In the Matters of Lohan; Paul; Way; Mahone; Mason; McCollum; Smith; Thiam* [2023] 1:23-cv-02433 (US), and *SEC v Payward Ventures, et al (d/b/a Kraken)* [2023] 3:23-cv-00588 (US).

through an effective registration statement before the referred instruments are offered and sold in the market. However, as this book has argued, cryptoassets can be designed to offer different solutions to different social systems. So, according to Article 3(10) of MiCA[24] we can define an 'issuer' as 'a natural or legal person, or other undertaking, who issues crypto-assets and distributes them to the participant's unique "wallet" address on the blockchain'.[25]

These shadow banks play additional roles to those in the most popular analyses on the shadow banking system. Why are they different? Well, as was seen in the previous chapter, these stakeholders develop and/or control – through the exercise of IPRs – the technological infrastructure needed to offer assets and liabilities that are accepted as substitutes of money. Additionally, based on this infrastructural control, they can structure and regulate the interactions developed around the networks of users, intermediaries and other technology providers that emerge from the traits that define the basic infrastructure. With that in mind we can say that there are two categories of issuers: 1) those that issue un-backed and pure algorithmic cryptoassets; and 2) those that tokenise tangible and intangible traditional assets and contracts. As we saw in chapter four, the first generation of cryptoassets was defined by the issuance of un-backed instruments through decentralised protocols and issuers that were not known.[26] Their name derives from the fact that they are not supported by any underlying financial asset nor sovereign claim and, consequently, these cryptographic assets have no inherent value. The value that we see in the news and markets is supported by the self-fulfilling expectation that these cryptoassets and/or their underlying infrastructure will be used in the future across different regulated industries, and that they constitute a 'fun investment', despite not offering any value to the social system.[27] It is possible to argue that this is the main reason behind the extreme volatility of the prices.[28] Consequently, as we can verify in cases like *SEC v Sun, et al and In the Matters of Lohan; Paul; Way; Mahone; Mason; McCollum; Smith; Thiam*,[29] *SEC v Payward Ventures, et al (d/b/a Kraken)*[30] and *SEC v Ripple Labs*,[31] among others, regulators often conclude that these un-backed cryptoassets behave more like speculative instruments.

In the case of the tokenisation of assets, we face a very interesting scenario, popularly illustrated through the case of stablecoins and non-fungible tokens

[24] Regulation 2023/1114 OJ L 150/40, 31 May 2023.

[25] *SEC v Crowd Machine, Inc, Metavine, Inc, and Craig Derel Sproule* [2022] 5:22-cv-00076 (US) 6.

[26] P Bains et al, 'Regulating the Crypto Ecosystem: The Case of Unbacked Crypto Assets' (2022), available at www.imf.org/en/Publications/fintech-notes/Issues/2022/09/26/Regulating-the-Crypto-Ecosystem-The-Case-of-Unbacked-Crypto-Assets-523715.

[27] House of Commons Treasury Committee, 'Regulating Crypto. Fifteenth Report of Session 2022–2023' (2023), available at committees.parliament.uk/publications/39945/documents/194832/default.

[28] W Bolt, V Lubbersen and P Wierts, 'Balancing Public and Private Interests: Crypto, Stablecoin, and Central Bank Digital Currency' (2022), available at www.suerf.org/docx/f_c2636c1bac9e9f0b4681955165240396_44617_suerf.pdf.

[29] [2023] 1:23-cv-02433 (US).

[30] [2023] 3:23-cv-00588 (US).

[31] [2020] 1:20-cv-10832 (US).

(NFTs), such as issuers employing DLT tokens as *reifiers* for the rights and/or assets that the stakeholders want to incorporate, store, distribute and, in some cases, destroy. In some jurisdictions, regulated institutions, such as banks and even central banks, are starting to employ DLT to tokenise monetary claims, and are fostering the emergence of new terms like 'tokenisation'[32] and 'tokenomics',[33] which are closely related to the verification of the content and the stability of the asset, and the role of these innovations in the economy of the DCS.

At the same time, issuers can distribute these assets in five main ways that combine off-chain and on-chain interactions: 1) pre-token sales; 2) initial coin offerings; 3) mining; 4) airdrops; and 5) forks, which together act as the *Bildungstrieb* of our *ius cudendae monetae*. Finally, these actions of creation and distribution are generally described by issuers in documents known as white papers, which were introduced by Satoshi Nakamoto with the aim of providing information on the assets, including their developers, objectives and other technical information. However, these documents can empower the next Waterlow & Sons to introduce informational asymmetries considering that white papers vary in their quality, with many containing incomplete or inaccurate information[34] that does not reflect the reality being coded in the respective smart contract.[35]

B. Miners

We have said the issuers develop and control the technological infrastructure that supports the creation and distribution of cryptoassets; however, just as in the case of other monetary expressions, these assets do not exist in isolation in their respective blockchains. Accordingly, the second constitutive element of our 'crypto shadow banking system' is the miner. If you wanted to obtain a Bitcoin back in 2010, online advice would tell you to act as a 'miner'[36] or pay one; these DLT nodes are an integral part of the scheme by which the network collects pending transactions, verifies their legitimacy and assembles them into a 'block candidate'.[37] Accordingly, we can define a 'miner' as:[38]

[32] '[T]he process of representing claims digitally on a programmable platform'. See Bank for International Settlements, 'Blueprint for the future monetary system: improving the old, enabling the new' (2023), available at www.bis.org/publ/arpdf/ar2023e3.htm.

[33] It is an emerging field that 'studies how tokens can be used as a form of currency for digital services'. See S Kampakis, 'Auditing Tokenomics: A Case Study and Lessons from Auditing a Stablecoin Project' (2022) 5 *The Journal of the British Blockchain Association* 1, 1.

[34] Bains et al (n 26).

[35] S Cohney et al, 'Coin-Operated Capitalism' (2018), available at papers.ssrn.com/sol3/papers.cfm?abstract_id=3215345.

[36] The term 'miner' is used as an analogy between the process of creating a new digital unit and unearthing gold.

[37] A Berensten and F Schär, 'A Short Introduction to the World of Cryptocurrencies' (2018) 100 *Federal Reserve Bank of St. Louis Review* 1, 5–6.

[38] *SEC in the Matter of BTC Trading, Corp and Ethan Burnside* [2014] 3-16307 (US), at 3.

> [A]n individual or entity that participates in a decentralized virtual currency network by running special software to solve complex algorithms in a distributed proof-of-work or other distributed proof system used to validate transactions in the virtual currency system. Certain virtual currencies (e.g., Bitcoin and Litecoin), self-generate units of the currency by rewarding miners with newly created coins.

In the initial stage of the evolution of the first-generation units, the idea was to create a uniform distribution of responsibilities through the network that would be the basis of the decentralisation idea, acting as the core of the arguments that support the development of these technologies. However, just as Falk MJ accurately describes, some very substantial commercial organisations are involved, and we have witnessed a gradual process of centralisation based on the rapid increase in computing power, the expansion of 'server farms', and the transition to other protocols like PoS, which are based on the amount of assets and/or time spent in the network to increase the opportunities to obtain more cryptographic incentives.[39]

Furthermore, we can argue that the role of these shadow banks within each network depends on the different views incorporated by different issuers, which, in turn, can be inferred by the management and enforcement of the IPRs involved. In *Tulip Trading Limited v Bitcoin Association for BSV*,[40] we can identify some of the moral issues presented in *Jacobsen v Katzer*[41] on the exercise of moral rights, which tend to be expressly discarded by some practitioners who have exchanged some ideas with the author on the relevance of these prerogatives in the constitution of FinTech start-ups. These colleagues have argued that within our FinTech dragon, the constitution, the marketing and the fast deployment of the products and services offered by the new generation of shadow banks is more important than the protection and understanding of IPRs. However, in *Tulip Trading* we have a perfect illustration of the exercise of moral rights in the hands of the developer and a misunderstanding of these prerogatives identified by Falk MJ[42] in the following terms:

> [T]here is no mechanism among miners that could allow for a collective refusal to accept a software update, the consensus mechanism that does exist being limited to the acceptance by nodes of blocks of transactions verified by other nodes (by using the hash value produced as the starting point for the next block), rather than relating to the protocols that govern the Network.

Consequently, in exercise of IPRs a few big players have installed huge computer capacity in large, dedicated premises and have applied for several patents relating to this process. Therefore, their exploitation of economies of scale has led, paradoxically, to the concentration of market power,[43] and to the development of

[39] *Tulip Trading Limited v Bitcoin Association for BSV* [2022] EWHC 667 (UK), at 6.
[40] [2022] EWHC 667 (UK).
[41] [2008] 535 F.3d 1373 (US).
[42] *Tulip Trading Limited v Bitcoin Association for BSV* [2022] EWHC 667 (UK), at 9.
[43] Office of the Chief Economist, 'Cryptocurrencies and Blockchain' (2018), available at documents.worldbank.org/curated/en/293821525702130886/pdf/125990-WP-7-5-2018-9-39-58-ECAEconomicUpdateCryptocurrenciesandBlockchainMayweb.pdf.

infrastructural power, just as other financial intermediaries have done throughout financial history.

This concentration of infrastructural power and evolution of protocols has fostered the development of cartels in which large owners of assets, commonly referred to as 'whales', know each other and coordinate their efforts to corner the market.[44] Given that these miners control a substantial part of the cryptoassets market, they are in a perfect position to manipulate transaction fees, refuse to process certain types of transactions, or deny service to users, independently that some of their actions, such a sudden sell of a portion of their cryptoassets, could result in acute price oscillations such as those that have characterised this market.[45] As an illustration of this potential, on 17 November 2017, one of these 'whales' moved approximately 25,000 Bitcoins to an online exchange, an action that worried speculators who argued that this move meant the owner was about to sell these assets.[46] It is certainly possible to argue that these 'whales' have the power to exercise a *crypto lex monetae* within their respective networks.

Given this situation, DLT communities have put in place efforts like the Blockchain Defensive Patent License[47] by which the purists and idealists who propounded the document encourage peaceful interaction among patent-holders who, in turn, are invited to generate open, zero-cost licences relating to their inventions in line with a utopian innovation system. Of course, as one can see through the analysis of the number of patent applications relating to mining processes, this effort can be labelled as irrelevant and ignorant of the dynamic nature of financial systems and IP strategies.

C. Exchanges/Trading Platforms

The emergence of the FinTech dragon has relied on the proliferation of digital platforms over the past 20 years. These platforms can be defined – building on the definition provided by the EBA – as a technical infrastructure that enables regulated and unregulated financial intermediaries to market customers, and/or conclude with customers' contracts for financial products and services.[48] So, if you do not want to spend the money, the time and the energy required to take part of the mining process – or to work on a patentable invention to ease your efforts – you can always look for a cryptoasset service provider to acquire the assets you

[44] I Cedillo, 'A New Approach for 'Cryptoassets' Regulation' (2019) 35 *Banking & Finance Law Review* 37, 50.

[45] Office of the Chief Economist (n 43).

[46] O Kharif, 'Thinking about Bitcoin? Beware the Whales' (2017) 4550 *Bloomberg Businessweek* 32, 32.

[47] See blockchaindpl.org.

[48] European Banking Authority, 'Report on the Use of Digital Platforms' (2021), available at www.eba.europa.eu/sites/default/documents/files/document_library/Publications/Reports/2021/1019865/EBA%20Digital%20platforms%20report%20-%20210921.pdf.

want, generally an exchange. In *US v Trendon T Shavers*,[49] the following definition of exchange for the purposes of this market is set out:

> In return for a commission, Bitcoin exchangers accept payments of currency in some conventional form (cash, wire transfer, or the like) and exchange the money for a corresponding number of Bitcoin, based on a fluctuating exchange rate. Exchangers also accept payments of Bitcoin and exchange the Bitcoin back for conventional currency, again, charging a commission for the service.

Although the role of these platforms is opaque, given the variety of assets and governance models that we can identify in contexts like the Chapter 11 declaration from FTX Trading Limited to the District Court of Delaware,[50] the primary function of these exchange platforms is to provide services to buy and sell different cryptoassets for sovereign currencies like the US dollar, the Mexican peso or the pound sterling, and other cryptoassets, with publicly posted prices and order books,[51] as explained in the recitals of MiCA:

> When a crypto-asset service provider executing orders for crypto-assets on behalf of clients is the client's counterparty, there might be similarities with the services of exchanging crypto-assets for funds or other crypto-assets. However, in exchanging crypto-assets for funds or other crypto-assets, the price for such exchanges is freely determined by the crypto-asset service provider as a currency exchange. Yet in the execution of orders for crypto-assets on behalf of clients, the crypto-asset service provider should always ensure that it obtains the best possible result for its client, including when it acts as the client's counterparty, in line with its best execution policy. The exchange of crypto-assets for funds or other crypto-assets when made by the issuer or offeror should not be a crypto-asset service.

Accordingly, the first generation of exchanges performed this function through two operational stages. In the first stage, these intermediaries set master nodes – acting as miners – to participate in 'on-chain' interactions in different DLT networks with the aim of offering to the public the cryptoassets obtained from these efforts. In the second stage, we witnessed the emergence of trading platforms know as P2P exchanges, which started to develop activities that are rather similar to those executed by conventional stock exchanges, matching buyers and sellers, even when they do not sell assets themselves.[52]

At the same time, these exchanges allow users to manage a digital wallet and even acquire products and services with institutions such as Visa and Mastercard that have signed agreements with them. Again, we start to witness a historical

[49] [2014] 4:13-CV-416 (US), at 3.

[50] *In re: FTX Trading Ltd, et al* [2022] 22-11068-JTD (US).

[51] S Lo and JC Wang, 'Bitcoin as Money?' (2014), available at www.bostonfed.org/publications/current-policy-perspectives/2014/bitcoin-as-money.aspx; Hileman and Rauchs (n 22).

[52] D Awrey and K van Zwieten, 'The Shadow Payment System' (2018) 43 *The Journal of Corporation Law* 102, 122–23; R Houben and A Snyers, 'Cryptocurrencies and Blockchain. Legal Context and Implications for Financial Crime, Money Laundering and Tax Evasion' (2018), available at www.europarl.europa.eu/cmsdata/150761/TAX3%20Study%20on%20cryptocurrencies%20and%20blockchain.pdf.

trend. Just as in most of the free banking experiences, some functions traditionally associated with clearing houses start to emerge from these exchanges, which, for a fee, receive cryptographic instruments from the user and forward the amount of sovereign currency to retailers.[53] Significantly, given the potential existence of frictions that result from these conversions, one might see differences in prices associated with cryptoassets that are strictly homogenous by design.[54]

In response to the introduction of these services and the risks that could derive from them, the European Commission stated under Section 2 of its draft Directive of the European Parliament and the Council amending Directive 2015/849 on the prevention of the use of the financial system for the purposes of money laundering and terrorist financing and amending Directive 2009/101/EC that:

> In respect of designing providers of exchange services between virtual currencies and fiat currencies as obliged entities, the proposed amendments respect the proportionality principle. In order to allow competent authorities to monitor suspicious transactions with virtual currencies, while preserving the innovative advances offered by such currencies, it is appropriate to define as obliged entities under the 4AMLD all gatekeepers that control access to virtual currencies, in particular exchange platforms and wallet providers.

This was addressed by the European Union on 10 January 2020 through the Commission's proposal known as 5MLD,[55] and incorporated into the Money Laundering, Terrorist Financing and Transfer of Funds (Information on the Payer) Regulations 2017[56] at the end of 2019, thus extending the Anti-Money Laundering/Combating the Financing of Terrorism Regulations to these intermediaries.[57] However, the regulatory efforts relating to these intermediaries did not end with these measures. MiCA, Article 77 looks to address the frictions that emerge from prices establishing that:

> 1. Crypto-asset service providers exchanging crypto-assets for funds or other crypto-assets shall establish a nondiscriminatory commercial policy that indicates, in particular, the type of clients they agree to transact with and the conditions that shall be met by such clients.
> 2. Crypto-asset service providers exchanging crypto-assets for funds or other crypto-assets shall publish a firm price of the crypto-assets or a method for determining the price of the crypto-assets that they propose to exchange for funds or other crypto-assets, and any applicable limit determined by that crypto-asset service provider on the amount to be exchanged.

[53] A Kroeger and A Sarkar, 'Is Bitcoin Really Frictionless' (2016), available at libertystreeteconomics.newyorkfed.org/2016/03/is-bitcoin-really-frictionless.html.

[54] ibid.

[55] Directive 2018/843 of the European Parliament and of the Council amending Directive (EU) 2015/849 on the prevention of the use of the financial system for the purposes of money laundering or terrorist financing, and amending Directives 2009/138/EC and 2013/36/EU OJ L 156/43, 30 May 2018.

[56] SI 2017, No 692.

[57] Financial Conduct Authority (n 16).

3. Crypto-asset service providers exchanging crypto-assets for funds or other crypto-assets shall execute client orders at the prices displayed at the time when the order for exchange is final. Crypto-asset service providers shall inform their clients of the conditions for their order to be deemed final. 4. Crypto-asset service providers exchanging crypto-assets for funds or other crypto-assets shall publish information about the transactions concluded by them, such as transaction volumes and prices.

D. Wallets

Among the arguments of decentralisation and disintermediation that characterise our cryptoassets market, one can find a functional equivalence in the software and hardware that allow users in traditional retail banking to hold and store these assets in 'wallets'.[58] In *United States v Ulbricht*,[59] the US Court of Appeals for the Second Circuit defined a wallet, in the context of assets of first generation as:

> [A] storage method for Bitcoins. The wallet is associated with a Bitcoin address, which is 'analogous to the account number for a bank account, while the "wallet" is analogous to a bank safe where the money in the account is physically stored'.

To complement this definition, and as can be seen in the repository of the files that constitute the underlying architecture for the European Digital Identity Wallet,[60] it is important to highlight that wallets are not proper storage for cryptoassets, but a set of online files (hot storage) and hardware devices (cold storage) used to manage and store cryptographic identities, commonly known as keys,[61] just as the old Mondex did.[62] In the context of DLT networks, we can identify two categories of keys: one public key that acts as an address and identifier for other nodes in the network; and a private individual key, which is employed to sign transactions and access the funds held in the account.[63] Therefore, these files and devices allow users to send and receive cryptoassets while they monitor their balances and automate certain functions, such as, estimating what fee to pay to achieve a desired transaction confirmation time.[64]

[58] T Barbereau and B Bodó, 'Beyond financial regulation of crypto-asset wallet software: In search of secondary liability' (2023) 49 *Computer Law & Security Review* 1–17, 2; C Hare, 'Cryptocurrencies and Banking Law. Are There Lessons to Learn?' in D Fox and S Green (eds), *Cryptocurrencies in Public and Private Law* (Oxford, Oxford University Press, 2019) 229–53, 231.

[59] [2017] 15-1815-CR (US), at 9.

[60] See github.com/eu-digital-identity-wallet/eudi-doc-architecture-and-reference-framework.

[61] Barbereau and Bodó (n 58).

[62] Hare (n 58) 233.

[63] European Securities and Markets Authority, 'Advice. Initial Coin Offerings and Crypto-Assets' (2019), available at www.esma.europa.eu/sites/default/files/library/esma50-157-1391_crypto_advice.pdf; H Hasanova et al, 'A Survey on Blockchain Cybersecurity' (2018) 29 *International Journal of Network Management* 1, 5; Barbereau and Bodó (n 58); Hileman and Rauchs (n 22).

[64] ibid.

Hot wallets such as Blockchain[65] or those managed by Bitso, are offered as applications that can be downloaded to our computers, tablets and mobile phones, or as wallets stored in the cloud, meaning that they can be accessible from any computing device or location.[66] Consequently, hot wallets are perceived as being less secure given their propensity to be influenced, stolen or relocated. Furthermore, users often fail to recall their protective PIN or password, or lose the hard drive where the private key is located.[67] In response, some developers have introduced hardware (cold) wallets, such as a USB key in the case of Lockbox,[68] which are not connected to the internet.

As set out in *United States v Ulbricht*,[69] these wallet services are comparable to those offered by traditional transaction accounts, such as a bank checking account or a money market mutual fund account. This similarity in functionality immediately poses the question of consumer protection.[70] In contrast to the regulatory proposals designed in response to the evolution of exchanges and the work of developers, wallets have been practically free of the regulation with which other intermediaries that provide similar services must comply.[71] One can reason that some regulatory efforts address wallets as integral parts of exchanges; however, the fact that 'pure' wallet providers are often operating globally, in contrast with exchanges and money transfer operators, which tend to limit services to particular jurisdictions, complicates wallets regulatory assessment.

With these obstacles in mind, some regulatory efforts have been developed on current anti-money laundering (AML) and countering the financing of terrorism (CFT) regulations, and the implementation of operational resilience principles, as seen in 'Targeted Update on Implementation of the FATF Standards on Virtual Assets and Virtual Asset Service Providers' published by the FATF,[72] under the following terms:

> The VA ecosystem is interconnected and jurisdictions need to take a holistic approach to risk assessments, to reflect the interconnectedness between DeFi arrangements, VASPs, unhosted wallets and P2P transactions.
>
> …
>
> While P2P transactions fall outside the scope of the FATF Standards, implementation of the Standards can still play a critical role in mitigating illicit finance risks of P2P transactions and unhosted wallets. The FATF 2021 Guidance provides a menu of options 40

[65] See www.blockchain.com.
[66] ESMA (n 63).
[67] ibid; Hasanova et al (n 63).
[68] See www.blockchain.com/lockbox.
[69] [2017] 15-1815-CR (US), at 9.
[70] Hare (n 58).
[71] Lo and Wang (n 51).
[72] Financial Action Task Force, 'Targeted Update on Implementation of the FATF Standards on Virtual Assets and Virtual Asset Service Providers' (2023), available at ww.fatf-gafi.org/en/publications/Fatfrecommendations/targeted-update-virtual-assets-vasps-2023.html.

> for how jurisdictions can address P2P transaction risks at the national level, such as improving P2P transaction market metrics and risk mitigation solutions, utilising blockchain analytics tools, and placing additional AML/CFT requirements on VASPs that allow transactions to or from non-obliged entities. At present, several delegations noted that they are assessing risk associated with P2P payments, albeit in some cases with challenges, and/or requiring VASPs to implement measures to mitigate risks associated with unhosted wallet transactions.

For instance, on this basis, the FCA in the UK requires these shadow banks to register with them, as set out in Regulations 8, 9 and 14A of the Money Laundering, Terrorist Financing and Transfer of Funds (Information on the Payer) Regulations 2017,[73] which define 'wallet'[74] for purposes of the regulations and the obligations related to relevant persons, including cryptoasset exchange providers. However, under Article 123 of MiCA,[75] the EBA has prerogatives to investigate the financial and technological operation of these intermediaries.

Additionally, if cryptoassets are legally considered to be money, as described in section VI of chapter 4 above, does that require companies providing basic cryptoasset storage services to comply with existing banking regulation, or does this only apply to wallet providers that take custody of user funds and/or provide integrated currency exchange services?[76] The answer to this question varies among jurisdictions and legal traditions, and the characteristics of specific assets, but we find an interesting model in the standard published by the BIS[77] on 'Prudential Treatment of Cryptoasset Exposures', where we can find – in the case of 'stablecoins' – that 'the "cryptoassets" must confer the same level of legal rights as cash held in custody', following the example set for cheques.

III. Regulating the New Generation of Shadow Banks

The emergence and evolution of the intermediaries mentioned above pose several risks given that innovators are entering the industry without a financial compliance culture and with limited pre-existing interaction with financial regulators.[78] On this point, critics of the public interest theory of regulation could argue that these markets and their algorithmic codes can take care of most market imperfections in the absence of any government intervention, and in cases where these

[73] See n 56.

[74] 'In these Regulations, "custodian wallet provider" means a firm or sole practitioner who by way of business provides services to safeguard, or to safeguard and administer – (a) cryptoassets on behalf of its customers, or (b) private cryptographic keys on behalf of its customers in order to hold, store and transfer cryptoassets.'

[75] See n 24.

[76] Hare (n 58) 236–48; Hileman and Rauchs (n 22).

[77] Bank for International Settlements, 'Prudential Treatment of Cryptoasset Exposures' (2022), available at www.bis.org/bcbs/publ/d545.pdf.

[78] T. Braithwaite and F Guerrera, 'Finance a Wider Divide' (2010), available at www.ft.com/content/4adcf1fc-6832-11df-a52f-00144feab49a.

markets and codes do not work perfectly, private litigation could address any resulting conflicts.[79] However, the experience of failures in projects like Ethereum Classic where a single attacker took advantage of the 51 per cent rule of the PoW protocols and gained control of more than half of the network's computing power with the aim of rewriting the transaction history,[80] and the potential of new models of attacks, such as, 'steal now decrypt later' based on quantum computing, offer strong evidence that a *crypto lex mercatoria* by itself is not as efficient as many libertarian enthusiasts believe.

Considering that 'algorithms are opinions embedded in code',[81] they, by themselves, cannot avoid the emergence of market imperfections –one could even argue that they constitute a market imperfection. On the one hand, it is possible to argue that these new shadow banks can be subjected to the spirit of current regulations, following Robert C Merton's[82] functional perspective. For instance, the US Treasury's Financial Crimes Enforcement Network (FINCEN) in 2013 issued several interpretations and guidance relating to the applicability of the Financial Record Keeping and Reporting of Currency and Foreign Transactions Act of 1970[83] – better known as the Bank Secrecy Act (BSA) – to DLT innovations.[84] Based on these latter, the FINCEN stated that although an ordinary user of cryptoassets would not be subject to the Act, exchanges would be considered 'money transmitters' for the purposes of the Act. Accordingly, on 18 April 2019, the FINCEN penalised an exchange operator (Eric Powers) for violating the BSA and for failing to register as a money services business.[85] Furthermore, as stated in section VI of chapter 4 above, the evolution of these assets and new shadow banks could eventually put them under the terms of regulations currently applicable to electronic money and payment systems, as set by the standard on cryptoasset exposure presented by the BIS.

[79] A Schleifer, 'Understanding Regulation' (2005) 11 *European Financial Management* 439, 440.

[80] S Ouimet, 'Ethereum Classic's Price Stumbles amid Suspected 51% Attack' (2019), available at www.coindesk.com/ethereum-classic-price-stumbles-amid-suspected-51-attack.

[81] C O'Neil, *Weapons of Math Destruction. How Big Data Increases Inequality and Threatens Democracy* (New York, Broadway Books, 2017) 21.

[82] Merton argues that the functional perspective takes as given six economic functions developed by financial intermediaries, independently of which institution develops them: 1) provision of a payments system; 2) provision of mechanisms for the pooling of funds; 3) provision of a way to transfer economic resources; 4) provision of a way to manage uncertainty and control risk; 5) provision of price information; and 6) provision of a way to deal with market failures. See RC Merton, 'A Functional Perspective of Financial Intermediation' (1995) 24 *Financial Management* 23–41, 24.

[83] Financial Record Keeping and Reporting of Currency and Foreign Transactions Act of 1970 84 Stat.1114.

[84] See Financial Crimes Enforcement Network, 'Application of FinCEN's Regulations to Persons Administering, Exchanging, or Using Virtual Currencies' (2013), available at /www.fincen.gov/sites/default/files/shared/FIN-2013-G001.pdf.

[85] Financial Crimes Enforcement Network, 'FinCen Penalizes Peer-to-Peer Virtual Currency Exchanger for Violations of Anti-Money Laundering Laws' (2019), available at www.fincen.gov/news/news-releases/fincen-penalizes-peer-peer-virtual-currency-exchanger-violations-anti-money.

On the other hand, one could be tempted to adopt an institutional perspective[86] and say that the technical complexities that characterise the new generation of shadow banks require the implementation of special regulations designed around the characteristics of the new environment. However, in scenarios of rapid social and technological transformation like ours, most of the regulatory answers issued along these lines tend to be based on the elements existent when the new regulation is studied. It is possible to represent this reactive behaviour through a set of different straight segmented arrows (x) that show how, as it can be evidenced through the proposals that currently try to address the evolving elements that configure our new generations of cryptoassets, legislators and regulators tend to respond to these scenarios with patchwork responses.[87] Thus, one can see that between the periods that constitute the analysis of a new proposal and its gradual introduction, the social/technological reality, which is represented by a solid line, has separated itself from the spirit of the original norm and its respective responses.[88] Consequently, we produce backward-looking regulations that take aim at yesterday's perceived problems rather than tomorrow's.[89]

Figure 11 Representation of a law that is modified in different occasions as reaction to several social/technological changes. Explanation: Point A = time when the referred law came into force; Point B = time when the law is modified for the first time; Point C = the second time the referred law is modified; segmented line A-M = evolution of a rigid law; solid line A-N = evolution of social necessities/technological developments; segmented line B-L = evolution of the first legislative modification; segmented line C-K = evolution of the second legislative modification[90]

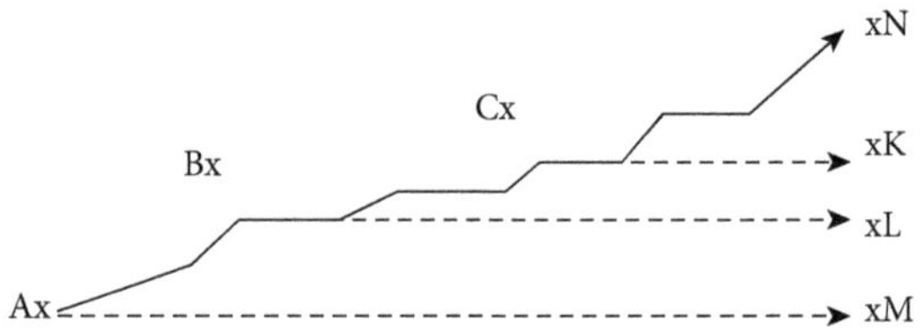

As an example of this reactive behaviour, one can read the Mexican FinTech Law[91] and its secondary instruments, such as Banxico's Circular 4/2019.[92] For instance,

[86] The institutional perspective takes as given the existing institutional structure of our financial systems and views the objective of regulation as a means to help the institutions currently in place to survive and flourish. See Merton (n 82) 23.

[87] F Fagan, 'Legal Cycles and Stabilization Rules' in F Fagan and S Levmore (eds), *The Timing of Lawmaking* (Cheltenham, Edward Elgar Publishing, 2017) 11–33, 12.

[88] E Novoa, *El Derecho como Obstáculo al Cambio Social* (Mexico City, Siglo XXI Editores, 1980) 37.

[89] MC Nussbaum, 'Janus-Faced Law: A Philosophical Debate' in F Fagan and S Levmore (eds), *The Timing of Lawmaking* (Cheltenham, Edward Elgar Publishing, 2017) 249–79, 250.

[90] Novoa (n 88) 36.

[91] Law for the Regulation of Financial Technology Institutions of Mexico.

[92] Circular 4/2019 addressed to Credit Institutions and Financial Technology Institutions related to the general provisions applicable to Credit Institutions and Financial Technology Institutions in the transactions conducted with virtual assets.

the last paragraph of Article 19 of the first draft of this law followed the spirit of the Volcker Rule found in Section 619 of the Wall Street Reform and Consumer Protection Act[93] (the Dodd-Frank Act), and restricted bank involvement in certain FinTech activities under the following terms:

> Credit institutions, credit unions, regulated multi-purpose financial companies, popular financial societies, community financial societies and popular savings and credit cooperatives, cannot act as investors through institutions of collective investment.

However, the version that was sent to the Senate was modified to eliminate this restriction; thus, the fourth paragraph of Article 21 of the new draft stated that:

> Credit institutions, credit unions, regulated multi-purpose financial companies, popular financial societies, community financial societies and popular savings and credit cooperatives with operative level I to IV, can act as investors through institutions of collective investment, subject to the rules set by the CNBV for this purpose.

It is important to note that, originally, the institutions regulated by the FinTech Law would have the option to include in their operations the management and exchange of digital instruments like cryptoassets. So, as we expressed in the consultation issued by the central bank regarding this law, this first effort emerged with gaps that could foster the development of systemic complexities in terms of the varieties and shapes of new financial products, financial institutions' exposures to them, and the interconnected markets within which they are bought and sold.[94] In other words, we could face a TCTF problem in the near future. Fortunately, Banxico issued Circular 4/2019[95] by which the central bank has stated that only regulated institutions can employ cryptoassets to conduct their internal transactions. However, the task is not complete. If we do not learn the lessons provided by the GFC and put in place a proper *ex ante* regulation, if a problem emerges and becomes systemic, it would be impossible for the political system not to intervene, even if they state the opposite on paper.

IV. Conclusion

It is a cliché to say that current financial innovations are sweeping the financial industry. The financial ecosystem in which we find our FinTech dragon has been subject to the evolutionary dynamics that define our financial *Bildungstrieb* since time immemorial. To illustrate this fact, we can build on Arner, Barberis and Buckley's model based on three main FinTech eras,[96] and refine it to present a

[93] Wall Street Reform and Consumer Protection Act 124 Stat 1376.

[94] C Ford, *Innovation and the State. Finance, Regulation and Justice* (New York,Cambridge University Press, 2017), 28–29.

[95] See n 92.

[96] Arner, Barberis and Buckley (n 12).

paradigm built upon five FinTech eras that highlight the role of 'shadowy innovation' in the evolution of money and of our financial markets:

FinTech 1.0. Incorporation of endogenous sources of liquidity within the first standardised monetary expressions, which resulted from the emergence and diffusion of new practices and technologies, such as, those related to the minting of the first metallic coins.

FinTech 2.0. Introduction and diffusion of different legal fictions that constituted a set of exceptions to the rule *nemo dat quod non habet*, by which we witnessed the emergence of innovations structured around the evolution of papermaking and printing, like bills of exchange, promissory notes and banknotes.

FinTech 3.0. In the context of the first age of financial globalization, it is possible to identify the role of the technologies developed during the First World War (WWI) and the Second World War (or WWII), particularly, those related to communication. The diffusion of these technologies fostered a transition from analogue processes to automated mechanisms during the decade of the 1960s represented by innovations, such as, ATMs and the infrastructural cornerstones of modern payment systems.

FinTech 4.0. This era is found in the transition between the Third and the Fourth Industrial Revolutions, and it can be identified with the incorporation of Internet to the practices developed by the financial industry; thus, configuring the e-banking model. Through this paradigm it was possible to remove the physical link between the consumer and the bank that we take for granted in our financial systems.

FinTech 5.0. The development of technologies, such as, Machine Learning, Cloud Computing, Open Source Software and mobile devices, has empowered different stakeholders to participate actively in the development of technological solutions, increasing the speed of the evolutionary dynamics that support the development of our financial systems. Consequently, we are witnessing how the new generation of infrastructural stakeholders and 'shadow banks' are extending the value chains that constitute the financial industry, and creating the bases of Decentralised Finance (DeFi).

As we can see through these five evolutionary stages, the *leitmotiv* of shadow banking has been the constitution and the diffusion of trust around legal and technological innovations developed by the endogenous needs of each dynamic social system. Accordingly, when we are analysing innovations like cryptoassets we have to understand – as it is evidenced in MiCA – that, just as in the past, monetary innovations do not emerge nor circulate in isolation: they rely on infrastructures and social systems to materialise their socioeconomic aims. It is important to note that the creation and primary diffusion of these innovations are not supported by traditional and regulated intermediaries, and they have needed the constitution of a new set of infrastructural stakeholders to address the endogenous needs of different social systems.

Consequently, legislators, regulators and supervisors worldwide have to pay attention to the fact that, just as other monetary innovations in the past, new crypto payment systems are structured around shadow banks like exchanges, wallets and miners. However, it could be argued that – prior to MiCA – we had been ignoring the most important element of the cryptoasset market: the issuer, who is the individual or institutional developer that creates a cryptoasset, the network, and the underlying obligations by which they will introduce a source of liquidity, taking the latter to a new era. Without it, the cryptoassets market would not exist and would not keep evolving. Accordingly, as I have mentioned throughout this work, and as will be developed further in the following chapter, I do not see issuers as shadow banks who will issue the money of the future under a *crypto lex monetae.* Just as in the past, these issuers and their infrastructural power will be subject to the sovereign exercise of *lex monetae.*

6

Designing a *Lex Monetae* for the Digital Commercial Society

I. Introduction

As seen in chapter four, DLT and cryptoassets do not offer something radically new. They simply replicate models created by the decentralised nature of the internet just as other technologies have done in the past and just as other technologies will do in the future. Meanwhile, innovations such as Bitcoin, XRP and JPMCoin are posing questions regarding fundamental issues on the post-Westphalian design and exercise of the normative framework that configures the *lex monetae*. As seen in previous chapters, cryptoassets emerged in response to these questions. However, as seen in crises such as the *Overend, Gurney & Co* panic of 1866, these monetary innovations tend to foster the emergence of non-regulated intermediaries, which highlight a pyrrhic pattern of legal cycles. These involve, first, innovation and deregulation, followed by crises and then reactive regulations that, in many cases, have not been appropriate responses.[1] Unfortunately, 'this dialectic illustrates the evolution of many financial systems'.[2]

Despite these fundamental changes and the historical lessons/warnings that one can take from them, legal scholars, legislators and regulators have failed to describe the world as it really is.[3] Consequently, the evolution of the intermediaries that support the diffusion of monetary innovations has made the effort of making them safe more challenging. The innovative minds behind the unregulated innovations that have been presented throughout this book are finding, in the suboptimal understanding and exercise of the *ius cudendae monetae*, the perfect conduits to generate links with regulated institutions. Building on instruments such as the

[1] S Deakin, 'The Evolution of Theory and Method in Law and Finance' in N Moloney, E Ferran and J Payne (eds), *Oxford Handbook of Financial Regulation* (Oxford, Oxford University Press, 2017) 13–40, 15; F Fagan, 'Legal Cycles and Stabilization Rules' in F Fagan and S Levmore (eds), *The Timing of Lawmaking* (Cheltenham, Edward Elgar Publishing, 2017) 11–33, 12; C Ford, *Innovation and the State. Finance, Regulation and Justice* (New York, Cambridge University Press, 2017) 17.

[2] P Artus and C de Boissieu, 'The Process of Financial Innovation: Causes, Forms, and Consequences' in A Heertje (ed), *Innovation, Technology, and Finance* (Oxford, European Investment Bank, 1988) 101–26, 109.

[3] G Calabresi, *The Future of Law & Economics. Essays in Reform and Recollection* (New Haven, Yale University Press, 2016) 3.

DebtRank[4] algorithm, these innovations are materialising a web of interconnections that, eventually, will cause shocks across our financial systems and their infrastructures.[5] In other words, our legal reality is not appropriately representing our current experience, and it is, instead, reflecting undesirable rules that in many occasions are not more than anachronisms.[6]

With this unfortunate fact in mind, we can be certain that the next crisis will be named after a constitutive element of our FinTech dragon. Will it be unleashed by cryptoassets or by algorithmic trading? We do not know. For now, this book aims to present a contribution to close the door to a Great Operational Crypto Crisis (GOCC).

II. Preparing for the Next Global Financial Crisis

The attempt in chapter two to define 'money' showed how difficult it is to balance economic and legal interests and to alight upon a definition that is acceptable in both spheres.[7] There is certainly friction in academia, which has two ways to describe the FWS. Within the first group are the efficient market economists who believe that we are all economically 'intelligent' adults interacting within the market, following Eugene F Fama's[8] definition:

> An 'efficient' market is defined as a market where there are large numbers of rational, profit-maximizers actively competing, with each trying to predict future market values of individual securities, and where important current information is almost freely available to all participants.

This means that, as long as the preferences exhibited by an individual satisfy certain basic axioms, as any rational agent should, as described by von Neumann and Morgestern,[9] then, the choices made by that individual can necessarily be described as maximising the expected value of a utility function.[10] However, it should be stated that, as we are seeing in different debates on AIs – particularly those related to machine learning (ML) – we have not reached a consensus on which behaviour should be classified as intelligent. In some cases, the term is related to the autonomy in decision-making as described in *Director of Child*

[4] S Battiston et al, 'DebtRank: Too Central to Fail? Financial Networks, the FED and Systemic Risk' (2012) 2 *Nature Scientific Reports* 1; S Battiston et al, 'Liaisons dangereuses: Increasing connectivity, risk sharing, and systemic risk' (2012) 36 *Journal of Economic Dynamics & Control* 1121.

[5] R Cranston et al, *Principles of Banking Law* (Oxford, Oxford University Press, 2017) 345; R Goode, *Goode on Commercial Law* (London, LexisNexis, 2009) 3.

[6] Calabresi (n 3) 6.

[7] RH Coase, 'The Nature of the Firm' (1937) 4 *Economica* 386, 386.

[8] EF Fama, 'Random Walks in Stock Market Prices' (1995) 51 *Financial Analysts Journal* 75, 76.

[9] J von Neumann and O. Morgenstern, *Theory of Games and Economic Behavior* (New Jersey, Princeton University Press, 1944).

[10] S Russell, *Human Compatible. Artificial Intelligence and the Problem of Control* (New York, Penguin Books, 2019) 23.

and Family Services (Man) v AC et al,[11] while in others it is associated with moral distinctions and the ability to communicate, as set out in *R v DI*.[12]

Independently of this lack of agreement, the members of this group, which tend to be associated with the Chicago School of Law and Economics, argue that markets and private models can take care of most market imperfections without sovereign intervention at all.[13] Where markets do not work perfectly, private litigation could address the potential conflicts that might emerge.[14] However, as one can see through the emergence of DLT protocols like PoW and PoS, private orderings tend to degenerate into paradigms where the strong imposes its own agenda, violating constitutional principles, such as no discrimination, transparency and due process as seen in *State v Loomis*,[15] where the operation of an algorithm employed in a judicial process is kept as a trade secret, thus configuring a black box.

Within the second group, are the behavioural economists, who believe that we are all irrational animals, driven by fear and greed like so many other species of mammals.[16] In other words, we fail to conform to the axioms in systematic ways; thus, we cannot say that humans behave rationally.[17] Consequently, our markets tend to fail as result of the 'animal spirits' described by George A Akerlof and Robert J Shiller,[18] which can be seen in the problems that are inherent in the structure of our markets, such as monopolies, information asymmetries and externalities. With that in mind, it has been argued that sovereign regulation is beneficial for the development of financial markets given that the role of our financial systems carries a public responsibility starting from the very incorporation of social trust within our dynamic social systems.[19]

Based on the experiences of September 2008, within the parameters set out in the Institutional Possibility Frontier developed by Djankov et al,[20] the second group is gaining momentum, and the names of authors such as Hyman P Minsky[21] have emerged. This group is putting on the table the need for sovereign regulation

[11] [2009] 390 NR 1 (SCC) (CA).

[12] *R v DI*, [2012] NR TBEd. FE.013 (CA).

[13] A Schleifer, 'Understanding Regulation' (2005) 11 *European Financial Management* 439, 441.

[14] ibid.

[15] [2016] 881 NW.2d 749 (US).

[16] AW Lo, *Adaptative Markets. Financial Evolution at the Speed of Thought* (New Jersey, Princeton University Press, 2017) 6–7.

[17] Russell (n 10) 25.

[18] GA Akerlof and RJ Shiller, *Animal Spirits. How Human Psychology Drives the Economy, and Why It Matters for Global Capitalism* (Princeton, Princeton University Press, 2019).

[19] H Kaufman, *The Road to Financial Reformation: Warnings, Consequences, Reforms* (New Jersey, John Wiley & Sons, 2019) 42; Schleifer (n 13) 442.

[20] This paradigm shows the transitions and trade-offs that regulators have to analyse regarding two social costs: disorder and dictatorship. See S Djankov, et al., 'The New Comparative Economics' (2003) 31 *Journal of Comparative Economics* 595–619.

Lo (n 16) 6–7.

[21] HP Minsky, 'The Financial Instability Hypothesis' (1992), available at www.levyinstitute.org/pubs/wp74.pdf.

following the Machiavellian approach to face our own nature. Even legendary central banker Alan Greenspan, who in 1994 said that 'there's nothing involved in Federal regulation which makes it superior to market regulation', admitted before a House Committee on Capitol Hill on 23 October 2008 that his thinking had to evolve on this matter.[22] Furthermore, he[23] has argued that regulators:

> [C]an never get more than a glimpse at the internal workings of the simplest of modern financial systems. Today's competitive markets, whether we seek to recognise it or not, are driven by an international version of Adam Smith's 'invisible hand' that is unredeemably opaque.

III. Facing Our Own 'Rationality'

Before the GFC, innovation was seen positively as a form of rational expression that generates an atmosphere of competition and 'creative destruction',[24] to the point that it has been influencing the trajectory of public policy and regulation since the collapse of the Bretton Woods System.[25] Consequently, regulatory frameworks that configured the New International Financial Architecture (NIFA), were focused on favouring financial innovation with a) financial stability and consumer protection based on risk-based prudential regulations; b) disclosure to provide market discipline; and c) enforcement to protect consumers.[26] However, these tools were mainly focused on safeguarding the resilience of individual firms[27] and avoided direct product regulation.[28]

In the G20's Declaration of the Summit on Financial Markets and the World Economy, it was agreed that all aspects of the financial sector should be subject to appropriate levels of regulation, and that 'regulation is first and foremost the responsibility of national regulators who constitute the first line of defence against market instability'.[29] Consequently, post-GFC efforts have been directed not only towards those institutions labelled as TBTF, but to all aspects of the financial

[22] S Mallaby, *The Man Who Knew. The Life and Times of Alan Greenspan* (London, Bloomsbury Paperbacks, 2017) 664–68.

[23] A Greenspan, 'Dodd-Frank Fails to Meet Test of Our Times' (2011), available at www.ft.com/content/14662fd8-5a28-11e0-86d3-00144feab49a.

[24] M Haiven, 'The Creative and the Derivative' (2014) 118 *Radical History Review* 113, 114.

[25] DA Zetzsche et al, 'Regulating a Revolution: From Regulatory Sandboxes to Smart Regulation' (2017) 23 *Fordham Journal of Corporate & Financial Law* 34, 34; H Mayer and J Kneeshaw, 'Financial Market Structure and Regulatory Change' in A Heertje (ed), *Innovation, Technology, and Finance* (Oxford, European Investment Bank. 1988) 126–57, 126; Ford (n 1) 6.

[26] Zetzsche et al (n 25) 47–48.

[27] L Enriques, A Romano and T Wetzer, 'Network-Sensitive Financial Regulation' (2019) 451 *ECGI Working Paper Series in Law* 1, 8–9.

[28] A Turner, 'The Turner Review. A Regulatory Response to the Global Banking Crisis.' (2009) available at www.fsa.gov.uk/pubs/other/turner_review.pdf.

[29] G20, 'Declaration of the Summit on Financial Markets and the World Economy' (2008), available at www.g20.utoronto.ca/2008/2008declaration1115.html#actions.

system, which were previously unregulated.[30] Therefore, it is possible at a basic level to say that our financial markets have been operating in a highly regulated environment. However, the rapid evolution of our FinTech dragon and the technologies related to it, and an international agenda to foster financial inclusion are putting some pressure on regulators to support innovation.[31] In many cases, one could even argue that they are fostering, again, subprime innovation.

Regulators and supervisors tend to act within the framework of the applicable legislation which sets their aims and the tools to reach those aims. When confronted with this framework, innovators tend to introduce new practices and financial instruments that are endogenous to the dynamic social system to circumvent regulations that bear a high cost of compliance.[32] Furthermore, innovators and financial intermediaries tend to adapt their strategies both in terms of the actions they undertake and the information they supply to the regulator, thus creating further restrictions for optimal regulatory efforts.[33] Therefore, considering the elements presented in the previous chapters relating to the nature of money and cryptoassets, the argument for a regulatory effort begins with a rather simple question: why do we need to exercise the *lex monetae* to face these innovations? This question, in turn, can be divided into two sub-questions: why does this market and its *crypto lex mercatoria* not suffice? And, if there is to be sovereign intervention, why does it take the form of the *lex monetae*?[34]

As a starting point, the notion that markets alone lead to efficient 'intelligent' outcomes has no theoretical justification.[35] As we can see through our monetary *res*, markets are the 'outcomes of a complex bundle of entitlements that determine the nature of power struggles'.[36] Consequently, in the absence of adequate regulation, firms such as IBM, JP Morgan or Meta, in exercise of their infrastructural power and the structure of democratic self-governance models,[37] could change the ground rules and engage in abusive anticompetitive practices. This behaviour would undermine the efficiency of *lex monetae* and the incentives to keep innovating,[38] thus increasing the possibility of systemic failures, considering that

[30] Zetzsche et al (n 25) 49.

[31] ibid.

[32] Artus and De Boissieu (n 2) 108.

[33] W Silber, 'The Process of Financial Innovation' (1983) 73 *American Economic Review* 89; MD McCubbins, 'The Legislative Design of Regulatory Structure' (1985) 29 *American Journal of Political Science* 721, 724.

[34] JE Stiglitz, 'Government Failure vs. Market Failure: Principles of Regulation' in EJ Balleisen and DA Moss (eds), *Government and Markets. Toward a New Theory of Regulation* (New York, European Cambridge University Press, 2010) Kindle EBook Loc 446–1370, at Loc 478.

[35] ibid, at Loc 493.

[36] F Pasquale et al, 'Eleven Things They Don't Tell You About Law & Economics: An Informal Introduction to Political Economy and Law' (2019) 37 *Law & Inequality* 95, 119.

[37] K Pistor, 'Regulating Financial Markets. An LTF Perspective' in E Avgouleas and DC Donald (eds), *The Political Economy of Financial Regulation* (Cambridge, Cambridge University Press, 2022) 19–37, 34–35.

[38] Stiglitz (n 34) Loc 513.

these innovators – and the intermediaries relating to them – have not yet developed more complex and challenging forms.

IV. Technology as a Market Imperfection

Following the description provided in section II above, we can define financial innovation as a 'long chain of innovations leading to the development of novel financial products and processes used to improve allocation of capital and risk management'.[39] However, as has been seen through the cases of Enron in the US, ABCP in Canada and the GFC,[40] over the past 20 years, a large number of these innovations has emerged entirely detached from the functions found in this definition,[41] and most of DLT innovations, as subprime derivatives of a subprime crisis, are not the exception. With these catastrophic experiences in mind, how can the law help to guide the DLT Cambrian explosion towards the spirit of this definition?

In accordance with the spirit of Recital 16 of MiCA,[42] we have the challenge to create, on the one hand, frameworks that can 'keep pace with innovation and technological development' and define 'crypto-assets' and 'distributed ledger technology' 'as widely as possible to capture all types of crypto-assets that currently fall outside the scope of Union legislative acts on financial services', while, on the other hand, restricting financial arms races that create risky and opaque interlinkages that present a superficial perception of growth and development while the institutional framework gets weaker.[43] So, it could be said that our legal structures have to face these changes in their environments and recognise that no version of the *ius cudendae monetae* was designed to stay static. As was highlighted through the words of Lord Wilberforce in *Miliangos v George Frank (Textiles) Ltd*,[44] at its base, law is coding and interpretation, and, accordingly, it has to follow the spirit of its own social, cultural, technological and political context.[45]

This sounds easy in theory, more so if one considers that, as developed in chapter two, money and the institutions that have emerged from it have become artificial creatures of the law, creations of legislators, as are the constitutions from

[39] E Avgouleas, 'Regulating Financial Innovation' in N Moloney, E Ferran and J Payne (eds), *Oxford Handbook of Financial Regulation* (Oxford, Oxford University Press, 2017) 660–692, 660.

[40] Ford (n 1) 27–34.

[41] Avgouleas (n 39) 668.

[42] Regulation 2023/1114 on markets in crypto-assets, and amending Regulations (EU) No 1093/2010 and (EU) No 1095/2010 and Directives 2013/36/EU and (EU) 2019/1937 OJ L 150/40, 31 May 2023.

[43] AG Haldane, 'Financial Arms Races.' (2012), available at www.bis.org/review/r120426a.pdf; RS Kroszner and PE Strahan, 'Financial Regulatory Reform: Challenges Ahead' (2011) 101 *The American Economic Review* 242, 243; H Kaufman, 'Financial Institutions in Ferment' (1983) 26 *Challenge* 20, 20–21.

[44] [1976] AC 443 (UK), at 460–70.

[45] Ford (n 1) 24; Schleifer (n 13) 24.

which they emerge.[46] In other words, money 'is not only regulated by law, it is made in law',[47] and its value depends, in large measure, on its legal vindication through the sovereign exercise of *lex monetae*.[48] However, a fact generally overlooked is that financial innovations include not only the new financial instruments that mathematicians, cryptographers and/or economists may help to design, and bankers to market. They also include the work that lawyers do in creatively deploying old instruments, such as bills of exchange, promissory notes and cheques in new contexts, reimagining market and regulatory structures, and identifying and helping their clients to take advantage of new opportunities.[49] In short, law and finance are intertwined in a dynamic process in which the *lex monetae* is continuously challenged by new contractual devices, which in turn seek legal recognition.[50]

Furthermore, legislators and regulators – like private parties – are limited by transaction costs, such as the time and money invested in understanding the technological and legal design of new products and services. This kind of expertise is much in demand throughout the private and public sectors, but the pay differential between them is so significant that states have some difficulty finding and keeping talented individuals with sufficient public sector commitment.[51] An illustration of this problem can be found in the case of Benjamin Lawsky, who was the mind behind the famous New York BitLicense and, who, in 2017, became a board member of Ripple.[52] This example is relevant for two reasons. On the one hand, the public sector lost knowledge to make proper case-by-case regulatory analyses in an evolving market and foster international coordination, given that few other regulators had the necessary expertise upon which to make sound judgements.[53] On the other hand, the private sector increased its agenda-setting power, which can be defined as the ability to decide what will be discussed in the regulatory agenda taking advantage of the talent gap between the public and private sector,[54] and its own capabilities to structure the constitutive elements of new markets.

This lack of regulatory talent, paired with decades of deregulation, has given current regulators the difficult task of trying to contain new elements that they barely understand. On this point lies one of the main criticisms of the standard

[46] K Pistor, *The Code of Capital. How the Law Creates Wealth and Inequality* (Princeton, Princeton University Press, 2019) 11; PR Wood, 'Lawyers and Economists: Who Rule the World' (2010) 11 *Business Law International* 145, 151.

[47] Pistor (n 37) 34.

[48] K Pistor, 'A Legal Theory of Finance' (2013) 41 *Journal of Comparative Economics* 315, 315.

[49] Ford (n 1) 13; Pistor (n 46) 20.

[50] Pistor (n 48) 315.

[51] DK Tarullo, *Banking on Basel. The Future of International Financial Regulation* (Washington, DC, Peterson Institute for International Economics, 2018) 169.

[52] Ripple, 'Ripple Appoints Former New York State Superintendent of Financial Services Benjamin Lawsky to Its Board and Ron Will as CFO' (2017) available at ripple.com/ripple_press/ripple-appoints-former-new-york-state-superintendent-financial-services-benjamin-lawsky-board-ron-will-cfo.

[53] Zetzsche et al (n 25) 62.

[54] Ford (n 1) 43.

public interest theory of regulation, given that thanks to this lack of understanding the exercise of the *ius cudendae monetae* tends to be captured by the industry and its own infrastructural power.[55]

A. The Rationale for Regulation

As we have seen throughout this book, the most important and sensitive functions of sovereign and private institutions are the efficient incorporation and transfer of rights, the constitution of infrastructural networks to ease these transfers, and the proper management of the *res* incorporated.[56] Consequently, financial systems require well-developed legal and information infrastructures to function appropriately; thus, as seen in chapters two and three, for as long as there has been money and banks, there has also been governments involved in their regulation.[57] Despite the apparent revolutionary nature of the DCS, these functions and necessities prevail. Just as the EBA's[58] FinTech Roadmap shows, among the most cited FinTech solutions that are viewed as sources of vulnerabilities and risks for our financial infrastructures are cryptoassets, which exploit the gaps found in current regulatory and supervisory environments, and new institutions' lack of experience in the sector. Therefore, to face the new wave of financial innovations and the *Bildungstrieb* that guides their evolution, it is important to improve our understanding of current paradigms and the context in which *lex monetae* has to be exercised.[59]

B. Obstacles to Regulation

Generally speaking, governments influence the operation of their respective markets through two tools that are closely related to the transition between the *proto lex monetae* and the *ius cudendae monetae*, as analysed in chapter two: taxation and regulation.[60] Following section III.A of chapter one, the two primary reasons for this sovereign intervention are either to ensure that markets work

[55] Schleifer (n 13) 441; Pistor (n 46) 20.

[56] C Mayer, 'Economic Development, Financial Systems, and the Law' in N Moloney, E Ferran and J Payne (eds), *Oxford Handbook of Financial Regulation* (Oxford, Oxford University Press, 2017) 41–67, 54.

[57] A Demirgüç-Kunt, 'Finance and Economic Development. The Role of Government' in AN Berger, P Molyneux and JO Wilson (eds), *The Oxford Handbook of Banking* (Oxford, Oxford University Press, 2010) 729–55, 740.

[58] European Banking Authority, 'The EBA's FinTech Roadmap. Conclusions from the Consultation on the EBA's Approach to Financial Technology (FINTECH).' (2018) available at www.eba.europa.eu/documents/10180/1919160/EBA+FinTech+Roadmap.pdf.

[59] Lo (n 16) 372.

[60] HM Schooner and MW Taylor, *Global Bank Regulation. Principles and Policies* (London, Academic Press, 2010) xii.

efficiently, or to alter market outcomes to achieve endogenous social objectives.[61] However, as in everything relating to economic policy, one will find frictions that, in this particular case, are identified with five main restrictions to the optimal exercise of *lex monetae*.[62] First, based on the agenda-setting power of the private sector, governments have imperfect knowledge of the structure of the economy emerging from these innovative efforts and their potential risks. In particular, it is important to highlight that many legal and operational decisions are made in a highly decentralised fashion and outside the public eye, their effects remaining hidden for years.[63] Second, building on this first restriction, private parties devise their own strategies of self-structuring, self-regulation and techno-regulation,[64] and react to – and anticipate – regulatory measures.[65] Third, as witnessed in Banxico's Circular 4/2019,[66] legislators and regulators may not be able to convince private parties that they will actually do what they have announced, which affects the behaviour of the private parties. Fourth, legislators, regulators and supervisors may not have the proper information they need to take decisions, as shown in the different calls for information issued by regulators, such as the Bank of England[67] and the FCA,[68] relating to the nature of DLT and the instruments that are emerging from it. Fifth and finally, just as it has been discussed in the context of cases such as *SEC v Citigroup Global Markets*,[69] legislators and regulators may pursue their own political interests or are captured by a particular group, including the regulated industry itself, which could exercise the *lex monetae* indirectly.[70]

Considering these restrictions, innovators argue that through the use of technologies such as DLT and AI it is possible to create maths-based money, optimal contracts and perfect regulatory frameworks that could act as a *crypto lex monetae* structured around the 'impartiality' of a machine in opposition to imperfect and capricious human bureaucracy.[71] Unfortunately, as evidenced by the cryptoparadox

[61] RJ Shiller, *Finance and the Good Society* (Princeton, Princeton University Press, 2012) 25.

[62] A Bénassy-Quéré et al, *Economic Policy. Theory and Practice* (New York, Oxford University Press, 2010) 63.

[63] E Avgouleas and DC Donald, 'Introduction' in E Avgouleas and DC Donald (eds), *The Political Economy of Financial Regulation* (Cambridge, Cambridge University Press, 2022) 1–16, 5.

[64] W Hoffmann-Riem, 'Artificial Intelligence as a Challege for Law and Regulation' in T Wischmeyer and T Rademacher (eds), *Regulating Artificial Intelligence* (Cham, Springer Nature, 2020) 2–29, 18–23.

[65] Silber (n 33).

[66] Circular 4/2019 addressed to Credit Institutions and Financial Technology Institutions related to the general provisions applicable to Credit Institutions and Financial Technology Institutions in the transactions conducted with virtual assets DOF 8 March 2019.

[67] Bank of England, 'Central Bank Digital Currency. Opportunities, Challenges and Design' (2020), available at www.bankofengland.co.uk/-/media/boe/files/paper/2020/central-bank-digital-currency-opportunities-challenges-and-design.pdf?la=en&hash=DFAD18646A77C00772AF1C5B18E63E71F68E4593.

[68] Financial Conduct Authority, 'Guidance on Cryptoassets' (2019), available at www.fca.org.uk/publication/consultation/cp19-03.pdf.

[69] [2012] 752F.3d 285 (US).

[70] McCubbins (n 33); Schleifer (n 13) 446.

[71] R Romano, 'Regulating in the Dark and a Postscript Assessment of the Iron Law of Financial Regulation.' (2015) 43 *Hofstra Law Review* 25, 27; Lo (n 16).

developed in section II of chapter 5, and by the lack of transparency and explainability described by Greenspan[72] and evidenced in *State v Loomis*,[73] this is a naïve understanding of these technologies. To start, when one talks about economic policymaking, it is vital to distinguish between enforcing the rules and making the rules, as has been seen through the discussions related to the *lex mercatoria* and arbitration in international trade.[74]

As seen in chapter three, current *lex monetae* is based on a set of laws that are created by each legislature through well-defined procedures found in constitutional documents and enforced by sovereign entities. However, given the organisation of our markets, their infrastructures mostly developed and provided by the private sector through self-organising and self-regulation paradigms, and GVCs, this regulatory framework requires the introduction of complementary governance models. For instance, SWIFT is structured around a complementary set of rules enforced by the G-10's central banks and the SWIFTNet, and created by the International Organization for Standardization and by the SWIFT's board of directors, which in turn are subject to a set of regulations issued by Belgian sovereign authorities applicable to the constitution of messaging systems without constituting a proper payments system.[75] In the particular case of cryptoassets, the analysis and the gradual recognition of the agreements that configure a DLT network will depend on which instrument one wants to focus on. For example, the Ripple Transaction Protocol is a set of rules created by Ripple Labs subject to the laws of California, while the protocol of the most famous unit of first generation, Bitcoin, was made anonymously and enforced by its distributed international network. Based on these different levels of decentralisation, one could argue that DLT may provide impartial rule-enforcement, but that could be problematic if the obfuscated rules are changed by anonymous parties who have the right and/or the power to do so in absence of proper sovereign guidance and regulation,[76] or if there is not a law chosen by the parties involved in the transactions as set in Article 3(1) of the Rome 1 Regulation 593/2008[77] on the law applicable to contractual obligations.

[72] Greenspan (n 23).

[73] [2016] 881 NW.2d 749 (US).

[74] V Lehdonvirta, 'The Blockchain Paradox: Why Distributed Ledger Technologies May Do Little to Transform the Economy' (2016), available at www.oii.ox.ac.uk/blog/the-blockchain-paradox-why-distributed-ledger-technologies-may-do-little-to-transform-the-economy.

[75] SWIFT, 'Information about SWIFT and Procurement and Compliance Departments' (2019), available at www.swift.com/about-us/legal.

[76] S Cohney et al, 'Coin-Operated Capitalism.' (2018) 39, available at papers.ssrn.com/sol3/papers.cfm?abstract_id=3215345; Lehdonvirta (n 74).

[77] 'A contract shall be governed by the law chosen by the parties. The choice shall be made expressly or clearly demonstrated by the terms of the contract or the circumstances of the case. By their choice the parties can select the law applicable to the whole or to part only of the contract.' Regulation 593/2008 of the European Parliament and of the Council on the law applicable to contractual obligations (Rome I) OJ L 177/6, 17 June 2008.

C. Market Imperfections

When facing issues of this nature, conventional economic theory recognises that public regulation is justified, along with other elements of public policy towards industry, by exogenous and endogenous shocks/distortions faced by every dynamic social system that could derive in market imperfections.[78] These imperfections – like those that have emerged from the *crypto lex mercatoria* – can emerge from market power, externalities, asymmetric information and/or the incomplete nature that defines every market.[79] The first is related to competition, considering that market power is undesirable and is generally prohibited by competition law.[80] If one or few dominant firms or individuals, as evidenced through the existence of issuers and 'whales' within DLT protocols such as PoW and PoS, and new intermediaries relating to them, have the power to restrict competition, they are likely to corner the market, charge prices significantly higher than the marginal costs of supply, offer suboptimal services, and restrict innovation, among other undesirable practices.[81] Consequently, it is important to put in place regulations designed to contain monopolistic behaviour, whilst maintaining and promoting competition paradigms[82] where the successful competitor is not punished 'when he wins'.[83] In the particular case of the cryptoassets market, one has to be careful with those special circumstances in which a firm or an individual are awarded potential monopoly rights across different jurisdictions, as one can verify with patent systems that take part in governance schemes such as that introduced through the Patent Cooperation Treaty.

Certainly, in the context of the FIR and the DCS, courts will face controversies, such as, the one found in *Gottshalk v Benson*,[84] which, in turn, could lead us to question the introduction of measures aimed to ensure that firms and individuals involved in the development of the algorithms and the infrastructure required by DLT projects do not abuse this benefit, extending their infrastructural power using utility models,[85] among other corporative strategies based

[78] E Avgouleas, *Governance of Global Financial Markets. The Law, the Economics, the Politics* (Cambridge, Cambridge University Press, 2012) 6.

[79] X Freixas and JC Rochet, *Microeconomics of Banking* (Cambridge, MIT Press, 2008) 306; J Kay et al, 'Regulatory Reform in Britain' (1988) 3 *Economic Policy* 285, 301; Stiglitz (n 34) Loc 546.

[80] AI Ogus, *Regulation: Legal Form and Economic Theory* (Oregon, Hart Publishing, 2014) Kindle EBook, at Loc 1119; Kay et al (n 79) 304.

[81] Kay et al (n 79) 304; Schooner and Taylor (n 60) xii.

[82] Kay et al (n 79) 304; Stiglitz (n 34) Loc 546.

[83] *US v Aluminum Co of America* [1945] 148 F 2d 416 (US) 430.

[84] Patents of software and software-related inventions have been rather controversial. In the case of *Gottshalk v Benson*, the US Supreme Court determined that algorithms by themselves are not patentable; however, it acknowledged that new technologies could be subject to new regimes based on the 'Mental Steps' Doctrine. See [1972] 409 US 63 (US).

[85] Utility models are protected under schemes similar to those applicable to patents, but they are focused on minor improvements on an existent invention; thus, if you own a patent, in certain jurisdictions, you could extend the life of your market power through this figure.

on network effects, scale, and winner-take-all-economies.[86] Furthermore, in a world of datafied finance where the intermediary with the best data and data analytics wins, projects such as DIEM could employ its substantial market power in different datafied markets to introduce a new offer of financial products and services.[87]

The second market imperfection emerges under the influence of externalities, or what are sometimes referred to as the problem of social costs.[88] As seen in cases such as *Sturges v Bridgman*[89] and *Bass v Gregory*,[90] externalities arise when the economic activities of one party (a consumer or a company) is negatively or positively[91] affected by the actions of another for which they neither compensate nor are compensated for.[92] As one could infer, regulation is typically employed to correct negative externalities or to promote good behaviour.[93] For this purpose, policymakers can select from a myriad of regulatory instruments, classifiable according to the level of sovereign intervention required following the Institutional Possibility Frontier.[94] In the financial sector, one can find an illustration of these measures in the form of capital adequacy to face potential bank runs triggered by doubts on banks' financial health[95] or by extreme circumstances such as that faced in the context of COVID-19.[96] The resulting externality among depositors is evident, and in the limit, there is a zero-sum game among them, in which each is scrambling for a portion of his/her underlying liquidity rights, just as was witnessed when long queues formed outside Northern Rock's premises in 2007. Accordingly, one of the purposes of capital adequacy, as set in the Basel Committee Standards (I, II and III), is to ensure that banks have enough funds available to cover these eventualities and thus avoid a potential contagion.[97]

[86] CV Chien, 'Software Patents as a Currency, Not Tax, on Innovation' (2016) 31 *Berkeley Technology Law Journal* 1669, 1675.

[87] DA Zetzsche, RP Buckley and DW Arner, 'Regulating Libra. The Transformative Potential of Facebook's Cryptocurrency and Possible Regulatory Responses' (2019) 47 *University of New South Wales Law Research Series* 1, 15–16.

[88] RH Coase, 'The Problem of Social Cost' (1960) 3 *The Journal of Law & Economics* 1; Schooner and Taylor (n 60) xiii.

[89] [1879] 1 Ch D 852 (UK).

[90] [1890] 25 QBD 481 (UK).

[91] An example of a positive externality would be a bank branch that attracts consumers to nearby businesses, but that is not compensated for the positive influence it generates. This topic was discussed recently by the Scottish Parliament through an evidence session held on 19 June 2018 regarding the reduction of bank branches across Scotland.

[92] Kay et al (n 79) 302; Schooner and Taylor (n 60) xiii; Stiglitz (n 34) Loc 546.

[93] Schooner and Taylor (n 60) xiii.

[94] Djankov et al (n 20).

[95] LE Panourgias, *Banking Regulation and World Trade Law. GATS, EU and 'Prudential' Institution Building* (Portland, Hart Publishing, 2006) 20; Ogus (n 80) Loc 1106.

[96] H Siekmann, 'Deposit Banking and the Use of Monetary Instruments' in. Fox and. Ernst (eds), *Money in the Western Legal Tradition. Middle Ages to Bretton Woods* (Oxford, Oxford University Press, 2016) 489–531, 493.

[97] Kay et al (n 79) 303.

The third conventional justification for regulation emerges from the existence of information asymmetries.[98] If one wants to assume that we are intelligent players in a well-functioning market, as described by Fama,[99] we need a set of regulations designed to ensure that, for example, the exchanges where we buy our cryptoassets are sufficiently sound. Naturally, if information was perfect – and we were rational – we would not put our money in an intermediary that could not repay it, or in one whose technological offer does not follow the spirit of its time.[100] There are two broad forms that these regulations can adopt. The first arises when government regulates the conduct/activities of the institutions that would have access to sovereign benefits, such as sovereign reserves and/or guarantees. In theory, as can be seen in the traditional TBTF approach diffused under NIFA, governments tend to bail out failing banks that develop certain activities, either because they worry about the systemic consequences related to the maturity mismatches between their assets and liabilities, or because depositors are treated quite unlike other creditors and protected by government-backed insurance or sovereign guarantees.[101]

The second category of measures that are designed to tackle information asymmetries concerns what might be called 'certification of the structure'.[102] All individuals want to be assured that if they put money in a bank, the bank will be there when the time comes to withdraw the money. Sovereign bank regulation is in part a certification, which sets certain standards that the infrastructure provided by a bank must satisfy, and inspections are carries out to ensure that it meets those standards. In the context of the cryptoassets market, this certification can be identified in Articles 16, 17 and 18 of MiCA[103] where legal persons and credit institutions can find the requirements to obtain an authorisation to offer asset-referenced tokens to the public. Consequently, as can be seen in the risk assessments introduced in the revised framework Basel II, independently of the infrastructural power of the private sector, the state establishes which firms are qualified to develop certain type of activities.[104]

Finally, there is a fourth justification that is not common in most of the works on regulation, which is relevant for the purposes of this book, which results from the fact that markets are incomplete as developed under the Lancasterian perspective.[105] The optimality of the competitive market equilibrium depends on the existence of markets for all necessary transactions at all relevant horizons.[106]

[98] Kay et al (n 79) 304; Ogus (n 80).

[99] Fama (n 8).

[100] Freixas and Rochet (n 79) 305; Stiglitz (n 34) Loc 562.

[101] S Bristoll and R Goode, '1992: The Insolvency Implications for Banks' in R Cranston (ed), *The Single Market and the Law of Banking* (London, Lloyd's of London Press, 1995) 121–138, 121; Avgouleas (n 78) 6; Stiglitz (n 34) Loc 562.

[102] Stiglitz (n 34) Loc 562.

[103] Regulation 2023/1114 on markets in crypto-assets, and amending Regulations (EU) No 1093/2010 and (EU) No 1095/2010 and Directives 2013/36/EU and (EU) 2019/1937 OJ L 150/40, 31 May 2023.

[104] Freixas and Rochet (n 79) 305; Stiglitz (n 34) Loc 562.

[105] Artus and de Boissieu (n 2) 110; Bénassy-Quéré et al (n 62) 29.

[106] Bénassy-Quéré et al (n 62) 29.

The theory of the demand for characteristics explains a demand for new financial products in the light of particular endogenous elements of the social system.[107] For example, in countries such as Mexico where only 49.1 per cent of the population over 18 years old have a bank account,[108] the absence of proper infrastructure to improve this number fosters private innovation, which, in turn, given the socio-economic conditions of the country, could be translated in sub-optimal solutions provided by the private sector.

The selection of the sovereign strategy to face these failures will depend on the exposure related to three sets of interests that are closely related to the incomplete nature of our post-Lehman Brothers markets. First, there is the interest of the state, understanding that money and financial stability are public goods whose nature is set into the constitutional agreement. On this point, most of the works relating to DLT innovations are focused on regulations against money laundering, financing crime and tax evasion, but, following the chapter three, special attention should – and will – be paid to the exercise of the *lex monetae*. With this cornerstone in place, the secondary issues addressed by the Financial Action Task Force (FATF) following the terms of the UN Convention against Illicit Traffic in Narcotic Drugs and Psychotropic Substances of 1988 and the UN Convention against Transnational Organized Crime 2000, could be solved once there is put in place a sound regulatory and institutional framework, taking advantage of what new technologies have to offer.

The next set of interests that has to be considered in any regulatory strategy are those of regulated and non-regulated intermediaries that constitute our payment systems. On the one hand, the existent payment intermediaries are concerned with the competition provided by the shadow payments system,[109] so they try to defend their infrastructural power through patents[110] and sovereign intervention under an institutional perspective. On the other hand, despite the popular views on decentralisation and disintermediation, innovators want to be incorporated into existent payment infrastructures and avoid public prosecutions such those related to the activities of Binance[111] and Kraken,[112] while, at the same time, play a pivotal role in the efforts aimed to foster financial inclusion. Finally, on this last point, ordinary consumers and unsophisticated investors do not have access to perfect information, as expressly acknowledged in *Bertrand v Ott*,[113] so they can influence the process of regulation from a marginal position, their only power being their

[107] Artus and de Boissieu (n 2) 110.
[108] National Institute of Statistics and Geography, 'National Survey on Financial Inclusion 2021' (2022), available at www.inegi.org.mx/contenidos/saladeprensa/boletines/2022/enif/ENIF21.pdf.
[109] D Awrey and K van Zwieten, 'The Shadow Payment System' (2018) 43 *The Journal of Corporation Law* 102, 103.
[110] It is important to highlight that commercial banks are among the main applicants for patents relating to DLT.
[111] *SEC v Binance* [2023] 1:23-cv-01599 (US).
[112] *SEC v Kraken* [2023] 3:23-cv-00588 (US).
[113] [1978] ECR 150/77 (EU).

decision to use a service or not. In all three cases, it is the state which, through its *lex monetae* and the institutions relating to it, can decide on and enforce the existence and conditions of the adoption of financial innovations.

V. Changing the Regulatory Approach

When studying current regulatory proposals, it is immediately apparent that they have followed two opposing schemes that, paradoxically, are structured around the idea of money as an asset that exists by itself within the institutional structure, which, in turn, is taken as a given. On the one hand are those efforts developed by institutions such as the FATF[114] and the Bank of England,[115] which aim to improve the existent international infrastructure by which payments are made and to face new challenges posed by *anti securitas* practices, such as money laundering. These proposals flow from the G20's[116] common principles, which acknowledges that:

> [O]ur financial markets are global in scope, therefore, intensified international cooperation among regulators and strengthening of international standards, where necessary, and their consistent implementation is necessary to protect against adverse cross-border, regional and global developments affecting international financial stability.

On the other hand, are the proposals developed in countries such as Gibraltar[117] and Switzerland,[118] which have been designed to face the characteristics of a Wallersteinian FWS. Under this line of regulation, these regulators consider that this system and its integral elements behave like an organism that through our *Bildungstrieb* change the composition of its boundaries, institutions, member groups, rules and coherence.[119] Therefore, following the trend that started with

[114] See Financial Action Task Force, 'FATF FinTech & RegTech Initiative' (2018), available at www.fatf-gafi.org/fintech-regtech/?hf=10&b=0&s=desc(fatf_releasedate).

[115] Bank of England, 'RTGS Renewal Programme Proof of Concept: Supporting DLT Settlement Models.' (2018), available at www.bankofengland.co.uk/news/2018/july/rtgs-renewal-programme-proof-of-concept-supporting-dlt-settlement-models.

[116] G20, 'Declaration of the Summit on Financial Markets and the World Economy' (2008) available at www.g20.utoronto.ca/2008/2008declaration1115.html#actions.

[117] On 12 October 2017, the Government of Gibraltar published in its gazette 4401 the Financial Services (Distributed Ledger Technology Providers) Regulations 2017 by which regulates the provision of financial services using DLT, a regulation that has attracted companies to issue ICOs in this jurisdiction in platforms like the Gibraltar Blockchain Exchange. See L Noonan, 'Gibraltar Wants to Rock to ICO Beat.' (2018), available at www.ft.com/content/48793616-2c13-11e8-9b4b-bc4b9f08f381.

[118] Following the words of Johann Schneider-Ammann, Economics Minister of Switzerland, this country aims to become a 'crypto-nation'. Accordingly, the Swiss Financial Market Supervisory Authority (FINMA) has issued several guidelines related to the issuance of ICOs and stablecoins, following the evolutionary trend described in ch 4 of this book. See F Atkins, 'Switzerland Embraces Cryptocurrency Culture' (2018), available at www.ft.com/content/c2098ef6-ff84-11e7-9650-9c0ad2d7c5b5; FINMA, 'FINMA Publishes ICO Guidelines' (2018), available at www.finma.ch/en/news/2018/02/20180216-mm-ico-wegleitung/; FINMA, 'FINMA Publishes "Stable Coin2 Guidelines.' (2019), available at www.finma.ch/en/news/2019/09/20190911-mm-stable-coins/.

[119] I Wallerstein, *World-Systems Analysis. An Introduction* (Durham, Duke University Press, 2004).

the 'spontaneous order' of the CGS, these measures aim to continually introduce conflicting innovative forces to hold the system together through innovation, thus seeking 'eternally' to remould it to their own advantage.[120]

One can acknowledge that both arguments have their strong and weak points; however, for our purposes, we will give the edge to the first approach. Of course, here the followers of the Wallersteinian argument could argue that 'public international law recognises the concept of money as a creature and creation of a national legal system'.[121] Therefore, it is possible to say that money is a public good characterised by two elements. First, non-exclusivity. Given that the government that emerges from the social contract is a public good, through its *lex monetae* it has the obligation to provide the ultimate means of payment to its citizens as integral parties of the agreement.[122] Furthermore, based on the incorporation of social liquidity, its use by one individual increases its value to other current or potential users.[123] The second element is non-rivalry. This means that our use of a fungible monetary asset in what would otherwise be barter has no effect on its general circulation.[124] These characteristics are perfectly reflected in the definition of money found in *Moss v Hancock*[125] and in the legal principle that states that '*money has no earmark*'.

In practice, it could be argued that the G20's[126] principles would involve two major obstacles: how to agree on what constitutes a global public good in the absence of a universal social contract? And what would be the appropriate rules to produce this good? Initially, one could argue that given that money is a public good subject to the *jus cudendae monetae* that characterises most post-Westphalian nations and the paradigm followed to protect IPRs as seen in cases, such as *Eldred v Ashcroft*,[127] it is impossible to constitute a global public good. However, following Merton's functional perspective of financial intermediation, it is possible to say that 'the basic functions of a financial system are essentially the same in all economies'.[128] Accordingly, as can be seen in the transition from cases, such as *Burton v Davy*[129] and *Miller v Race*,[130] to the international adoption of the principles found in the

[120] Haldane (n 43).

[121] C Proctor, 'Cryptocurrencies in International and Public Law Conceptions of Money' in D Fox and S Green (eds), *Cryptocurrencies in Public and Private Law* (Oxford, Oxford University Press, 2019) 33–55, 37.

[122] J Tobin, 'Discussion' (1980), available at www.minneapolisfed.org/~/media/files/pubs/books/models/cp83.pdf?la=en.

[123] N Kiyotaki and R Wright, 'On Money as a Medium of Exchange' (1989) 97 *Journal of Political Economy* 927, 928; Tobin (n 122).

[124] Panourgias (n 95) 20.

[125] [1899], 2 QB 111 (UK), at 116.

[126] G20 (n 116).

[127] This case highlighted the differences between Anglo-Saxon and continental Europe traditions regarding the extension of the term of the post-mortem protection for works subject to copyright. See [2003] 537 US 186 (US).

[128] RC Merton, 'A Functional Perspective of Financial Intermediation' (1995) 24 *Financial Management* 23, 24.

[129] H Hall, *Select Cases Concerning the Law Merchant AD 1251–1779. Vol III* (London, Selden Society, 1932) 117–19.

[130] [1758] 97 ER 398 (UK), at 401.

Convention Providing a Uniform Law For Bills of Exchange and Promissory Notes of 1930, and from this to normative instruments such as the General Law of Negotiable Instruments and Credit Operations[131] of Mexico, this socio-legal institution has relied on standards that have worked as a set of 'universal' principles, as evidenced in *Swift v Tyson*[132] where Joseph Story J argued that:

> Undoubtedly, the decisions of the local tribunals upon such subjects are entitled to, and will receive, the most deliberate attention and respect of this court; but they cannot furnish positive rules, or conclusive authority, by which our own judgments are to be bound up and governed. The law respecting negotiable instruments may be truly declared in the languages of Cicero, adopted by Lord MANSFIELD in Luke v. Lyde, 2 Burr. 883, 887, to be in a great measure, not the law of a single country only, but of the commercial world. Non erit alia lex Romae, alia Athenis; alia nunc, alia posthac; sed et apud omnes gentes, et omni tempore una eademque lex obtinebit.

Although this case was overruled by the US Supreme Court in *Erie v Tompkins*,[133] the spirit of *Swift v Tyson* highlights that, despite the irrefutable existence of legal traditions, generally speaking, mini-systems constrained by a single cultural framework are an academic fiction,[134] as verified through the very existence of 'comity'.[135] As it was explained by Atkins J in *Dubai Islamic Bank PJSC v Paymentech Merchant Services INC*,[136] we interact within a complex web of transnational regulatory and monetary networks and agreements put in force by the private sector that, in the opinion of some authors,[137] have eroded the role of the *lex monetae*. On this point, there is a lack of understanding of the full reach of *lex monetae*.

These networks and agreements by which nations permeate the exercise of their *ius cudendae monetae* follow the work of bodies with no legal status as international organisations, such as the International Organization for Standardisation (ISO). that set the standards for the infrastructures that constitute the global financial sector. Through these efforts, convergence has increasingly been sought on certain core principles and standards, such as the Core Principles for Systemically Important Payment Systems set by the Basel Committee on Payment and Settlement Systems.[138] These models are structured

[131] General Law General Law of Negotiable Instruments and Credit Operations DOF, 27 August 1932.

[132] [1842] 41 US 1 (US).

[133] [1938] 304 US 64 (US).

[134] Wallerstein (n 119) 5.

[135] '"Comity," in the legal sense, is neither a matter of absolute obligation, on the one hand, nor of mere courtesy and good will, upon the other. But it is the recognition which one nation allows within its territory to the legislative, executive or judicial acts of another nation, having due regard both to international duty and convenience, and to the rights of its own citizens or of other persons who are under the protection of its laws.' See *Hilton v Guyot* [1895] 159 U. 113 (US), at 163–64.

[136] [2001] 1 Lloyd's Rep 65 (UK), at 517–18.

[137] See K Sono and H Kanda, 'In Search of Order in the World Monetary System: State Intervention after the Decline of the Lex Monetae' in M Giovanoli and D Devos (eds), *International Monetary and Financial Law. The Global Crisis* (Oxford, Oxford University Press, 2010) 506–16.

[138] Bank for International Settlements, 'Core Principles of Systemically Important Payment Systems' (2001), available at www.bis.org/cpmi/publ/d43.htm.

around soft and flexible models,[139] where the state is seen as a semi-endogenous normative order, which to some degree reflects the conditions in the economy.[140] Furthermore, the continual stream of technological developments in payment services over the last two decades has dematerialised our interactions across multiple jurisdictions. This change has led to a large number of regulatory efforts to support and encourage these new developments and to promote competition by fostering the emergence of new non-bank payment services providers into the market, but also to ensure that these new developments are regulated appropriately[141] without granting normative hegemony to those countries that are leading thecurrent technological arms race.

A. From the Assets to the Technology

Institutions such as the ECB[142] have acknowledged that the actions taken by sovereign entities to face these changes tend to lag behind private sector innovations by several years. As seen throughout history, from the 'Grandsons of Egibi' in Babylon to the very network of agreements that constitute RTGSs, this advantage can be identified in the very infrastructure of our payment systems where, although we have acknowledged that money is a public good, we also need to recognise that this public good has been subject to the infrastructural power – and even abuses[143] – of the private sector.

The dominant body of literature on the legal aspects of money tends to ignore this fact; most tend to be focused on the current designs, the behaviour and the sovereign *diktats* of central banks, thus leaving aside the very relevant operational details of the payment systems employed to exercise these monetary prerogatives. Consequently, it should not be surprising that when we talk about the regulation of cryptoassets, the dominant opinion is based on the creation of CBDCs to face specific antagonists such as Bitcoin and certain stablecoins. Yes, as section III of chapter two showed, there was a time when the state provided and controlled the infrastructure required to put money in circulation in the form of mints; however, financial innovation has increased the role played by the private sector in the development of these infrastructures. Accordingly, the exercise of the *lex monetae* has to be understood beyond the mere monopoly over money creation and include the prerogatives related to the design of the infrastructure that supports the interactions between inside money and outside money.

[139] K Alexander, R Dhumale and J Eatwell, *Global Governance of Financial Systems. The International Regulation of Systemic Risk* (New York, Oxford University Press, 2006) 79; Cranston (n 5) 19; Goode (n 5) 517; Avgouleas (n 78) 190; Schooner and Taylor (n 60) xi.

[140] Deakin (n 1) 25.

[141] C Proctor and V Dixon, *Goode on Payment Obligations in Commercial and Financial Transactions* (London, Thomson Reuters, 2016) 203.

[142] European Central Bank, 'Virtual Currency Schemes.' (2012) 44, available at www.ecb.europa.eu/pub/pdf/other/virtualcurrencyschemes201210en.pdf.

[143] See *Banco de Portugal v Waterlow & Sons Ltd* [1932] AC 452 (UK).

This is not to say that central banks are institutional anachronisms. After all, as will be seen in the following section, we will need a sovereign source of liquidity to *reify* in the fourth generation of cryptoassets and/or sovereign units of reference to act as the anchors of new crypto payment systems. Furthermore, the lack of attention to the monetary governance arrangements is perfectly reflected in most of our regulatory analyses and proposals. In these, the idea that prevails is that these innovations could challenge the power of the fourth constitutional power and, as can be seen through the excessive focus on PoW protocols, ignore the need for a well-defined underlying *res* and the evolution of the infrastructure provided by DLT developers towards that aim following the example set by electronic money.

B. Money for Datafied Markets

The first analyses relating to electronic money were heavily focused on the assets and the hypothetical risks that these latter would pose on the *ius cudendae monetae*; for example, the Report on Electronic Money published in August 1998 by the ECB,[144] and academic efforts such as *The New Virtual Money: Law and Practice*[145] written by Olivier Hance and Suzan Dionne Balz. However, after these initial arguments, the technology – but not the instruments – has been widely introduced in our economies and payment systems, and regulated accordingly throughout the world. These efforts were gradual. First, the legal definitions of writing and signature were revised and modified to include any medium of communication and cryptographic systems of authentication so long as the message is capable of being represented in a computer following the principles set in instruments such as Article 6(1) of the 1996 UNCITRAL Model Law on Electronic Commerce, which states that 'Where the law requires information to be in writing, that requirement is met by a data message if the information contained therein is accessible so as to be usable for subsequent reference.' This, in turn, was included in national legislation, such as Regulation 7 of the Electronic Communications Act 2000[146] where, with the aim to ease commerce:

> [A]n electronic signature incorporated into or associated with a particular electronic communication or particular electronic data is certified by any person if that person (whether before or after the making of the communication) has made a statement confirming that—
>
> (a) the signature,
> (b) a means of producing, communicating or verifying the signature, or
> (c) a procedure applied to the signature,

[144] European Central Bank, 'Report on Electronic Money.' (1998), available at www.ecb.europa.eu/pub/pdf/other/emoneyen.pdf.

[145] O Hance and SD Balz, *The New Virtual Money: Law and Practice* (The Hague: Kluwer Law International, 1999) 391.

[146] Electronic Communications Act 2000.

> is (either alone or in combination with other factors) a valid means of establishing the authenticity of the communication or data, the integrity of the communication or data, or both.

And Article 89 of the Mexican Commercial Code,[147] where the legislator specified that:

> The interpretation and execution of the activities regulated by this Title, will be subject to the principles of technological neutrality, autonomy of the will, international compatibility and functional equivalency of the Data Message, in relation to the information documented in non-electronic mediums, and the Electronic Signature in relation to the autograph signature.

Or in cases such as *Your Response Ltd v Datateam Business Media Ltd*[148] by which-Floyd LJ argued that:

> When information is created and recorded there are sharp distinctions between the information itself, the physical medium on which the information is recorded and the rights to which the information gives rise. Whilst the physical medium and the rights are treated as property, the information itself has never been.

Accordingly, regulators have recognised the existence of intangible electronic markets and contracts, and issued instruments, such as the Electronic Commerce Directive[149] introduced by the EU in 2000, implemented in the UK through the Electronic Commerce Regulations 2002,[150] the Digital Services Act[151] and the Digital Markets Act[152] published in the Official Journal of the European Union in 2022, and the reform of 29 August 2003 by which an entire title on electronic commerce was included within the Mexican Commercial Code.[153] In these examples, it is possible to see how legislators introduced harmonised frameworks for electronic commerce that include a quasi-universal recognition of these electronic contracts,[154] which has eased the interoperability of the global infrastructure and the contractual networks that allow us to make payments throughout the world.

[147] Commercial Code DOF.

[148] [2015] QB 41 (UK), at 56.

[149] Directive 2000/31/EC of the European Parliament and of the Council on certain legal aspects of information society services, in particular electronic commerce, in the Internal Market (Directive on electronic commerce) OJ L 178/1, 8 June 2000.

[150] Electronic Commerce (EC Directive) Regulations 2002 (SI 2002/2013).

[151] Regulation (EU) 2022/2065 of the European Parliament and of the Council on a Single Market for Digital Services and amending Directive 2000/31/EC (Digital Services Act) OJ L 277/1, 19 October 2022.

[152] Regulation (EU) 2022/1925 of the European Parliament and of the Council on contestable and fair markets in the digital sector and amending Directives (EU) 2019/1937 and (EU) 2020/1828 (Digital Markets Act) OJ L 265/1, 14 September 2022.

[153] Commercial Code DOF.

[154] Proctor and Dixon (n 141) 203.

Following this recognition, the next stage was the introduction of instruments such as the Electronic Money Directive 2000/46/EC,[155] which was eventually replaced by the 2EMD,[156] which sets out the legal framework for issuing electronic money in the EU and which is implemented in the UK through the Electronic Money Regulations 2011,[157] with the aim of dealing with these electronic payments and the landscape of intermediaries that was emerging within these markets. Regarding the infrastructure of new electronic payment systems, a number of other regulations have been introduced, including MiCA,[158] the Circular 1/2006 issued by Banxico and the Payment Services Directive 2007/64/EC,[159] which was intended to promote competition by providing a framework for service providers other than banks that provide payment services. On this latter, the PSD2[160] continues with this spirit that has been put in force in the UK through the Payment Services Regulations 2017.[161] These regulations were designed to include new FinTech service providers, as one can see through the recognition and incorporation of TransferWise to the Bank of England payment system,[162] and the current efforts to materialise a PSD3, which will be focused on 'open banking' services, including the secure exchange of financial data among banks, and the constitution and operation of FinTechs.[163]

The main lesson that we can take from this is that we need to stop focusing our efforts on fantastic scenarios where Bitcoin and PoW protocols will challenge the *lex monetae*. Instead, following the evolution of this market, we have to understand that the private sector will eventually will introduce a refined version of DLT that will allow it to develop infrastructural power under existent regulations applicable to payment systems, payment instruments and electronic money as a new stage of this process of digitisation.

[155] Directive 2000/46/EC of the European Parliament and of the Council on the taking up, pursuit of and prudential supervision of the business of electronic money institutions OJ L 275/39, 18 September 2000.

[156] Directive 2009/110/EC of the European Parliament and of the Council on the taking up, pursuit and prudential supervision of the business of electronic money institutions amending Directives 2005/60/EC and 2006/48/EC and repealing Directive 2000/46/EC OJ L 267/7, 16 September 2009.

[157] The Electronic Money Regulations 2011 (SI 2011/99).

[158] Regulation 2023/1114 on markets in crypto-assets, and amending Regulations (EU) No 1093/2010 and (EU) No 1095/2010 and Directives 2013/36/EU and (EU) 2019/1937 OJ L 150/40.

[159] Directive 2007/64/EC of the European Parliament and of the Council on payment services in the internal market amending Directives 97/7/EC, 2002/65/EC, 2005/60/EC and 2006/48/EC and repealing Directive 97/5/EC OJ L 319/1, 13 November 2007.

[160] Directive 2015/2366 of the European Parliament and of the Council on payment services in the internal market, amending Directives 2002/65/EC, 2009/110/EC and 2013/36/EU and Regulation (EU) No 1093/2010, and repealing Directive 2007/64/EC OJ L 337/35, 25 November 2015.

[161] The Payment Services Regulations 2017 (SI 2017/752).

[162] N Megaw, 'TransferWise Becomes First Non-Bank to Join BoE Payment System. (2018), available at www.ft.com/content/78886740-42e9-11e8-803a-295c97e6fd0b.

[163] European Commission, 'Modernising Payment Services and Opening Financial Services Data: New Opportunities for Consumers and Businesses' (2023), available at ec.europa.eu/commission/presscorner/detail/en/ip_23_3543.

VI. Money for the Digital Commercial Society

Authors such as Cristie Ford[164] argue that financial innovations have shattered the concept of property to the point that we should not get too comfortable in our understanding of what certain terms, such as 'money' actually are. However, generally, when a new technology is introduced, it fosters a behaviour that can be compared with a new theory of physics given that, as can be seen in Nakamoto's paper,[165] the 'revolution' never completely displaces what came before.[166] On this point, it can be argued that in debates concerning the legal implications of electronic/digital business environments, there is an unfortunate tendency to over-emphasise and idealise the virtues of technologies such as blockchain and AI, and to assume that they automatically change everything as far as legal relationships are concerned.[167] This perception is something that we have to overcome if we want to describe legal reality as it is and to generate optimal solutions. Whether one is talking about electronic money or the development of cryptoassets, it is necessary to ask why, if the *res* incorporated within these instruments is the same, its legal meaning and effects should be affected by the technological medium employed to send it.

Some arguments relating to the virtues of decentralisation, the 'cypherpunk' movement, and alternative governance models, among others, claim that these are very different instruments, but there is nothing further from the truth. Here one will find the charm of the Socio-Legal theory of money and the evolution of the 'sacred' source of liquidity, both introduced in chapter two. Based on this approach, one could refine the previous question and ask what is the difference between an incorporation and transfer of liquidity using a stablecoin like JPMCoin and the delivery of a bill of exchange, a promissory note, a cheque, a bank note or a coin? The answer is rather simple. The only difference lies in the technology available to uphold the underlying obligations, which is introduced by merchants and diffused by an evolving offer of intermediaries following the rules set by a sovereign stakeholder for this purpose.

A. What is Special about DLT?

So, what is so special about DLT? Why should cryptoassets necessitate different rules of law, such as MiCA? The general answer found in practically every source relating to the regulation of these innovations starts by arguing that cryptoassets do not fit into the definitions provided by those regulations applicable to electronic

[164] Ford (n 1) 142.

[165] S Nakamoto, 'Bitcoin: A Peer-to-Peer Electronic Cash System' (2008), available at bitcoin.org/bitcoin.pdf.

[166] K Werbach, *The Blockchain and the New Architecture of Trust* (Massachusetts, MIT Press, 2018) 2.

[167] R Goode, *Commercial Law in the Next Millennium* (London, Sweet & Maxwell, 1998) 97.

money or other payment instruments. Therefore, although there are instruments in force, such as the Consumer Rights Directive,[168] it is argued that there is very little protection for users of these instruments either in terms of standardising the conditions for the incorporation of underlying obligations, compensating in the case of unauthorised transactions or theft, or facing scenarios where the issuer of the asset becomes insolvent.[169] These are rather valid concerns, but the creation of an entire body of regulations focused exclusively on cryptoassets is not the answer.

Despite the current state of the legal-institutional frameworks applicable to payment orders and instruments, the same rules could eventually apply to both electronic money and cryptoasset transactions, and some existent regulations could be adjusted to the new environment, without losing their original spirit. For instance, as mentioned in chapter four, if the emergence of currency-backed stablecoins continues, regulations such as the Scottish and Northern Ireland Banknote Regulations 2009[170] could be amended and applied to new instruments and institutions, and/or act as a guide for future legal transfers. Furthermore, the intermediaries that are emerging within this market could eventually be subject to regulations such as PSD2,[171] Recital 21 of which states that 'The definition of payment services should be technologically neutral and should allow for the development of new types of payment services, while ensuring equivalent operating conditions for both existing and new payment service providers.' This would not be a new practice. Throughout history of money, formats of monetary institutions have been transferred from country to country. For example, the Venetian Banco della Piazza di Rialto inspired the constitution of the Amsterdamsche Wisselbank, which in turn inspired, through the observations made by Johan Palmstruch, the creation of the Sveriges Riksbank in 1668.[172] In this respect, the evolution of financial institutions has been truly international.

Furthermore, as seen in previous chapters, issues relating to the protection of IPRs have to be considered in our regulatory strategies. These rights are the cornerstone of the digital infrastructure that is provided by the private sector, which is designed not only on the interoperability of DLT networks, but also on the interoperability of these latter with technologies, such as AI and 5G, as expressed by Dr Frank Tong, CEO of HSBC Innovations, during a visit to the University of Edinburgh. As one would expect, these interactions will force us to keep an eye on

[168] Directive 2011/83/EU of the European Parliament and of the Council OJ L 304/64, 25 October 2011.

[169] Proctor and Dixon (n 141) 269.

[170] Scottish and Northern Ireland Banknote Regulations 2009 (SI 2009/3056).

[171] Directive 2015/2366 of the European Parliament and of the Council on payment services in the internal market, amending Directives 2002/65/EC, 2009/110/EC and 2013/36/EU and Regulation (EU) No 1093/2010, and repealing Directive 2007/64/EC OJ L 337/35, 25 November 2015.

[172] R Edvinsson, T Jacobson and D Waldenström, 'Introduction' in R Edvinsson, T Jacobson and D Waldenström (eds), *Sveriges Riksbank and the History of Central Banking* (Cambridge, Cambridge University Press, 2018) 1–25, 22; K Fregert, 'Sveriges Riksbank: 350 Years in the Making' in R Edvinsson, T Jacobson and D Waldenström (eds), *Sveriges Riksbank and the History of Central Banking* (Cambridge, Cambridge University Press, 2018) 90–142, 95.

potential problems, such as those relating to the identification of data controllers and processors, given that in digital environments money could become a personal piece of information, as described in Article 4 of the new European General Data Protection Regulation[173] (GDPR), which defines personal data as:

> [A]ny information relating to an identified or identifiable natural person ('data subject'); an identifiable natural person is one who can be identified, directly or indirectly, in particular by reference to an identifier such as a name, an identification number, location data, an online identifier or to one or more factors specific to the physical, physiological, genetic, mental, economic, cultural or social identity of that natural person.

As seen in the new generation of shadow banks, the ease and speed with which large sums of money and data can be moved around the world in complex digital environments creates the potential for large-scale losses of datasets through fraud or operational failure[174] that could challenge not only financial regulations, but also other legal-institutional frameworks, such as GDPR.

In the DCS, supervisory and regulatory concerns relating to the structure of the governance arrangements that configure payment systems around the world fall under various heads who should have the legal power to ensure it.[175] For example, Part 5 of the Banking Act 2009[176] of the UK and Article 2 of the Law of Banxico[177] empower their respective central banks to supervise inter-bank payment systems. Of course, they are not the only institutions involved in this task. For instance, in the US there are academic and public discussions over the legal nature of cryptoassets (are they commodities or securities?), which give rise to a very interesting question: Which agency is empowered to regulate cryptoassets: the Commodity Futures Trading Commission (CFTC) or the Securities Exchange Commission (SEC)?[178] Additionally, a concern about the difficulty facing new entrants in accessing payment systems could attract the attention of competition regulators.[179]

B. Designing a New Crypto Payments System

After the GFC, central bankers and policymakers spent many hours discussing and working on the design of unconventional monetary policies, such as quantitative easing and negative interest rates; however, there has more recently been a shift to

[173] Regulation 2016/679 of the European Parliament and of the Council on the protection of natural persons with regard to the processing of personal data and on the free movement of such data, and repealing Directive 95/46/EC (General Data Protection Regulation) OJ L 119/1, 27 April 2016.
[174] Goode (n 167) 97–98.
[175] Cranston et al (n 5) 354.
[176] Banking Act 2009.
[177] Law of the Bank of Mexico DOF.
[178] TA Moffett, 'CFTC & SEC: The Wild West of Cryptocurrency Regulation' (2023) 57 *University of Richmond Law Review* 715.
[179] Cranston et al (n 5) 355.

the issues at the very heart of the *lex monetae*.[180] Back in 2013, during the conference *Shadow Banking: An European Perspective* organised by the City University London, I argued that, given the gradual emergence of innovations like Bitcoin, we would eventually have to create digital sovereign currencies such as a digital euro.[181] At the time, many people thought that such idea was interesting but irrelevant. However, the 'spirit of the times' has changed and over the last couple of years, central banks and institutions such as the BIS have been publishing documents, such as 'The Riksbank's E-Krona Project',[182] 'Central Bank Cryptocurrencies',[183] 'Central Bank Digital Currency in Denmark?',[184] 'Rafkróna? Central Bank Digital Currency',[185] and even a proposal for a Regulation of the European Parliament and of the Council on the establishment of the digital euro,[186] just to name a few. After all, any financial system reform has to start with the understanding that Information Technology is the story of our time.[187]

However, these documents – including my own 2013 opinion – show different analyses and proposals regarding projects structured around CBDCs aimed at challenging existent cryptoassets and/or defending current regulatory prerogatives. As an exercise, it is okay, but we have to ask if the creation of these assets is the final aim or only an integral part of a more complex governance model. In the current academic and regulatory environment, the answer to this question is not an easy one. We are so certain about the 'neutral' virtues of algorithmic codes that we tend to think of these technologies as something so perfectly materialised that has already changed our monetary paradigms.

In opposition to the arguments presented by innovators and enthusiasts, it is possible to affirm that there would not be a radical innovation in the provision of these digital versions.[188] First, we agree that anyone can hold and use banknotes

[180] A Carstens, 'Money in the Digital Age: What Role for Central Banks?' (2018), available at www.bis.org/speeches/sp180206.pdf.

[181] I Cedillo, 'The Historical Role of the European Shadow Banking System in the Development and Evolution of Our Monetary Institutions' (2013), available at papers.ssrn.com/sol3/papers.cfm?abstract_id=2220167.

[182] Sveriges Riksbank, 'The Riksbank's E-Krona Project. Report 1' (2017), available at www.riksbank.se/globalassets/media/rapporter/e-krona/2017/rapport_ekrona_uppdaterad_170920_eng.pdf.

[183] M Bech and R Garratt, 'Central Bank Cryptocurrencies' (2017), available at www.bis.org/publ/qtrpdf/r_qt1709f.htm.

[184] Danmarks Nationalbank, 'Central Bank Digital Currency in Denmark?' (2017), available at www.nationalbanken.dk/en/publications/Documents/2017/12/Analysis%20-%20Central%20bank%20digital%20currency%20in%20Denmark.pdf.

[185] Central Bank of Iceland, 'Rafkróna? Central Bank Digital Currency.' (2018), available at www.cb.is/library/Skraarsafn---EN/Reports/Special_Publication_12.pdf.

[186] European Commission, 'A proposal for a Regulation of the European Parliament and of the Council on the Establishment of the Digital Euro' (2023), available at finance.ec.europa.eu/system/files/2023-06/230628-proposal-digital-euro-regulation_en.pdf.

[187] RJ Shiller, *The Subprime Solution. How Today's Global Financial Crisis Happened, and What to Do about It* (Princeton, Princeton University Press, 2008) 117.

[188] J Barrdear and M Kumhof, 'The Macroeconomics of Central Bank Issued Digital Currencies' (2016), available at www.bankofengland.co.uk/research/Documents/workingpapers/2016/swp605.pdf; Y. Mersch, 'Virtual or Virtueless? The Evolution of Money in the Digital Age' (2018), available at www.ecb.europa.eu/press/key/date/2018/html/ecb.sp180208.en.html.

and coins in a cash transaction and remain anonymous, given that these instruments do not carry any information other than value and cultural traits related to the issuer.[189] In other terms, there is no need for a trusted third party to keep a record of the transfer of cash from one party to another.[190] As mentioned at the opening of chapter four, this is the reason for the old doctrine of the Common Law found in cases such as *Moss v Hancock*,[191] which stated that 'money has no earmark'. This principle is necessary by the very nature of commerce and the 'open bag' doctrine analysed in *Folley v Hill*,[192] because no transactions can take place if the seller is bound in every sale to inquire into the right of the buyer to the money.[193] As one can see through reports and warnings published by institutions such as the FATF[194] regarding the risks related to anonymity in cryptoassets markets, cash has also been subject to similar reports.[195]

Second, with the advent of the digital age, the private sector has developed solutions that meet new endogenous demands within different dynamic social systems. The COVID-19 crisis demonstrated that the vast majority of money in a modern economy is already electronic, while bills and coins make up only a tiny part of the money in circulation. Locally, commercial banks have always offered deposit accounts, but now customers have access to digital account balances through online banking. Globally speaking, EFT infrastructures keep evolving; for example, SWIFT has announced that it is working on trials to use DLT to 'connect SWIFT's GPI Link gateway with R3's Corda platform to monitor payment flows and support application programming interfaces (APIs), as well as SWIFT, and NIST and ISO standards.'[196]

Furthermore, one was able to see the effect of the evolution of our payment systems in an interesting exercise in which the Bank of England challenged users that rely on cash to go digital for a week and, if they relied on electronic money, to use only cash,. The results of this activity show that 58.3 per cent relied heavily on card payments, while cash payments represented almost the half of that figure (28.6 per cent).[197] The output of this exercise confirms the fall from 62 per cent of

[189] H Nakaso, 'Future of Central Bank Payment and Settlement Systems under Economic Globalization and Technological Innovation' (2017), available at www.bis.org/review/r170425h.pdf.

[190] W Engert and BSC Fung, 'Central Bank Digital Currency: Motivations and Implications' (2017) available at www.bankofcanada.ca/wp-content/uploads/2017/11/sdp2017-16.pdf.

[191] [1899], 2 Q.B. 111 (UK), at 114.

[192] [1848] 2 HLC 28 (UK), at 36.

[193] PJ Eder, 'Legal Theories of Money' (1934) 20 *Cornell Law Review* 52, 56.

[194] Financial Action Task Force, 'Virtual Currencies. Key Definitions and Potential AML/CFT Risks' (2014) available at www.fatf-gafi.org/media/fatf/documents/reports/Virtual-currency-key-definitions-and-potential-aml-cft-risks.pdf.

[195] One of the most referenced works on this matter is Kennett Rogoff's 'The Curse of Cash.' See KS Rogoff, *The Curse of Cash* (Princeton, Princeton University Press, 2016).

[196] I Allison, 'SWIFT Chief Announces Trail DLT Integration with R3' (2019), available at www.coindesk.com/swift-chief-announces-integration-with-r3-at-paris-fintech-forum.

[197] Bank of England, 'Future Forum 2018: The Highlights' (2019), available at www.bankofengland.co.uk/outreach/future-forum-2018.

transactions in 2006 to 40 per cent in 2016, a trend that has been accelerated by the COVID-19 crisis.[198] In addition, there are sovereign efforts to eliminate physical money in countries such as South Korea and Sweden, which have projects to 'go coinless'. South Korea aims to generating 1.2 per cent extra economic growth a year[199] in doing so, while Sweden plans to create a digital alternative to cash such as the e-Krona,[200] in collaboration with companies such as Accenture[201] and R3[202] who have provided the technology for this purpose.

One can therefore conclude that the creation of a cryptographic instrument of this nature is necessary, but it should not be considered as the ultimate aim. If that was our purpose, we should be restricting our time on the application of normative instruments such as the Bills of Exchange Act 1882 under a technology-neutral approach. Following the evolution of the cryptoassets market, a proper cryptocurrency has to act as an infrastructural asset within a new payments system, which would allow us to improve the current state of our financial infrastructure and offer better products and services based on the best technology available for each dynamic social system.

i. Sovereign Cryptoassets

Almost every day there are proposals regarding new regulatory paradigms that will use governance theory, DLT and AI to solve problems regarding monetary functions in digital environments. Despite these entertaining efforts, this is not something radically new. Digital money structured around sovereign units of reference and governance arrangements already circulates throughout our payment systems. Independently of this fact, the first wave of proposals that involved the creation of 'sovereign cryptoassets' was initiated by individuals who, following the prominence gained by Bitcoin, tried to build a momentum by appealing to people of different nationalities and cultural backgrounds.[203] Consequently, it was possible to witness the emergence of new units, k including the Scotcoin,[204] the

[198] C Segal-Knowles, 'Payments after the COVID Crisis. Emerging Issues and Challenges' (2020), available at www.bankofengland.co.uk/-/media/boe/files/speech/2020/payments-after-the-covid-crisis-emerging-issues-and-challenges-speech-christina-segal-knowles.pdf?la=en&hash=5398FAD3D7005A5D7CC9E87EE9FDD72C9E093B94.

[199] B Harris, 'South Korea to Kill the Coin in Path towards "cashless society"' (2016), available at www.ft.com/content/bf5c929c-b78d-11e6-ba85-95d1533d9a62.

[200] Sveriges Riksbank (n 182).

[201] Sveriges Riksbank, 'Riksbank Develops an E-Krona in A Test Environment' (2019), available at www.riksbank.se/en-gb/press-and-published/notices-and-press-releases/notices/2019/riksbank-develops-an-e-krona-in-a-test-environment.

[202] Sveriges Riksbank, 'E-Krona Pilot. Phase 2' (2022), available at www.riksbank.se/globalassets/media/rapporter/e-krona/2022/e-krona-pilot-phase-2.pdf.

[203] A Kristof, 'National Cryptocurrencies' in DL Kuo Chen (ed), *Handbook of Digital Currency. Bitcoin, Innovation, Financial Instruments, and Big Data* (San Diego, Academic Press, 2015) 67–80, 67–68.

[204] See scotcoinproject.com/.

PesetaCoin,[205] the GreeceCoin,[206] the CryptoEscudo[207] and the eGulden.[208] Some of the common elements that these units share look to foster national identities through cultivating a collective memory, a nationalist culture, and even a numismatic nostalgia,[209] even though none of these projects involved a central bank or sovereign entity.

However, cryptoassets under a sovereign initiative have start to emerge. For instance, Ecuador, relying on the exercise of its *lex monetae*, started to reserve for itself the power to issue cryptoassets. Article 94(3) of the Monetary and Financial Organic Code[210] states that:

> The Central Bank of Ecuador is the only entity empowered to provide and manage national metallic and electronic currency in the Republic of Ecuador, equivalent and convertible to dollars of the United States of America, according to the conditions of this Code, and the regulations and authorization of the Monetary and Financial Policy and Regulation Board.

In the case of the regulatory proposal for the establishment of the digital euro, the same normative spirit is present in its Article 4:

> 1. In accordance with the Treaties, the European Central Bank shall have the exclusive right to authorise the issue of the digital euro, and the European Central Bank and the national central banks may issue the digital euro.
> 2. The digital euro shall be a direct liability of the European Central Bank or of national central banks towards digital euro users.

In stark contrast, there has been a very interesting exercise of the *lex monetae* in El Salvador through the issuance of its controversial Bitcoin Law.[211] In this case, as one can infer from Articles 2,[212] 6[213] and 13[214] reflect that these monetary prerogatives are subject to the action of the *ius cudendae monetae* exercised in the US and the governance arrangements put in place by a long chain of private and public stakeholders distributed around the world. In other words, the sovereign exercise of the *lex monetae* in El Salvador is in the hands of third parties whose behaviour will not be necessarily aligned with the interests of El Salvador under a single mandate.

Here it is important to note that this kind of effort is not new nor bound exclusively to the 'cypherpunk' movement or to the development of DLT. Back in

[205] See pesetacoin.info/.

[206] The information of this project was available in greececoin.net/; however, according to deadcoins.com, this asset –based on its extended periods of inactivity with zero transactions – has disappeared.

[207] See www.cryptoescudo.pt/.

[208] See e-gulden.org/.

[209] E Helleiner, 'National Currencies and National Identities' (1998) 41 *The American Behavioral Scientist*, 1414.

[210] Monetary and Financial Organic Code RO 332.

[211] Bitcoin Law DO 57.

[212] 'The exchange rate between bitcoin and the United States dollar, subsequently USD, will be freely established by the market.'

[213] 'For accounting purposes, the USD will be used as the reference currency.'

[214] 'All obligations in money expressed in USD, existing before the effective date of this law, may be paid in bitcoin.'

2002, the Board of Commissioners of Currency of Singapore was working on a Singapore Electronic Legal Tender (SELT) by which its units would be generated through an extension of the existing system.[215] Based on this extension, each bank would draw SELT value from the Board and the assets would be loaded remotely into the bank's designated computer. In turn, each person that requiring Singapore currency would draw down from his/her account with the bank and download SELT value into a smart chip.[216]

Following these first attempts, since 2016 a myriad of proposals sponsored by central banks around the world regarding the creation of CBDCs have been made, among which are two basic paradigms. The first, looks to increase efficiency, reduce settlement costs and ensure immediate finality.[217] This model is related to prototypes for domestic interbank settlement systems using DLT developed jointly by some central banks, commercial banks and IT developers.[218] The early stages of these projects were proof-of-concept tests that explored the opportunities for DLT to improve the existing RTGS infrastructures. For example, the CAD-coin, which was the result of the project Jasper developed by R3, six private Canadian banks, Payments Canada and the Bank of Canada.[219] Through this project, the institutions involved simulated a funds transfer using DLT by which the Bank of Canada issued CAD-coins once the participants had pledged cash collateral into a special pooled account held by the central bank.[220] Once this *res* was deposited in this wholesale payment system, participating banks could then send payments of CAD-coin to each other in real time to meet the payment obligations that they had agreed to settle, and sent payments back to the Bank of Canada in order to 'cash-out' and convert the referred digital asset into Canadian dollars.[221]

In the UK – in stark contrast to the words of Sir Robert Peel, who quoted one Mr Smith, who argued that the pound was 'something that has existed without variation in this country for eight hundred years'[222] – the Bank of England has run proofs-of-concept with companies such as Baton Systems, Clearmatics Technologies Ltd, R3 and Token to see how a renewed RTGS service could be compatible with new payment technologies, particularly DLT.[223] Under these

[215] LS Kok, 'Singapore Electronic Legal Tender (SELT) – A Proposed Concept.' (2002), available at www.oecd.org/futures/35391062.pdf.

[216] ibid.

[217] ML Bech and B Hobjin, 'Technology Diffusion within Central Banking. The Case of Real-Time Gross Settlement' (2006) 260 *Federal Reserve Bank of New York Staff Reports* 1, 2.

[218] Sveriges Riksbank (n 182).

[219] R Garratt, 'CAD-coin Versus Fedcoin' (2016), available at www.r3.com/wp-content/uploads/2017/06/cadcoin-versus-fedcoin_R3.pdf.

[220] ibid.

[221] ibid.

[222] R Peel, 'Bank of England – Resumption of Cash Payments' (1819) available at api.parliament.uk/historic-hansard/commons/1819/may/24/bank-of-england-resumption-of-cash.

[223] Bank of England, 'RTGS Renewal Programme Proof of Concept: Supporting DLT Settlement Models' (2018) available at www.bankofengland.co.uk/news/2018/july/rtgs-renewal-programme-proof-of-concept-supporting-dlt-settlement-models.

exercises, the central bank hosts the core ledger and an application programming interface (API) by which private sector firms can access the ledger in order to offer and provide user services.[224] Based on this exercise the central bank is currently working in the development of different account structures and cryptographic proofs such as Proof-of-Identity (PoI), while it keeps working closely with different FinTech firms to see if they could provide better technological options or structural arrangements to improve current RTGS services[225] or even to introduce a UK CBDC through a second paradigm available for households and businesses.[226]

Through the second paradigm, central banks are analysing the potential opportunities and risks related to M0 crypotassets available to a broad general public. In other words, proper electronic cash. Within this group one can find the Fedcoin,[227] the digital yuan,[228] the UKCBDC,[229] and proofs-of-concept such as the digital currencies issued by the Central Bank of Uruguay.[230] These assets would be designed using DLT – or other technology – as sovereign units, but unlike other cryptoassets that have been analysed in this book, only the respective central bank would be able to create them, based on a one-for-one convertibility with cash and reserves.[231] Therefore, these CBDCs would be created following two schemes. First, if an equivalent amount of cash or reserves were cancelled at the same time by the central bank. For example, if one wanted to hold a certain amount of CBDCs, one would have to turn over tangible currency for new cryptoassets of the same nominal quantity.[232] Second, preallocating the entire supply of units, as seen in the precedent set by Ripple, which, at its constitution, created the entire supply of 100 billion XRP, with 61 billion XRP under the control of Ripple itself.[233]

A third complementary category that is emerging from the two basic CBDC design paradigms is related to different projects that are looking to constitute a multi-CBDC platform, thus fostering the use of retail CBDCs in the context

[224] Bank of England, 'The Digital Pound. Technology Working Paper' (2023), available at www.bankofengland.co.uk/-/media/boe/files/paper/2023/the-digital-pound-technology-working-paper.pdf.

[225] Bank of England (n 223).

[226] Bank of England (n 67).

[227] JP Koning, 'Fedcoin: A Central Bank-Issued Cryptocurrency' (2016) available at static1.squarespace.com/static/55f73743e4b051cfcc0b02cf/t/58c7f80c2e69cf24220d335e/1489500174018/R3+Report-+Fedcoin.pdf.

[228] Y Zhao and E Lam, 'China's PBOC Says Its Own Cryptocurrency Is "Close" to Release' (2019), available at www.bloomberg.com/news/articles/2019-08-12/china-s-pboc-says-its-own-cryptocurrency-is-close-to-release.

[229] Bank of England (n 67).

[230] Banco Central del Uruguay, 'El BCU Presentó un Plan Piloto para la Emisión de Billetes Digitales' (2017) available at www.bcu.gub.uy/Comunicaciones/Paginas/Billete_Digital_Piloto.aspx.

[231] S Gupta, P Lauppe and S Ravishankar, 'Fedcoin. A Blockchain-Backed Central Bank Cryptocurrency' (2017) available at law.yale.edu/system/files/area/center/global/document/411_final_paper_-_fedcoin.pdf; Bank of England (n 67); Bech and Garratt (n 183).

[232] Bech and Garratt (n 183); Koning (n 227).

[233] M del Castillo and B Reutzel, '$100 Billion Controversy: XRP's Surge Raises Hard Questions for Ripple' (2018), available at www.coindesk.com/100-billion-controversy-xrps-surge-raises-hard-questions-ripple.

of cross-border and cross-currency transactions between different sovereign cryptoassets systems, such as the cases tested under projects Icebreaker[234] and Dunbar.[235]

Considering the outcomes of these tests and proposals, this chapter will argue that refined versions of these units could act as the cornerstones of new crypto payment systems. From the 'sacred, a proposal will be developed, structured around the supremacy of constitutional arrangements, as developed by Marshall CJ in *Marbury v Madison*[236] and exercised through the *lex monetae*. On this basis, there is then a choice between granting a monopoly to central banks on the issuance of CBDCs and/or defining the role of the sovereign unit of reference independently if the central bank is involved or not in the direct provision of these *reifiers*, based on the preferences and needs of each system.

One could initially argue that this *crypto lex monetae* would be irrelevant in a digital environment based on the increasing infrastructural power of the private sector by which 'transactions are made by book-entries across bank accounts outside the reach of monetary authorities'.[237] However, a monetary regime of this nature would be materialised as a transitional form where monetary assets such as coins and notes will play a pivotal role in the configuration of the new payments system. So, the *lex monetae* would allow us to create cryptoassets that will have to be universal, electronic, 24/7, denominated in the sovereign unit of reference, provide certain level of anonymity, and, like cash, not bear interest.[238] It could be assumed that most of the transaction balances would continue to be held as deposits with commercial banks as described in *Folley v Hill*,[239] while these intermediaries continue to provide the infrastructure required to circulate money within the economy.[240] Consequently, under this scheme, the central bank would exchange reserves, banknotes and cryptographic instruments at par with those financial institutions that have an account at the central bank, just as reserves and banknotes are exchanged at par under our current paradigm.[241]

[234] Bank for International Settlements, 'Project Icebreaker concludes experiment for a new architecture for cross-border retail CBDCs' (2023), available at www.bis.org/about/bisih/topics/cbdc/icebreaker.htm.

[235] Bank for International Settlements, 'Project Dunbar: international settlements using multi-CBDCs' (2021), available at www.bis.org/about/bisih/topics/cbdc/dunbar.htm.

[236] [1803] 5 US 137 (US), 177–80.

[237] Sono and Kanda (n 137) 507.

[238] Michael Kumhof and Clare Noone argue that these units could 'be interest bearing, under realistic assumptions paying a rate that would be different to the rate on reserves'. See M Kumhof and C Noone, 'Central Bank Digital Currencies – Design Principles and Balance Sheet Implications' (2018), available at www.bankofengland.co.uk/-/media/boe/files/working-paper/2018/central-bank-digital-currencies-design-principles-and-balance-sheet-implications.pdf?la=en&hash=11469281B32821BCFD85B4A5483AB3577E38B2DD; Barrdear and Kumhof (n 188; Bank of England (n 67); Bech and Garratt (n 183).

[239] [1848] 2 HLC 28 (UK), at 36.

[240] Barrdear and Kumhof (n 188).

[241] Engert and Fung (n 190).

ii. Issuing a Fourth Generation of Cryptoassets

As this book has shown, in relation to CBDCs, arguments are often structured – or even attacked – on the characteristics that define units of first generation such as Bitcoin. Within these arguments, it is possible to find different opinions structured around an aversion to put in place a sovereign instrument of this nature given that the direct provision of these assets could open the central bank's balance sheet to a wider variety of non-bank institutions, and even individual households,[242] as seen in the case of the *Amsterdamsche Wisselbank.*[243] However, despite the talent shown in these analyses, throughout 2022 the share of central banks that are working on CBDC projects rose to 93 per cent, within both retail and wholesale payment systems.[244]

As explored in chapter two, and as can be verified in the technical descriptions that support most CBDC projects – the evolution of our monetary institutions results from the interaction between the infrastructural power developed by the private sector and the sovereign prerogatives of the public sector that have evolved from our 'sacred' source of liquidity, with each sector taking turns to create, develop and adopt monetary innovations. Under our current paradigm, authors such as Milton Friedman[245] have recognised that:

> [A] moderately stable monetary framework seems an essential prerequisite for the effective operation of a private market economy. It is dubious that the market can by itself provide such a framework. Hence, the function of providing one is an essential governmental function on a par with the provision of a stable legal framework.

Historically, many central banks were established to ensure or restore stability in payments and settlements after the creation of nation-states and during the transition from the modern era to the postmodern era.[246] The paradigm of strict bank regulation and supervision and central banks' monopoly on the issue of banknotes and operation of the payment and settlement systems that has emerged over the last century or so has proven to be the most effective way to avoid the instability and high economic costs associated with the proliferation of private and public monies.[247] These facts imply that there is a strong common economic rationale for central banks to act as the cornerstones of these infrastructures.[248]

[242] B Broadbent, 'Central Banks and Digital Currencies' (2016), available at www.bankofengland.co.uk/-/media/boe/files/speech/2016/central-banks-and-digital-currencies.pdf?la=en&hash=8D9B0F2911064BD7570B10370DF521FAE174217D; Bank of England (n 67); Bech and Garratt (n 183); Nakaso (n 189).

[243] J Frost, HS Shin and P Wierts, 'An Early Stablecoin? The Bank of Amsterdam and the Governance of Money' (2020), available at www.bis.org/publ/work902.pdf.

[244] Bank for International Settlements, 'Making Headway – Results of the 2022 BIS Survey on Central Bank Digital Currencies and Crypto' (2023), available at www.bis.org/publ/bppdf/bispap136.pdf.

[245] M Friedman, *A Program for Monetary Stability* (New York, Fordham University Press, 1960) 8.

[246] Nakaso (n 189).

[247] Carstens (n 180); Nakaso (n 189).

[248] Nakaso (n 189).

Following the tests and the proposals examined in this section and the set of interests that justify regulation as presented in section IV.A of this chapter, one can think that central banks, based on their sovereign cryptoasset and their control over the infrastructure, could be the cornerstone of permissioned networks by which they could be empowered to issue a fourth generation of cryptoassets or, at least, keep acting as the constitutional guardians of the sovereign unit of reference. The argument/proposal of this book builds upon the evolutionary trend relating to the development of the protocols employed to create assets and run transactions within each network, which, in this context, follows an historical path towards centralisation and intermediation compatible with the historical evolution of the *lex monetae.*

Figure 12 Proof-of-Authority model

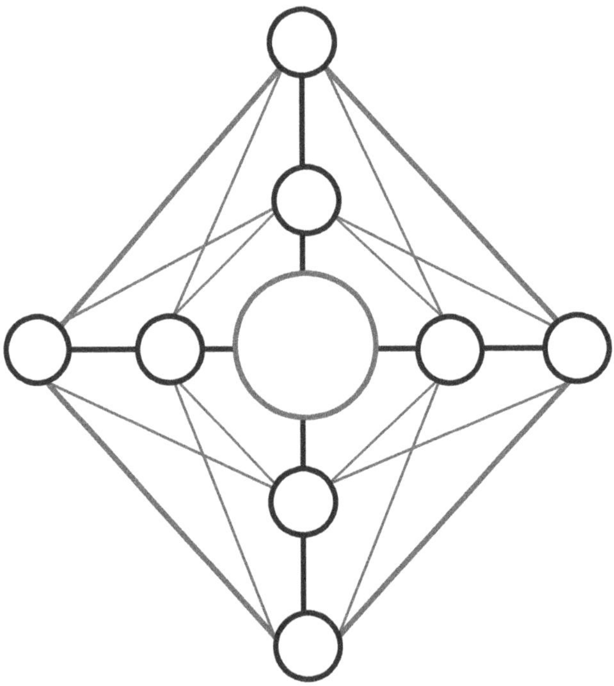

Accordingly, it is not surprising that we are starting to see the diffusion of more centralised protocols, such as PoA (Figure 12). PoA can be defined as an algorithm that delivers faster transactions through a consensus mechanism based on identity, which configures the authority of the DLT nodes.[249] Based on the evolutionary trend highlighted by these protocols, we argue that, building on the spirit of

[249] T Kozak, 'Consensus Protocols that Serve Different Business Needs. Part II' (2018), available at blockchain.intellectsoft.net/blog/consensus-protocols-that-serve-different-business-needs-part-2/#Proof-of-Authority.

projects, such as Project Aurum,[250] it is possible to design a permissioned network in which regulated institutions act as nodes with access to our sovereign blockchain. As Figure 12 shows, as well as patent applications such as 201610179399.3,[251] 201610178662.7,[252] 201710494547.5[253] and 201710494152.5,[254] filled by the Digital Currency Institute of the People's Bank of China, a well-defined stakeholder appears in the centre, who will exercise the *lex monetae*. In our hypothetical case, building upon the words of Charles Goodhart[255] who stated that 'central banks are unlikely to be forced to the sidelines by technological innovation', the main stakeholder would be a central bank.

It is important to note that these are not the only protocols employed to develop DLT networks; others include Proof-of-Capacity (PoC), Proof-of-Burn (PoB) and Proof-of Contribution (PoCo). However, PoA is the focus here given its potential for the development of this market and in the configuration of the governance scheme by which the private and public sectors could set the new payments infrastructure. Once selected, if one desires to use DLT to generate a CBDC, there is a choice between two network designs. On the one hand, following the institutional perspective of financial intermediation,[256] we can put in place a DLT network where – just as in the case of RTGS and Project Aurum – only commercial banks would have access to the software that would allow them to act as nodes within this payments model.

On the other hand, based on Merton's functional perspective[257] and following the example of countries such as Japan where cryptoasset exchange businesses have been included in Chapter III-2 of the Payment Services Act,[258] this network could be opened to other shadow banks, after they have demonstrated their compliance with the requirements set by each national regulator. These requirements could include the prohibition of holding and dealing with non-infrastructural cryptoassets. Therefore, while the central bank acts as the stakeholder of the new payments system with its native sovereign unit, well-defined institutions would provide the infrastructure and act as delegated monitors for the interactions developed directly on the chain ('on-chain') and among different nodes and third parties outside the

[250] Bank for International Settlements, 'Project Aurum: A Prototype for Two-Tier Central Bank Digital Currency (CBDC)' (2022), available at www.bis.org/publ/othp57.htm.

[251] [2016] Patent application CN107230070: 'Digital Currency System'.

[252] [2016] Patent application CN107230077: 'Digital Currency Exchange Method, Digital Currency Payment Method and Digital Currency Systems'.

[253] [2017] Patent application CN107358521: 'Method and System for Using Digital Currency to Exchange Deposit'.

[254] [2017] Patent application CN107358436: 'Method and System for Payment by Accessing Digital Currency Wallet through Bank Account.'

[255] CAE Goodhart, 'Can Central Banking Survive the IT Revolution?' (2000) 3 *International Finance* 189, 207.

[256] The institutional perspective of financial intermediation takes as given the existing institutional structure of our financial intermediaries. See Merton (n 128) 23.

[257] ibid.

[258] Payment Services Act, Act No 59.

chain ('off-chain') related to our hypothetical network,[259] following the spirit of the Child Report described in section VI.B of chapter three of this work.[260]

For that purpose, and considering that governments affect financial intermediation as market participants, industry competitors or benefactors of innovation, legislators and enforcers, negotiators and unwitting intervenors,[261] any fully decentralised protocol whose source code could eventually be subject to any claim related to moral and/or economic rights, or that could empower a shadow bank to act as the paymaster of the entire system can be discarded. Accordingly, our network would be structured around a network of licences by which well-defined providers of the technology would transfer the source code and the rights necessary to put the respective payments system in place, and these developers could not offer the referred code and rights to any third party in the absence of the consent of the central bank taking advantage of the Work for Hire (WFH) doctrine. These hypothetical systems would work through a platform model based on a core ledger and an API layer to which four types of DLT nodes assigned to a single or multiple parties at the same time (participants, doormen, notaries and oracles)[262] can connect, with the aim of providing services to users.[263]

Building on the cases of the digital pound and Project Aurum, the organisation of these nodes and infrastructures would not require substantial normative creation or reform. It would be based on the constitutional prerogatives and regulations that currently configure our *lex monetae*. For instance, following the developments presented by UBS[264] and JP Morgan,[265] participant DLT nodes could be assigned to regulated intermediaries covered by regulations such as the Financial Services and Markets Act 2000,[266] the Banking Act 2009[267] or the Mexican Credit Institutions Law[268] to allow them to transact with each other and manage the off-chain transactions developed by consumers.

Additionally, within this category one could assign a unique issuer node to the central bank based on its constitutional mandates. Furthermore, one could even foster the creation of free banking models, such as that covered by the Scottish and

[259] F Allen and E Carletti, 'The Roles of Banks in Financial Systems' in AN Berger, P Molyneux and JO Wilson (eds), *The Oxford Handbook of Banking* (Oxford, Oxford University Press, 2010) 37–57, 41; Freixas and Rochet (n 79) 29–30.

[260] A Arora, *Electronic Banking and the Law* (London, Banking Technology, 1993) 9.

[261] Merton (n 128) 36.

[262] A McMyn and M Sim, 'Networks in Trade Finance: Balancing the Options' (2017), available at www.r3.com/wp-content/uploads/2018/04/Networks-in-trade-finance.pdf.

[263] Bank of England, 'The Digital Pound: Technology Working Paper' (2023), available at www.bankofengland.co.uk/paper/2023/the-digital-pound-technology-working-paper.

[264] L Noonan, 'Top Banks Push Ahead with Digital Coins for 2020' (2019), available at www.ft.com/content/9fd8e8ea-83e5-11e9-b592-5fe435b57a3b.

[265] H Son, 'JP Morgan Is Rolling out the First US Bank-Backed Cryptocurrency to Transform Payment Business' (2019), available at www.cnbc.com/2019/02/13/jp-morgan-is-rolling-out-the-first-us-bank-backed-cryptocurrency-to-transform-payments--.html.

[266] Financial Services and Markets Act 2000.

[267] Banking Act 2009.

[268] Credit Institutions Law DOF.

Northern Ireland Banknote Regulations 2009,[269] by which certain nodes could be empowered to issue new instruments structured around a sovereign unit of account.[270] All these activities would be monitored by regulator nodes assigned by the state, probably to the same regulated intermediaries and/or even to those financial intelligence units described in Article 7(1) of the United Nations Convention against Transnational Organized Crime, with the aim of receiving and processing reports relating to legal and illegal transactions developed in the network, but through these nodes one would not be empowered to make updates on the ledger.

The second category of DLT nodes would be structured around a doorman service based on the spirit of regulations, such as Chapter 2 of Part 1A of the Financial Services Act 2012[271] of the UK and Article 8 of the Mexican Credit Institutions Law,[272] by which the central bank and/or other sovereign institution would receive, study and, if applicable, approve the addition of a new DLT node in the network. Following the content of the same regulations, these nodes could provide certain services for the arrangement, including dispute resolution, standard-setting, regulatory reporting, and even those provided by the third category of nodes: the notary nodes. Under this paradigm, the central bank will operate a service within the network with the aim of easing the safe execution of transactions by verifying that each transaction is unique and does not represent double spending,[273] as set out in Articles 28–34 and Annex 1 of the Regulation 910/2014[274] on electronic identification and trust services for electronic transactions in the internal market, and Articles 89–98 of the Mexican Commercial Code.[275]

Finally, considering that our network and its applications would be developed through smart contracts and virtual machines, it would need to incorporate oracle nodes; after all, despite the denomination of these agreements, they are not complete agents that can access information that is found off-chain.[276] Replicating the old paradigm introduced by the introduction of the EMIDEC 1100 computer by Barclays in 1959, by which less powerful machines transferred, through communication cables, information processed by branches with the aim of underpinning institutional processes,[277] our system would require mediators to provide

[269] Scottish and Northern Ireland Banknote Regulations 2009 (SI 2009/3056).

[270] Bank for International Settlements, 'Distributed Ledger Technology in Payment, Clearing and Settlement. An Analytical Framework' (2017), available at www.bis.org/cpmi/publ/d157.pdf.

[271] Financial Services Act 2012.

[272] Credit Institutions Law DOF.

[273] Bank for International Settlements (n 270); Bank of England (n 263); McMyn and Sim (n 262).

[274] Regulation 910/2014 of the European Parliament and of the Council on electronic identification and trust services for electronic transactions in the internal market and repealing Directive 1999/93/EC OJ L 257/73, 23 July 2014.

[275] Commercial Code DOF.

[276] Bank for International Settlements, 'The crypto ecosystem: key elements and risks' (2023), available at www.bis.org/publ/othp72.htm.

[277] A Sweetman, *Cyber and the City. Securing London's Banks in the Computer Age* (Cham, Springer Nature, 2002) 58.

market information related to the contract code execution, but, just as in the case of regulator nodes, they would not be in position to make changes on the ledger.[278]

The constitution of a network of this nature would be based on asymmetric interconnection agreements, which would reflect vertical relationships, whereby commercial banks and new service providers, as secondary paymasters, need central banks for their own service provision.[279] The fourth constitutional power – who owns the infrastructure and/or the rights related to it – would be in the situation of a regulator of the competition game, a position that, in absence of this sovereign stakeholder, could be taken by a dominant player within the private sector, such as Meta or Amazon Web Services (AWS).

Any decision to introduce an instrument of this nature has to start by assessing the opportunities and risks associated with the transition to a digital regime.[280] Despite the enthusiasm of innovators and their followers, people generally hesitate to adopt a monetary unit different from the one they currently accept, considering that economic agents may not adopt the new units as consequence of coordination problems such as network effects.[281] There are several historical examples to illustrate this point: the refusal by Nigerians to accept British currency at the end of the nineteenth century;[282] the failure to launch the Susan B Anthony dollar in the United States at the end of the 1970s;[283] the resistance of Mexica communities in Mexico to use metallic coins during the sixteenth century;[284] and the emergence of the 'cypherpunk' movement after the introduction of electronic money. So, it is not a surprise that most of the respondents of the 2014 Commonwealth of Massachusetts Division of Banks and the Conference of State Bank Supervisors consumer survey,[285] the 2019 Oesterreichische Nationalbank Ownership and Purchase Intention of Crypto-Assets Survey[286] and the 2022 Ontario Securities

[278] McMyn and Sim (n 262).

[279] G Dang-Nguyen and T Pénard, 'Interconnection Agreements in Telecommunications Networks: From Strategic Behaviours to Property Rights' in E Brousseau and JM Glachant (eds), *The Economics of Contracts. Theories and Applications* (Cambridge, Cambridge University Press, 2002) Kindle EBook Loc 4806–5004, at Loc 4835.

[280] Barrdear and Kumhof (n 188).

[281] S Lotz and G Rocheteau, 'On the Launching of a New Currency' (2002) 34 *Journal of Money, Credit and Banking* 563, 564; D Pfajfar, G Sgro and W Wagner, 'Are Alternative Currencies a Substitute or Complement to Fiat Money? Evidence form Cross-Country Data' (2012) 16 *International Journal of Community Currency Research* 46, 46.

[282] WI Ofonagoro, 'From Traditional to British Currency in Southern Nigeria: Analysis of a Currency Revolution' (1979) 39 *Journal of Economic History* 623.

[283] JP Caskey and S St Laurent, 'The Susan B. Anthony Dollar and the Theory of Coin/Note Substitutions' (1994) 26 *Journal of Money, Credit and Banking* 495.

[284] A Caplan, '"Cada uno en su bolsa llevar lo que cien indios no llevarían": Mexica Resistance and the Shape of Currency in New Spain, 1542–1552' (2013) 25 American Journal of Numismatics 333.

[285] Commonwealth of Massachusetts Division of Banks and the Conference of State Bank Supervisors, '2014 Survey: Consumer Attitudes on Bitcoin and Other Virtual Currencies' (2014), available at www.csbs.org/regulatory/ep/Documents/Final%20Report-VirtualCurrencySurvey2014.pdf.

[286] Oesterreichische Nationalbank, 'Ownership and Purchase Intention of Crypto-Assets Survey' (2019), available at www.ecb.europa.eu/pub/conferences/shared/pdf/20191126_payments_conference/academic_paper_stix.pdf.

Commission Crypto Asset Survey[287] relating to attitudes on digital means of payment, answered that it was somewhat or very unlikely that they would purchase or use digital instruments mainly because these innovations are not regulated nor supported by the state.

These cases raise the following questions: if one wants to introduce a new monetary *reifier*, should the old versions be left in circulation, or should the government withdraw the competing form of currency, such as coins and banknotes? Should the conversion of the old versions into the new one be voluntary or compulsory?[288] The first immediate answer is that coins and banknotes would be left in circulation given that these tangible monetary expressions are perceived as store of value. On this point, as mentioned in section VI.B, it must be remembered that countries, such as Sweden, are putting in place efforts to become cashless societies. However, from May 2018 to the end of February 2019 Sweden witnessed the demand for cash increase by 7.23 per cent following the introduction of high-denomination banknotes.[289] Furthermore, although that one can find different sources that these technologies will foster financial inclusion, more than four billion people, mostly in developing countries, do not have access to the internet;[290] consequently, the introduction of a CBDC would rely on, at least for a transitional period in the best-case scenarios, the parallel existence of coins and banknotes.

iii. The 'Scottish' Recipe

Providing a CBDC is only a partial solution to the current challenge posed on the dynamic social systems in the DCS. The existence of this new generation of outside monies by itself would not eliminate the emergence of private options issued by the DeFi ecosystem and regulated intermediaries. Consequently, one could be tempted to pose the following question: could central banks eventually retreat from their functions as providers of the unit of account and the standard for discharge contractual obligations? The answer to this question has to be, at least partially, negative. In his famous work, *An Inquiry into the Nature and Causes of the Wealth of Nations*, Adam Smith[291] argued that:

> To restrain private people, it may be said, from receiving in payment the promissory notes of a banker, for any sum whether great or small, when they themselves are willing to receive them; or, to restrain a banker from issuing such notes, when all his neighbours

[287] Ontario Securities Commission, 'Crypto Asset Survey' (2022), available at www.osc.ca/sites/default/files/2022-10/inv_research_20220928_crypto-asset-survey_EN.pdf.

[288] Lotz and Rocheteau (n 281) 564.

[289] G Lepecq, 'The Great Swedish Cash-Back' (2019), available at cashessentials.org/the-great-swedish-cash-back.

[290] E Luxton, '4 Billion People Still Don't Have Internet Access. Here's How to Connect them' (2016), available at www.weforum.org/agenda/2016/05/4-billion-people-still-don-t-have-internet-access-here-s-how-to-connect-them.

[291] See A Smith, *An Inquiry into the Nature and Causes of the Wealth of Nations* (Oxford, Oxford University Press, 2008) 188.

> are willing to accept of them. Is a manifest violation of that natural liberty which it is the proper business of law, not to infringe, but to support. Such regulations may, no doubt, be considered as in some respect a violation of natural liberty. But those exertions of the natural liberty of a few individuals, which might endanger the security of the whole society, are, and ought to be, restrained by the laws of all governments; of the most free, as well as of the most despotical.

Following the words of Smith, historically, as explored in chapters two and three, it has been the state, in exercise of its *lex monetae*, that has provided, at least, the unit of reference for the standardisation of the economic interactions that derive from our post-Westphalian social contracts. Even during the free banking eras in the United States and Scotland during the nineteenth century, private intermediaries did not introduce their own units of account,[292] demonstrating how the sovereign unit of reference acts as the cornerstone of our monetary systems.

Many would argue that a striking feature of the last decade of central banking is that an ever-growing share of payments is performed electronically following a set of rules and formulas enforced by each payments system, and which do not require any settlement in cash nor the expression in any sovereign unit of reference.[293] Yes, it is conceivable that future central banks may no longer function as providers of the means of payment, but it is possible to think that, as the heart of our DLT networks, they could evolve as they did when they retreated from their functions as commercial banks in the nineteenth century and early twentieth centuries, while they keep their prerogatives relating to the unit of account and the system that supports it.

a. The 'Cryptocharter'

In the context of this book, in the middle of the transition between the cryptoassets of third generation that were represented by LIBRA/DIEM and the fourth generation, such as the digital pound, even if the supply of one type of cryptoasset is restricted, the Cambrian explosion related to DLT and other complementary technologies, such as Machine Learning (ML), means that the total supply of all forms of these assets is unlimited. Given the experience with currency debasement as seen through the *Case of Mixed Money in Ireland*,[294] the proliferation of such private units should lead us to think in a complementary and transitional framework. From an initial analysis, the figure of the issuer will disappear in favour of those developers who, under asymmetric interconnection agreements, will provide the technology to materialise the payments network described in the previous section. However, some free banking models could emerge as result of the evolution of DLT protocols, and new types of negotiable instruments might be recognised and even tolerated by the state in exercise of its *lex monetae*.

[292] Edvinsson, Jacobson and Waldenström (n 172) 22.
[293] Sono and Kanda (n 137) 509.
[294] *Gilbert v Brett (The Case of Mixed Money)* [1605] Cobb St Tr 114 (UK), at 125–26.

With that potential in mind, the second element of the current proposal would be based on a cryptocharter, which would be designed to control issuers' behaviour and set vertical and horizontal interconnection and interaction rules. This complementary strategy would be applicable in systems such as the Scottish, where private institutions, following the requirements set in Part 6 of the Banking Act 2009[295] and Part 3 of the Scottish and Northern Ireland Banknote Regulations 2009,[296] are in charge of providing banknotes that circulate together with those assets considered legal tender by Regulation 2(1A) of the Coinage Act 1971;[297] or in jurisdictions such as Switzerland[298] and El Salvador, which have stated that they want to foster the development of 'crypto nations'. In these scenarios, to be considered as a participant DLT node in the network proposed lines above, and *ergo* to issue cryptoassets, issuers would have the option to apply for a cryptocharter.

b. 'On-Chain' and 'Off-Chain' Transactions

With the aim of applying to this charter, these institutions should set their on-chain and off-chain operations on the data sovereignty of each nation, structuring them around different standards and rules proposed and/or enforced by international standards development organisations and national regulators,[299] such as the ISO 22739:2020.[300] First, the on-chain elements would have their cornerstone on the proper constitution of their respective networks, which should be designed around an intermediary, a well-defined asset, and a set of rules that would allow them to interact with the sovereign network. As it was stated in *Fair Housing Council of San Fernando Valley v* Roomates.com[301] our starting point is the intermediary given that:

> The Internet is no longer a fragile new means of communication that could easily be smothered in the cradle by overzealous enforcement of laws and regulations applicable to brick-and-mortar businesses. Rather, it has become a dominant-perhaps the preeminent-means through which commerce is conducted. And its vast reach into the lives of millions is exactly why we must be careful not to exceed the scope of the immunity provided by Congress and thus give online businesses an unfair advantage over their real-world counterparts, which must comply with laws of general applicability.

[295] Banking Act 2009.

[296] Scottish and Northern Ireland Banknote Regulations 2009 (SI 2009/3056).

[297] Section 2(1A) of the Coinage Act 1971 states that 'coins of cupro-nickel, silver or bronze shall be legal tender as follows: a)coins of cupro-nickel or silver of denominations of more than 10 pence, for payment of any amount not exceeding £10; b) coins of cupro-nickel or silver of denominations of not more than 10 pence, for payment of any amount not exceeding £5; c) coins of bronze, for payment of any amount not exceeding 20 pence.'

[298] Atkins (n 118).

[299] D Hyland-Wood and S Khatchadourian, 'A Future History of International Blockchain Standards' (2018) 1 *The Journal of the British Blockchain Association* 25.

[300] (en) Blockchain and distributed ledger technologies – Vocabulary.

[301] [2008] 521 F.3d 1157 (US), at 1164.

Despite the arguments and the desires of Bitcoin enthusiasts related to a decentralised and disintermediated world, nations can command considerable control over the internet based on their control over the physical components of the network within their borders,[302] as seen through the deployment of China's Great Firewall, which has blocked the access to some sources of Ethereum blockchain data.[303] It is also important to establish what kind of intermediary is being employed. Rowland, Kohl and Charlesworth[304] argue that currently we have five types of intermediaries:

1. **Access/Connectivity**: These intermediaries provide or facilitate access to the internet. This class includes cable companies, telecommunications providers and internet access providers, among others.
2. **Navigation**: Within this group, we find those intermediaries like Google and Yahoo! that index online content and make it easily accessible to users.
3. **Content-hosting**: This category of intermediaries provides online services that allow the storage of content and platforms for user-generated content, for commercial and social purposes. Among the most famous examples are companies like Facebook and Amazon.
4. **Providers of the sharing economy**: Illustrated through the cases of Uber and Airbnb, these intermediaries do not support online services as such, but they provide means of interaction that are materialised through the execution of services outside the cyberspace.
5. **Traditional commercial facilitators**: Finally, within this group, we find those traditional commercial intermediaries or their online equivalents, such as financial institutions and Open Banking, whose main focus is to facilitate online interactions

In particular, it can be argued that our new crypto intermediaries can be identified as traditional commercial facilitators, which in turn can be separated in two categories: i) those that create inside money demanded by their respective payment networks, as described in *Moss v Hancock*[305] and *Miller v Race*,[306] and identified with the three first generations of cryptoassets; and ii) those intermediaries that act as the payment service providers defined in Article 4(11) of the PSD2,[307] and as the *Bildungstrieb* that fosters the transition between the third and fourth generation of

[302] AK Woods, 'Litigating Data Sovereignty' (2018) 128 *The Yale Law Journal* 328, 360.

[303] F Zhao, 'China's Internet Firewall Has Blocked Access to Ethereum Block Explorer Etherscan.io' (2019), available at www.coindesk.com/chinas-internet-firewall-has-blocked-access-to-ethereum-block-explorer-etherscan-io.

[304] D Rowland, U Kohl and A Charlesworth, *Information Technology Law* (Abingdon, Routledge, 2017) 75–76.

[305] [1899], 2 QBD 111 (UK), at 116.

[306] [1758] 97 ER 398 (UK), at 401.

[307] Directive 2015/2366 of the European Parliament and of the Council on payment services in the internal market, amending Directives 2002/65/EC, 2009/110/EC and 2013/36/EU and Regulation (EU) No 1093/2010, and repealing Directive 2007/64/EC OJ L 337/35, 25 November 2015.

these cryptographic instruments. Accordingly, for the purposes of our proposal, the focus here is on the second category.

Building upon the argument of this book, these networks would follow the four DLT node category described in section VI.B.ii, and they would have to demonstrate their interoperability with the sovereign and the other regulated networks through their respective regulator nodes, which could be a bank, a financial intelligence unit, an exchange and/or the respective issuer, as tested in projects Helvetia and Icebreaker. As developed by Goodhart[308] when he explained the transition between monetary technologies, the state has the power to push new intermediaries to select between two options: on the one hand, there is an asymmetric relationship for vertical compatibility related to the access to an essential facility, for example, access to RTGSs. On the other, if new intermediaries foster the adoption of horizontal compatibility among competing services, they would not have the power to fully exploit the outcomes of the network effects that the new regulated system would provide (for example, the state could impose taxes payable in regulated cryptoassets) and, eventually, they would be pushed to extinction.

Consequently, once new intermediaries have constituted the structural basis of the network, issuers would be subject to a series of tests conducted with the authorities within regulatory sandboxes and/or periodic supervisory visits with the aim to verify that the DLT protocols and smart contracts employed to issue their cryptoassets fulfil minimum design and operational requirements. These requirements will be focused on explainability. This is a rather important point. Many works on cryptoassets regulation are focused on security issues, and very few pay attention to the important issue of the confidence structured around the formal requirements that have standardised the incorporation of our monetary *res* throughout our history. Accordingly, to avoid biases regarding the interpretation of the term 'money' and its underlying sources of liquidity, and concerns centred on the lack of information regarding how the protocol works, applicants will have to present a meaningful explanation regarding the operation of their cryptoassets through the very lines of code, documents and visual presentations.

If these protocols and smart contracts are modified or designed through non-locked algorithms, they should be subject to periodic stays in the sandbox and/or additional tests and supervisory visits with the aim to verify that the cryptoasset keeps developing its original function in the absence of black boxes. This would be relevant for the execution of the unlimited liability mentioned in section V of this chapter given that we could include and exercise the *contra preferentem* rule which states the words of deed are to be taken more strongly against the one who put them forward.[309] Additionally, potential developers would have to empower

[308] CAE Goodhart, 'The Two Concepts of Money. Implications for the Analysis of Optimal Currency Areas' (1998) 14 *European Journal of Political Economy* 407, 413–416.

[309] E Coke, *The First Part of the Institutes of the Laws of England, or, A Commentary upon Littleton* (Philadelphia, Robert H. Small, 1853) 42a–42b.

doormen nodes to set standards, execute regulations and solve disputes, among other functions.

The interoperability of the networks through these DLT nodes would be particularly relevant, given that these assets would be considered as public goods based on constitutional prerogatives; therefore, through these inter-network interactions one could require potential issuers to back their cryptoassets with an underlying sovereign source of liquidity under a set of conditions similar to those found in the Scottish and Northern Ireland Banknote Regulations 2009[310] and in the General Law of Credit Institutions of 1897 of Mexico.[311] Accordingly, new cryptoassets would circulate as money within the jurisdictions that decide to adopt this strategy, just as those bank notes issued by authorised banks in Scotland do today, thus avoiding those scenarios where companies such as Tether issue stablecoins not properly backed with sovereign assets to engage in illegal practices.[312]

The off-chain transactions would be heavily focused on the user experience. Given that individual users would not control individual DLT nodes to interact with the network, they would have access to this new payments system through cold wallets and cards such as those devised by Coinbase and Bitso with VISA and Mastercard respectively, thus reflecting perfectly the analysis provided by Lord Mance, who in *Office of Fair Trading v Lloyds TSB Bank plc*[313] accurately argued that 'large scale consolidation has led to card issuers becoming members of one of the two main international credit card networks: Visa and MasterCard'. This argument is rather interesting given that, with the help of Lord Mance, we can see how the cryptoassets market is starting to consolidate, through Merton's functional perspective,[314] towards the paradigm presented in section 6.B.ii of this work.

iv. Operational Risk and Resilience

As has been seen throughout this book, the private sector tends to provide the infrastructure to implement new payment systems or to improve the existent arrangements. Accordingly, under the current state of DLT, one could ask what happens if the algorithms involved in these arrangements are sub-optimally designed. After all, these codified opinions are designed by humans and, consequently, subject to the *Animal Spirits* described by Akerlof and Shiller.[315] For example, on 18 October 2017, the FCA imposed a financial penalty of £34,524,000

[310] Scottish and Northern Ireland Banknote Regulations 2009 (SI 2009/3056).

[311] Memoria Política de México, 'Ley General de Instituciones de Crédito, de Porfirio Díaz' (2023), available at www.memoriapoliticademexico.org/Textos/5RepDictadura/1897LGD.html.

[312] NY Attorney General, 'Attorney General James Announces Court Order Against "Crypto" Currency Company Under Investigation for Fraud' (2019), available at ag.ny.gov/press-release/attorney-general-james-announces-court-order-against-crypto-currency-company-under.

[313] [2008] 1 AC 316 (UK), at 325.

[314] Merton (n 128).

[315] Akerlof and Shiller (n 18).

to Merrill Lynch International, who did not make the reports required by Article 9 of the European Markets Infrastructure Regulation (EMIR).[316] What is interesting here is that this failure derived from: 1) a shortage of expertise; and 2) an error on a static data table within the ETD reporting syste, that, in fact, was not appropriately designed and tested.

With the increasing digitisation of our interactions, and the rise of the IoT, operational risk needs to be considered a central feature in all the products and services developed in the FIR.[317] Accordingly, independently of the arguments that state these innovations improve the speed and security of transactions, most current DLT consensus architectures and their related innovations are particularly vulnerable to double spending, re-entrance vulnerabilities, 51 per cent network-level and pool attacks, container breakouts, among other risks[318] that certainly will be highlighted with the development of new technologies such as quantum computing. Even Satoshi Nakamoto acknowledged some of these risks in the original Bitcoin white paper[319] and considered the creation of centralised networks, such as the one proposed in this chapter, in the following terms:

> As such, the verification is reliable as long as honest nodes control the network, but is more vulnerable if the network is overpowered by an attacker. While network nodes can verify transactions for themselves, the simplified method can be fooled by an attacker's fabricated transactions for as long as the attacker can continue to overpower the network. One strategy to protect against this would be to accept alerts from network nodes when they detect an invalid block, prompting the user's software to download the full block and alerted transactions to confirm the inconsistency. Businesses that receive frequent payments will probably still want to run their own nodes for more independent security and quicker verification.

Considering these important – and potentially systemic – risks related to DLT, these intermediaries should put in place measures to certify the integrity of their premises, equipment, software and hardware, among other critical structural elements following the content of regulatory instruments, such as the FCA Handbook. Consequently, to complement the content of these documents, we have to consider that the development of a payments system similar to the one presented in this chapter will require the identification of the infrastructural stakeholders that will play a role in the processing of data. Accordingly, one first parameter that could be considered for the creation and operation of a CBDC such as the FedCoin can be found in the Cybersecurity Maturity Model Certification, commonly known as the CMMC 2.0.[320]

[316] Financial Conduct Authority, 'Final Notice to Merryll Lynch International.' (2017), available at www.fca.org.uk/publication/final-notices/merrill-lynch-international-2017.pdf.

[317] W Isaacson, *The Industries of the Future* (London, Simon & Schuster, 2016) 146.

[318] H Hasanova et al, 'A Survey on Blockchain Cybersecurity' (2018) 29 *International Journal of Network Management* 1, 5.

[319] Nakamoto (n 165).

[320] Chief Information Officer, 'Cybersecurity Maturity Model Certification' (2021), available at dodcio.defense.gov/CMMC/, *US Department of Defense.*

Under the CMMC 2.0. presented in November 2021 in the US, we can identify a very interesting transition from a paradigm structured around five tiers to one based on three tiers which considers elements such as self-structuration, self-regulation and corporative governance in the first level; an obligation to map and assess interrelations and dependencies to third parties on the development and deployment of technological infrastructures; and, of course, the prerogatives of the state to verify the soundness of the mapping and the operation of the systems throughout their respective value chains. Although this standard is currently notional while its supportive regulations are completed, we can verify in it another interesting transition. The term employed up to this point is 'cybersecurity', which is defined within Article 6(2) of the Directive on measures for a high common level of cybersecurity across the Union (commonly known as the NIS2 Directive)[321] as:

> [T]he ability of network and information systems to resist, at a given level of confidence, any event that may compromise the availability, authenticity, integrity or confidentiality of stored, transmitted or processed data or of the services offered by, or accessible via, those network and information systems.

However, this argument should not be restricted to the ability of networks and systems to resist, given that it has to flow around a different one: operational resilience. This is particularly evident in the context of the financial industry, which, in March 2021, was presented with the Principles for Operational Resilience issued by the BIS,[322] and the consultative document on Enhancing Third-Party Risk Management and Oversight developed by the FSB.[323]

The principles found in these documents certainly reflect the spirit of our context and they are relevant for the optimal exercise of the *lex monetae*. Financial intermediaries (including those labelled as P2P), following the infrastructural trends unleashed by the FIR, rely on GVCs, which are constituted by networks of actors that are linked through different sets of agreements with the aim to develop and offer financial services. Within our financial markets, intermediaries can be identified as the main stakeholders; however, behind them are hierarchies structured around the power held by certain companies that exercise certain level of infrastructural control based on their ownership of IPRs and their power to process of data, including personal data through algorithmic black boxes.

[321] Directive 2022/2555 of the European Parliament and of the Council on measures for a high common level of cybersecurity across the Union, amending Regulation (EU) No 910/2014 and Directive (EU) 2018/1972, and repealing Directive (EU) 2016/1148 (NIS 2 Directive) OJ L 333/80, 14 December 2022.

[322] Bank for International Settlements. 'Principles for Operational Resilience' (2021), available at www.bis.org/bcbs/publ/d516.htm.

[323] Financial Stability Board, 'Enhancing Third-Party Risk Management and Oversight' (2023), available at www.fsb.org/2023/06/enhancing-third-party-risk-management-and-oversight-a-toolkit-for-financial-institutions-and-financial-authorities-consultative-document.

Based on this, it is useful to highlight the following elements within the principles developed by the BIS that could improve their gradual incorporation in positive hard law:

1. **Explicability within Principle 2**[324]
   One of the greatest challenges of the technologies adopted and diffused throughout our financial infrastructures in the FIR is their lack of explainability. Lawmaking, regulation and supervision of financial markets rely on the analysis and forecasting of participants' behaviour. Unfortunately, just as it was verified in the context of the GFC, and in the words of Alan Greenspan,[325] current financial alchemy relies on asymmetries of information.
   This increased complexity and the product variability that results from it poses challenges not only for regulation, but also for those institutions that create and deal with new instruments and technologies, such as cryptoassets. Consequently, in order to improve operational risk management, Principle 2 could include or highlight a subprinciple based on the selection of explainable technology with the aim of simplifying or standardising algorithmic finance to minimise the risks that could emerge from its complexity.
   One of the normative elements that could emerge from this subprinciple could be an integral part of our 'cryptocharter' by which the incorporation of certain explainable applications would require financial institutions to be licensed to do so.[326] Of course, those applications that could not comply under well-defined explainability requirements – particularly during their stay in a regulatory sandbox – should be banned from their incorporation within our financial infrastructures unless reasonable explanation for their operation and the reasoning behind their selection is presented.[327]

2. **Identifying stakeholders for purposes of Principles 4 and 5**
   Complementing the comment issued on Principle 2, it is possible to argue that Principles 4[328] and 5[329] are very relevant to: 1) identifying the infrastructural stakeholders involved; and 2) setting the agreements by which intermediaries will have to answer for the failures of their systems and support the

[324] Principle 2 states: 'Banks should leverage their respective functions for the management of operational risk to identify external and internal threats and potential failures in people, processes and systems on an ongoing basis, promptly assess the vulnerabilities of critical operations and manage the resulting risks in accordance with their operational resilience approach.'

[325] Greenspan (n 23).

[326] E Kahana, 'Quantum Computing and AI Algorithmic Bias' (2020), available at law.stanford.edu/2020/02/06/quantum-computing-and-algorithmic-bias.

[327] J Schemmel, 'Artificial Intelligence and the Financial Markets: Markets as Usual?' in T Wischmeyer and T Rademacher (eds), *Regulating Artificial Intelligence* (Cham, Springer Nature, 2020) 255–276, 270.

[328] 'Once a bank has identified its critical operations, the bank should map the internal and external interconnections and interdependencies that are necessary for the delivery of critical operations consistent with its approach to operational resilience.'

[329] 'Banks should manage their dependencies on relationships, including those of, but not limited to, third parties or intragroup entities, for the delivery of critical operations.'

selection of the infrastructures deployed. In other words, independently of the existence of the networks of stakeholders and agreements, intermediaries must have control of their infrastructures. Consequently, this argument presents a complementary proposal to identify the relevance of the stakeholders and refine the requirements set for the agreements referred within Principle 5.

Figure 13 Map of operational interactions between IPRs and processing of personal data

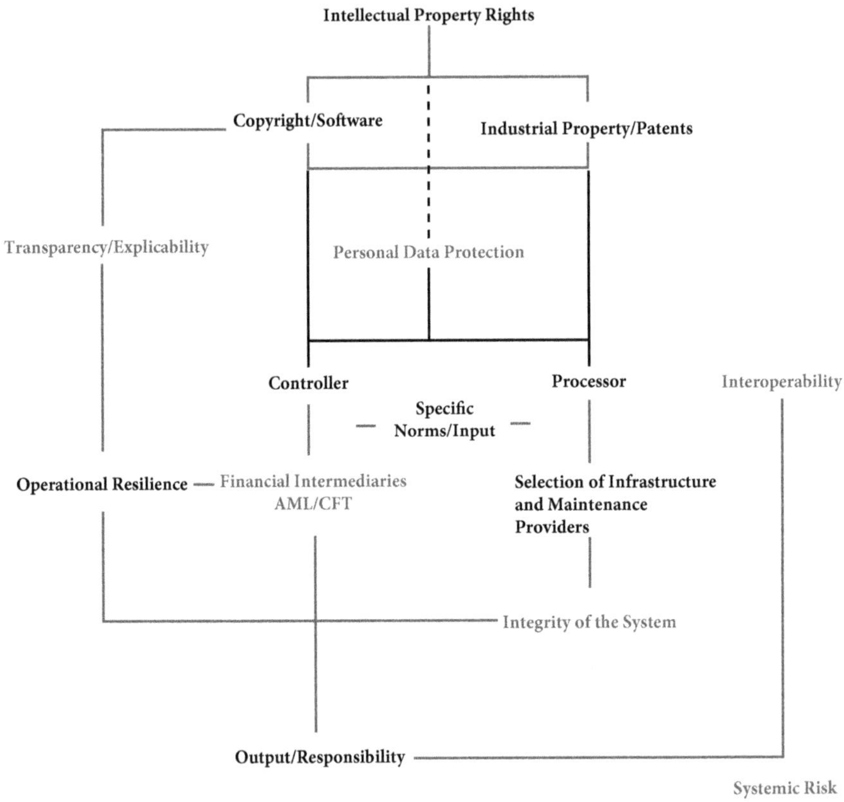

In the figure shown above, a scheme represents the interaction of several stakeholders within a single service under the light of three regulatory spheres (IP Law, Personal Data Protection and Anti-Money Laundering/Combating of Financing of Terrorism (AML/CFT)), which – as an integral elements of our *ius cudendae monetae* – could be useful to manifest the mapping described in Principle 4. At the first level are the owners of IPRs. Within this level, we have to separate/identify: 1) the owners of moral and economic rights related to copyright elements, such as software; and 2) the owners of the industrial property rights related to the inventions and innovations protected by patents, utility models, among other figures, that support the operation of the referred software. With the exception of those intermediaries that develop and control their own infrastructures, we need to verify that financial intermediaries have the rights that will allow them to control the selected infrastructures, particularly if they rely on smart applications, such as DevOps, to develop their products and services. As an illustration of this point, a survey developed by the Bank of England[330] mentions that some intermediaries employ OS software; however, care must be taken given that most of the time we do not consider the existence of moral rights that give certain control to the original author, as we can infer from the case *Jacobsen v Katzer*.[331] With these elements in mind, the cryptocharter has to consider these elements in the agreements referred in Principle 5.

Within the second level are the controllers and processors of personal data, which can be identified following the chain of transfers of IPRs. For instance, a financial institution that acquires the economic rights or a licence on the components of a technological infrastructure used to process personal data for purposes of credit scoring, will be considered the controller for purposes of regulations such as GDPR. At the same time, if the infrastructure is supported/controlled by a third party, this would be considered as a processor within the chain of processing. Again, these relationships have to be developed appropriately in the respective agreements reflecting the requirements set by GDPR; a relevant point if we consider the reports required by the FATF, which could rely on technologies such as ML to process personal data and avoid the 'crying wolf' problem.

From the content of the principles under analysis and these comments, we can conclude that risks and their contagion will not depend on Eugene Fama's rationality, but on the interaction among infrastructures, which are based on 'irrational' coded algorithms, which, in turn, will not react on a coordinated way. Building upon this fact, through the gradual implementation of these principles, we have to highlight the risks behind financial black boxes that could give form to the next generation of financial infrastructures and their systemic relevance, and propose a set of standards to uniform these structures to coordinate actions and avoid contagion in Machine-to-Machine (M2M) interactions within the next generation of payment systems.

From the spirit of these instruments, issuers could be exhorted to comply with different governance paradigms and international standards, such as the NIST framework, ISO 200220[332] and the CPMI-IOSCO guidance for cyber-resilience of financial market infrastructures that could be developed specifically for them and include the implementation of measures such as CASPER protocols[333] and

[330] Bank of England, 'Machine Learning in UK Financial Services' (2019), available at www.bankofengland.co.uk/report/2019/machine-learning-in-uk-financial-services.

[331] [2008] 535 F.3d 1373 (US), at 1381.

[332] A single standardisation approach (methodology, process, and repository) to be used by all financial standards initiatives.

[333] CASPER is a partial consensus mechanism that relies on smart contracts to track stakes and funds created within a specific network.

'Hawk' tools.[334] These standards could ease the transfer of knowledge and best practices by helping to ensure common understanding of concepts, terms and definitions, which prevent errors.[335] Furthermore, these types of standards would play a prominent role in harmonisation across jurisdictions given that these practices tend to be employed as the technical basis for domestic regulation. If devices from different manufacturers within our GVCs do not use the same standards, creating interoperability among them, extra gateways will be required to translate from one standard to another, thus leading to a substantial increase in legacy systems and transaction costs.[336]

v. Unlimited Liability

Among the most important aspects – if not the most important – regarding the constitution of these intermediaries and networks is the potential of default. While it is common to ignore the possibility of default in analyses, for financial intermediaries with principal businesses that involve issuing payment instruments to their customers, default and systemic risk are central financial issues.[337] The prospect of a future default by an intermediary of this nature can substantially reduce the effectiveness of the main economic function served by it.[338] Given the relevance and the involvement of public goods in these activities, the transition to a regulatory regime that can optimally mitigate these risks in a hyper-connected system such as that presented here, will not be complete if without an acknowledgement of the interconnections among its components.[339]

Considering these interconnections, it would be important to include – together with the *contra preferentem* rule – an unlimited liability relating to their operations, following the historical example set in Regulation 182 of the Companies Act of 1862, which stated:

> No Banking Company claiming to issue Note in the United Kingdom shall be entitled to limited liability in respect of such Issue, but shall continue subject to Unlimited Liability in respect thereof, and, if necessary, the Assets shall be marshalled for the Benefit of the general Creditors, and the Members shall be liable for the whole Amount of the Issue, in addition to the Sum for which they would be liable as Members of a Limited Company.

[334] 'Hawk' is a framework designed to enhance privacy and preserve smart contracts by which the compiler automatically generates a cryptographic protocol that uses zero-knowledge proofs.

[335] S Peng, 'Cybersecurity Standards. Cyberspace Governance, Multistakeholderism and the (Ir) Relevance of the TBT Regime' (2018) 51 *Cornell International Law Journal* 445, 447.

[336] ibid, 455.

[337] CAE Goodhart and DP Tsomocos, 'The Role of Default in Macroeconomics' (2011) 23 *IMES Discussion Papers* 1.

[338] Merton (n 128) 24.

[339] Enriques, Romano and Wetzer (n 27) 4.

This unlimited liabilities model found also in cases that involved money issuance, such as *Douglas, Heron, and Company v Alexander Hair*,[340] in Scotland from 1716 to 1845, would be designed upon the fact that managers and directors of financial intermediaries lack the incentives to account for the systemic relevance of their firms when they are deciding the respective courses of action.[341] This measure would not be very popular, but it could offer us an answer for the current state of the market. After all, the referred period is widely considered among economic and financial historians to have been one of the closest approximations to the implementation of an optimal 'free banking' model.[342]

Licensing of new intermediaries under this cryptocharter would be essential for the exercise of the *lex monetae* in the DCS. As Stiglitz[343] has noted, confidence in the financial system requires public awareness that financial intermediaries can only be operated by entities that are licensed to do so.[344] From a prudential supervision perspective, this cryptocharter should prevent institutions that would not be safe and sound, or that could pose a threat to the stability of our financial systems, from entering the banking market in the first place. When granting authorisations through this cryptocharter, central banks such as the ECB, the Bank of England and Banxico, would continue as gatekeepers, whose task would be, as it is today, to ascertain that new entrants to the banking market are robust and comply with national regulatory requirements.[345]

This proposal could generate some questions, among which one of the most relevant would be: what would happen with the existent cryptoassets generated based on the protocols of the generations covered in chapter four? Given that most of these assets – if not all of them – would not be included in the system presented above, the answer can be found in cases such as *Commodity Futures Trading Commission v Patrick K McDonnell and Cabbagetech, Corp d/b/a Coin Drop Markets*,[346] where the CFTC has classified these innovations as commodities. After all, independently of the argument related to the futures market, one can argue that, based on *Your Response Ltd v Datateam Business Media Ltd*[347] and *AA v Persons Unknown & Ors, Re Bitcoin*,[348] these assets are not very different from those numismatic properties found in collections around the globe.

[340] W Maxwell, *The Decisions of the Court of Session. Vol. XVII* (Edinburgh, Bell & Bradfute, 1804) 14668.

[341] Enriques, Romano and Wetzer (n 27) 4.

[342] TB Goodspeed, *Legislating Instability. Adam Smith, Free Banking, and the Financial Crisis of 1772* (Cambridge, Harvard University Press, 2016) 7.

[343] Stiglitz (n 34) Loc 562.

[344] European Central Bank, 'Guide to Assessments of License Applications. License Applications in General.' (2018) available at www.bankingsupervision.europa.eu/legalframework/publiccons/pdf/licensing_and_fintech/ssm.guide_to_assessment_of_credit_institution_licensing_applications_draft.en.pdf.

[345] ibid.

[346] [2018] 18-CV-361 (US), at 17–20.

[347] [2015] QB 41 (UK), at 56.

[348] [2019] EWHC 3556 (Comm) (UK).

VII. Do We Need a New Definition of Electronic Money?

Authors such as Sarah Green[349] argue that commercial practices require that the spirit of the instruments that currently cover sovereign forms of money should be extended to assets such as Bitcoin. An interesting argument – more so if we consider that she writes in the context of private law – but, unfortunately, one that does not consider the systemic implications of an action of this nature. To reduce these risks, in the preceeing sections, the basic structure for a transitional and/or alternative payments system based on the current state of the cryptoassets market has been presented. However, its viability and proper execution would depend on the answer to a single question: can we include this fourth generation of cryptoassets in the current definition of electronic money?

As seen in chapter four, cryptoassets under their current design cannot be subject to existent regulations applicable to electronic money. For example, in Article 2(2) of the 2EMD,[350] electronic money is defined as:

> [M]eans electronically, including magnetically, stored monetary value as represented by a claim on the issuer which is issued on receipt of funds for the purpose of making payment transactions as defined in point 5 of Article 4 of Directive 2007/64/EC, and which is accepted by a natural or legal person other than the electronic money issuer.

This definition was incorporated practically word-for-word in Article 2 of the Electronic Money Regulations 2011[351] of the UK. From these definitions, paired with the opinion in *Skatteverket v Hedqvist*,[352] we can say that most of the current cryptoassets cannot be considered as electronic money mainly because they: 1) are not issued on receipt of funds for the purpose of making payments; 2) they are not accepted by a person other than the electronic money issuer; 3) they tend to be structured under their own units of reference; and 4) they are not centrally issued. Additionally, in the context of those issuers found in the transition between the third and fourth generations of cryptoassets covered by MiCA,[353] we find, in Article 3(7) of that Regulation, the definition of 'electronic money token', which, including the sovereign unit of reference states that these tokens are 'a type of crypto-asset that purports to maintain a stable value by referencing the value of one official currency'.

So, do we need a new definition of electronic money? The answer is no. Following the evolution of the instruments developed using DLT and the potential

[349] S Green, 'It's Virtually Money' in D Fox and S Green (eds), *Cryptocurrencies in Public and Private Law* (Oxford, Oxford University Press, 2019) 13–31, 30–31.

[350] Directive 2009/110/EC of the European Parliament and of the Council on the taking up, pursuit and prudential supervision of the business of electronic money institutions amending Directives 2005/60/EC and 2006/48/EC and repealing Directive 2000/46/EC OJ L 267/7, 16 September 2009.

[351] The Electronic Money Regulations 2011 (SI 2011/99).

[352] [2015] C-264/14 (EU).

[353] Regulation 2023/1114 on markets in crypto-assets, and amending Regulations (EU) No 1093/2010 and (EU) No 1095/2010 and Directives 2013/36/EU and (EU) 2019/1937 OJ L 150/40, 31 May 2023.

adoption of the system proposed in this chapter – or others similar to it – a fourth generation of cryptoassets could fit perfectly in the current definitions of electronic money. First, as seen in the case of Fedcoin, these assets would be issued on receipt of funds for the purpose of making payments within and outside their respective networks to avoid entering in the exceptions covered by regulations, such as Article 2(3) of the Electronic Money Regulations 2011.[354] Second, building upon our *lex monetae* and the transition evidenced in MiCA, these cryptoassets would be structured around sovereign units of reference reflecting the continuity of our 'sacred' source of liquidity; and third, their issue would be subject to the conditions set by a sovereign stakeholder, throughout a system of compatible payment networks structured around PoA protocols.

Furthermore, the reference to the Directive 2007/64/EC[355] found in the definition provided by the 2EMD[356] highlights the existence of a different category of regulations that, despite its relevance, tends to be ignored in regulatory discussions. These regulations are those focused on the constitution of payment systems. As seen in section VI.A of chapter three following the content of instruments such as the ECB's Regulation 795/2014[357] and the Directive 2007/64/EC[358] of the European Parliament and the Council, payment systems have been developed and legally recognised as governance models by which different regulated institutions constitute a network of agreements that allow them to set common rules for the processing, clearing and/or settlement of payment transactions. Consequently, following the evolution of the market under a functionalist approach, it could be argued that the gradual regulation and incorporation of new intermediaries in these arrangements would ease the adoption of the proposal presented in this chapter and take it beyond its transitional nature with the incorporation of other technologies, such as AI and 5G.

VIII. Conclusion

In clear opposition to those purists that claim that DLT or – worse – Bitcoin will displace current constitutional arrangements, this chapter offers an alternative

[354] The Electronic Money Regulations 2011 (SI 2011/99).

[355] Directive 2007/64/EC of the European Parliament and of the Council on payment services in the internal market amending Directives 97/7/EC, 2002/65/EC, 2005/60/EC and 2006/48/EC and repealing Directive 97/5/EC OJ L 319/1, 13 November 2007.

[356] Directive 2009/110/EC of the European Parliament and of the Council on the taking up, pursuit and prudential supervision of the business of electronic money institutions amending Directives 2005/60/EC and 2006/48/EC and repealing Directive 2000/46/EC OJ L 267/7, 16 September 2009.

[357] Regulation of the European Central Bank 795/2014 on oversight requirements for systemically important payment systems OJ L 217/16, 3 July 2014.

[358] Directive 2007/64/EC of the European Parliament and of the Council on payment services in the internal market amending Directives 97/7/EC, 2002/65/EC, 2005/60/EC and 2006/48/EC and repealing Directive 97/5/EC OJ L 319/1, 13 November 2007.

argument. Building upon the three generations of cryptoassets introduced in chapter four, it has argued that this market emerged with imperfections that require the exercise of the *lex monetae*. To confront these imperfections, this chapter introduced a proposal that goes beyond the simple creation of a CBDC, taking as its starting point current constitutional prerogatives by which central banks are put at the core of a system that could allow us to issue a fourth generation of cryptoassets. It is important to highlight that the very creation of these assets is not the main target of this proposal, but the constitution of new regulated payment networks.

These networks could be structured around current commercial banks and new payment service providers as those described in PSD2 and – eventually – in PSD3.[359] All these intermediaries would have assigned specific regulated nodes to interact with each other on-chain following a PoA protocol, while they offer services off-chain under the trend described by Lord Mance in *Office of Fair Trading v Lloyds TSB Bank plc*.[360] The aim of this is to replicate historical trends by which the private sector introduces the technology while the gradual legal recognition and sovereign adoption fosters its diffusion.

Currently, the constitution of these payment systems could find a sound basis in existent projects developed by very well-known players. For example, although attention is focused on Bitcoin and its PoW protocol, JP Morgan Chase on 3 January 2017 filled a patent application[361] to introduce DLT to more familiar environments. Furthermore, this institution could be a systemic relevant element in a new payments system as the one presented above, depending on the results of the tests of its own stablecoin and the evolution of its Interbank Information Network,[362] which could increase its own infrastructural power.

Finally, following the words of Dr Frank Tong, this process will not end with the configuration of this payments system. The gradual development and inclusion of AI and 5G would require the development and refinement of alternative DLTs to blockchain based on the example set by projects, such as Iota, which is structured around a technology known as Tangle.[363] Through its own cryptoasset, Iota aims to address the problems of scalability that characterise most of the assets mined within blockchain networks. For this purpose, Tangle eliminates the figure of the miners and introduces what Serguei Popov[364] names 'local modifiers' by which

[359] Directive 2015/2366 of the European Parliament and of the Council on payment services in the internal market, amending Directives 2002/65/EC, 2009/110/EC and 2013/36/EU and Regulation (EU) No 1093/2010, and repealing Directive 2007/64/EC OJ L 337/35, 25 November 2015.

[360] [2008] 1 AC 316 (UK), at 325.

[361] [2017] Patent application 62446185: 'Systems and Methods for Management of Asset or Obligation-Backed Virtual Receipts on a Distributed System'.

[362] J.P. Morgan, 'J.P. Morgan Interbank Information Network Expands to More than 75 Banks' (2018) available at www.jpmorgan.com/country/GB/en/detail/1320570135560.

[363] S Popov, 'The Tangle.' (2018), available at assets.ctfassets.net/r1dr6vzfxhev/2t4uxvsIqk0EUau6g2sw0g/45eae33637ca92f85dd9f4a3a218e1ec/iota1_4_3.pdf.

[364] S Popov, 'Local Modifiers in the Tangle' (2018) available at assets.ctfassets.net/r1dr6vzfxhev/4p2Jh4jQzYwmQSqScgKW2G/6bd776742d48e6a44fca66845e956e8e/Local_Modifiers_in_the_Tangle.pdf.

each node interacts with the network based on the information available to them, in opposition to the uniformity found in DLT protocols such as PoW. Currently, Tangle is in its first stages of development, but the goal of its developers is to create a protocol that could foster secure exchanges of data for the IoT, which currently enables many banking applications and fostering the development of models such as Open Banking.

7

Epilogue

Throughout this book, the history of money has been presented as a history of social structures. Money represents the endogenous needs that emerge and evolve within our dynamic social systems, which, in turn, are materialised in the form of transitional rules within which we find our *lex monetae*. In other words, and as stated by Knapp,[1] money is a creature of law; a law that emerges and evolves from dynamic social needs. This is the reason behind the need for the Socio-Legal theory of money that is presented in this work. Through this approach, this work aims to clarify our understanding of some of the main lessons to be learned from the evolution of money and the institutions related to it around the world. For instance, there are parallels between instruments such as bills of exchange, electronic money and cryptoassets and contexts, such as the Middle Ages, the post-Bretton Woods environment and the Digital Commercial Society. Based on this exercise, it can be concluded that societies and their monetary expressions do not evolve through the influence of a single and static *Bildungstrieb*. After all, we have different legal traditions, different central bank designs, different technologies supported by different GVCs, and even different models and infrastructures for the creation of money, as we can verify through the multiple designs tested for the development of CBDCs around the world.

Within this framework, this book has emphasised the argument that we should not rely only on a 'purist' version of the Mengerian/Metallist, the State/Chartalist and/or the Societary theories to understand what money is in law beyond its economic functions. After all, an attempt to characterise cryptoassets through the application of principles developed in the era of the gold standard or during the development of complementary instruments like the Bristol pound is not only unwise, but unjustifiable,[2] as can be inferred from stories such as the following that circulates in different collectors' circles:

> Abe bought a shipment of sardines that had already been traded many times and each time profitably. Unlike previous buyers, Abe took the trouble of procuring a box of his purchase. The sardines were terrible. He telephoned Joe, from whom he had bought them, only to be told, 'But Abe, those sardines are for trading, not eating.'[3]

[1] GF Knapp, *The State Theory of Money* (London, Macmillan & Company Limited, 1924) 1.

[2] S Gleeson, *The Legal Concept of Money* (New York, Oxford University Press, 2018) 26.

[3] B Wallace, *The Billionaire's Vinegar. The Mystery of the World's Most Expensive Bottle of Wine* (New York, Broadway Books, 2009) 206.

Through the multidisciplinary analysis of this book, it is possible to conclude that money and its manifestations – among which we find cryptoassets – are dynamic social creations that are perfected periodically by law, reflecting the relevance of the *lex monetae* in monetary innovation.[4] The concept of *lex monetae* is relevant within this framework given that it goes beyond the common descriptions related to the monopoly over money creation and include the power of the state over the design and structure of the monetary system beyond the simple issuance of national currencies. As has been developed throughout this book, outside money has never formed the whole of the circulating monetary instruments of any economy, as can be seen in the existence – even today – of different expressions of inside money[5] that are generally accepted following the words of Lord Mansfield in *Miller v Race*[6] and Darling J in *Moss v Hancock*.[7]

In particular, it is relevant to show how the law has reacted to the innovative transitions that emerge from the endogenous needs within each dynamic system. In the concrete case of the Digital Commercial Society, those needs tend to be structured around enthusiast arguments based on perfect algorithmic reasoning, global coins, and the end of the nation-state as we know it, built on what Reinhart and Rogoff[8] call the 'this-time-is-different-syndrome'. Through these arguments, enthusiasts aim to unleash our FinTech dragon as an alternative paradigm to that which fostered the development of the GFC. However, despite the compelling arguments related to democracy and financial inclusion that support this objective, one can be certain that this FinTech dragon can (and will) evolve into a new version of *The Dragon of Profit and Private Ownership* presented in the introductory part of this work.

With that in mind, it can be stated that the future of money is and will be the future of financial crises. Despite the virtues attributed to the technologies that define the FIR, DLT is an expression of the endogenous needs of our societies. Consequently, as stated in the introduction to chapter six, it is clear that the next big financial crisis will be named after a FinTech innovation; a matter of concern that has motivated this work. Among the innovations that could unleash such a crisis, this book is concerned with the proper understanding and regulation of the cryptoassets market beyond Bitcoin and its PoW protocol, in stark contrast to most legal scholarship and case law on the subject.

For that purpose, efforts must be focused on the role of evolving cryptographic instruments as infrastructural elements for the exercise of *lex monetae* in new digital environments and the development of a new generation of payment systems

[4] Gleeson (n 2) 4.

[5] ibid, 46.

[6] [1758] 97 ER 398 (UK), at 401.

[7] [1899] 2 QBD 111 (UK), at 116.

[8] This syndrome is described as in the common belief that financial crises are things that happened in the past to other people in other countries, and that, accordingly, these crises do not happen to us, here and now. See CM Reinhart and KS Rogoff, *This Time is Different. Eight Centuries of Financial Folly* (New Jersey, Princeton University Press, 2009) 1.

that build on the interoperability among different technologies. This argument is illustrated through the segmentation of the cryptoassets market in three main generations, considering IPRs and the role of global value chains. Consequently, this work identifies the following lessons for the present and the future:

(1) Money tends to be defined based on its traditional functions – means of payment, unit of account and store of value – which can be found in practically every economics and banking law textbook. With that in mind, legal scholarship tends to rely on different theories with the aim of presenting different explanations related to the legal nature of money. Among the most famous money theories, are the Mengerian/Metallist theory, the State/Chartalist theory, and the Societary theory. After analysis, the Mengerian/Metallist theory has been discarded, and both the State Theory and the Societary Theory of money are accurate but incomplete approaches that complement each other to configure a Socio-Legal theory of money that will allow us to identify different monetary expressions in the Digital Commercial Society and beyond.
(2) Within Socio-Legal theory, it is possible to argue that cryptoassets do not represent a monetary revolution, but only a new link of the evolutionary chain of money, which has been built – and will continue to grow – following the diffusion of the best technologies available for each dynamic social system to fulfil not only its economic functions, but also to *reify* new underlying governance arrangements. The arguments found in many sources evidence the combination of ever-present technical uncertainties and funding commitments.[9]
(3) Given that money is not a static socio-legal innovation, defining it has historically proved difficult. As explained by Lord Chancellor Viscount Simon in *Perrin v Morgan*,[10] money cannot be defined only by its natural economic functions, given that it 'has several meanings, each of which in appropriate circumstances may be regarded as natural'.[11] In the context of judicial and regulatory history, this has been verified through the difficulties faced in defining innovations, such as promissory notes, banknotes, electronic money, and currently cryptoassets.
(4) Building on the previous point, money and its different manifestations tend to have their genesis in needs and solutions developed within the private sector in specific socio-economic circumstances as inside monies,[12] but they are perfected and diffused outside their original contexts first by commercial uses and customs, and then consolidated by law. This process has left traces

[9] V. Smil, *Invention and Innovation. A Brief History of Hype and Failure* (Massachusetts, The MIT Press, 2023) 146.
[10] [1943] AC 399 HL (UK), at 406–07.
[11] ibid.
[12] CAE Goodhart, 'The Two Concepts of Money. Implications for the Analysis of Optimal Currency Areas' (1998) 14 *European Journal of Political Economy* 407, 13.

identified with the emergence of coins, the evolution of paper instruments from bills of exchange to banknotes as verified in cases such as *Miller v Race*[13] and *Suffel v Bank of England*,[14] and the gradual regulation of electronic money and the diffusion of RTGSs. Consequently, after the segmentation of the cryptoassets market in three generations, as seen in chapter four, it can be inferred that these cryptographic innovations are following the same path.

(5) Law has standardised and stabilised the main economic functions that tend to be used to define money through the invention of currencies, the design of legal tender rules, and the sovereign nominalism, all of them designed under the *ius cudendae monetae*. On this point, there is an incomplete understanding related to the reach of *lex monetae*. It should not be restricted to the simple monopoly over the creation of money, but also has to consider the prerogatives of the state over the design of the financial infrastructure, including the power to tolerate or forbid the creation of complementary inside monies, as developed in chapters two and three.

Figure 14 Monies under the Socio-Legal exercise of the *lex monetae*

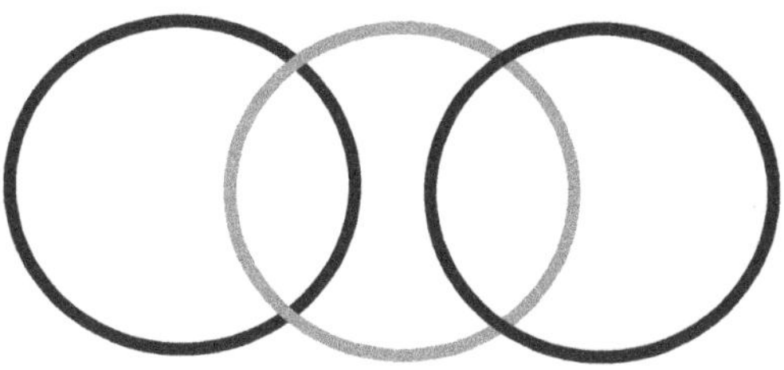

This can be verified through the fact that courts and legislators are prepared to recognise not only barter agreements as described in § 2-304 (1) of the Uniform Commercial Code of the USA,[15] but also private payment *reifiers* as money as we can verify in *Vick v Howard*[16] and *White v Elmdene Estates Ltd*:[17]

(1) Bagehot[18] stated that 'money will not manage itself' and, certainly, money does not emerge nor evolve in isolation. It relies on intermediaries, network effects, GVCs and technological infrastructures developed by the private sector,

[13] [1758] 97 ER 398 (UK), at 401.
[14] [1882] 9 QBD 555 (UK), at 563.
[15] '[T]he price can be made payable in money or otherwise. If it is payable in whole or in part in goods each party is a seller of the goods which he is to transfer.'
[16] [1923] 116 SE 465 (US), at 214.
[17] [1959] 2 All ER 605 (US), at 610–11.
[18] W Bagehot, *Lombard Street. A Description of the Money Market* (London, Kegan Paul, Trench, Trübner & Co, 1896) 20.

which, as witnessed throughout different periods of free banking and by the very existence of Gresham's Law, during their first stages of development, are defined by market imperfections that have to be addressed through sovereign regulation. The best example of these interactions and their diffusion can be found in the existence of payment systems and their regulations, as verified through the ECB's regulation 795/2014[19] and the PSD2,[20] among others. From the experiences of these systems and their network effects, it should be recognised that the cryptoassets market has fostered the development of a new generation of shadow banks that could be – or should be – regulated as such. MiCA is an illustration of such efforts.

(2) The perception that cryptoassets are a revolutionary expression reflects the decentralised nature not only of the technologies involved but of the internet itself, and the state of what Frank Pasquale[21] termed the Black Box Society. Accordingly, it is not surprising that there has been an emergence of centralised networks and a new generation of intermediaries, thus replicating historical trends associated with the internet and the FWS. The creation of a fourth generation of cryptoassets can therefore be anticipated as a future RegTech strategy to protect not only sovereign monetary prerogatives, but also digital sovereignty. After all, DLT is useful in designing new networks within the network of networks, not to create a new global decentralised financial network.

(3) Building upon the experience of electronic money and the prerogatives related to *lex monetae*, it is possible that, eventually, cryptoassets of the fourth generation introduced in chapter four, will be regulated and labelled as infrastructural elements within regulated electronic payment systems, not as individual monetary assets. Consequently, the big winners within the cryptoassets market will be those regulated institutions that are not focused on the creation of a GlobalCoin based on decentralised paradigms, but on the design and development of the new payments infrastructure for the DCS.

(4) Relatedly, it is important to highlight the relevance of IPRs in the development of such infrastructures. As seen throughout this book, through the access obtained to study several work documents, and through the interactions and feedback received in different academic and professional activities, users and developers ignore the existence of IPRs simply because the licences state that they are open-sourced. Furthermore, building on this lack of understanding, developers and service providers often offer black boxes that they barely understand, highlighting the existence of information asymmetries, just as was seen in the case of derivatives contracts before the GFC.

[19] Regulation of the European Central Bank 795/2014 on oversight requirements for systemically important payment systems OJ L 217/16, 3 July 2014.

[20] Directive 2015/2366 of the European Parliament and of the Council on payment services in the internal market, amending Directives 2002/65/EC, 2009/110/EC and 2013/36/EU and Regulation (EU) No 1093/2010, and repealing Directive 2007/64/EC OJ L 337/35, 25 November 2015.

[21] F Pasquale, *The Black Box Society. The Secret Algorithms that Control Money and information* (Massachusetts, Harvard University Press, 2015).

I. Designing the Future of Cryptocurrencies

Building on these lessons, chapter six presented a proposal built upon a new approach that goes beyond a simple analysis of Bitcoin. That proposal includes: 1) the role of IPRs in the development and the diffusion of technological infrastructures beyond the utopian decentralised ideal; 2) the power of the state to tolerate and adopt financial infrastructures through the exercise of *lex monetae*; and 3) the conception of payment systems as governance paradigms where the private and public sectors collaborate to place the fourth constitutional power in new contexts under principles of operational resilience.

To illustrate how this proposal would look in practice, the tests developed by institutions such as the Bank of England[22] and the People's Bank of China[23] can be taken as a starting point. It is possible that from these tests the first standards will emerge in private environments and will be gradually diffused through different ISO standards, such as the ISO 22739:2020 (en),[24] which in turn will be globally adopted as soft law through the work of international organisations such as the G20 and the BIS. Based on this soft law, the gradual prohibition and/or the classification of 'cryptoassets' of first, second and third generation as commodities is likely, following the spirit of cases such as *CFTC v Patrick K. McDonnell and Cabbagetech, Corp. d/b/a Coin Drop Markets*,[25] or as simple property as developed in *AA v Persons Unknown & Ors, Re Bitcoin*[26] with the aim of harmonisating payment systems around a fourth generation of infrastructural assets.

Building upon the case of the Bank of England and its royal/constitutional prerogatives that evolved from cases such as the *Case of Mixed Money in Ireland*[27] and inserted in instruments sich as Regulation XXVII of the Bank Charter Act 1844, the central bank would be the cornerstone of a new crypto payments system. This follows an historical trend. Considering the crises unleashed by the failures of institutions such as the Ayr Bank in the eighteenth and nineteenth centuries, the creation of a uniform CBDC structured around the exercise of the *lex monetae* could allow uniform interactions around a nominal anchor within the payments system and even improve the exercise of traditional functions, such as the lender of last resort in digital environments.

Once the stakeholder for the new payments system is defined, the concern will be avoiding the introduction of black boxes in payment infrastructures. Following the new standards, the Bank of England would need to develop proprietary technology –

[22] Bank of England, 'Future Forum 2018: The Highlights.' (2019), available at www.bankofengland.co.uk/outreach/future-forum-2018.

[23] Y Zhao and E Lam, 'China's PBOC Says Its Own Cryptocurrency Is "Close" to Release.' (2019), available at www.bloomberg.com/news/articles/2019-08-12/china-s-pboc-says-its-own-cryptocurrency-is-close-to-release.

[24] Blockchain and distributed ledger technologies – Vocabulary.

[25] [2018] 18-CV-361 (US), at 17–20.

[26] [2019] EWHC 3556 (Comm) (UK).

[27] [1605] Cobb St Tr 114 (UK), at 125–26.

avoiding working on source codes whose authors cannot be identified or hiring providers that barely understand what they are offering – or sign different agreements with well-defined institutions. For example, providers such as R3, Ripple, Ethereum, Microsoft Azure and Token own the IPRs needed to issue exclusive licences and offer the necessary rights to put in place a payments network, while the central bank exercises its own digital sovereignty. After all, this regulatory panopticon has to be controlled exclusively by a sovereign entity to work optimally as a RegTech strategy.

Following the terms of legislation such as s 55A(2) of the Financial Services Act 2012, the central bank would have control of the doorman, the notary and the oracle nodes by which it will manage the exercise of the rights found in the acquired licences and the respective smart contracts if these latter are required, whicht does not differ from the current infrastructural agreements that configure RTGSs. To access the network, commercial banks and/or other FCA-authorised payment service providers would need to demonstrate that they have the infrastructure set by the new standards and the FCA Handbook to run the software required to act as participant nodes within the new payments system. Non-bank participants should comply with the terms set by regulations such the forthcoming PSD3, and by regulations on operational resilience that are emerging around the world.

The regulator nodes would be assigned to the Prudential Regulation Authority (PRA), the FCA,[28] and probably to a financial intelligence unit as described in Article 7(1) of the United Nations Convention against Transnational Organized Crime, with the aim of processing reports relating to the transactions developed within the network. Finally, in this case, the issuer node would be assigned exclusively to the central bank by which it can control its RTGS and the supply of sovereign cryptoassets based on the deposits constituted by each participant node for purposes of on-chain clearing and settlement. Does the final user have access to the network? The answer is no. Given that the fourth generation of cryptoassets would be considered a form of electronic money based on a hypothetical Electronic Money Regulations 2024/25, electronic cards and electronic devices would remain in use to issue payment orders. The only change would be the technology that supports the payments system and the parties involved in the on-chain and off-chain agreements that will constitute the payments system.

In theory, this scheme could lead to the emergence of an international cryptowire. The technology available would enable an international set of payment chains to be run, as seen in the first outputs of projects Icebreaker[29] and Dunbar.[30] But

[28] On 10 January 2020, the FCA was set as the anti-money laundering and counter-terrorist financing (AML/CTF) supervisor of UK cryptoassets businesses. See Financial Conduct Authority (f), 'Cryptoassets: AML/CTF Regime' (2020) available at www.fca.org.uk/firms/financial-crime/cryptoassets-aml-ctf-regime.

[29] Bank for International Settlements. 'Project Icebreaker concludes experiment for a new architecture for cross-border retail CBDCs' (2023), available at www.bis.org/about/bisih/topics/cbdc/icebreaker.htm.

[30] Bank for International Settlements. 'Project Dunbar: international settlements using multi-CBDCs' (2021), available at www.bis.org/about/bisih/topics/cbdc/dunbar.htm.

would it be possible to materialise the world coin as dreamt by Scaruffi under a uniformed set of terms and conditions? As LIBRA/DIEM has evidenced, the final answer will depend on the level of technological standardisation and the level of digital sovereignty that each nation is willing to sacrifice. These networks rely on different categories of nodes, and the interoperability among central banks and their respective payment networks would require the assignment of some of these nodes to third parties in other jurisdictions. This is a relevant issue, particularly because these networks and the technologies involved can be employed as RegTech strategies with the potential to configure transnational regulatory panopticons structured around the normative hegemony exercised by the USA and/or China[31] on the internet. Consequently, the potential configuration of these raises the question: who can be trusted to control the panopticon, and under what conditions?

II. The Future of Money and Payments

As already stated, the main motivation and the intellectual cornerstones of this work emerged from the GFC. It is vital to avoid the 'madness' associated with the legal and financial complexity of human interactions and wihtin dynamic social systems, described in Chapter 10 of the 2011 Report published by the National Commission on the Causes of the Financial and Economic Crisis in the United States.[32] Certainly, a 'black box society' defined by very long GVCs will in the future unleash an 'algorithmic madness that will be faced by every payments system. This has to be covered in a separate work.

Accordingly, the scenarios and forecasts found within this book do not provide a conclusion or represent the final solution for the challenges that regulators around the world have to face in the context of the Digital Commercial Society. The analysis and proposals in this book represent a transitional paradigm for the diffusion and gradual consolidation of new payment systems; a single view of the cathedral. Certainly, it is more useful in initiating regulatory efforts than other works on Bitcoin, but it does not offer the final solution. As stated in chapter six, every major, far-reaching advance represents by itself a market imperfection, whether immediately appreciated or apparent only much later.[33] Given the nature of the technologies developed under the FIR and their increasing interoperability through the IoT, and the rise of quantum computing,

[31] The codes and contracts employed in the development of new infrastructures and services on the internet tend to reproduce the terms employed in the original sources that can be found in US or China. See GN La Diega and I Walden, 'Contracting for the "Internet of Things": Looking into the Nest' (2016) 7 *European Journal of Law and Technology* 1, 2.

[32] National Commission on the Causes of the Financial and Economic Crisis in the United States, 'The Financial Crisis Inquiry Report' (2011), available at fcic-static.law.stanford.edu/cdn_media/fcic-reports/fcic_final_report_full.pdf.

[33] Smil (n 9) 151.

we will probably never find a definite solution to the 'algorithmic madness' that is coming. Independently of this, this book presents a framework that could be employed to look beyond DLT.

For instance, the sociolegal analyses of the concept of 'money' found in chapters two and three could be useful in facing future monetary innovations that not necessarily will be designed around DLT or even around current definitions of electronic money. The analysis in the first three chapters of this work of instruments such as stablecoins under the terms of the Bills of Exchange Act 1882 could be used to define and use these instruments as cryptographic bills of exchange, promissory notes and/or cheques. This would help us to identify useful elements of new technologies to exercise acts like the protest and the indorsement in digital contexts, following the example set by cryptographic signatures.

Another project that could emerge the analysis of stablecoins in this book is a more refined work on the potential use of the Scottish and Northern Ireland Banknote Regulations 2009 to propose/create a set of Scottish stablecoins if the Bank of England decides to issue a digital pound. Furthermore, based on stablecoins, one could present an argument for the creation of a free-banking paradigm in Scotland similar to that witnessed in the eighteenth century for the post-Brexit context. This framework could be extended further to develop a deeper analysis on the role of the *lex monetae* to constitute that hypothetical free-banking system.

Another interesting element that could be used to develop new work can be found in the explainability requirements for cryptoassets and the introduction of the *contra preferentem* rule in their digital environments. Although in cases such as *Multiplex Construction (Europe) v Dunne*[34] there are arguments stating that this rule is a useless anachronism, it could become a useful tool to remove certain incentives to introduce algorithmic black boxes within financial infrastructures and smart contracts. Furthermore, following the diffusion process that is leading to the gradual introduction of CBDCs, the Yacatecuhtli approach introduced in chapter three could be useful in analysing the interactions among different CBDCs and other stablecoins.

Additionally, given that better financial instruments are needed to reduce the risk of financial crises in the future,[35] it is useful to think about complementary elements within this proposal that could lead to deeper analyses based on the interoperability of different technologies. For instance, given that we are leaving behind the winter of AI and the arguments set out in the Lighthill Report,[36] could we design a crypto payments system structured around an algorithmic central bank? Or a smart network of e-money tokens, as described in MiCA, issued by artificial agents? If this is possible, how should we regulate them? Should we design them around an expert program or around a specific number of neural networks?

[34] [2017] EWHC 3073 (TCC) (UK), at 27.

[35] R Shiller, *Finance and the Good Society* (New Jersey, Princeton University Press, 2012) xi.

[36] J Lighthill, 'Artificial Intelligence: A General Survey' (1973) available at www.chilton-computing.org.uk/inf/literature/reports/lighthill_report/p001.htm.

The answers to questions like these could represent academic and professional opportunities. Perhaps we could even reach a point that forces us to think – building upon Alan Turing's[37] original question, can machines think? – about whether money in the future will require human intervention for its definition, reinvention, diffusion and/or regulation. Of course, the final question must be: how can we face the next financial crisis? After all, the *lex monetae* has to be human, not perfect.

[37] AM Turing, 'Computing Machinery and Intelligence' (1950) 49 *Mind* 433, 433.

BIBLIOGRAPHY

Abrazhevich, D, 'Classification and Characteristics of Electronic Payment Systems' in K Bauknecht, S Kumar Madria and G Pernul (eds), *Electronic Commerce and Web Technologies* (Berlin, Springer-Verlag, 2001) 81–90.

Accominotti, O, 'International Monetary Regimes: The Interwar Gold Exchange Standard' in S. Battilossi et al (eds), *Handbook of the History of Money and Currency* (Singapore, Springer Nature, 2018) 1–32.

Aglietta, M, *Money. 5,000 Years of Debt and Power* (New York, Verso, 2018).

Akerlof, GA, 'The Market for "Lemons": Quality Uncertainty and the Market Mechanism' (1970) 84 *The Quarterly Journal of Economics* 488–500.

Akerlof, GA and Shiller, RJ, *Animal Spirits. How Human Psychology Drives the Economy, and Why It Matters for Global Capitalism* (Princeton, Princeton University Press, 2009).

Alexander, K, Dhumale, R and Eatwell, J, *Global Governance of Financial Systems. The International Regulation of Systemic Risk* (New York, Oxford University Press, 2006).

Allen, F and Carletti, E, 'The Roles of Banks in Financial Systems' in AN Berger, P Molyneux and JO Wilson (eds), *The Oxford Handbook of Banking* (Oxford, Oxford University Press, 2010) 37–57.

Amend-Traut, A, 'Monetary and Currency Problems in the Light of Early Modern Litigation' in D Fox and W Ernst (eds), *Money in the Western Legal Tradition. Middle Ages to Bretton Woods* (Oxford, Oxford University Press, 2016) 295–316.

Angeles, J, *Fundamentals of Robotic Mechanical Systems. Theory, Methods, and Algorithms* (Cham, Springer, 2014).

Aristophanes, *The Frogs* (1908, London, George Allen & Sons.).

Aristotle, *Nicomachean Ethics* (London, Kegan Paul, Trench, Trübner & Co, 1906).

—— *Politics* (Oxford, Clarendon Press, 1908).

—— *The Athenian Constitution, The Eudemian Ethics, and Virtues and Vices* (London, Harvard University Press, 1952).

Arner, DW, Barberis J and Buckley, RP, '150 Years of Fintech. An Evolutionary Analysis' (2016) 3 *The Finsia Journal of Applied Finance* 22.

—— 'The Evolution of FinTech: A New Post-Crisis Paradigm?' (2016) 47 *Georgetown Journal of International Law* 1271.

Arora, A, *Electronic Banking and the Law* (London, Banking Technology, 1993).

Arrow, KJ and Debreu, G, 'Existence of an Equilibrium for a Competitive Economy' (1954) 22 *Econometrica* 265.

Artus, P and de Boissieu, C, 'The Process of Financial Innovation: Causes, Forms, and Consequences' in A Heertje (ed), *Innovation, Technology, and Finance* (Oxford, European Investment Bank, 1988) 101–26.

Aschheim, J and Park, YS, 'Artificial Currency Units: The Formation of Functional Currency Areas' (1976) 114 *Essays in International Finance* 1.

Ashworth, WJ, 'Metrology and the State: Science, Revenue, and Commerce' (2004) 306 *Science* 1314.

Avgouleas, E, *Governance of Global Financial Markets. The Law, the Economics, the Politics* (Cambridge, Cambridge University Press, 2012).

—— 'Regulating Financial Innovation' in N Moloney, E Ferran and J Payne (eds), *Oxford Handbook of Financial Regulation* (Oxford, Oxford University Press, 2017) 660–92.

Avgouleas, E and Blair, W, 'The Concept of Money in the 4th Industrial Revolution. A Legal and Economic Analysis' (2020) *Singapore Journal of Legal Studies* 4.

Awrey, D and van Zwieten, K, 'The Shadow Payment System' (2018) 43 *The Journal of Corporation Law* 102.

Badour, A and Presta, D, 'Open Banking: Canadian and International Developments' (2018) 34 *Banking and Finance Law Review* 41.

Bagehot, W, *Lombard Street. A Description of the Money Market* (London, Henry S King & Co, 1873).

Baker, JH, 'The Law Merchant and the Common Law before 1700' (1979) 38 *Cambridge Law* Journal 295.

Balch, TW, 'The Law of Oresme, Copernicus and Gresham' (1908) 47 *Proceedings of the American Philosophical Society* 18.

Banerjee, AV and Maskin, ES, 'A Walrasian Theory of Money and Barter' (1996) 111 *Quarterly Journal of Economics* 955.

A Bank Manager, *Papers on Banking & Finance* (London, Bemrose and Sons, 1871).

Baron, JP, 'Making Money in Mesoamerica: Currency Production and Procurement in the Classic Maya Financial System' (2018) 5 *Economic Anthropology* 210.

Battiston S et al, 'DebtRank: Too Central to Fail? Financial Networks, the FED and Systemic Risk' (2012) 2 *Nature Scientific Reports* 1.

—— 'Liaisons dangereuses: Increasing connectivity, risk sharing, and systemic risk' (2015) 36 *Journal of Economic Dynamics and Control* 1121.

Becerra-Ramíres, M, *La Propiedad Intelectual en Transformación* (Porrúa, Mexico City, 2009).

Bech, ML and Hobjin, B, 'Technology Diffusion within Central Banking. The Case of Real-Time Gross Settlement' (2006) 260 *Federal Reserve Bank of New York Staff Reports* 1.

Beck, T, Demirgüç-Kunt A and Levine, R, 'Law and Finance. Why Does Legal Origin Matter?' (2002) 9379 *National Bureau of Economic Research Working Papers* 1.

Bénassy-Quéré, A et al, *Economic Policy. Theory and Practice* (New York, Oxford University Press, 2010).

Berensten, A and Schär, F, 'A Short Introduction to the World of Cryptocurrencies' (2018) 100 *Federal Reserve Bank of St Louis Review* 1.

Bernanke, BS, Geithner TF and Paulson, HM, *Firefighting the Financial Crisis and Its Lessons* (London, Profile Books, 2019).

Billio, M et al, 'Econometric Measures of Connectedness and Systemic Risk in the Finance and Insurance Sectors' (2012) 104 *Journal of Financial Economics* 535.

Byttebier, K, *Towards a New International Monetary Order* (Cham, Springer, 2017).

Blumenbach, JF, *De generis human varietate nativa* (Göttingen: Vandenhoek, 1795).

Bordo, MD and Redish, A, 'Putting the 'System' in the International Monetary System' in D Fox and W Ernst (eds), *Money in the Western Legal Tradition. Middle Ages to Bretton Woods* (Oxford, Oxford University Press, 2016) 595–610.

Bordo, MD and Siklos, PL, 'Central Banks. Evolution and Innovation in Historical Perspective' in R Edvinsson, T Jacobson and D Waldenström (eds), *Sveriges Riksbank and the History of Central Banking* (Cambridge, Cambridge University Press, 2018) 26–89.

Brady, F, 'So Fast to Ruin. The Ayr Bank Crash' (1973) 11 *Ayrshire Collection* 27.

Brindle, M and Cox, R, 'Introduction' in M Brindle and R Cox (eds), *Law of Bank Payments* (London, FT Law & Tax, 1996) 1–23.

Bristoll, S and Goode, R, '1992: The Insolvency Implications for Banks' in R Cranston (ed), *The Single Market and the Law of Banking* (London, Lloyd's of London Press, 1995) 121–38.

Bromberg, B, 'The Origin of Banking: Religious Finance in Babylonia' (1942) 2 *The Journal of Economic History* 77.

Buchanan, G, *De Jure Regni apud Scotos Dialogus* (Glasgow, Ronerti Urie, 1750).

Calabresi, G, 'Property Rules, Liability Rules, and Inalienability: One View of the Cathedral' (1972) 85 *Harvard Law Review* 1089.

—— *The Future of Law & Economics. Essays in Reform and Recollection* (New Haven, Yale University Press, 2016).

Campbell, D, 'Virtual Economics: Economists Explore the Research Value of Virtual Worlds' (2008) 12 *Region Focus* 18–22.

Caplan, A, '"Cada uno en su bolsa llevar lo que cien indios no llevarían": Mexica Resistance and the Shape of Currency in New Spain, 1542–1552' (2013) 25 *American Journal of Numismatics* 333.

Caskey, JP and St Laurent, S, 'The Susan B. Anthony Dollar and the Theory of Coin/Note Substitutions' (1994) 26 *Journal of Money, Credit and Banking* 495.

Castronova, E, 'On the Research Value of Large Games: Natural Experiments in Norrath and Camelot' (2005) 1621 *CESifo Working Papers* 1.

Cedillo, I, 'A new Approach for "Cryptoassets" Regulation' (2019) 35 *Banking and Finance Law Review* 37.

Chick, V, 'Unresolved Questions in Monetary Theory: A Critical Review' (1978) 126 *De Economist* 37.

Chien, CV, 'Software Patents as A Currency, Not Tax, on Innovation' (2016) 31 *Berkeley Technology Law Journal* 1669.

Chubb, H, 'The Bank Act and the Crisis of 1866' (1872) 35 *Journal of the Statistical Society of London* 171.

Chung, JJ, 'Money as Simulacrum: The Legal Nature and Reality of Money' (2009) 64 *Roger Williams University Legal Studies Research Paper Series* 108.

Clarke, R, 'The Digital Persona and Its Application to Data Surveillance' (1994) 10 *The Information Society* 77.

Clower, R, 'A Reconsideration of the Microfoundations of Monetary Theory' (1967) 6 *Western Economic Journal* 1.

Coase, RH, 'The Nature of the Firm' (1937) 4 *Economica* 386.

—— 'The Problem of Social Cost' (1960) 3 *The Journal of Law & Economics* 1.

Coggan, JP, *Paper Promises. Money, Debt, and the New World Order* (London, Penguin, 2011).

Coin Collector, 'Before the Empire' (2023) 18 *Coin Collector* 36.

Coke, E, *The First Part of the Institutes of the Laws of England, or, A Commentary upon Littleton* (Philadelphia, Robert H Small, 1853).

Cooper, GS, *The Origin of Financial Crises. Central Banks, Credit Bubbles, and the Efficient Market Fallacy* (New York, Vintage Books, 2008).

Copernicus, N, *On the Minting of Money* (New York, Laissez Faire Books, 2013) Kindle EBook.

Cox, RW and Wartembe, M, 'The Politics of Global Value Chains' in R Kiggins (ed), *The Political Economy of Robots. Prospects for Prosperity and Peace in the Automated 21st Century* (Cham, Palgrave Macmillan, 2018) 17–40.

Cranston, R et al, *Principles of Banking Law* (Oxford, Oxford University Press, 2017).

Crockett, A, *Money. Theory, Policy and Institutions* (London, Thomas Nelson and Sons, 1939).

Dang-Nguyen, G and Pénard, T, 'Interconnection Agreements in Telecommunications Networks: From Strategic Behaviours to Property Rights' in E Brousseau and JM Glachant (eds), *The Economics of Contracts. Theories and Applications* (Cambridge, Cambridge University Press, 2002) Kindle EBook Loc 4806–5004.

Davies, C, *A History of Money. From Ancient Times to the Present Day* (Cardiff, University of Wales Press, 1994).

Deakin, S, 'The Evolution of Theory and Method in Law and Finance' in N Moloney, E Ferran and J Payne (eds), *Oxford Handbook of Financial Regulation* (Oxford, Oxford University Press, 2017) 13–40.

Deeks, A, 'The Judicial Demand for Explainable Artificial Intelligence' (2019) 119 *Columbia Law Review* 1829, 1837–38.

Dell'Erba, M, 'Stablecoins in Cryptoeconomics: From Initial Coin Offerings to Central Bank Digital Currencies' (2019) 22 *Legislation and Public Policy* 1.

Demirgüç-Kunt, A, 'Finance and Economic Development. The Role of Government' in AN Berger, P Molyneux and JO Wilson (eds), *The Oxford Handbook of Banking* (Oxford, Oxford University Press, 2010) 729–55.

Desan, CA, 'Money as a Legal Institution' in D Fox and W Ernst (eds), *Money in the Western Legal Tradition. Middle Ages to Bretton Woods* (Oxford, Oxford University Press, 2016) 18–35.

Dhillon, V, Metcalf, D and Hooper, M, *Blockchain Enabled Applications. Understand the Blockchain Ecosystem and How to Make It Work for You* (California, APress Media, 2017).
Dickinson, A, 'Cryptocurrencies and the Conflict of Laws' in D Fox and S Green (eds), *Cryptocurrencies in Public and Private Law* (Oxford, Oxford University Press, 2019) 93–137.
Diffie, W and Hellman, ME, 'New Directions in Cryptography' (1976) 22 *IEEE Transactions on Information Theory* 644.
Dixit, A, 'Governance Institutions and Economic Activity' (2009) 99 *The American Economic Review* 3.
Djankov, S et al, 'The New Comparative Economics' (2003) 31 *Journal of Comparative Economics* 595.
Dodd, N, *The Social Life of Money* (Princeton, Princeton University Press, 2014).
—— 'Utopian Monies' in N Bandelj, FF Wherry and VA Zelizer (eds), *Money Talks. Explaining How Money Really Works* (Princeton, Princeton University Press, 2017) 230–47.
Doguet, JJ, 'The Nature of the Form: Legal and Regulatory Issues Surrounding the Bitcoin Digital Currency System' (2013) 73 *Lousiana Law Review* 1119.
Donald, DC, 'Information, and the Regulation of Inefficient Markets' in E Avgouleas and DC Donald (eds), *The Political Economy of Financial Regulation* (Cambridge, Cambridge University Press, 2022) 38–62.
Dooley, J, *History of Cryptography and Cryptanalysis* (Cham, Springer International Publishing, 2018).
Dondorp, H, 'The Effect of Debasements on Pre-existing Debts in Early Modern Jurisprudence' in D Fox and W Ernst (eds), *Money in the Western Legal Tradition. Middle Ages to Bretton Woods* (Oxford, Oxford University Press, 2016) 247–66.
Doty, R, *Money of the World* (London, Ridge Press, 1978).
Dowd, K, 'Free Banking' in CJ Coyne and PJ Boettke (eds), *The Oxford Handbook of Austrian Economics* (Oxford, Oxford University Press, 2015).
—— 'Contemporary Private Monetary Systems' in LH White, VJ Vanberg and EA Köhler (eds), *Renewing the Search for a Monetary Constitution. Reforming Government's Role in the Monetary System* (Washington, Cato Institute, 2015) Kindle EBook Loc 3442–4029.
Dylag, M, 'The Negotiability of Promissory Notes and Bills of Exchange in the Time of Chief Justice Holt' (2010) 31 *The Journal of Legal History* 149.
Eagleton, C and Williams, J, *Money. A History* (London, The British Museum Press, 2013).
Eder, PJ, 'Legal Theories of Money' (1934) 20 *Cornell Law Review* 52.
Edgar, L, 'Electronic Money' in C Reed, I Walden and L Edgar (eds), *Cross-Border Electronic Banking. Challenges and Opportunities* (London, LLP Professional Publishing, 2000) 201–21.
Edvinsson, R, Jacobson, T and Waldenström, D, 'Introduction' in R Edvinsson, T Jacobson and D Waldenström (eds), *Sveriges Riksbank and the History of Central Banking* (Cambridge, Cambridge University Press, 2018) 1–25.
Eha, BP, *How Money Got Free. Bitcoin and the Fight for the Future of Finance* (London, Oneworld Publications, 2017).
Eich, S, *The Currency of Politics. The Political Theory of Money from Aristotle to Keynes* (New Jersey, Princeton University Press, 2022).
Eichengreen, B, 'Introduction' in B Eichengreen (ed), *The Gold Standard in Theory and History* (New York, Methuen, 1985) 1–35.
Eichengreen, B, Mehl, AJ and Chitu, L,'Mars or Mercury? The Geopolitics of International Currency Choice' (2017) 24145 *NBER Working Papers* 1.
Eisenstein, C, *Sacred Economies. Money, Gift & Society in the Age of Transition* (California, Evolver Editions, 2011).
Ellinger, P, 'Electronic Funds Transfer as a Deferred Settlement System' in RM Goode (ed), *Electronic Banking. The Legal Implications* (London, The Institute of Bankers, 1985) 29–44.
Enriques, L, Romano, A and Wetzer, T, 'Network-Sensitive Financial Regulation' (2019) 451 *ECGI Working Paper Series in Law* 1.
Ernst, W, 'The Legists' Doctrines on Money and the Law from the Eleventh to the Fifteenth Centuries' in D Fox and W Ernst (eds), *Money in the Western Legal Tradition. Middle Ages to Bretton Woods* (Oxford, Oxford University Press, 2016) 110–35.

—— 'Mensura et mensuratum: money as measure and measure for money' in J von Hagen and M. Welker (eds), *Money as God? The Monetization of the Market and its Impact on Religion, Politics, Law, and Ethics* (Cambridge, Cambridge University Press, 2014) 60–79.

Eusebius, *The Life of the Blessed Emperor Constantine* (London, Samuel Bagster and Sons, 1845).

Fagan, F, 'Legal Cycles and Stabilization Rules' in F Fagan and S Levmore (eds), *The Timing of Lawmaking* (Cheltenham: Edward Elgar Publishing, 2017) 11–33.

Falkner, RP, 'The Currency Law of 1900' (1900) 16 *Annals of the American Academy of Political and Social Science* 33.

Fama, EF, 'Mandelbrot and the Stable Paretian Hypothesis' (1963) 36 *Journal of Business* 420.

—— 'Random Walks in Stock Market Prices' (1995) 51 *Financial Analysts Journal* 75.

Fazio, A and Zuffranieri, F, 'Interbank Payment System Architecture from a Cyber Security Perspective' (2018) 418 *Questioni di Economia e Finanza* 1.

Ferguson, N, *The Ascent of Money. A Financial History of the World* (New York, The Penguin Press, 2018).

Ford, C, *Innovation and the State. Finance, Regulation and Justice* (New York, Cambridge.

Fox, D, 'The Anglo-Scots Monetary Union of 1707' (2018) 24 *Edinburgh School of Law Research Paper Series* 1.

—— 'The Case of Mixt Monies' in D Fox and W Ernst (eds), *Money in the Western Legal Tradition. Middle Ages to Bretton Woods* (Oxford, Oxford University Press, 2016) 224–43.

—— 'The Case of Mixt Monies: Confirming Nominalism in the Common Law of Monetary Obligations' (2011) 70 *Cambridge Law Journal* 144.

Fox, D and Green, S (eds), *Cryptocurrencies in Public and Private Law* (Oxford, Oxford University Press, 2019).

Frame, WS and White, LJ, 'Empirical Studies of Financial Innovation: Lots of Talk, Little Action?' (2004) 42 *Journal of Economic Literature* 116.

Franco, P, *Understanding Bitcoin. Cryptography, Engineering and Economics* (West Sussex, John Wiley & Sons, 2015).

Frankel, SH, *Money: Two Philosophies. The Conflict of Trust and Authority* (Bristol, Basil Blackwell, 1977).

Frankopan, P, *The Earth Transformed. An Untold History* (London, Bloomsbury, 2023).

Frederick, DE, 'Libraries, Data and the Fourth Industrial Revolution' (2016) 33 *Library Hi Tech News* 9.

Freeman, C, 'Diffusion: The Spread of New Technology to Firms, Sectors and Nations' in A Heertje (ed), *Innovation, Technology, and Finance* (1988, Oxford, European Investment Bank) 38–70.

Fregert, K, 'Sveriges Riksbank: 350 Years in the Making' in R Edvinsson, T Jacobson and D Waldenström (eds), *Sveriges Riksbank and the History of Central Banking* (Cambridge, Cambridge University Press, 2018) 90–142.

Freixas, X and Rochet, JC, *Microeconomics of Banking* (Cambridge, MIT Press, 2008).

Friedman, M, *A Program for Monetary Stability* (New York, Fordham University Press, 1960).

—— 'The Island of Stone Money' (1991) 91 *Hoover Institution Working Papers* 1.

—— *The Optimum Quantity of Money and Other Essays* (New York, Macmillan, 1969).

Friedman, M and Schwartz, AJ, 'Has Government Any Role in Money?' in AJ Schwartz (ed), *Money in Historical Perspective* (Chicago, University of Chicago Press, 1987) 289–314.

Fröwis, M and Böhme, R, 'In Code We Trust? Measuring the Control Flow Immutability of All Smart Contracts Deployed on Ethereum' in J Garcia-Alfaro et al (eds), *Data Privacy Management, Cryptocurrencies and Blockchain Technology* (Cham, Springer International Publishing, 2017) 357–72.

Furht, B and Villanustre, F, 'Introduction to Big Data' in B Furht and V Villanustre (eds), *Big Data Technologies and Applications* (Cham, Springer International Publishing, 2016) 3–11.

Galbraith, JK, *Money. Whence It Came, Where It Went* (London, Andre Deutsch, 1975).

Geva, B, 'The Concept of Payment Mechanism' (1986) 24 *Osgoode Hall Law Journal* 1.

—— 'The Order to Pay Money in Medieval Continental Europe' in D Fox and W Ernst (eds), *Money in the Western Legal Tradition. Middle Ages to Bretton Woods* (Oxford, Oxford University Press, 2016) 409–440.

—— *The Payment Order of Antiquity and the Middle Ages. A Legal History* (Oxford, Hart Publishing, 2011).
Geva, B and Peari, S, *International Negotiable Instruments* (Oxford, Oxford University Press, 2020).
Gleeson, S, *The Legal Concept of Money* (New York, Oxford University Press, 2018).
Goetzmann, WN, *Money Changes Everything. How Finance Made Civilization Possible* (New Jersey:, Princeton University Press, 2016).
Goldthwaite, RA, *The Economy of Renaissance Florence* (Maryland, Johns Hopkins University Press, 2009).
Goode, R, *Commercial Law in the Next Millennium* (London, Sweet & Maxwell, 1998).
—— *Goode on Commercial Law* (London, LexisNexis, 2009).
Goodhart, CAE, 'Can Central Banking Survive the IT Revolution?' (2000) 3 *International Finance* 189.
—— *Money, Information and Uncertainty* (Hong Kong, The Macmillan Press, 1975).
—— 'The Bank of England, 1694–2017' in R Edvinsson, T Jacobson and D Waldenström (eds), *Sveriges Riksbank and the History of Central Banking* (Cambridge, Cambridge University Press, 2018) 143–71.
—— *The Evolution of Central Banks* (Massachusetts, MIT Press, 1988).
—— 'The Two Concepts of Money. Implications for the Analysis of Optimal Currency Areas' (1998) 14 *European Journal of Political Economy* 407.
Goodhart, CAE and Tsomocos, DP, 'The Role of Default in Macroeconomics' (2011) 23 *IMES Discussion Papers* 1.
Goodspeed, TB, *Legislating Instability. Adam Smith, Free Banking, and the Financial Crisis of 1772* (Cambridge, Harvard University Press, 2016).
Graeber, D, *Debt: The First 5,000 Years* (New York, Melville House, 2011).
—— 'Notes on the Politics of Divine Kingship, or Elements for an Archaeology of Sovereignty' in D Graeber and M Sahlins (eds), *On Kings* (Chicago, Hau Books, 2017) 377–464.
Granovetter, M, 'The Nature of Economic Relations' (1992) 10 *Understanding Economic Process* 21.
Green, S, 'Cryptocurrencies: The Underlying Technology' in D Fox and S Green (eds), *Cryptocurrencies in Public and Private Law* (Oxford, Oxford University Press, 2019) 1–12.
—— 'It's Virtually Money' in D Fox and S Green (eds), *Cryptocurrencies in Public and Private Law* (Oxford, Oxford University Press, 2019) 13–31.
Gurley JG and Shaw, ES, *Money in a Theory of Finance* (Washington DC, The Brookings Institution, 1960).
Gurrea-Martínez, A and Remolina, N, 'The Law and Finance of Initial Coin Offerings' in C Brummer (ed), *Cryptoassets. Legal, Regulatory and Monetary Perspectives* (New York, Oxford University Press, 2019) 117–56.
Haiven, M, 'The Creative and the Derivative' (2014) 118 *Radical History Review* 113.
Hall, H, *Select Cases Concerning the Law Merchant AD 1251–1779. Vol III* (London, Selden Society, 1932).
Hance, O and Balz, SD, *The New Virtual Money: Law and Practice* (The Hague, Kluwer Law International, 1999).
Hare, C, 'Cryptocurrencies and Banking Law. Are There Lessons to Learn?' in D Fox and S Green (eds), *Cryptocurrencies in Public and Private Law* (Oxford, Oxford University Press, 2019) 229–53.
Harris, R and Hutton, C, *Definition in Theory and Practice: Language, Lexicography and the Law* (London, Continuum, 2007).
Hasanova, H et al, 'A Survey on Blockchain Cybersecurity' (2018) 29 *International Journal of Network Management* 1.
Hawking, S, *Brief Answers to the Big Questions* (London, John Murray, 2018).
Hayek, FA, *Choice in Currency* (London, The Institute of Economic Affairs, 1976).
—— *Denationalisation of Money. The Argument Refined* (London, Institute of Economic Affairs, 1978).
Hayman, PA and Williams, J, 'Westphalian Sovereignty. Rights, Intervention, Meaning and Context' (2006) 20 *Global Society* 521.
Heertje, A, 'Technical and Financial Innovation' in A. Heertje (ed), *Innovation, Technology, and Finance* (Oxford, European Investment Bank, 1988) 1–13.

Helleiner, E, 'National Currencies and National Identities' (1998) 41 *The American Behavioral Scientist* 1409.

Hellwig, D, Karlic, G and Huchzermeier, A, *Build Your Own Blockchain. A Practical Guide to Distributed Ledger Technology* (Cham, Springer Nature, 2020).

Herrman, C and Dornacher, C, *International and European Monetary Law* (Cham, Springer Nature, 2017).

Hess B, 'Standardization and Monetization: Legal Perspectives' in J von Hagen and M Welker (eds), *Money as God? The Monetization of the Market and its Impact on Religion, Politics, Law, and Ethics* (Cambridge, Cambridge University Press, 2014) 80–95.

Hicks, J, *A Market Theory of Money* (Oxford, Oxford University Press, 1989).

Hirst, FW, *Money. Gold, Silver & Paper* (London, Charles Scribner's Sons, 1932).

Hirth, K, *The Aztec Economic World. Merchants and Markets in Ancient Mesoamerica* (New York, Cambridge University Press, 2016).

Hobbes, T, *Leviathan* (Oxford, Oxford University Press, 2008).

Hoffmann-Riem, W, 'Artificial Intelligence as a Challege for Law and Regulation' in T Wischmeyer and T Rademacher (eds), *Regulating Artificial Intelligence* (Cham, Springer Nature, 2020) 2–29.

Hohfeld, W, 'Some Fundamental Legal Conceptions as Applied in Judicial Reasoning' (1914) 16 *Yale Law Journal* 16.

Hooley, R and Taylor, JC, 'Payment by Funds Transfer' in M Brindle and R Cox (eds), *Law of Bank Payments* (London, FT Law & Tax, 1996) 25–142.

Huber, J, *Sovereign Money. Beyond Reserve Banking* (Cham, Palgrave Macmillan, 2017).

Hume, D, 'Of Commerce' in A Broadie (ed), *The Scottish Enlightenment. An Anthology* (Edinburgh: Canongate Books, 1997) 385–97.

Hunt, RM, 'Ten Years After: What Are the Effects of Business Method Patents in Financial Services?' (2008) 3 *Business Review* 21.

Hyland-Wood, D and Khatchadourian, S, 'A Future History of International Blockchain Standards' (2018) 1 *The Journal of the British Blockchain Association* 25.

Ingham, G, *The Nature of Money* (Cambridge, Polity Press, 2004).

Ingves, S, 'Going Cashless' (2018) 55 *Finance & Development* 11.

Ioini, NE and Pahl, C, 'A Review of Distributed Ledger Technologies' in H Panetto; et al (eds), *On the Move to Meaningful Internet Systems* (Cham, Springer Nature, 2018) 277–88.

Isaacson, W, *The Industries of the Future* (London, Simon & Schuster, 2016).

Jackson, P, 'Shadow Banking and New Lending Channels. Past and Future' in M Balling and E Gnan (eds), *50 Years of Money and Finance. Lessons and Challenges* (Brussels, Larcier, 2013) 377–414.

Jevons, WS, *Money and the Mechanism of Exchange* (New York, D Appleton and Company, 1875).

Joia, A and Coche, J, 'Framework and Process for Strategic Asset Allocation in Central Bank Foreign Exchange Reserves Management' in AB Berkelaar, J Coche and K Nyholm (eds), *Central Bank Reserves and Sovereign Wealth Management* (Hampshire, Palgrave Macmillan, 2018) 41–72.

Jones, D, *Magna Carta. The Making and Legacy of the Great Charter* (London, Head of Zeus, 2014).

Kahn, CM, McAndrews, J and Roberds, W, 'Money Is Privacy' (2005) 46 *International Economic Review* 377.

Kahn, RE and Lyons, PA, 'Representing Value as Digital Objects: A Discussion of Transferability and Anonymity' (2006) 5 *Journal on Telecommunications and High Technology Law* 189.

Kampakis, S, 'Auditing Tokenomics: A Case Study and Lessons from Auditing a Stablecoin Project' (2022) 5 *The Journal of the British Blockchain Association* 1.

Kaufman, H, 'Financial Institutions in Ferment' (1983) 26 *Challenge* 20–25.

—— *The Road to Financial Reformation: Warnings, Consequences, Reforms* (New Jersey, John Wiley & Sons, 2009).

Kay, J et al, 'Regulatory Reform in Britain' (1988) 3 *Economic Policy* 285.

Kayaoglu, T, 'The Extension of Westphalian Sovereignty. State Building and the Abolition of Extraterritoriality' (2007) 51 *International Studies Quarterly* 649.

Kelly, K, *What Technology Wants* (New York, Viking Press, 2010).

Kelsen, H, *Introduction to the Problems of Legal Theory* (tr BL Paulson and SL Paulson) (New York, Oxford University Press, 2002).
Keynes, JM, *A Treatise on Money. Vol I* (London, MacMillan and Co, 1914).
—— 'Propuestas para un Fondo de Compensación Internacional' (1985) 44 *Investigación Económica* 21.
Kharif, O, 'Thinking about Bitcoin? Beware the Whales' (2017) 4550 *Bloomberg Businessweek* 32.
Kindleberger, C, *A Financial History of Western Europe* (London, Routledge, 1984).
King, M, *The End of Alchemy. Money, Banking and the Future of the Global Economy* (London, Little, Brown, 2016).
Kiyotaki, N and Wright, R, 'On Money as a Medium of Exchange' (1989) 97 *Journal of Political Economy* 927.
Knapp, GF, *The State Theory of Money* (London, Macmillan & Company Limited, 1924).
Knight, JTP, *Canadian Banking Practice* (Montreal, F Wilson-Smith, 1908).
Kohl, U, 'The Rise of Online Intermediaries in the Governance of the Internet and Beyond' (2012) 26 *International Review of Law, Computers & Technology* 185.
Kreitner, R, 'Legal History of Money' (2012) 8 *The Annual Review of Law and Social Science* 415.
Kristof, A, 'National Cryptocurrencies' in DL Kuo Chen (ed), *Handbook of Digital Currency. Bitcoin, Innovation, Financial Instruments, and Big Data* (San Diego, Academic Press, 2015) 67–80.
Kroszner, RS, 'Free Banking. The Scottish Experience as a Model for Emerging Economies' (1995) 1536 *World Bank's Policy Research Working Papers* 1.
Kroszner, RS and Strahan, PE, 'Financial Regulatory Reform: Challenges Ahead' (2011) 101 *The American Economic Review* 242.
Kwarteng, K, *War and Gold. A Five-Hundred-Year History of Empires, Adventures and Debt* (London, Bloomsbury Publishing, 2014).
La Diega, GN and Walden, I, 'Contracting for the 'Internet of Things': Looking into the Nest' (2016) 7 *European Journal of Law and Technology* 1 2.
Lagos, R, 'Inside and Outside Money' (2006) 374 *Federal Reserve Bank of Minneapolis Research Department Staff Report* 1.
Lamport, L, Shostak, R and Pease, M, 'The Byzantine Generals Problem' (1982) 4 *ACM Transactions on Programming Languages and Systems* 382.
Lane, PR and Milesi-Ferretti, GM, 'The Drivers of Financial Globalization' (2008) 98 *American Economic Review* 327.
La Porta, R, Lopez-de-Silanes, F and Shleifer, A, 'The Economic Consequences of Legal Origins' (2008) 46 *Journal of Economic Literature* 285.
Law, J, *Money and Trade Considered with a Proposal for Supplying the Nation with Money* (Glasgow, R. & A. Foulis, 1750).
Leeson, PT and Suarez, PA, 'An Economic Analysis of Magna Carta' (2016) 47 *International Review of Law and Economics* 40.
Leibert, F, 'New Computing in Digital Marketplaces Unleashed' in C Linnhoff-Popien, R Schneider and M Zaddach (eds), *Digital Marketplaces Unleashed* (Berlin, Springer-Verlag, 2018) 13–16.
Lemley, MA et al, *Software and Internet Law* (New York, Aspen Law & Business, 2000).
—— *Software and Internet Law* (New York, Walters Lower Law & Business, 2011).
Li, W et al, 'Securing Proof-of-Stake Blockchain Protocols' in J García-Alfaro; et al (eds), *Data Privacy Management, Cryptocurrencies and Blockchain Technology* (Cham, Springer International Publishing, 2017) 297–315.
Liao, GY and Caramichael, J, 'Stablecoins. Growth Potential and Impact on Banking' (2022) 1334 *International Finance Discussion Papers* 1.
Limantour, JY, *Apuntes Sobre Mi Vida Política* (Mexico City, Editorial Porrúa, 1965).
Lipton, A, 'Toward a Stable Tokenized Medium of Exchange' in C Brummer (ed), *Cryptoassets. Legal, Regulatory and Monetary Perspectives* (New York, Oxford University Press, 2019) 89–115.
Llewellyn, DT, 'Fifty Years in the Evolution of Bank Business Models' in M Balling and E Gnan (eds), *50 Years of Money and Finance. Lessons and Challenges* (Brussels, Larcier, 2013) 319–54.

Lo, AW, *Adaptative Markets. Financial Evolution at the Speed of Thought* (New Jersey, Princeton University Press, 2017).
Locke, J, *Two Treatises of Government* (London, Whitmore and Fenn and C Brown, 1821).
Lotz, S and Rocheteau, G, 'On the Launching of a New Currency' (2002) 34 *Journal of Money, Credit and Banking* 563.
Machiavelli, N, *Discursos Sobre la Primera Década de Tito Livio* (Madrid, Alianza Editorial, 1996).
—— *Escritos Políticos e Históricos. El Príncipe, Reforma de la Constitución de Florencia, Vida de Castruccio Castracani, Informe Sobre el Duque de Valentinois* (Barcelona, Librería Científico-Literaria de Toledano, López y Cía, 1900).
MacLeod, HD, *Theory and Practice of Banking* (London, Longmans, Green and Co, 1906).
Malinowski, B, *Argonauts of the Western Pacific. An Account of Native Enterprise and Adventure in the Archipelagos of Melanesian New Guinea* (London, Routledge & Kegan Paul, 1966).
Mallaby, S, *The Man Who Knew. The Life and Times of Alan Greenspan* (London, Bloomsbury Paperbacks, 1966).
Mann, FA, *The Legal Aspect of Money* (London, Oxford University Press, 1938).
—— *The Legal Aspect of Money* (Oxford, Clarendon Press, 1992).
—— 'The Proper Law in the Conflict of Laws' (1987) 36 *The International and Comparative Law Quarterly* 437.
Marrella, F and Yoo, CS, 'Is Open Source Software the New Lex Mercatoria' (2007) 47 *Virginia Journal of International Law* 808.
Mason, S, *Electronic Signatures in Law* (London, University of London, 2016).
Maurer, B and Swartz, L, 'Introduction. Curating Transactional Things' in B Maurer and L Swartz (eds), *Paid. Tales of Dongles, Checks, and Other Money Stuff* (Massachusetts, The MIT Press, 2017) xv–xxv.
Mauss, M, *The Gift* (London, Routledge Classics, 2002).
Maxwell, W, *The Decisions of the Court of Session. Vol. XVII* (Edinburgh, Bell & Bradfute, 1804).
Mayer, C, 'Economic Development, Financial Systems, and the Law' in N Moloney, E Ferran and J Payne (eds), *Oxford Handbook of Financial Regulation* (Oxford, Oxford University Press, 2017) 41–67.
Mayer, H and Kneeshaw, J, 'Financial Market Structure and Regulatory Change' in A Heertje (ed), *Innovation, Technology, and Finance* (Oxford, European Investment Bank, 1988) 126–57.
McCorry, P, Heilman, E and Miller, A, 'Atomically Trading with Roger. Gambling on the Success of a Hardfork' in J Garcia-Alfaro et al (eds), *Data Privacy Management, Cryptocurrencies and Blockchain Technology* (Cham, Springer International Publishing, 2017) 334–53.
McCubbins, MD, 'The Legislative Design of Regulatory Structure' (1985) 29 *American Journal of Political Science* 721.
Meder, S, 'Giro Payments and the Beginnings of the Modern Cashless Payment System' in D Fox and W Ernst (eds), *Money in the Western Legal Tradition. Middle Ages to Bretton Woods* (Oxford, Oxford University Press, 2016) 441–60.
Meigs, J, 'Recent Innovations in the Functions of Banks' (1966) 56 *The American Economic Review* 167.
Menger, K, 'On the Origin of Money' (1892) 2 *The Economic Journal* 239.
Merivale, JH, *Reports of Cases Argued and Determined in the High Court of Chancery. Vol 1* (London, Joseph Butterworth and Son, 1817).
Merton, RC, 'A Functional Perspective of Financial Intermediation' (1995) 24 *Financial Management* 23.
Minto, A, Voelkerling, M and Wulff, M, 'Separating Apples from Oranges: Identifying Threats to Financial Stability Originating from FinTech' (2017) 12 *Capital Markets Journal* 428.
Monteagudo, M, 'Neutrality of Money and Central Bank Independence' in M Giovanoli and D Devos (eds), *International Monetary and Financial Law. The Global Crisis* (Oxford, Oxford University Press, 2010) 484–505.
Moore, T, '"According to the Law of Merchants and the Custom of the City of London": Burton v. Davy (1436) and the Negotiability of Credit Instruments in Medieval England' in M Allen and M Davies

(eds), *Medieval Merchants and Money. Essays in Honour of James L Bolton* (London, University of London, 2016) 305–22.

Moore, T and Christin, N, 'Beware the Middleman: Empirical Analysis of Bitcoin-Exchange Risk' in AR Sadeghi (ed), *Financial Cryptography and Data Security* (Berlin, Springer, 2013) 25–33.

Morgan-Webb, C, *The Money Revolution* (New York, Economic Forum Inc, 1935).

Muñoz, ML, *Tlacos y Pilones. La Moneda del Pueblo de México* (Mexico City, Fomento Cultural Banamex, 1976).

Murray, AL, 'Sir Isaac Newton and the Scottish Recoinage, 1707–1710' (1997) 127 *Proceedings of the Society of Antiquaries of Scotland* 921.

Ndaw, M, Mendy G and Ouya, S, 'Modelling the Effect of Security Measures on Electronic Payment Risks' in A Abraham et al (eds), *Innovations in Bio-Inspired Computing and Applications* (Cham, Springer, 2017) 255–65.

Nian, LP and Kuo Chuen, DL, 'Introduction to Bitcoin' in DL Kuo Chuen (ed), *Handbook of Digital Currency. Bitcoin, Innovation, Financial Instruments, and Big Data* (San Diego, Academic Press, 2015) 6–29.

Nixey, C, *The Darkening Age. The Christian Destruction of the Classical World* (London, Pan Books, 2018).

Nosal, E and Rocheteau, G, *Money, Payments, and Liquidity* (Massachusetts, The MIT Press, 2011).

Norman, J, *Adam Smith. What He Thought, and Why it Matters* (Milton Keynes, Allen Lane, 2018)

Novoa, E, *El Derecho como Obstáculo al Cambio Social* (Mexico City, Siglo XXI Editores, 1981).

Nussbaum, A, 'A Note on the Idea of World Money' (1949) 64 *Political Science Quarterly* 420.

—— 'Basic Monetary Conceptions in Law' (1937) 35 *Michigan Law Review* 865.

Nussbaum, MC, 'Janus-Faced Law: A Philosophical Debate' in F Fagan and S Levmore (eds), *The Timing of Lawmaking* (Cheltenham: Edward Elgar Publishing, 2017) 249–79.

O'Keefe, JA, *The Law of Weights and Measures* (London, Butterworths, 1966).

O'Neil, C, *Weapons of Math Destruction. How Big Data Increases Inequality and Threatens Democracy* (New York, Broadway Books, 2017).

Officer, LH, 'International Monetary Regimes: The Gold Standard' in S Battilossi et al (eds), *Handbook of the History of Money and Currency* (Singapore, Springer Nature, 2018) 1–33.

Ofonagoro, WI, 'From Traditional to British Currency in Southern Nigeria: Analysis of a Currency Revolution' (1979) 39 *Journal of Economic History* 623.

Ogus, AI, *Regulation: Legal Form and Economic Theory* (Oregon, Hart Publishing, 2014), Kindle EBook.

Orrell, D and Chlupatý, R, *The Evolution of Money* (New York, Columbia University Press, 2016).

Panetta, F, '21st Century Cash: Central Banking, Technological Innovation and Digital Currencies' in E Gnan and D Masciandaro (eds), *Do We Need Central Bank Digital Currency?* (Oregon, Hart Publishing, 2018) 23–32.

Panourgias, LE, *Banking Regulation and World Trade Law. GATS, EU and 'Prudential' Institution Building* (Portland, Hart Publishing, 2006).

Papadopoulos, G, 'Between Rules and Power: Money as an Institution Sanctioned by Political Authority' (2009) XLIII *Journal of Economic Issues* 951.

—— 'Blockchain and Digital Payments: An Institutional Analysis of Cryptocurrencies' in DL Kuo Chuen (ed), *Handbook of Digital Currency. Bitcoin, Innovation, Financial Instruments, and Big Data* (San Diego, Academic Press, 2015) 153–72.

Parks, T, *Medici Money. Banking Metaphysics and Art in the Fifteenth-Century Florence* (London, Profile Books, 2006).

Parton, J, *Life of Voltaire*. Vol 1 (Cambridge, The Riverside Press, 1881).

Pasquale, F, *The Black Box Society. The Secret Algorithms that Control Money and information* (Massachusetts, Harvard University Press, 2015).

Pasquale, F et al, 'Eleven Things They Don't Tell You About Law & Economics: An Informal Introduction to Political Economy and Law' (2019) 37 *Law & Inequality* 95.

Paton, GW, *A Text-Book of Jurisprudence* (London, Oxford University Press, 1964).

Peng, S, 'Cybersecurity Standards. Cyberspace Governance, Multistakeholderism and the (Ir)Relevance of the TBT Regime' (2018) 51 *Cornell International Law Journal* 445.

Pereira, AC, *Lecciones de Teoría Constitucional* (Porrúa. Mexico City, 2018).

Perman, R, *The Rise and Fall of the City of Money. A Financial History of Edinburgh* (Edinburgh, Birlinn, 2020).

Pettifor, A, *The Production of Money. How to Break the Power of Bankers* (London, Verso, 2017).

Pfajfar, D, Sgro, G and Wagner, W, 'Are Alternative Currencies a Substitute or Complement to Fiat Money? Evidence form Cross-Country Data' (2012) 16 *International Journal of Community Currency Research* 46.

Pistor, K, 'A Legal Theory of Finance' (2013) 41 *Journal of Comparative Economics* 315.

—— 'Regulating Financial Markets. An LTF Perspective' in E Avgouleas and DC Donald (eds), *The Political Economy of Financial Regulation* (Cambridge, Cambridge University Press, 2022) 19–37.

—— *The Code of Capital. How the Law Creats Wealth and Inequality* (Princeton, Princeton University Press, 2019).

Polanyi, K, *The Great Transformation. The Political and Economic Origins of Our Time* (Boston, Beacon Press, 2001).

Polo, M, *The Travels of Marco Polo the Venetian* (London, JM Dent & Sons, 1908).

Proctor, C, 'Cryptocurrencies in International and Public Law Conceptions of Money' in D Fox and S Green (eds), *Cryptocurrencies in Public and Private Law* (Oxford, Oxford University Press, 2019) 33–55.

—— *Mann on the Legal Aspect of Money* (Oxford, Oxford University Press, 2012).

Proctor, C and Dixon, V, *Goode on Payment Obligations in Commercial and Financial Transactions* (2016, London, Thomson Reuters).

Quinn, S and Roberds, W, 'Death of a Reserve Currency' (2016) 12 *International Journal of Central Banking* 63.

—— 'Responding to a Shadow Banking Crisis. The Lessons of 1763' (2015) 47 *Journal of Money, Credit and Banking* 1149.

Rackham, H, *Pliny. Natural History with an English Translation in Ten Volumes. Volume V* (Massachusetts, Harvard University Press, 1950).

Rahmatian, A, 'Money as a Legally Enforceable Debt' (2018) 29 *European Business Law Review* 205.

—— 'Money as a Normative Text' (2014) 13 *Journal of International Business and Law* 221.

Reed, C, *Electronic Finance Law* (Cambridge, Woodhead-Faulkner, 1991).

Reinhart, CM and Rogoff, KS, *This Time is Different. Eight Centuries of Financial Folly* (New Jersey, Princeton University Press, 2009).

Richards, RJ, 'Kant and Blumenbach on the Bildungstrieb: A Historical Misunderstanding' (2000) 31 *Studies in History and Philosophy of Biological and Biomedical Sciences* 11.

Richey, S, 'Manufacturing Trust: Community Currencies and the Creation of Social Capital' (2007) 29 *Political Behavior* 69.

Rifkin, J, *The Third Industrial Revolution. How Lateral Power is Transforming Energy, the Economy, and the World* (New York, St Martin's Press, 2011).

Roberds, W and Velde, FR, 'The Descent of Central Banks (1400–1815)' in MD Bordo et al (eds), *Central Bans at a Crossroads* (New York, Cambridge University Press, 2016) 18–61.

Rochon, LP and Vernengo, M, 'State Money and the Real World: Or Chartalism and Its Discontents' (2003) 26 *Journal of Post Keynesian Economics* 57.

Rogoff, KS, *The Curse of Cash* (Princeton, Princeton University Press, 2016).

Romano, R, 'Regulating in the Dark and a Postscript Assessment of the Iron Law of Financial Regulation' (2015) 43 *Hofstra Law Review* 25.

Rose-Ackerman, S, 'The Regulatory State' in M Rosenfeld and A Sajo (eds), *The Oxford Handbook of Comparative Constitutional Law* (Oxford, Oxford University Press, 2012) 671.

Rosner, MT and Kang, A, 'Understanding and Regulating Twenty-First Century Payment Systems: The Ripple Case Study' (2016) 114 *Michigan Law Review* 650.

Ross, A, *The Industries of the Future* (London, Simon & Schuster, 2016).

Rowland, D, Kohl, U and Charlesworth, A, *Information Technology Law* (Abingdon, Routledge, 2017).

Rüfner, T, 'Money in the Roman Law Texts' in D Fox and W Ernst (eds), *Money in the Western Legal Tradition. Middle Ages to Bretton Woods* (Oxford, Oxford University Press, 2016) 93–109.

Russell, S, *Human Compatible. Artificial Intelligence and the Problem of Control* (New York, Penguin Books, 2019).

Sahagun, B, *Historia General de las Cosas de la Nueva España* (Madrid, Dastin, 2003).

Sahlins, M, 'The Original Political Society' in D Graeber and M Sahlins (eds), *On Kings* (Chicago, Hau Books, 2017) 23–64.

Salop, SC, 'Monopolistic Competition with Outside Goods' (1979) 10 *The Bell Journal of Economics* 141.

Sargent, T and Wallace, N, 'The Real Bills Doctrine versus the Quantity Theory. A Reconsideration' (1982) 90 *The Journal of Political Economy* 1212.

Scaruffi, G, *L'alitinonfo* (Reggio, Hercoliano Bartoli, 1582).

Schaps, DM, *Invention of Coinage and the Monetization of Ancient Greece* (2013, Michigan, The University of Michigan Press).

—— 'What Was Money in Ancient Greece?' in WV Harris (ed), *The Monetary System of the Greeks and Romans* 39–48.

Scheidel, W, 'The Divergent Evolution of Coinage in Eastern and Western Eurasia' in WV Harris (ed), *The Monetary Systems of the Greeks and Romans* (Oxford, Oxford University Press, 2008) 268–85.

Schenk, C and Straumann, T, 'Central Banks and the Stability of the International Monetary Regime' in MD Bordo et al (eds), *Central Banks at a Crossroads* (New York, Cambridge University Press, 2016) 319–55.

Schleifer, A, 'Understanding Regulation' (2005) 11 *European Financial Management* 439–51.

Schmandt-Besserat, D, 'The Invention of Tokens' in A Crisà, M Grikaki and C Rowan (eds), *Tokens. Culture, Connections, Communities* (London, Royal Numismatic Society, 2019) 11–18.

Schmitt, C *Political Theology: Four Chapters on the Concept of Sovereignty* (Massachusetts, MIT Press, 1985).

Schoenmaker, D, *Governance of International Banking. The Financial Trilemma* (New York, Oxford University Press, 2013).

Schoenmakers, 2013 and van Tilborg, HCA, 'What Cryptology Can Mean for Electronic Commerce' in JEJ Prins et al (eds), *Trust in Electronic Commerce. The Role of Trust from a Legal, and Organizational and a Technical Point of View* (The Hague, Luwer Law International, 2002) 45–54.

Schooner, HM and Taylor, MW, *Global Bank Regulation. Principles and Policies* (London, Academic Press, 2010).

Schuler, K, 'The World History of Free Banking. An Overview' in K Dowd (ed), *The Experience of Free Banking* (London, Routledge, 1992) 7–47.

Schumpeter, JA, *Business Cycles: A Theoretical, Historical and Statistical Analysis of Capital Process* (New York, McGraw-Hill, 1939).

—— 'Money and Currency' (1991) 58 *Social Research* 499.

Schwab, K, *The Fourth Industrial Revolution* (London, Portfolio Penguin, 2017).

Selgin, G, 'Gresham's Law' in S Battilossi et al (eds), *Handbook of the History of Money and Currency* (Singapore, Springer Nature, 2018) 2–21.

Shiller, RJ, *Finance and the Good Society* (Princeton, Princeton University Press, 2012).

—— *The Subprime Solution. How Today's Global Financial Crisis Happened, and What to Do about It* (Princeton, Princeton University Press, 2008).

Sieghart, P, *The Lawful Rights of Mankind. An Introduction to the International Legal Code of Human Rights* (Oxford, Oxford University Press, 1985).

Siekmann, H, 'Deposit Banking and the Use of Monetary Instruments' in D Fox and W Ernst (eds), *Money in the Western Legal Tradition. Middle Ages to Bretton Woods* (Oxford, Oxford University Press, 2016) 489–531.

Silber, W, 'The Process of Financial Innovation' (1983) 73 *American Economic Review* 89.

Simmel, G, *The Philosophy of Money* (New York, Routledge Classics, 2004).

Sissoko, C, 'Why Inside Money Matters?' (2007) 39 *Journal of Money, Credit and Banking* 2097.

Skidelsky, R, *Money and Government. A Challenge to Mainstream Economics* (London, Allen Lane, 2018).

Smart, E, 'Electronic Banking. An Overview of the Legal Implications' in RM Goode (ed), *Electronic Banking. The Legal Implications* (London, The Institute of Bankers, 1985) 1–4.

Smil, V, *Invention and Innovation. A Brief History of Hype and Failure* (Massachusetts, The MIT Press, 2023).

Smith, A, *An Inquiry into the Nature and Causes of the Wealth of Nations* (Oxford, Oxford University Press, 2008).

—— 'The Origin and Development of our Property Rights' in A Broadie (ed), *The Scottish Enlightenment. An Anthology* (Edinburgh, Canongate Books, 1997) 475–87.

Smith, CA, 'Economics of Marketing Systems: Models from Economic Geography' (1974) 3 *Annual Review of Anthropology* 167.

Smith, ME, 'The Archaeology of Ancient State Economies' (2004) 33 *Annual Review of Anthropology* 73.

Smith, V, *The Rationale of Central Banking and the Free Banking Alternative* (Indianapolis, Liberty Fund, 1990).

Solomon, EH, *Virtual Money. Understanding the Power and Risks of Money's High-Speed Journey unto Electronic Space* (New York, Oxford University Press, 1997).

Sono, K, 'The Changing Role of Currency. Toward a Catastrophe or a New System?' (1995) 38 *The Japanese Annual of International Law* 83.

Sono, K and Kanda, H, 'In Search of Order in the World Monetary System: State Intervention after the Decline of the Lex Monetae' in M Giovanoli and D Devos (eds), *International Monetary and Financial Law. The Global Crisis* (Oxford, Oxford University Press, 2010) 506–16.

St Augustine, *The City of God (De Civitate Dei)* (Edinburgh, John Grant, 1909).

Starr, RM, 'Why is there Money? Endogenous Derivation of 'Money' as the Most Liquid Asset: A Class of Examples' (2003) 21 *Economic Theory* 455.

Stevens, ME, *Temples, Tithes, and Taxes. The Temple and Economic Life of Ancient Israel* (Massachusetts, Hendrickson Publishers, 2006).

Stiglitz, JE 'Government Failure vs. Market Failure: Principles of Regulation' in EJ Balleisen and DA Moss (eds), *Government and Markets. Toward a New Theory of Regulation* (New York, European Cambridge University Press, 2010) Kindle EBook.

Stone, CW, 'A Common Coinage for All Nations' (1896) 163 *The North American Review* 47.

Strahan, PE, 'Liquidity Production in Twenty-First-Century Banking' in AN Berger, P Molyneux and JO Wilson (eds), *The Oxford Handbook of Banking* (Oxford, Oxford University Press, 2010) 112–45.

Strange, S, 'The Westfailure System' (1999) 25 *Review of International Studies* 345.

Sweetman, A, *Cyber and the City. Securing London's Banks in the Computer Age* (Cham, Springer Nature, 2022).

Tarasiewicz, M and Newman, A, 'Cryptocurrencies as Distributed Community Experiments' in DL Kuo Chuen (ed), *Handbook of Digital Currency. Bitcoin, Innovation, Financial Instruments, and Big Data* (San Diego: Academic Press, 2015) 201–22.

Tarullo, DK, *Banking on Basel. The Future of International Financial Regulation* (Washington, DC, Peterson Institute for International Economics, 2008).

Téllez-Valdés, J, *Derecho Informático* (Mexico City, McGraw-Hill, 2008).

Thier, A, 'Money in Medieval Canon Law' in D Fox and W Ernst (eds), *Money in the Western Legal Tradition. Middle Ages to Bretton Woods* (Oxford, Oxford University Press, 2016) 136–66.

Trakman, LE, 'From the Medieval Law Merchant to E-Merchant Law' (2003) 53 *The University of Toronto Law Journal* 265.

Tu, KV and Meredith, MW, 'Rethinking Virtual Currency Regulation in the Bitcoin Age' (2015) 90 *Washington Law Review* 271.

Tucker, P, *Unelected Power. The Quest for Legitimacy in Central Banking and the Regulatory State* (New Jersey, Princeton University Press, 2018).

Turing, AM, 'Computing Machinery and Intelligence' (1950) 49 *Mind* 433.
Turrent, E, *Historia del Banco de México. Antecedentes, Fundación y Despegue. Volumen I* (Mexico City, Banco de México, 2015).
Ugolini, S, 'The Historical Evolution of Central Banking' in S Battilossi et al (eds), *Handbook of the History of Money and Currency* (Singapore, Springer Nature, 2018) 1–22.
Usher, AP, 'The Origin of the Bill of Exchange' (1914) 22 *Journal of Political Economy* 566.
Vargyas, P, 'Sennacherib's Alleged Half-Shekel Coins' (2002) 61 *Journal of Near Eastern Studies* 111.
Velde, FR, 'Experiments with Paper Money' in S Battilossi et al (eds), *Handbook of the History of Money and Currency* (Singapore, Springer Nature, 2018) 2–12.
—— 'Technological Change and the Future of Cash' (2017) 15 *SUERF Policy Note* 1.
Vigna, P and Casey, MJ, *Cryptocurrency. The Future of Money?* (London, Vintage, 2015).
Villela, S, *Tópicos de Antropología Económica* (Mexico City, INAH, 1997).
Wallace, B, *The Billionaire's Vinegar. The Mystery of the World's Most Expensive Bottle of Wine* (New York, Broadway Books, 2009).
Wallerstein, I, *World-Systems Analysis. An Introduction* (Durham, Duke University Press, 2004).
Walras, L, *Elements of Pure Economics* (Illinois: Richard D Irwin, 1926).
Watson, G, 'The Provincial Coinage of Aemilian: A Study in Imperial Communication' (2018) 178 *The Numismatic Chronicle* 184.
Weber, RH and Weber, R, *Internet of Things. Legal Perspectives* (Heidelberg, Springer, 2010).
Werbach, K, *The Blockchain and the New Architecture of Trust* (Massachusetts, MIT, 2018).
Wetterberg, G, *Money and Power. From Stockholms Banco 1656 to Sveriges Riksbank Today* (Stockholm, Atlantis, 2009).
White, LH, *Free Banking in Britain: Theory, Experience and Debate 1800–1845* (London, The Institute of Economic Affairs, 1995).
—— 'The World History of Free Banking. An Overview' in K. Dowd (ed), *The Experience of Free Banking* (1992, London, Routledge) 157–186.
Withers, H, *The Meaning of Money* (London, John Murray, 1948).
Wood, PR, 'Lawyers and Economists: Who Rule the World' (2010) 11 *Business Law International* 145.
Woods, AK, 'Litigating Data Sovereignty' (2018) 128 *The Yale Law Journal* 328.
Woodward, BK, 'The Roles of Non-State Actors in Lawmaking within the Global Intellectual Property Regimes of WIPO and TRIPs' (2012)14 *International Community Law Review* 33.
Woytek, BE, 'Monetary Innovation in Ancient Rome: The Republic and its Legacy' in P Bernholz and R Vaubel (eds), *Explaining Monetary and Financial Innovation. A Historical Analysis* (Cham, Springer, 2014) 197–226.
—— 'The Denarius Coinage of the Roman Republic' in BE Woytek (ed), *The Oxford Handbook of Greek and Roman Coinage* (Oxford, Oxford University Press, 2012) 316–32.
Wray, LR, 'From the State Theory of Money to Modern Money' in D Fox and W Ernst (eds), *Money in the Western Legal Tradition. Middle Ages to Bretton Woods* (Oxford, Oxford University Press, 2016) 631–52.
—— 'Money' in GC Harcourt and P Kriesler (eds), *Oxford Handbook of Post-Keynesian Economics, Volume 1: Theory and Origins* (Oxford, Oxford University Press, 2013) 139–51.
Yadav, AS, Singh, N and Kushwaha, DS, 'Evolution of Blockchain and Consensus Mechanisms & its Real-World Applications' (2023) 82 *Multimedia Tools and Applications* 1.
Yang, BZ, 'What is (not) Money? Medium of Exchange ≠ Means of Payment' (2007) 51 *The American Economist* 101.
Yeager, LB, 'The Continuing Search for a Monetary Constitution' in LH White, VJ Vanberg and EA Köhler (eds), *Renewing the Search for a Monetary Constitution. Reforming Government's Role in the Monetary System* (Washington, Cato Institute, 2015) Kindle EBook Loc 229–550.
Zelizer, V, 'The Social Meaning of Money: "Special Monies"' (1989) 95 *American Journal of Sociology* 342.

Zetzsche, DA et al, 'Regulating a Revolution: From Regulatory Sandboxes to Smart Regulation' (2017) 23 *Fordham Journal of Corporate &Financial Law* 34.

Zetzsche, DA, Buckley, RP and Arner, DW, 'Regulating Libra. The Transformative Potential of Facebook's Cryptocurrency and Possible Regulatory Responses' (2019) 47 *University of New South Wales Law Research Series* 1.

Ziegler, R, 'What Makes the Kula Go Round? A Simulation Model of the Spontaneous Emergence of a Ceremonial Exchange System' (2008) 30 *Social Networks* 107.

INDEX

www.ingramcontent.com/pod-product-compliance
Ingram Content Group UK Ltd.
Pitfield, Milton Keynes, MK11 3LW, UK
UKHW020136290926
15471UKWH00003B/517

9 781509 969678